CW00687557

WARSHIP 1999-2000

VALEUR
DISCIPLINE

WARSHIP 1999-2000

Edited by Antony Preston

Frontispiece
A late view of the French battleship Strasbourg *taken on 18 June 1942. (Marius Bar) John Jordan describes the history of* Strasbourg *and her sistership* Dunkerque *in this volume.*

First published in Great Britain in 1999 by Conway Maritime Press,
a division of Chrysalis Books Ltd,
a member of the Chrysalis Group plc,
9 Blenheim Court, Brewery Road,
London N7 9NT

British Library Cataloguing in Publication Data
A record of this title is available on request from the British Library.

ISBN 0 85177 724 4

Project Editor: Daniel Mersey
Typesetting and layout by Stephen Dent
Printed and bound in Spain

CONTENTS

EDITORIAL

This latest issue of *Warship* has been severely delayed as a result of the change of ownership of Conway Maritime Press, and we can do no more than apologise profusely to both readers and authors, who have had to wait for much longer than the original publication date. We also hope that the next issue of the journal will not suffer the same delays.

That being said, this issue of *Warship* offers the readers the same high standard set in previous issues. There is a strong flavour of the mid-19th Century, with one feature by your editor on the 'Great Armament' of 1854-56, intended (successfully) to force Russia to the conference table; another article considers the Sea of Azov operations in 1855, written by David K Brown, a noted Conway author and *Warship* contributor. The obsession of army historians with the siege of Sevastopol and the sufferings of the British Army has resulted in a serious underestimation of the role played by the Royal Navy, and to a lesser extent the French Navy, in bringing pressure to bear on the Russians. The Azov Campaign showed that ships could prevent supplies from reaching Sevastopol at negligible cost, and at the same time improve conditions for the besiegers.

The Battle of the Yalu, fought between Japanese and Chinese ships during the Sino-Japanese War of 1896 is often quoted, but almost always with only the sketchiest details of the background or the outcome. Peter Brook has remedied this with a detailed analysis of the battle, shedding light on the first action fought between modern European-built warships since Lissa 30 years before.

Another relatively obscure campaign is the naval side of the War of the Triple Alliance, fought in 1865-70 between Argentina, Brazil and Uruguay on one side, against Paraguay. George Gratz writes about the Brazilian ironclads which took part in this bloody conflict, showing that the war involved modern ships, guns and mines. Although fought just after the American Civil War in rather similar circumstances, it never received the same attention from naval historians.

Arnold Putnam looks at the intricate diplomatic manoeuvring which went on during the building of the so-called Laird Rams in Birkenhead during the American Civil War. Embarrassed by the depredations of the Laird-built raider CSS *Alabama*, Lord Palmerston's government was determined to avoid a rupture with the United States, and eventually took them over for the Royal Navy. By making extensive use of correspondence between his masters in Richmond, the author creates a detailed picture of the process of building advanced ironclad turret ships in one of the most advanced shipyards in the world.

Frido Kip examines the complex story of the Imperial Japanese Navy's experimental light cruiser *Yûbari*. This little ship was the precursor of the large and powerful heavy cruisers which saw so much action in the Pacific in the Second World War. Although some of the structural innovations had been used first in the Royal Navy's *Arethusa* design of 1912, notably longitudinal framing and destroyer-type fast-running machinery, others were very unusual, and reflect great credit on the designer, Captain Hiraga.

John Jordan writes with his usual authority on the French battlecruisers *Dunkerque* and *Strasbourg*, magnificent ships which suffered the ignominy of being bombed by their allies and scuttled to avoid capture. Built to counter the German *panzerschiffe*, they demonstrated their potential in the hunt for the *Admiral Graf Spee* in 1939, but the collapse of France in June 1940 robbed them of any chance to distinguish themselves action.

Moving to more modern times, Paul French describes the planning of the passage of the aircraft carrier HMS *Victorious* through the Lombok Strait in September 1964, at a time of great tension between the United Kingdom and Indonesia. With hindsight, it is easy to see that the will of President Sukarno to attack the British ships was greatly over-estimated, but at the time this operation seemed fraught with risk, not least because Indonesia possessed modern Russian missiles and aircraft.

Getting the balance right has always been a priority for the Editor. Critics have complained about too much emphasis on Scandinavian cost defence ships, others would like the whole content to be devoted to the Second World War, and so on *ad infinitum*. Small navies with special requirements often produced unique solutions, so they cannot be ignored, even if their navies have never fired a shot in anger. Large navies, on the other hand, include minor vessels (in wartime, hordes of them), and although humble in purpose, taken as a whole they have often been decisive. One can cite landing craft in the Second World War, but in 1914-18 there were hundreds of purpose-built and converted civilian ships serving in navies of the Allies and the Central Powers, as well as gallant survivors of the Victorian Age. To ignore them is to give an unbalanced view of how control of the sea is exercised. So, as all volumes of *Warship* have done since day one, we doggedly persist in trying to please all of the readers *some* of the time, as we know that we cannot please *all* of them *all* of the time! As always, contributions and comments are welcome.

Antony Preston

THE BUILDING OF NUMBERS 294 & 295:

The Laird Rams

The depredations of Confederate commerce-raiders bought from British owners and even built in British shipyards were a major source of friction between Washington and London during the American Civil War. After the escape of the *Alabama*, the British government was forced to take action to stop two ironclad turret-ships from leaving Laird's shipyard at Birkenhead. **Arnold A Putnam** gives an absorbing account of the building of these controversial ships as well as the diplomatic manoeuvering to prevent their delivery.

By 1862 the American Civil War was entering its second year. To break the ever-tightening Union naval blockade the Confederate States Navy was constructing several casemated ironclads, similar to the CSS *Virginia* (ex-USS *Merrimack*). Overall design of the vessels was similar: shallow draft, at least for later vessels, low freeboard, sloped armour, and driven solely by a steam-powered screw propeller. These warships were designed to operate in defence of harbours and rivers and not to cruise the Atlantic coast. The naval shipbuilding capacity of the Confederacy was hampered by its inability to produce sufficient iron plate required for an armoured cruising vessel. The Secretary of the Confederate Navy, Steven R Mallory, looked to Europe, principally England and France with their superior shipbuilding technologies. He sought to purchase sea-going armoured warships, which could cruise the Atlantic and Gulf coasts, and lift the blockade.

Captain James D Bulloch, having successfully brought the blockade runner *Fingal* into Savannah in the late fall of 1861, was preparing to leave for England. At the time, it was intended that he take command of the nearly completed Confederate commerce raider, CSS *Alabama*. Although a competent commander, Bulloch proved to be of even greater value as a purchasing agent. Command of the *Alabama* was given instead to Raphael Semmes.

Mallory amended Bulloch's initial orders to include negotiations with British shipbuilders to 'commence construction of an ironclad sloop of war of four to six guns.' Three days later, on 14 January 1862, Mallory wrote that he wanted 'an armored steam slope [sic] of moderate size, say about 2000 tons, and to carry eight or ten heavy guns.' He enclosed a drawing of a vessel in which the guns were 'placed amidships in an iron casemate, the two after and forward guns in which are so pivoted as to fire in broadside or fore and aft.'

Upon his arrival in Liverpool on 10 March, Bulloch began consultations with the Laird Brothers, owners of the Birkenhead Iron Works, and builders of the *Alabama*. Lairds had experience in construction of ironclad vessels, the Admiralty having contracted the firm to build the 10,600 ton, 50-gun armoured 'frigate' HMS *Agincourt* in 1861. John Laird built his first iron vessel, the *Lady Lansdowne*, at the Wallasey Pool Yard, Liverpool, in 1837. By 1857 Laird had moved his operations across the River Mersey to Birkenhead, but he retired in 1861 and turned over operations of his yard to his sons, John (1834-98), William (1831-99) and Henry (1838-93).

Laird Brothers' yard covered 'an area of about 15 acres and [had] a frontage to the river of some 900 feet.' There were two graving (dry) docks, '410ft long by 85ft wide'. At the south end of the yard was:

> the building in which the machines for shearing, punching, drilling and preparing the plates, frames, &c, are situated; they are of the class usually found in such yards, with one exception, viz: a very large machine for planing the edges of ships' plates; it is 36 feet long, has a moving and revolving tool, which cuts both going ahead and back, and is capable of planing a plate 33 feet in length. There is also an immense pair of rollers operated by steam power, the barrels being 18ft in length by 28ins in diameter.

'The building slips occupied are of the following lengths: 240ft, 250ft, and 400ft'. The 'extreme left [north] of the works is a timber yard, behind which, and near the docks and building slips, are grouped the erecting, fitting, millwright, pattern, smith's and boiler shops, rigging and mould lofts, the sheds containing the armor-plate bending, planing and drilling machinery, the furnaces and tools for preparing the materials for the vessels building on the stocks.' In addition, there was a 10-ton crane in the timber yard and a 50-ton crane at the southernmost, or number 4, graving dock.

Due to the shallow waters and sand bars of Southern harbours and river mouths it was necessary to determine 'the minimum draft compatible with seaworthiness and invulnerability.' It was found by 'close calculation of weights and form of model that by using turrets instead of broadside batteries, whereby the sides would be relieved of much strain and the heavy weights thrown near the center,' a vessel, 'of 220ft and 1800 tons, might be built,' with a draft of 15ft. By the time Bulloch, now promoted to Commander, received Mallory's letter of 30 April instructing him to proceed on his own initiative, plans and drawings were nearly complete.

Bulloch informed Mallory in July that he had contracted with Lairds for two ironclad vessels, Yard Numbers 294 and 295, the first to be ready for sea in March and the second in May 1863. 'Cost of each fully equipped, except batteries and magazine fittings, £93,750'. The general dimensions were to be: 'Length overall about 235ft, Breadth Extreme to outside of plates, 42ft 4ins, Depth of hold from top of floor to upper side of deck beam, 17 feet 6 inches' and 'Tonnage builders measurement (BOM) abt 1896 tons'. The vessel would include 'A poop and topgallant forecastle fitted in such a manner that they can be removed at any time without breaking into the body of the vessel'. The [poop and forecastle] 'are of light structure, sufficiently strong to resist any force of the sea, but are not permanently connected with the hull proper, and could be shot away or otherwise entirely removed without injury to the main structure or any disarrangement of the armor plating.' To allow for a greater arc of fire and achieve a higher freeboard in rough seas, 'The bulwarks [were] made to be hinged down when the guns [were] worked.'

The keel consisted of a vertical plate '2ft 3ins' high by 11/16 inch wide extending from the lower part of the stem to the lower part of the stern frame.' The frames were to be made of angle iron 5in x 3in and 'spaced 21ins apart (centre to centre).' The skin of the vessel was to be composed of 1/2in iron plate. A forged iron stem was 'formed as a projecting beak below the waterline to give the blow when the vessel [was] used as a ram.' It was mistakenly believed by most naval experts at that time that the ram was the decisive offensive weapon for steam-powered warships.

The hull was 'clothed with 4 1/2in armour plates, tapering around the stem and stern to three-and-a-half and three inches.' This armour also ran to 3 1/4ft below the waterline. Twelve watertight bulkheads forming compartments were provided, 'six of these main athwartship compartments in the main body of the ship, besides smaller ones in the bow and stern.' In addition, a double watertight bottom was formed by having the floor tops 'plated over for the length of the Engine Room and Boiler Room.'

The ships were to have two direct-acting horizontal steam engines of 350 horsepower and be able to achieve 61 revolutions per minute. These engines would drive a single 14ft propeller. There were to be four tubular boilers, two on each side of the ship, each boiler providing steam pressure of 20lbs per square inch. The ironclads would carry 350 tons of coal, enough for about eleven days steaming at full power. In addition to steam power, the ship was bark-rigged – i.e. three masts with the foremost and mainmast square rigged and the mizzenmast fore-and-aft rigged. Number 295, later HMS *Wivern*, was equipped with tripod fore and main masts designed by Captain Cowper Phipps Coles RN.

Although initial consultations had convinced Bulloch that the guns should be housed in turrets rather than disposed on the broadside, he was unsure as to whether they

HMS Wivern, *with tripod fore and main masts.* (CPL)

should be revolving or fixed turrets. In July 1862 he considered mounting three fixed turrets in each ship, made of 5 ½in iron, backed with 12ins of teak. However, by early September he had reduced the number of turrets to two and had 'resolved to construct the turrets to revolve.' In each turret there were to be a pair of guns, parallel to each other and 4 ½ft apart. Laird Brothers signed a Licence Agreement with Captain Coles to use a turret of his design on 10 December.

The turret, a turntable and its turning mechanisms were supported:

> by a series of stanchions resting upon what may be called a circular keelson, built upon the main Keelsons and floors. The wheels upon which the turrets turn rest upon a circular race or girder of iron, and the revolving motion is referred to a wrought-iron pivot by means of radiating arms, also of wrought iron.

The turntable consisted of a circular bed 26ft in diameter, composed of teak timbers 30ins square and located on the berthing deck. Attached to the pivot was a brass cylinder from which radiated 24 arms. These arms connected to beveled iron wheels, 18ins in diameter, at widest, by 24ins long.

The turret proper was 23ft in internal diameter, polygonal in shape and composed of 21 plates. The turrets were so shaped because 'their cost is considerably less, and there is also a considerable saving in time and labor.' It consisted of an inner layer, or 'skin' of ½in iron boiler plate, to the outside of which T-shaped beams were bolted on at intervals of 20in around the circumference of the turret. The web of each beam was 10in in length with the area between the web of the beams filled in with teak. Over this was placed a crossed iron trelliswork of ¾in thickness and covered, in turn, by another 8ins of teak. Finally, solid, rolled iron plate, 5 ½in thick, was bolted to the outside using bolts running all the way through to the inner iron 'skin'. An additional layer of iron plate 4 ½in thick was placed on the facing of the turret around the gun ports, giving a total of 10in of armour at this point. The iron plate extended to below the level of the main deck.

The turret roof was composed of a layer of T-shaped beams covered over with 1in iron plates. Holes were cut through the roof to provide ventilation and access to the top of the turret. One of the holes allowed the Gun Captain to sight from the rear of the turret, over the top, while directing the training of the turret on a target.

Turning of the turrets was accomplished by hand, both from inside the turret and outside by means of a rack and pinion system, using gears attached to the turntable. It required a crew of eighteen men one minute to turn the turret one full revolution. The turret could also be turned by means of a block and tackle mechanism or by handspikes shipped and manned by capstan bars.

In addition to the hinged bulwarks, a leather flap, extending around the outside bottom of the turret and over the gap between the turret and the deck reduced the water flow through the gap. The freeboard of these vessels was such that pumps could easily handle any water entering the hull between the turret and the main deck before it threatened to sink the ship.

The ironclads were built beside each other at the southern end of the Birkenhead Ironworks yards. Bulloch supervised the laying of the keel of Number 294 in July 1862. By mid-September Captain James H North, a fellow purchasing agent, wrote that this vessel was 'half in frame, and the other [had] her keel down.' By November Number 294, designated by Mallory the CSS *North Carolina*, was '... about one third plated and the second, CSS *Mississippi* (No. 295) ... half in frame.'

As fall turned to winter and the days grew shorter, Lairds constructed over the two vessels 'eight comfortable sheds, and ... introduced gas, so as to insure additional hours for work during the short foggy days.' But, despite the upbeat reports there were serious problems. Bulloch reported in February 1863:

> Unforeseen causes have kept back work on iron ships; can not be ready at time first specified. Have tried very hard to hasten completion, but insurmountable difficulties have occurred. [W]hole character of work new and builders cannot make close calculations, great labor and unexpected time required to bend armor plates, and the most important part of the work, the riveting, is far more tedious than anticipated.

Another more serious problem began to rear its head. Since the escape of the *Alabama* in July 1862, the American Consul, Charles Francis Adams, had been pressing the Palmerston government to intercede and seize the rams building at Lairds. Stung by the escape of the British-built *Florida* and *Alabama*, the British Government had begun to take action to preserve its neutrality. The Foreign Enlistment Act, passed by Parliament in 1819, forbade British subjects to build or arm any ships of war for governments at war with any government friendly to England. At first, Bulloch intended 'to avoid every possible appearance of intent to arm [the ironclads] within British jurisdiction, it was arranged that no magazines were to be placed in either ship, nor any special places for stowing shells and ordnance stores.'

Now, as Bulloch had feared, the Government 'ordered the [Customs] collectors to examine and report frequently upon all vessels building in their districts, and armored ships cannot escape notice.' He wrote to Mallory that 'Lord Russell says in effect that the 290 [*Alabama*] evaded the law, and rather indicates that it shall not be done again.'

Early in April 1863 both hulls 'were complete, and the sides covered with slabs of teak [and the 294] had a great number of her iron armour-plates [sic] fixed'. Again, in June, Bulloch complained to Mallory that 'the engines of both ships have been ready for several months. One ship is entirely plated, and could have been in the water six weeks'.

Bullock informed Lairds, and they pretended to believe him, that his obviously war-like vessels were being built for the Pasha of Egypt. *El Toussan*, for Number 294, and *El Monnassir*, for Number 295, were used as cover names

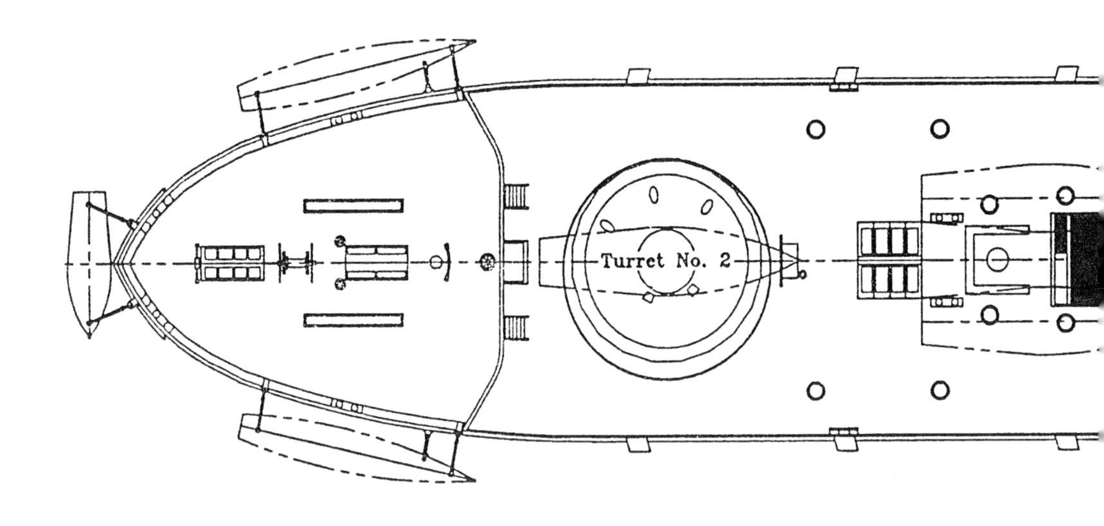

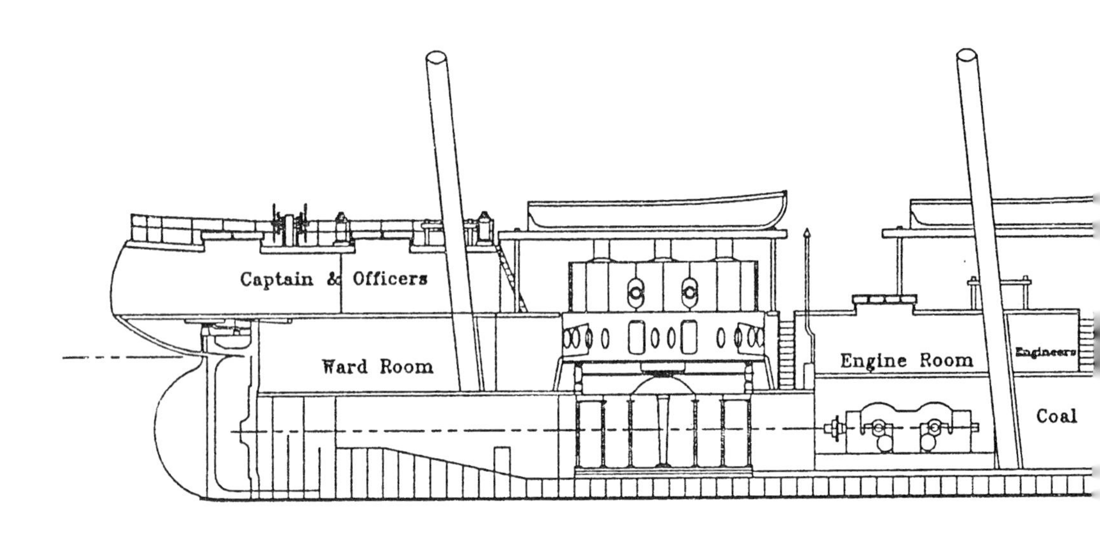

General Plans for Yard Nu

Built for Confederate States

by Laird Bros., Birkenhea

Later: H.M.S. SCORPION and

Deck Plan and Longitudinal Section of the Laird Rams. (Drawn by the author)

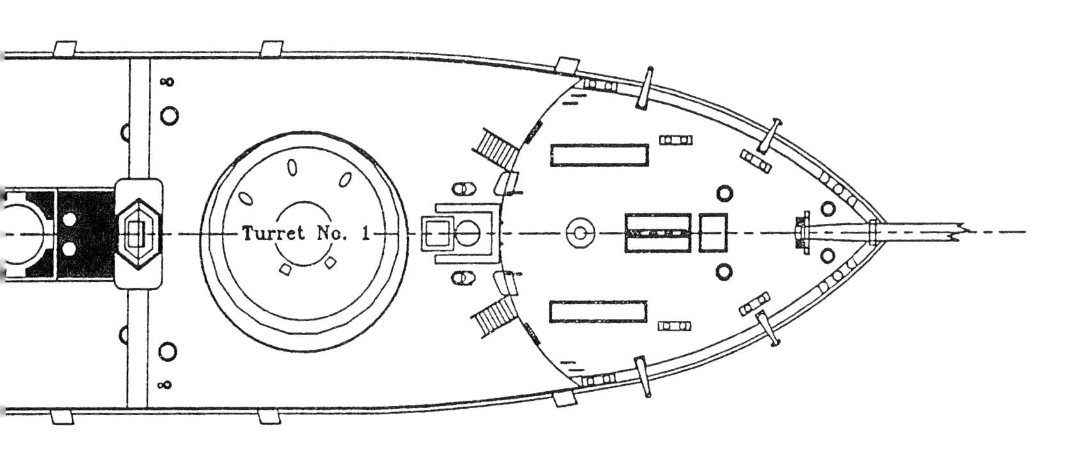

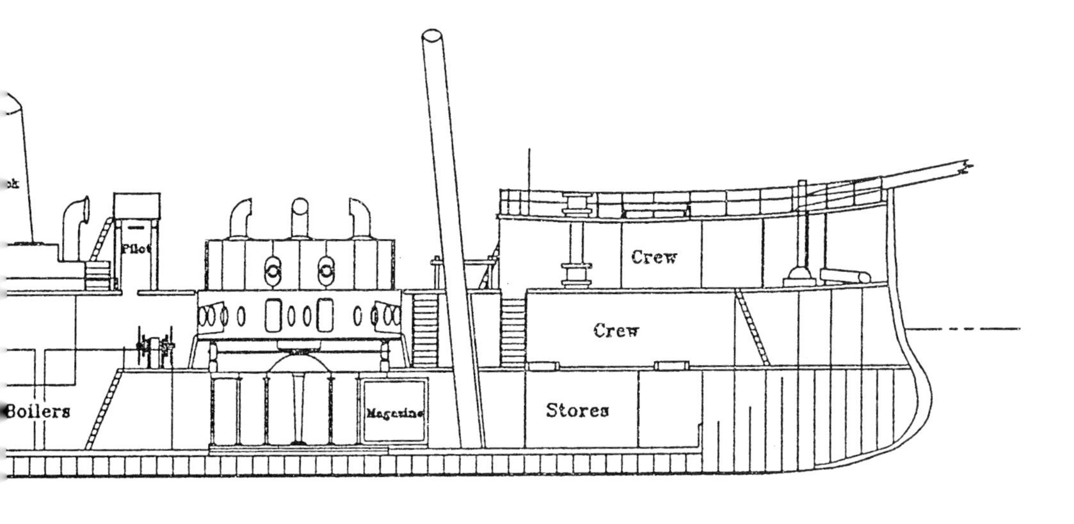

rs 294 & 295
62–1864
orks
IVERN

Length: 259 feet
Width: 43 Feet
Displacement: 3,000 tons
Armor: 4.5 Inches
Armament: 4 300–pounders
Crew: 150

Arnold A. Putnam, Kennebunkport, Maine
January 27, 1998

Captain James D Bullock. (US Naval Historical Foundation, Washington, DC)

for the two warships. To further obscure their destination, he transferred ownership of the vessels in June 1863 to Messrs Bravay & Cie of Paris, supposedly for the Pasha of Egypt. They had agreed to hold the vessels and return them at sea to Bullock, for a nominal fee, upon completion. The subterfuge fooled no one, and an inquiry with the Government of Egypt confirmed that the vessels were not bound for the Pasha.

The *El Toussan* was finally launched at about eleven o'clock on Saturday 4 July 1863. By 7 August the workers had her masts up, boilers and machinery in. The funnel was up and the 150-ton forward turret was on board *El Toussan* when her sister ship, *El Monnassir*, was launched on 29 August.

No one was deceived by the spurious names, and an inquiry by the British Government to the Egyptian Government confirmed that the vessels were not destined for their navy. After a request by Lairds for a trial trip by *El Toussan* in September, the Surveyor of Customs in Liverpool granted, then denied the request. The Palmerston government, which had been carefully watching the progress of the ironclads, finally took action. Lord Russell, the Home Secretary had earlier ordered the Admiralty to dispatch a guardship, HMS *Majestic*, to watch over the newly launched *El Toussan*. In addition, the Liverpool Collector of Customs was instructed not to allow the ship to leave the graving dock under any circumstances. The Surveyor of Customs finally seized the rams on 9 October.

To placate the politically well-connected Lairds, the Admiralty signed an agreement on 8 August 1864, stipulating that the Admiralty would pay Lairds £25,000 for completion of the *El Toussan* and *El Monnassir*. In July 1865 the former *El Toussan* was commissioned as HMS *Scorpion* at Portsmouth Dockyard. HMS *Wivern*, formerly *El Monnassir*, hoisted her commissioning pennant in October. Both vessels were armed with four 9in muzzle-loading rifled guns on iron mountings and slides. These were cumbersome and slow-firing. According to Parkes, the change from full elevation to full depression took one hour in smooth water with an even keel.

Following commissioning, the *Wivern* underwent speed trials on 4 October 1865, over the measured mile, attaining a speed of over 11kts. The ironclad made six runs at full power averaging just over 10kts. Both vessels passed their steam , sail and gunnery trials successfully. The two served briefly with the Channel Fleet, but HMS *Scorpion* was ordered to Bermuda to serve as a harbour defence ship. She served in this capacity for thirty years until decommissioned, and was sunk as a target in 1901. Raised in 1902, she sank while being towed to Boston. HMS *Wivern* was sent to Hong Kong in 1880, also as a harbour defence vessel. She later became a water distilling ship before being sold for scrap in 1922.

A final question: Would the rams have had a decisive effect on the outcome of the American Civil War? 'What if' questions always run the risk of relying on too many assumptions, but based on the available evidence, the answer has to be 'little'. The rams could have caused considerable damage, perhaps even lifting the blockade temporarily. They would, after an ocean voyage, need a friendly port to rest the crew and resupply for combat. It is unlikely that the ironclads could have reached the American coast before the winter, possibly even the spring, of 1864. Other than Charleston and Mobile, there were no deep-water ports in Confederate hands. The Union Navy had enough warships available at that time to overwhelm the two rams. They would simply have been too little, too late.

Sources

US Government. *Official Records of the Union and Confederate Navies in the War of Rebellion*. Government Printing Office, Washington, DC. 1899.

Parkes, Oscar. *British Battleships*. Naval Institute Press, Annapolis, MD. 1990.

Bowcock, A & Taylor, J. *Laird History*. Cammell Laird Archives, Birkenhead Town Hall, Birkenhead, Wirral. 1988.

King, J W. *Report on the Dockyards and Iron Works of Great Britain and France*. 38th Congress, 2nd Session, Washington, DC. 1865.

Plans: Birkenhead Iron Works, 1856 and 1859. Cammell Laird Archives.

Contracts Package. Cammell Laird Archives. Location No. 005/0195/039 & /040 General Dimensions. Sheet 1.

Bulloch, James D. *The Secret Service of the Confederate States in Europe*. G. P. Putnam's Sons, New York, NY. 1884. 2 Vols.

The Times, July- October 1865

Correspondence Respecting Iron-clad Vessels Building at Birkenhead, Parliamentary Papers, British Sessional Papers, House of Commons, Vol. LXII, No. 5, 1864.

THE SEA OF AZOV EXPEDITION, 1855

The Royal Navy's entry into the Sea of Azov behind the Crimean peninsula in 1855 provided a welcome alternative to the largely static siege of Sevastopol, in which Navy guns and personnel had been making good the deficiencies of the Army. **Eur Ing David K Brown, RCNC** shows how this relatively small-scale but cost-effective operation allowed sea power to exert pressure on the Russians by destroying food and forage for the garrison. Although short in duration, it did much to bring the siege to a successful conclusion.

Introduction

The value of the gunboats described by Antony Preston (see *Creating an Inshore Navy* article in this issue) was never made clearer than in the operations in 1855 against Russian supply depots around the very shallow waters of the Sea of Azov. The siege of Sevastopol was never a complete stranglehold; the besieged Russian troops relied on supplies from outside, particularly food from the vast granaries around the Azov, from which 1500 wagons a day passed through Kertch on the way to Sevastopol (Hamilton Williams). Arms and ammunition

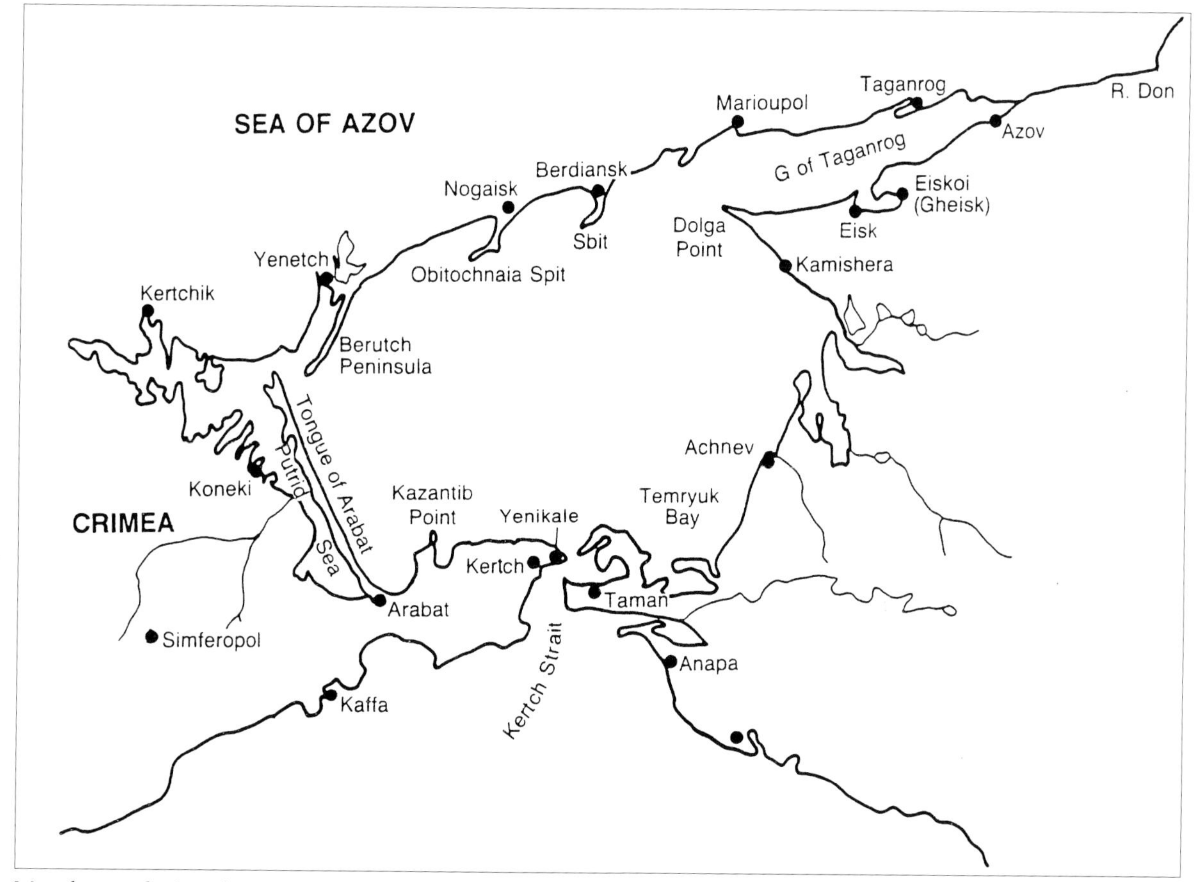

Map showing the Sea of Azov campaign. (Drawn by the author)

Operations in the Baltic, carried out in a very similar manner to those of the Azov Campaign. (National Maritime Museum, Greenwich, London)

came through Rostov on the Don, whilst there were plentiful sources of fodder and of fish.

Planning and Preparation

By the end of 1854 it was clear to Admiral Lyons, commanding the Royal Navy's Black Sea fleet, that this supply route could be closed by quite a small operation to capture Kertch at the entrance to the Azov (see map). Although Lyons was supported by Lord Raglan (the British army commander), by Graham (First Lord of the Admiralty), and by the French Admiral Bruat, the French generals under Canrobert were opposed to such an operation, seeing any diversion as weakening the main attack on Sevastopol.

Nothing could be done until Captain Giffard in HMS *Leopard* reported in early February 1855 that the ice had cleared from the Straits of Kertch and the line of scuttled ships had been broken. In March, Canrobert 'hoped' to be able to provide 12,000 troops in April, the majority of whom were French. The lengthy bombardment of Sevastopol in early April had consumed so much ammunition that it was clear that no major operation against the town could take place until mid May at the earliest.

Embarkation began on the afternoon of 3 May with many of the French troops being carried in British warships for want of transports. Some 56 ships sailed after dark that night and by the evening of 4 May they were close to the planned landing beach near Kertch. In the meantime, Canrobert had received a telegram from the Emperor in Paris, which he interpreted as requiring the recall of the expedition. (See Lambert for a discussion of this interpretation).

However, a new expedition was soon organised with 7000 French, 5000 Turkish and 3500 British troops embarking on 22 May. The fleet was led by nine line-of-battleships (the six British being screw-propelled) with 50 smaller ships. After a demonstration off Kaffa on the morning of 23 May the real landing took place the next morning at Kamisch Borru some five miles south of Kertch. The small vessels pushed on to Kertch and Yenikale, while the Russians retreated. Both towns were abandoned and three small ships previously engaged by the gunvessel HMS *Snake* were destroyed; they also left some 17,000 tons of coal behind. Discipline broke down and the towns were sacked by troops of all three armies and by the local Tartars. The departing Russians also destroyed 4,000,000lbs of grain and 500,000lbs of flour.

The defences were strengthened and a garrison of 7500, the majority of whom were Turkish, was left at Yenikale. On 25 May Captain Lyons (son of the Admiral) in HMS *Miranda* led the light squadron[1] into the Sea of Azov. Hamilton Williams describes the expedition in poetic style:

> The door of the Sea of Azov was now open to us, and fourteen British steamers, aided by four or five French vessels, poured eagerly into the almost unknown sea. It was like bursting into a vast treasure-house crammed with wealth of inestimable value. For miles along the shore stretched the countless storehouses packed with the accumulated harvests of the great corn provinces of Russia. From them the Russian armies in the field were fed; from them the beleaguered population of Sevastopol looked for preservation from the famine which already pressed hard upon them.

Action began on 26 May when some coasters and large stores of grain were burnt at Berdiansk. HMS *Swallow* and HMS *Wrangler* were then detached to control the entrance to the Putrid Sea at Genitchi whilst the rest of the flotilla went on to attack Fort Arabat (30 guns) two days later. After 1½ hours' bombardment the fort blew up, but the garrison was too numerous for a landing to be possible. The following day the force attacked Genitchi and after silencing the batteries a landing party was put ashore to destroy vessels and stores for which three officers received the Victoria Cross (VC). Lyons claimed that in the first four days the flotilla had destroyed four small warships, 246 merchant vessels and coal and flour worth £150,000 and sufficient food to feed 100,000 men for nearly four months.

The force moved on to the even shallower waters of the Gulf of the Don at Taganrog, where they were joined by two small steamers[2] and twelve launches from the fleet armed with 24pdr howitzers and rockets for use in water too shallow even for the gunboats. The force anchored about 8 ½ miles off Taganrog in 18ft of water on 1 June but, due to an easterly wind, the sea level fell three feet and the ships had to move a further 1 ½ miles out. The town governor Count Tolstoi rejected a call to surrender and fire was opened by the *Recruit*, covering a number of boats using their howitzers and rockets. A four-oared gig, manned by volunteers put men ashore, burning several stores and winning two more VCs. Mariopol was taken on 5 June, without opposition, and Gheisk the following day, all government property being destroyed. Detached ships carried out similar operations at Temriouk and Kiten after which the squadron returned to Kertch. Lyons planned an attack on the Tchongar bridge which involved dragging a boat over the Arabat Spit into the Putrid sea but the crew were forced to give up only three miles short of the objective. Captain Lyons and *Miranda* returned to Sevastopol where he was fatally wounded on 17 June, dying a week later.

The light squadron returned to the Azov under Commander Sherard Osborne, the boats of HMS *Vesuvius* destroying a small vessel at Kamieshwa and routing a force of Cossacks on 22 June. And so it went on; rather than attempting to describe every event, they are listed below in note form (see Laird Clowes for a fuller account):

June

24 *Vesuvius* destroyed guns at Petrovski.
27 Boats destroyed a wagon convoy near Genitchi.
27 Landing party from *Beagle* destroyed a floating bridge to Arabat at Genitchi – another VC. HMS *Curlew* later destroyed the only remaining bridge to the Spit of Arabat.

July

Bad weather prevented much activity in the first half of the month.
15 Corn stacks burnt at Berdiansk.
16 Fort Petrovski destroyed. Forage and fisheries destroyed at the mouth of the River Berda.
17 An attempt was made to attack stores at Glofira (Glafirovka) near Gheisk, but a strong force of cavalry prevented any landing. However, corn and fish stocks on a nearby spit were destroyed. The water was too shallow for *Vesuvius* and *Swallow* but the six *Gleaner* class gun boats could get in.
18 Fisheries on the Crooked Spit destroyed.
23 The gunboat *Jasper* ran aground on the Crooked Spit while her exhausted captain, the only officer on board, was asleep and was abandoned and blown up. (See Preston & Major, *Send a Gunboat* for further detail).

Before the end of the month further destructive visits were paid to Genitchi and Berdiansk.

August

5 Guns captured at Taganrog.
6-7 Barracks and stores destroyed at Petrushena.
23 Genitchi shelled.
23-24 Stores destroyed at Kiril and Gorelia.
27 Genitchi attacked.
30-31 Bay of Arabat attacked by *Weser* and *Cracker*; *Vesuvius* at Maripol.

September

13 *Cracker*'s boats destroyed fisheries and stores at Perebond.
24 The Azov flotilla joined with Captain Hall's Kertch squadron to land a considerable force of troops at Taman and Fanagoria, where the Russians had built barracks. These were destroyed together with sixty-two guns and stores. As a diversion, three gunboats and three French ships entered Temriouk Lake.

October

The shallow-draught *Gleaner* class gunboats were withdrawn for the Kinburn operation for most of the month, but the remaining ships kept up the work of destruction.
10 *Weser*'s boats entered the Salgir River.
15&18 *Recruit* at White House Spit.
20 *Arrow* at Crooked Spit.
24 *Vesuvius*' boats at Bieloserai Spit, *Recruit* at Mariopol.

November

3-6 The whole force including those from Kinburn carried out a series of major attacks on stores in the Gheisk region, using a large landing party. On 4 October it was estimated that fires extended over a two-mile front.

Ice was beginning to form in the Azov and the flotilla withdrew, although *Snake* remained off Kertch until 1 December. Planning for an 1856 campaign was in hand when the war ended.

What Effect Did It Have?

Military historians unfamiliar with sea power have tended either to ignore this expedition or to dismiss it as a sideshow, whereas Russian accounts used by Seaton suggest that it was an ineffective "terror" campaign. Almost certainly they are wrong; as Lambert's carefully reasoned

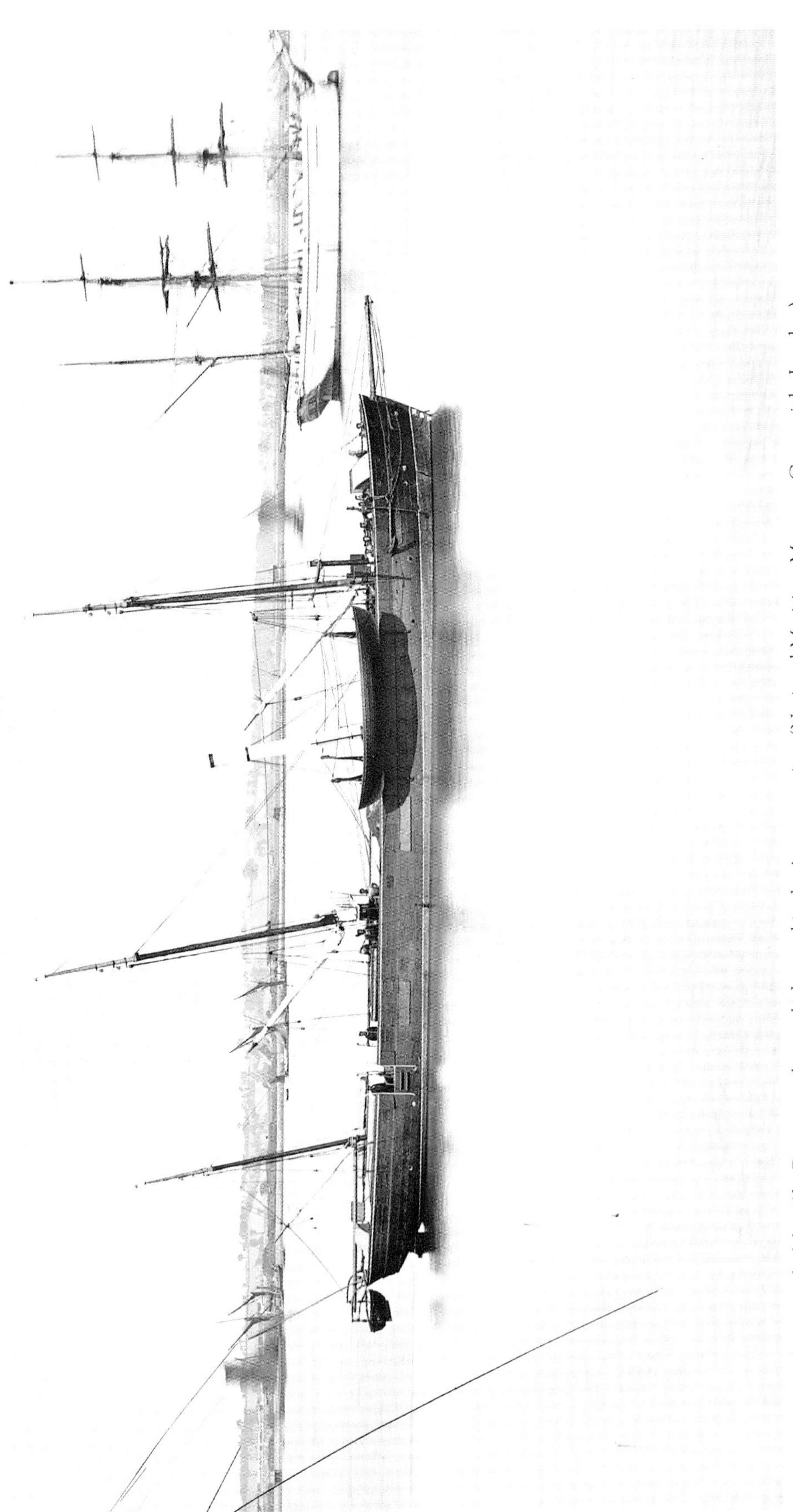

HMS Magnet*, 1858 - typical of the 60hp* Dapper *gunboats which served in the Azov campaign.* (National Maritime Museum, Greenwich, London)

account shows, the Russians deployed a very large number of troops in a vain attempt to protect the shores of the Azov, and installed a considerable number of batteries and earthworks.

Even by the end of June fodder was very scarce and the Russian supply wagons ceased to travel, which in turn meant that their cavalry in the Crimea was no longer able to keep the supply route to Sevastopol open.

The destruction of fodder, food, fish and other supplies, together with interruption to supply routes, must have been a major factor in the Russian decision to evacuate Sevastopol. The destruction of property was immense and many innocent Russians must have suffered in consequence. It anticipated Sherman's destructive march through Georgia by a decade.

Finally, one may see that the planning of both Admiral and Captain Lyons and Commander Osborne's execution of this operation, together with Sulivan's plans in the Baltic, should dispel the myth of Victorian admirals interested in "spit and polish" alone, as well as the canard of the Royal Navy achieving nothing in the Russian War. Only just in time the need for shallow-draught warships had been appreciated and the Royal Navy had become the finest coast-attack navy in the world. Quite correctly, Antony Preston has written 'It was the last old-fashioned war for the Army, but the first modern war for the Navy'.

Principal Sources

Lambert, A D. *The Crimean War*. Manchester University Press, 1990.

Clowes, W L. *The Royal Navy*. London, 1901 (Reprinted London, 1997).

Williams, H. *Britain's Naval Power*. London, 1898.

Preston, A & Major, J. *Send a Gunboat*. London, 1967.

Seaton, A. *The Crimean War, A Russian Chronicle*. London, 1977.

Eardley Wilmot, S. *The Life of Lord Lyons*.

Dewar, A (Ed). *The Russian War 1855; the Black Sea*. Navy Records Society, 1945.

Acknowledgements

My thanks are due to Dr Andrew Lambert for his help and advice.

Notes

1 Royal Navy: *Vesuvius* (paddle), *Curlew*, *Swallow*, *Stromboli* (paddle), *Ardent* (paddle), *Medina* (paddle), *Wrangler*, *Viper*, *Lynx*, *Recruit* (paddle), *Arrow*, *Snake* and *Beagle*. (screw except as noted) and four (later six) French steamers.

2 *Danube* and *Sulina*.

CREATING AN INSHORE NAVY:

Royal Navy Littoral Warfare Forces in the Russian War 1854-56

Continuing the Crimean theme, **Antony Preston** examines the role of inshore bombardment as a decisive factor in forcing the Russians to admit defeat. Military historians are generally obsessed with land operations in the Crimea, and ignore naval operations, yet the Admiralty always saw the Baltic as the most important theatre, and created a specialised inshore bombardment force to implement its strategy. It is a remarkable story of mass-production of a huge force in a very short time, during a period of great technological change.

The problems encountered by the Royal Navy in the Baltic and Black Sea campaigns of 1854 against Russia are well documented, but details of the response are less well known. The floating batteries have been fully described elsewhere, but they were only one solution to the problem of waging war against an enemy who refused to leave his fortified harbours. There is also the problem of contemporary public perceptions of the war, which assumed that the Crimea was the primary objective. Nor have many historians managed to penetrate the fog, and I have followed the suggestion of Andrew Lambert in reviving the old name, the Russian War, in place of the misleading 'Crimean'. The Royal Navy's main objective was Kronstadt, to bring pressure to bear on the Tsar and his ministers, and the Army's disasters in the Crimea merely diverted resources earmarked for operations in the Eastern Baltic. To achieve that aim the Royal Navy ordered six wooden-hulled and three iron-hulled floating batteries, and in parallel built a fleet of small craft to operate in very shallow water. Collectively this shipbuilding effort was known as the Great Armament, intended to be completed by 1 March 1856.

Although a number of minor warships had been built pre-war, most of them drew too much water, notably those with Symondite hull-forms. Even the new *Arrow* class gunvessels were found to draw too much water when operating in the Black Sea, and clearly a new approach was needed. By June 1854 W H Walker, a constructor in the Surveyor's Department, had completed a design for a new class of gunboats with a draught of only 6ft 6in (2m). The first six were known as the *Gleaner* class, and were ordered in the same month at an average price of £8200. The builder was responsible for the hull, while engines would be installed by the machinery contractor and armament by the Royal Dockyards.

Name	*Builder*	*Launched*
Gleaner	Deptford Dyd	7 October 1854
Ruby	Deptford Dyd	7 October 1854
Badger (ex-*Ranger*)	Pitcher, Northfleet	23 September 1854
Pelter	Pitcher, Northfleet	26 August 1854
Pincher	Pitcher, Northfleet	5 September 1854
Snapper	Pitcher, Northfleet	4 October 1854

Tonnage: 218-tons bom (average)
Dimensions: 100ft (pp) x 22ft x 6ft 6in
Depth of Hold: 7ft 9in
Machinery: 1-shaft horizontal reciprocating, 3 boilers, 270 ihp = 7.5kts

The hull was flat-bottomed, with a false keel about 3in deep, with a full bow and stern and a long parallel body with vertical sides. The turn of bilge was tight, and heavy bilge keels were fitted. The stem was slightly cut away, with no knee, and the stern was a square transom. As designed they were given a simple fore and aft schooner rig. Three boats were carried, two seaboats on davits port and starboard of the funnel and a gig on davits at the taffrail. A large tiller was provided. Between decks a single-shaft 60hp (nominal) horizontal direct-acting two-cylinder engine and three cylindrical boilers (two in Penn-engined gunboats) produced 270hp (indicated) for a theoretical maximum speed of 7.5kts. Coal 'boxes' (the term used in original documents, not bunkers) accommodated 25 tons, and the entire installation accounted for the midships half of the hull. The propeller was two-bladed, 6ft diameter and non-hoisting.

Ratings berthed forward, with a single stove for cooking and heating. The shell room was positioned forward of the boilers and funnel uptake, with water tanks on either side affording some protection. The machinery was abaft the boilers, and the magazine was positioned further aft, also protected by water tanks on either side. Officers lived aft, with a wash basin the only concession to personal cleanliness. Sanitary arrangements were primitive: 'seats of ease' forward and aft – in effect a plank with a hole in it, set into the 4ft high bulwarks forward and aft (port or starboard, according to builder's preference).

HMS *Seagull* (one of the later *Albacore* class) ran a series of trials off Greenhithe on 8 January 1856, She took on board forty-nine 68pdr round shot as movable ballast, and had all guns shipped, as well as 27.5 tons of coal and 4.5 tons of water. With the shot moved aft and a trim of 6ft 11in aft/7ft 9in forward her speed was 8kts. When the shot were moved forward abreast of the mainmast she floated on an even keel at 7ft.

Complement was 36 on average. According to work done by the late George Osbon and confirmed by my own sampling of logbooks, the complement broke down as follows:

1 Lieutenant or Mate
1 Boatswain
1 Gunner
1 Carpenter
3 Assistant Engineers
1 Leading Stoker
10 Stokers
12 Seamen
2 Boys
4 Royal Marines

36 Total

Designed armament was two single 68pdr 95cwt smooth-bore muzzle-loaders (ML), carried on iron slides and positioned forward and aft of the funnel, and two 24pdr ML howitzers on truck carriages, positioned abaft the mainmast to port and starboard. This proved too heavy, and in most a 32pdr 56cwt ML replaced the forward 68pdr. For special operations, notably the bombardment of Sveaborg in 1855, some gunboats shipped a heavier armament. HMS *Snapper* is credited with carrying three Lancaster 68pdr rifled ML guns; HMS *Gleaner* is credited with a number of armament changes; HMS *Pincher* carried three 68pdr smooth-bore MLs at one time. These were, however, exceptional, and only suitable when the gunboats were operating in sheltered waters. In the open sea the weight of the large guns

Lancaster 68pdr rifled muzzle-loader (the first rifled gun in the Royal Navy), on board HM gunvessel Snake *in the Black Sea, 1854.* (National Maritime Museum, Greenwich, London)

Practising 68pdr gun-drill aboard the gunboat Starling. *Note the 24pdr howitzers port and starboard.* (National Maritime Museum, Greenwich, London)

made them difficult to handle, and training both on the beam pivots caused a considerable heel and reduced range. For open sea passages the heavy guns were shipped aboard larger , accompanying warships, although the howitzers were left in place.

In October 1854, not long after work started on the *Gleaner* class, a further twenty were ordered. Although slightly longer and deeper (107ft and 7ft 10in respectively, on average) they were very similar to the original design. Costs of material and labour were already rising because of the wartime boom, and average cost went up to nearly £10,000. A wider range of builders was used for this group.

Name	*Builder*	*Launched*
Lark	Deptford Dyd	15 March 1855
Magpie	Deptford Dyd	15 March 1855
Starling	Pitcher, Northfleet	1 February 1855
Snap	Pitcher, Northfleet	3 February 1855
Thistle	Pitcher, Northfleet	3 February 1855
Dapper	Pitcher, Northfleet	31 March 1855
Fancy	Pitcher, Northfleet	31 March 1855
Redwing	Pitcher, Northfleet	19 March 1855
Weazel	Pitcher, Northfleet	19 March 1855
Boxer	Pitcher, Northfleet	7 April 1855
Clinker	Pitcher, Northfleet	2 April 1855
Cracker	Pitcher, Northfleet	2 April 1855
Stork	Pitcher, Northfleet	7 April 1855
Biter	Pitcher, Northfleet	5 May 1855
Skylark	Pitcher, Northfleet	3 May 1855
Swinger	Pitcher, Northfleet	10 May 1855
Hind	Thompson, Rotherhithe	3 May 1855
Jackdaw	Thompson, Rotherhithe	18 May 1855
Hind	Thompson, Rotherhithe	3 May 1855
Jackdaw	Thompson, Rotherhithe	18 May 1855
Grinder	White, Cowes	7 March 1855
Jasper	White, Cowes	2 April 1855

The placing of such a large order, against a background of accelerated building in the Royal Dockyards, required a major effort on the part of small commercial shipyards, particularly on the Thames. To ease the problems of fitting out, the Admiralty later built a new Gunboat Yard at Haslar, where the hulls could be coppered, rigged and armed. Isambard Brunel designed a traversing steam-powered carriage to allow the gunboats to be moved for re-launching from under cover to the slipway.

Builders were paid in installments, in the case of the *Dapper* class £1600 each. The first was payable when framing was complete, the second on launch, and the third on delivery. With so much work available labourers

The bombardment of Sveaborg, 1855. Historians and contemporary commentators have dismissed this bombardment as a 'three day firework display' – in fact it was a rehearsal for the attack on Kronstadt. (National Maritime Museum, Greenwich, London)

were able to hawk their services from one firm to another, and there were also strikes, 'go-slows' and absenteeism, much of the latter in the form of 'long lunches' in taverns. Wages rose from 7 shillings an hour to an eventual peak of 15 shillings. Although shift-working, resorted to during the winters of 1854-55 and 1855-56, was in theory a more efficient way of working, the dilution of the labour-force reduced the quality of workmanship. There was also a great deal of pilfering, leading in many cases to sub-standard construction.

The most severe problem was, however, the shortage of seasoned timber. The specification called for oak or elm to be used for the keel, oak for the stem and stern, 3-5in oak planking for the side, and fir planking on the deck. Because there were insufficient Admiralty overseers some contractors used green timber, a problem which caused a major scandal subsequently.

Despite the size of the order, only two firms were contracted to supply machinery: Maudslay, Son & Field of Lambeth and John Penn of Greenwich, who were awarded contracts for ten sets each in October 1854. The two firms resorted to some sub-contracting to cope with the volume of work, with Thames Iron Works forging crankshafts for Penn, for example. Both types of engine used boilers working at 35lbs/square in, regarded as a very high pressure at the time. These boilers were similar to those in railway locomotives, but working at half the pressure because they were using salt water. They gave considerable trouble through tube plates burning, and the machinery tended to suffer from wear through high rotational speed, and poor lubrication led to worn bearings.

Because of their cramped accommodation and limited endurance the gunboats sent to the Baltic and the Black Sea in 1855 were normally employed as tenders to larger ships. Although in theory this provided them with a ready source of ammunition, fresh water and provisions to extend their operating radius, it proved unsatisfactory, and for the 1856 operations they were to be grouped in three divisions: six gunvessels and 40 gunboats in each, headed by the partly-disarmed steam battleships *Algiers*, *Brunswick* and *Colossus*, with a fourth division of two gunvessels and 20 gunboats headed by the *Sans Pareil*. They ranged freely around the islands between Sweden and Finland and the Sea of Azov, destroying stores and harassing scattered Russian garrisons (see D K Brown's account in this issue). The major action in the second Baltic campaign was the bombardment of Sveaborg on 9-11 August 1855, in which all the available gunboats and mortar vessels took part. According to Laird Clowes nineteen gunboats (twenty-two according to Lambert)

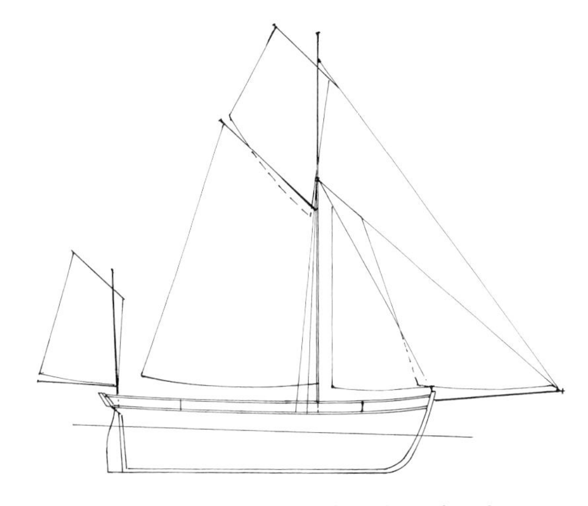

Sail plan of the mortar vessel Sinbad *(Redrawn by John Roberts)*

were sent to the Baltic: *Badger*, *Biter*, *Dapper*, *Gleaner*, *Jackdaw*, *Lark*, *Magpie*, *Pelter*, *Pincher*, *Redwing*, *Ruby*, *Skylark*, *Snap*, *Snapper*, *Starling*, *Stork*, *Swinger*, *Thistle* and *Weazel*. Of these only *Jackdaw*, *Ruby* and *Swinger* were absent at Sveaborg. Six gunboats were ordered to the Black Sea, arriving in June 1855: *Boxer*, *Clinker*, *Cracker*, *Fancy*, *Grinder* and *Jasper*. They operated in the Sea of Azov, and the *Boxer*, *Clinker*, *Cracker* and *Fancy* were also present at the bombardment of Kinburn on 14 October.

The success of the *Gleaners* and *Dappers* led to huge orders for repeat *Dappers* (also known as the *Albacore* class) in 1855; 23 in May-June, 23 more in July and 52 in October-November. As with the *Dappers*, Maudslay and Penn received all the engine orders, 49 sets each between May and November 1855. None of this group was completed in time for the end of the war, although all were afloat in June 1856. Orders were spread over a wide area of the country, presumably because the Thames yards were fully occupied.

Briggs, Sunderland
Magnet, Manly, Mastiff, Mistletoe

Fletcher, Limehouse
Firm, Flamer, Fly, Julia, Louisa

Green, Blackwall
Camel, Caroline, Cherokee, Cochin, Confounder, Crocus, Fervent, Forester, Griper, Spanker, Thrasher, Traveller

Hill, Bristol
Hardy, Havock, Highlander

Laird, Birkenhead
Beacon, Blazer, Brave, Brazen, Rainbow, Raven, Redbreast, Rocket, Rose

Mare, Blackwall
Bouncer, Hyaena, Nightingale, Savage, Violet, Wolf

Pitcher, Northfleet
Banterer, Bullfrog, Bustard, Carnation, Charger, Charon, Cockchafer, Dove, Forward, Grasshopper, Hasty, Haughty, Herring, Insolent, Leveret, Magnet, Mayflower, Peacock, Pheasant, Pickle, Plover, Porpoise, Primrose, Procris, Prompt, Sandfly, Seagull, Shamrock, Sheldrake, Skipjack, Spey, Staunch, Tickler, Tilbury

Patterson, Bristol
Escort

Smith, North Shields
Erne, Lively, Sepoy, Spider, Surly, Swan

White, Cowes
Albacore, Amelia

Wigram, Northfleet
Beaver, Delight, Goldfinch, Goshawk, Grappler, Growler, Parthian, Quail, Ripple, Wave, Whiting

Wigram, Blackwall
Foam, Opossum, Partridge, Wave, Whiting

Experience in the Baltic showed that even the 6ft 6in draught of the *Gleaner* design was too deep for the shallow inlets and channels. To meet this need W H Walker produced a design drawing only 4ft, the so-called 20hp type, otherwise known as the *Cheerful* class. The specification seems to have carried weight-saving too far, and they were the least successful of all the Crimean gunboats. The machinery was a Penn single-cylinder horizontal direct-acting single-piston engine developing 92ihp, equivalent to a speed of 6.75kts. Steam was generated by two cylindrical boilers. Armament was two 32pdr 56cwt smooth-bores and complement was 30 officers and ratings. The two-masted rig could only set 1919 sq ft of canvas, as against 2426 sq ft in the original *Gleaner* rig before it was modified.

Orders were placed in July-November 1855, and average cost was £7000.

Devonport Dockyard
Angler, Ant

Laird, Birkenhead
Blossom, Gadfly, Garland, Gnat

Deptford Dockyard
Cheerful

Sheerness Dockyard
Chub

Westbrook, Blackwall
Daisy, Dwarf

Joyce, Greenwich
Fidget, Flirt

Young & Son, Limehouse
Midge, Onyx, Pert, Tiny

Pembroke Dockyard
Decoy, Nettle, Pet, Rambler

Tonnage:	212-tons bom (average)
Dimensions:	100ft x 21ft 10in x 6ft 6in
Depth of hold:	6ft 7in (average)
Machinery:	Single-shaft horizontal direct-acting, two cylindrical boilers, 92ihp = 8kts
Complement:	30 officers and ratings

To rectify the faults of the 20hp type, an improved design was prepared, the 40hp *Clown* type, with a longer hull and more powerful machinery. Orders were placed in January 1856 and cost rose to £9500-£10,000, the same as the larger *Dapper*/*Albacore* design. The enlarged hull enabled the armament to be increased to a 68pdr 95cwt smooth-bore and a 32pdr 56cwt.

Briggs, Sunderland
Ready, Thrush

Miller, Liverpool
Clown, Kestrel

Pembroke Dockyard
Drake, Janus

Pitcher, Northfleet
Fenella, Garnet, Handy, Hunter

Smith, North Shields
Watchful, Woodcock

Tonnage:	238-tons bom (average)
Dimensions:	110ft x 22ft x 4ft
Depth of Hold:	6ft 7in (average)
Machinery:	Single-shaft horizontal direct-acting, two cylindrical boilers, 145ihp = 7.5kts
Complement:	30 officers and ratings

Other Russian War gunboats should also be mentioned. The *Azov* and *Kertch* were schooner-rigged sailing gunboats, built in an attempt to improvise from local resources. They were ordered from Messrs German at Malta, both being launched on 14 July 1855. They measured 94 tons (bom) and were 64ft long, and were armed with two guns of unidentified calibre, probably 32pdrs. The Australian colonial government of Victoria, worried about possible Russian raids in the Pacific, ordered a ketch-rigged gunboat from John Cuthbert of Miller's Point. The *Spitfire* was launched on 4 April 1855. She measured 60 tons (bom) and was 62ft (pp) in length; armament was a single 32pdr 56cwt smooth-bore ML. Two more are recorded as having been built in 1854-56 for Brazil. The *Japura* was a 120ft wooden vessel armed with two 68pdrs and two 32pdrs, and the *Maracana*, a 102ft composite vessel built by an unidentified Falmouth yard, and armed with two 32pdr guns. The latter is recorded as a 'Baltic gunboat' – the only known export order, although the *Japura* has dimensions similar to the post-war *Algerine* class.

13in mortar on board an unknown mortar vessel, probably photographed in April 1856 at the Spithead Review. This was the last time these ships were seen in their original state. (National Maritime Museum, Greenwich, London)

As David Brown has pointed out, the truly remarkable feature of the Great Armament was the speed with which over 250 gunboats and mortar vessels were built (see tables), while at the same time the Royal Dockyards were also working to capacity on new construction, conversions and repairs to neutralise any post-war threat from France. The impact of wartime inflation on the yards was disastrous; by 1857 Pitcher and Mare were in receivership, and other yards were in such financial difficulties that the Surveyor of the Navy, Captain Sir Baldwin Walker, authorised *ex gratia* payments to yards to compensate them for their exertions at a time of perceived national crisis. David Brown and other authorities agree that the financial problems marked the beginning of the end for shipbuilding on the Thames.

The Mortar Vessels

In parallel with the gunboat programme the Admiralty also funded a large programme of mortar vessel construction. Although long regarded as obsolete, the high-angle 13in mortar, with its fuzed 196lb bomb, was the only weapon capable of destroying dockyard buildings and magazines, so it was needed for the planned attack on Kronstadt. Fixed in its octagonal well (but, see below), the 5.5-ton mortar fired at a fixed elevation of 45°. Range was altered by the provision of variable charges and appropriate fuze-settings, and lateral corrections by warping to and fro. They were cheap, costing as little as £28 to make.

Charge	*Range*	*Time of Flight*	*Fuze-length*
2lbs	690yds	13 secs	2.7ins
8lbs	2575yds	24.75 secs	5.09ins
12lbs	3500yds	29 secs	6.02ins
20lbs	4200yds	31 secs	6.44ins

In addition to the fuzed bomb, they fired 'carcasses' to set fire to building and stores of timber. These were fuzed, like the bombs, but were filled with highly combustible material intended to burn for several minutes:

ground saltpetre	6lb 4oz
sulphur	2lb 8oz
powdered resin	1lb 14oz
sulphurate of antimony	10oz
tallow	10oz
Venice turpentine	10oz

Two 1834-vintage dockyard lighters, the *Drake* and *Sinbad*, started conversion in October 1854, the former at Portsmouth Dockyard, the latter at Deptford Dockyard. On 19 October 1855 *Drake* was named *Mortar Vessel No.1*, and *Sinbad* became *Mortar Vessel No.2*. Chris Ware suggests that they were armed with a 10in mortar, but the drawings of *Sinbad* refer to 13in, and in any case the 10in had not been in service since 1815.

Tonnage:	105 bom
Dimensions:	60ft 1in x 20ft 9in
Depth of Hold:	9ft
Armament:	1 13in mortar

The mortar vessel HMS Pickle *(MV22) at Sveaborg, August 1855.* (National Maritime Museum, Greenwich, London)

At the same time ten purpose-built craft were ordered, very similar to the *Drake* and *Sinbad*. Although only half the length of the 60hp gunboats the depth of hold was similar, reflecting the weight of the mortar and the stiffening needed under the well.

Name	*Builder*	*Launched*
Blazer	Mare, Blackwall	5 May 1855
Havock	Mare, Blackwall	14 March 1855
Mastiff	Mare, Blackwall	5 May 1855
Manly	Thompson, Rotherhithe	16 May 1855
Porpoise	Thompson, Rotherhithe	26 May 1855
Firm	Wigram, Blackwall	1 March 1855
Flamer	Wigram, Blackwall	1 March 1855
Growler	Wigram, Blackwall	31 March 1855
Surly	Wigram, Blackwall	31 March 1855
Hardy	Wigram, Blackwall	14 March 1855

Tonnage:	117-tons bom
Dimensions:	65ft x 20ft 10in
Depth of Hold:	7ft 8in (average)
Armament:	1 13in mortar

Like the two converted mortar vessels, all ten were renumbered on 19 October 1855:
Blazer = *MV.3*; *Growler* = *MV.4*; *Havock* = *MV.5*; *Manly* = *MV.6*; *Mastiff* = *MV.7*, *Porpoise* = *MV.8*; *Surly* = *MV.9*; *Flamer* = *MV.10*; *Firm* = *MV.11*; *Hardy* = *MV.12*

A further ten of slightly enlarged type were ordered in October:

Name	*Builder*	*Launched*
Raven	Green, Blackwall	19 April 1855
Redbreast	Green, Blackwall	5 May 1855
Rocket	Green, Blackwall	5 May 1855
Pickle	Mare, Blackwall	23 May 1855
Prompt	Mare, Blackwall	23 May 1855
Beacon	Wigram, Blackwall	21 April 1855
Camel	Wigram, Blackwall	21 April 1855
Carron	Wigram, Blackwall	28 April 1855
Grappler	Wigram, Blackwall	1 May 1855
Magnet	Wigram, Northam	2 May 1855

They were also given numbers on 19 October 1855:
Raven = *MV.13*; *Camel* = *MV.14*; *Magnet* = *MV.15*; *Beacon* = *MV.16*; *Carron* = *MV.17*; *Grappler* = *MV.18*; *Redbreast* = *MV.19*; *Rocket* = *MV.20*; *Prompt* = *MV.21*; *Pickle* = *MV.22*

Tonnage:	160-tons bom
Dimensions:	70ft x 23ft 4in
Depth of Hold:	9ft 6in
Armament:	1 13in mortar

The substitution of numbers for names caused confusion for many years, leading authorities like Lecky to refer to 'mortar vessels converted to gunboats', while Laird Clowes referred to them as having 60hp engines. This was understandable as the named mortar vessels disappeared from the Navy List at the end of 1855, yet some of the names reappeared in 1856 as gunboats. The mystery was finally solved by George Osbon of the National Maritime Museum. The *Camel*, *Firm*, *Flamer*, *Hardy*, *Magnet* and *Raven* were present at Kinburn, according to Admiral Sir Edmund Lyons' dispatch dated 18 October 1855, the day before the Admiralty ordered the renumbering. Some time would have elapsed before the change was executed.

Seventeen mortar vessels (twenty-two according to Lambert) left for the Baltic in late March-early April 1856: the *Beacon*, *Blazer*, *Carron*, *Drake*, *Grappler*, *Growler*, *Havock*, *Lively*, *Manly*, *Mastiff*, *Pickle*, *Porpoise*, *Prompt*, *Redbreast*, *Rocket*, *Sinbad* and *Surly*. Of these, only *Lively* appears to have been absent from the bombardment of Sveaborg. The mortars were manned by the Royal Marine Artillery, as the Corps had done since 1804. The complement was even smaller than the gunboats, usually a mate in command, a dozen seamen and four or five marines. The light single-masted rig was for passage only; mortar vessels fired at anchor to achieve maximum accuracy.

A further thirty-two numbered craft were ordered in November-December 1855, but saw no service. They were virtually identical to the *Raven* class:

Briggs, Sunderland
MV.53-54

Hoad Bros
MV.35-36

Harvey, Ipswich
MV.45-48

Hessel & Holmes
MV.44

Inman
MV.37

Lungley, Deptford (*MV.28* built at Northam, possibly sub-contracted to Wigram).
MV.23-28

Patterson, Bristol
MV.49-52

Scott & Long
MV.38-43

Thompson, Rotherhithe
MV.29-34

White, Cowes
MV.55-56

In addition 50 unnamed iron mortar floats were ordered in November 1855. These lacked even the vestigial rig of the mortar vessels, and were no more than dumb lighters.

They were slightly smaller than the mortar vessels: 60ft in length, 6ft 9in depth of hold and displacing 104ft (average figures).

Laird, Birkenhead (possibly not Birkenhead)
No.103, Nos.136-150

Mare, Blackwall
Nos.104-111

Samuda, Poplar
No.101

Scott Russell, Millwall
No.102, 124-135

Unknown
Nos.112-113

Tonnage:	100-tons bom
Dimensions:	60ft x 20ft x 5ft 8in
Depth of Hold:	6ft 6in (average)
Armament:	1 13in mortar

Five frigates were selected for conversion to 'mortar frigates', with two 13in mortars and a mixed armament of 68pdrs and 32pdrs. All ran trials, but only one, HMS *Horatio*, appears to have received her armament, and she saw no action.

Foreign Acquisitions

In addition to these massive construction programmes the Admiralty also succeeded in acquiring two unusual double-ended iron paddle gunboats from the Prussian Navy. The *Nix* and *Salamander* had been built to a specification framed by Prince Adalbert and were ordered from Scott Russell in 1849. The *Nix* was launched in 1850 and was commissioned on 29 July 1851; her sister *Salamander* was launched in 1850 and commissioned on 1 July 1851. This contradicts all British sources consulted, who say that the two ships were purchased while under construction (or fitting out) by Scott Russell, whereas German records are quite clear that the ships had been in service with the Prussian Navy for over three years.

The design was unorthodox, with rudders forward and aft. They proved good seaboats, but the turning circle was larger than predicted because the bow rudder proved useless, and they were virtually unmanageable under unassisted sail.

Tonnage:	430-tons(bom)
Dimensions:	53.05m wl x 7.2m (hull) x 2.00m
Armament:	4 25pdr ML howitzers
	4 12pdr ML (intended)
Machinery:	2 2-cylinder oscillating direct-acting engines, 4 boilers, 600ihp = 13kts
Endurance:	2500 nm @ 10kts
Complement:	74 officers and ratings

The Prussian Navy needed a frigate for training, and after negotiations HMS *Thetis* was handed over on 12 January 1855 in exchange, the *Nix* becoming HMS *Recruit* and *Salamander* becoming HMS *Weser*. They were rearmed with four 8in 65cwt shell guns, and drew favourable comments when operating in the Sea of Azov in 1855.

Two diminutives were ordered from Scott Russell in November 1855 at a cost of £11,400 each. On a tonnage of 267 (bom) and a draught of only 4ft, HMS *Bann* and HMS *Brune* carried two 8in shell guns and two short 32pdr 25cwt guns. Their oscillating two-cylinder engines developed 364ihp, equivalent to 10.5kts. Both were delivered shortly after the end of the war.

Lambert mentions 'half-hearted' attempts by the Admiralty in 1854 to buy four Brazilian gunboats building on the Thames. These were delivered as the *Beberibe* class, and Brazil also bought a composite copy of the *Recruit* design, the *Paraguacu*, from R & H Green.

Epilogue

The signing of the peace treaty on 30 March 1856 brought this huge building programme to an end. It also put an end to the planned seaward assault on Kronstadt, in which the gunboats, mortar vessels and mortar floats would have played a major role alongside the floating batteries. The bombardment of Sveaborg proved that great damage could be done to dockyard facilities, but stone forts continued to be virtually indestructible by naval bombardment alone. On the morning of the third day the bombardment was called off because ammunition was running short, but as a dress rehearsal for the assault on Kronstadt it had achieved its purpose.

In the post-mortem there were complaints about the mortars bursting. During the first hour, HMS *Growler*'s mortar, cast in 1813, fired over 30 rounds, whereas many of the newly-cast mortars proved incapable of sustained firing. HMS *Havock*'s, for example, fired only 94 rounds before bursting, whereas the *Growler*'s fired 355 times. Nine of the 16 mortars fired fewer than 200 rounds, and only two managed more than 300. HMS *Sinbad* stowed 86 filled bombs and 20 incendiary 'carcasses', as well as 40 more unfilled bombs, a total of 146 rounds. David Brown suggests that the figures for rounds fired per mortar vessel could not have exceeded 200 rounds, but Lambert quotes official papers for these figures. and notes that eleven were repaired on station by the factory ship *Volcano*, using molten zinc. Captain Julius Roberts RMA's suspension gear, which allowed the barrel to train, was given its first combat trial at Sveaborg, in the *Drake*, *Surly* and *Growler*, and three others. The system might have been adopted had the mortar not fallen out of favour immediately after the war. For the 1856 campaign it was decided that mortars should be treated as expendable stores, to be replaced from stock.

The immense effort put into creating the Great Armament is easy to criticise, on the grounds that only a small number of ships saw action. However, the prodigality must be set against the purpose for which the gunboats and mortar vessels were ultimately intended: the

TABLE 1: *BUILDERS OF GUNBOATS, MORTAR VESSELS AND FLOATS*

Builder	GBs	MVs	Floats	Total
Briggs, Sunderland[1]	6	2		8
Deptford Dyd	5	1[2]		6[2]
Devonport Dyd	2			2
R H Fletcher, Limehouse	5			5
R&H Green, Blackwall[3]	12	3		15
Harvey, Ipswich		4		4
Hessel & Holmes, Rye		1		1
Charles Hill, Bristol	3			3
Hoad Bros, Rye[4]		2		2
G Inman, Lymington		1		1
Wm Joyce & Co, Greenwich		2		2
Laird, Birkenhead[5]	13		16	29
Chas Lungley, Deptford[6]		6		6
C&J Mare, Blackwall	6	5	18	29
W C Miller, Liverpool[7]	2			2
Patterson & Son, Bristol	1	4		5
Pembroke Dyd	6			6
W&H Pitcher, Northfleet	56			56
Portsmouth Dyd		1[2]		1[2]
Samuda Bros, Poplar			1	1
Scott & Long[8]		6		6
J Scott Russell, Millwall			13	13
Sheerness Dyd	1			1
T&W Smith, N Shields	8			8
J Thompson, Rotherhithe	4	8		12
Westbrook, Blackwall	2			2
White, Cowes[9]	4	2		6
M Wigram & Son, Blackwall	5	9		14
M Wigram & Son, Northam	11	1		12
S Young & Co, Limehouse	4			4
Unknown			2	2
Total	156	56	50	262

Notes:

1 There were three Sunderland yards: James Briggs of North Hylton and Pallion, and William Briggs of Low Southwick.
2 Converted.
3 The Blackwall site appears to have been shared with Wigram, although up to 1843 the name Wigram & Green was used, and the two companies operated separately.
4 There appears to have been a second yard at Sandwich.
5 Two new yards existed at the time: John Laird of Wallasey Pool, and John Laird of Birkenhead, and more than one was involved in building GBs and mortar floats.
6 At least one of these MVs was built at Northam, Southampton, suggesting that these hulls may been sub-contracted to Wigram's Northam yard. There is no record of a Lungley yard there.
7 In addition to the yard at Brunswick Dock, a new yard, Miller & Johnstone, was opened in 1855.
8 No record of this yard can be found.
9 Two yards existed at this time: T & J White at Medina Dock, and J & S White at East Cowes.

great assault on Kronstadt planned for the summer of 1856. Captain Sulivan's plan envisaged the deployment of thirty gunboats and thirty mortar vessels, as well as eight floating batteries. Although parallel schemes for the Black Sea were discussed informally, that was now seen correctly as a secondary theatre. The Royal Navy's newly created inshore offensive capability also proved very relevant to its needs in the next fifteen years or so.

The British public was given a chance to see what its taxes had paid for at the great Victory Review of the Fleet in Spithead on 23 April 1856. In addition to major warships, 120 gunvessels and gunboats and 50 mortar vessels and floats were present. As part of the public entertainment (and to impress the French) the gunboats took part in a mock attack on Southsea Castle, but for most of them it was their only service. The peacetime navy had no use for the mortar vessels and floats because the 13in mortar was quickly declared obsolete, and many became dockyard lighters or coast guard watch vessels. In these humble roles some survived for 30 or 40 years. The gunboats were, however, ideal for local conflict, and a few remained in commission for service in China, where the second Opium War was beginning. Two played a minor role in the Jamaica Rebellion in 1865, and one was given to the fledgling Imperial Japanese Navy. The *Dapper* outlasted them all, surviving until 1922 as a hulk. In 1860 Parliament became aware of problems affecting the later 60hp gunboats and the 20hp and 40hp types. The use of green timber caused 32 to fall to pieces, even though laid up at Haslar, and dry rot continued to plague the rest through the 1860s. They had, however, achieved their purpose, and the design cannot be blamed for sub-standard materials and workmanship. Two classes of similar design were built very shortly after the war, and served with distinction on foreign stations.

References

Brown, David K. *Before the Ironclad* . CMP, 1990.

Brown, David K. *Paddle Warships*. CMP, 1993.

Clowes, Sir Wm Laird. *The Royal Navy Vol VI*. Sampson Low, Marston 1901.

Colledge, J J. *Ships of the Royal Navy Vols I/II*. David & Charles, 1969/1970.

Eardley-Wilmot, Capt S. *Life of VAdm Lord Lyons*. Sampson Low, 1898.

Greenhill, Basil and Giffard, Anne. *The British Assault on Finland*. CMP, 1988.

Gröner, Erich (revised by Dieter Jung & Martin Maass). *German Warships 1815-1945*. CMP, 1990.

Lambert, Andrew. *The Crimean War*. Manchester University Press, 1990.

Osbon, G A. 'The Crimean Gunboats' Parts I/II. *Mariner's Mirror* May and August 1965.

Preston, Antony and Major, John. *Send a Gunboat*. Longmans, 1966.

Ships' Logs etc. PRO

Ships' Plans etc. NMM

Ware, Chris *The Bomb Vessel*. CMP, 1994.

Acknowledgements

I must also acknowledge the help of a number of people, including Bob Todd and David Taylor of the National Maritime Museum, Sr Robert Graz of Rio de Janeiro, Freddi Lindegaard and Ian Buxton of the British Shipbuilding Survey and the late Adrian Caruana of the Royal Artillery Historical Department. Comments and additions are welcome.

THE BATTLE OF THE YALU

17 September 1894

The Battle of the Yalu is of great historical importance, as it was the first naval battle involving large fleets of steel-built warships armed with breech-loading guns and torpedoes. It is also of interest as it marked the beginning of Japanese imperial expansion; on a more domestic note, ships built by the great North Eastern firm of Armstrongs, gunmakers and warship builders, fired on and damaged each other. **Peter Brook** details the lead up to the battle, the action itself, and the outcome and its consequences.

More properly, the Battle of the Yalu should be known as the Battle of the River Tayang, which is situated some 23 miles to the west of the River Yalu, the boundary between Korea and China. Overshadowed four years later by the Spanish-American War and quite eclipsed by the vaster scale and decisive battles of the Russo-Japanese War of 1904-1905, nothing original has appeared in English for 100 years with the exception of an important article by Dr J C Perry which appeared in *Mariners Mirror* in 1964; the campaign remains largely forgotten.

The Background

China claimed suzerainty over the Kingdom of Korea, an assertion strongly resisted by Japan. In 1894 there was an uprising in the south of Korea, possibly instigated by Japan. The King of Korea called on China, as suzerain, to provide troops to put down the rebellion and a force of 2000 men was sent in early June to the port of Asan, some 70 miles to the south of the capital, Seoul, but near to the rebel HQ. In accordance with the 1885 treaty of Tientsin, Japan was informed and in response the government began to pour in troops to the port of Chemulpo north of Asan and near to Seoul, so that by the end of June more than 8000 soldiers had been landed. At this stage, Japan proposed a joint commission to reform Korea which the Chinese rejected out of hand, a response doubtless anticipated by the Japanese, whose real aim was to control Korea. Late in July the Japanese delivered an ultimatum to China to withdraw all her troops, backing this up with a request from the Korean government that the Chinese be expelled.

The unfortunate Koreans had, in fact, completely lost their freedom of action as the Japanese had seized the King in his royal palace on 23 July. Two days later, without any formal declaration of war, a Japanese squadron fired on two Chinese warships, the cruiser *Chi Yuan* (*Tsi Yuan*) and a sloop, severely damaging the former and forcing the latter ashore. The Japanese cruiser *Naniwa*, under the command of Captain Togo, the victor at Tsushima eleven years later, stopped a British merchant ship, the *Kowshing*, carrying 1100 Chinese troops. After *Naniwa*'s order for *Kowshing* to follow her was not complied with, she sank the merchant ship, and ensured that there would be few survivors by firing at boats and swimmers.

The formal declaration of war was not made until 1 August. By mid September the Japanese troops had advanced northwards as far as Pyongyang, where the defending Chinese army was decisively defeated with heavy losses. During this whole period the Chinese fleet under the command of Admiral Ting made no effort to intercept troopships passing between Japan and Korea, apparently under orders from Li Hung Chang, the Viceroy of Chihli, that the primary function of the fleet was to protect the gulf of Chihli, which was the sea approach to Peking. Both fleets engaged in patrolling and convoying troops, although the Japanese did make an ineffective bombardment of Wei-hai-Wei, one of the two Chinese bases in the North.

The Two Fleets Compared

The Chinese navy was not a unified force, despite the efforts of Li Hung Chang to make it one, but consisted of four almost independent navies each located in a different region and under different civil authorities. From North to South and in order of size they were:

Fleet	Region	Responsible Official
Peiyang	Shantung; Yellow Sea	Northern Commissioner of Trade, Tientsin
Nanyang	Shanghai; Lower Yangtse	Southern Commissioner of Trade, Nanking
Fukien	Foochow	Superintendent, Foochow Dockyard
Kwang tung	Canton	Governor-General of Canton

(Source: Roberts)

During the war almost all warships were drawn from the Peiyang fleet; it had two fortified naval bases, Port Arthur and Wei-hai-Wei. The former was situated at the end of the Liao-Tung peninsula at the northern end of the gulf of Chihli, and the latter at the southern entrance; Port Arthur's dock facilities were superior to those at Wei-hai-Wei.

The Chinese naval commander was Admiral Ting, personally brave, but as an ex-cavalryman totally dependent on the advice of his professionally trained naval colleagues. China, like Japan, had used foreign naval advisers while building up a modern fleet, but the last, Captain Lang RN had resigned in 1890, leaving behind about four English and German engineers and gunners. Not long before the battle the Chinese had appointed a German artillery officer, Constantine von Henneken (who had survived the *Kowshing* sinking) to act as co-Admiral with Ting.

Admiral Ting. (Ogawa)

There were two English-speaking volunteer officers, Philo McGiffin and William Tyler. McGiffin had graduated from the US Naval Academy in 1881 but as only the top twelve in his class were commissioned he was discharged, but determined to pursue a naval career, he joined the Chinese Navy as an instructor in navigation at the naval academy at Wei-hai-Wei. He left what appears to be the only contemporary account in English of the Yalu battle but he cannot be regarded as a trustworthy witness. His brother officer W F Tyler described him as 'not quite all there'; put out of action during the battle by blast effect, he wrote articles 'giving wondrous but entirely imaginary descriptions of what he had seen and done and illustrations of himself with his many bandaged wounds', while Fred Jane commenting on his being photographed wounded against the background of the damaged Chen Yuan, remarked 'that he was not blind to dramatic effect. His narrative can hardly be accepted as historical events save in a general way'. His health deteriorated and at the time of his death by suicide in a New York hospital in February 1897 he was bed-ridden and in danger of losing his eyesight, or sanity, or both. It seems likely that he had a progressive neurological illness.

W F Tyler was of quite a different calibre, occupying a responsible post in the maritime branch of the Imperial Customs, and subsequently went on to a long and distinguished career in that service. He had joined the Customs as a young merchant navy officer, having just completed a year with the Royal Navy as a Sub-Lieutenant RNR. He published his reminiscences, including the Yalu fight, in 1929; the book does contain some inaccuracies but he was almost certainly the author of an article on the battle which appeared in *Blackwoods Magazine* in 1895. Also, he probably assisted in the compilation of the restricted Admiralty Intelligence Department account contained in *Modern Naval Operations 1884-1900*. Curiously, he is not listed in that account as one of the Europeans in the Chinese fleet. Almost certainly the reason was that he was still a serving officer in the RNR and was therefore breaking the terms of the Foreign Enlistment Act, so that an official blind eye was turned on his presence as co-commander on the *Ting Yuan*. He remained on the active list of the RNR until the turn of the century, and on the retired list until his death many years later.

The two most powerful units in the Chinese fleet were two small battleships: the *Ting Yuan* and the *Chen Yuan* built by the Vulcan shipyard at Stettin from 1881 to 1884. They resembled HMS *Colossus* in that their main armament of two pairs of 12in 25 calibre Krupp BL were placed *en echelon* but the guns were in a common barbette, each pair protected by a 1in shield. At bow and stern there was a 5.9in Krupp BL, each mounted in a small turret. The two ships were designed on the central citadel system, with a 14in compound armour belt amidships; buoyancy fore and aft was given by an underwater

The Chinese battleship Chen-Yuan. (MPL)

deck, 3in thick with cellular compartments above filled with coal and stores surmounted by a high superstructure fore and aft to give seaworthiness and stability.

Before the battle the thin gunshields were removed as experience had shown that they would merely act as shell traps; the 6in turrets had to be retained to protect them from the blast from the 12in guns firing right forward or aft. These two ships absorbed much punishment, but inflicted much less damage than they could have because they carried very little explosive shell. Also, solid armour piercing shot was not very effective against the unarmoured Japanese ships; it usually passed straight through their hulls, inflicting little damage. The shortage of explosive shell was known, but despite protests from ships' officers, insufficient numbers were delivered due to a combination of bureaucracy and graft.

Next in importance were two armoured cruisers *King Yuan* and *Lai Yuan* both built by Vulcan. They were protected by a narrow, 6ft wide belt surmounted by an armour deck, with an 8in barbette forward with a thin shield protecting a pair of 8.2in Krupp BL and a 5.9in Krupp BL sponsoned on each side. The smallest armoured vessel was the *Ping Yuan* built in China and armed with a 10.2in Krupp gun in a turret forward and two 5.9in. Her speed was only a nominal 10.5kts and she took no active part in the battle.

The *Chih Yuan* and *Ching Yuan* were a pair of Armstrong-built deck-protected cruisers armed with a twin 8.2in mounting forward, a single 8.2in aft and a 6in gun sponsoned on each side. Both had made 18kt in trials, but in practice they were slower. The *Chi (Tsi) Yuan* was a Vulcan-built protected cruiser mounting a pair of 8.2in in a barbette forward and a single 5.9in in a turret aft.

Vice Admiral Ito. (Author's collection)

The Imperial War Museum has suggested that this is a photograph of Chien Yuan, *but the Illustrated London News for 17 September 1887 identifies the ship as the Chinese* Ching Yuan, *Portsmouth 1887.* (IWM)

The Japanese protected cruiser Akitsushima. (World Ship Society)

Table 1: *The Two Fleets Compared*

Japanese

Name	Type	Displacement	Speed (kts)	Armament	Launch Year & Place
Matsushima	PC	4277	15.5	1-12.6in12-4.7in Q	1890, France
Itsukushima	PC	4277	15.5	1-12.6in11-4.7in Q	1889, France
Hashidate	PC	4277	15.5	1-12.6in11-4.7in Q	1891, Japan
Chiyoda	BC	2450	17.0	10-4.7in Q	1889 Great Britain
Fuso	Battleship, 3rd Class	3717	11.5	4-9.4in2-6.6in	1877, Great Britain
Hiei	AC	2200	10.8	3-3.6in2-5.9in	1878, Great Britain
Yoshino	PC	4150	19.5	4-6in Q8-4.7in Q	1892, Great Britain [1]
Naniwa	PC	3650	17.0	2-10.2in6-5.9in	1885, Great Britain [2]
Takachiho	PC	3650	17.0	2-10.2in6-5.9in	1885, Great Britain [2]
Akitsushima	PC	3150	17.5	4-6in Q6-4.7in Q	1892, Japan
Akagi	GB	615	11.2	1-9.4in1-4.7in	1888, Japan
Saikyo Maru	Transport	2913	11.0	2 small Q	1888, Great Britain

Chinese

Name	Type	Displacement	Speed (kts)	Armament	Launch Year & Place
Ting Yuan	Battleship	7330	12.0	4-12in2-5.9in	1881, Germany
Chen Yuan	Battleship	7330	12.0	4-12in2-5.9in	1882, Germany
King Yuan	AC	2850	13.5	2-8.2in2-5.9in	1887, Germany
Lai Yuan	AC	2850	14.0	2-8.2in2-5.9in	1887, Germany
Chi Yuan	PC	2355	13.0	2-8.2in2-5.9in	1883, Germany
Chih Yuan	PC	2300	15.0	3-8.2in2-5.9in	1886, Great Britain [2]
Ching Yuan	PC	2300	15.0	3-8.2in2-5.9in	1886, Great Britain [2]
Ch'ao Yung	GB	1350	13.0	2-10in4-4.7in	1880, Great Britain [2]
Yang Wei	GB	1350	13.0	2-10in4-4.7in	1881, Great Britain [2]
Kuang Chia	Sloop	1296	13.8	2-6in4-4.7in	1887, China
Ping Yuan	Armoured Vessel	2100	9.0	1-10.2in2-5.9in	1889, China
Kuang Ping	GB	1000	9.5	3-4.7in	1890, China

Notes:
AC: Armoured Cruiser; PC: Deck Protected Cruiser; BC: Belted Cruiser; GB: Gunboat.
[1] Built at Armstrongs Elswick Yard.
[2] Built at Armstrongs Low Walker Yard.
(Sources: *Brassey's Naval Annual 1895*, p102; Roberts, S. *The Imperial Chinese Steam Navy 1862-1895*; *Warship International* 1/74, pp19-57)

The Imperial Japanese Navy was closely modelled on the RN, but did not have a separate minister responsible for it; a minister of cabinet rank (and always a serving officer) was responsible for both Army and Navy. The fleet was commanded by Vice Admiral Ito, a professional naval officer of high calibre, but inclined to be cautious and lacking in dash and initiative. On this occasion however, he was accompanied by Vice Admiral Count Kabayama, Chief of the Naval General Staff, who was ostensibly inspecting the fleet, his headquarters being in a small liner the *Saikyo Maru* armed with only a few small guns. Kabayama has been described as the antithesis of Ito, impetuous and full of verve and enthusiasm. Beatty to Ito's Jellicoe perhaps?

The Japanese had no modern battleships. The core of their fleet comprised three large deck-protected cruisers of French design each armed with a powerful 12.6in gun mounted in a thick but shallow barbette surmounted by a thin cupola. They were capable of being loaded at any angle of training or elevation; in practice they proved almost useless, the three ships firing a total of 13 rounds between them in the five hours of battle. The *Matsushima* mounted her big gun aft with six 4.7in Armstrong QF on each broadside forward, all only protected by thin shields. The other two, *Itsukushima* and *Hashidate* had their big gun forward and eleven 4.7in QF aft.

Chiyoda was a small cruiser with a thin narrow belt and with her ten 4.7in QF shield-protected. *Fuso* was a small old ironclad rated as a 3rd class battleship, slow and mounting four 9.4in BL and six 6in BL on the broadside. An even smaller and very slow ironclad, the *Hiei*, mounted three 6.6in BL and two 5.9in BL. These ships formed the Main Squadron, with Ito flying his flag in the *Matsushima*, while the four fastest cruisers comprised the Flying Squadron under Rear Admiral Tsuboi.

The Japanese fleet at anchor on the day before the battle. (Ogawa)

The newest cruiser was the Armstrong-built *Yoshino*, armed entirely with QF guns, four 6in and eight 4.7in, and at the time of her completion the fastest cruiser in the world. Armstrong QF guns were up to six times faster than the old fashioned breech loaders and in addition were more accurate as the trainer and layer could keep their sights continually on the target. The *Naniwa* and *Takachiho*, also built by Armstrong, were older mounting a 10.2in Krupp BL at bow and stern and three 5.9in on each broadside. Completing the squadron was the *Ikitsushima*, armed with four 6in and six 4.7in guns, all of which were QF.

The Japanese had fifty-eight 4.7in and eight 6in QF, while the Chinese had a few small QF only. Completing the fleet was the small, very slow gunboat Akagi, useful only for reconnoitring the poorly-charted, treacherous shoal waters off the coast of Korea.

The Battle – Preliminaries

The Japanese fleet escorted a twenty ship convoy carrying large numbers of reinforcements for the army in Korea, landing the troops at Chemulpo (present day Inchon) on 12 September. Admiral Kabayama persuaded Ito to go north to the Taedong river in order to support the crossing of that river by the force massing to advance on the key fortress of Pyongyang. The fleet sailed north on 14 September leaving behind a number of older ships to cover Chemulpo, reaching the mouth of the Taedong on the next day. Three gunvessels and all the torpedo boats attached to the fleet were sent up the river; the latter would have little value in covering a river crossing, and would have been better employed in accompanying the fleet.

The fleet headed south for Cape Choppek (present day Changsangot) the westernmost tip of Korea, and anchored for the night. On 16 September the fleet sortied northwest, following intelligence sent to Kabayama and Ito, in order to intercept Chinese troops being sent to Takushan and to bring the Chinese fleet to action. The Japanese headed for the island of Haiyang, centrally situated in the Gulf of Korea and a likely place to intercept any convoy proceeding from Talienwan to Takushan (which was situated at the mouth of the Tayang). Reaching the island at 6.30am the fleet headed for Takushan in bright weather and a calm sea, with the Flying Squadron in the lead. At 10.23 am the *Yoshino* signalled that she had seen smoke to the NE and shortly after, several more columns of smoke were observed; the Chinese fleet had been sighted. The Flying Squadron was ordered to slow down and the vulnerable *Saikyo Maryu* and *Akagi* were placed on the disengaged port side of the fleet.

How had the Chinese fleet come to be at that particular spot at that particular time? Admiral Ting had received orders on 12 September to escort five transports carrying 4000 men from Talienwan to Takushan to reinforce the army in Korea; landing them at the mouth of the Yalu 23 miles to the east was not feasible because of the shallow water at that river's mouth. Ting wished to bring the Japanese fleet to action before undertaking the

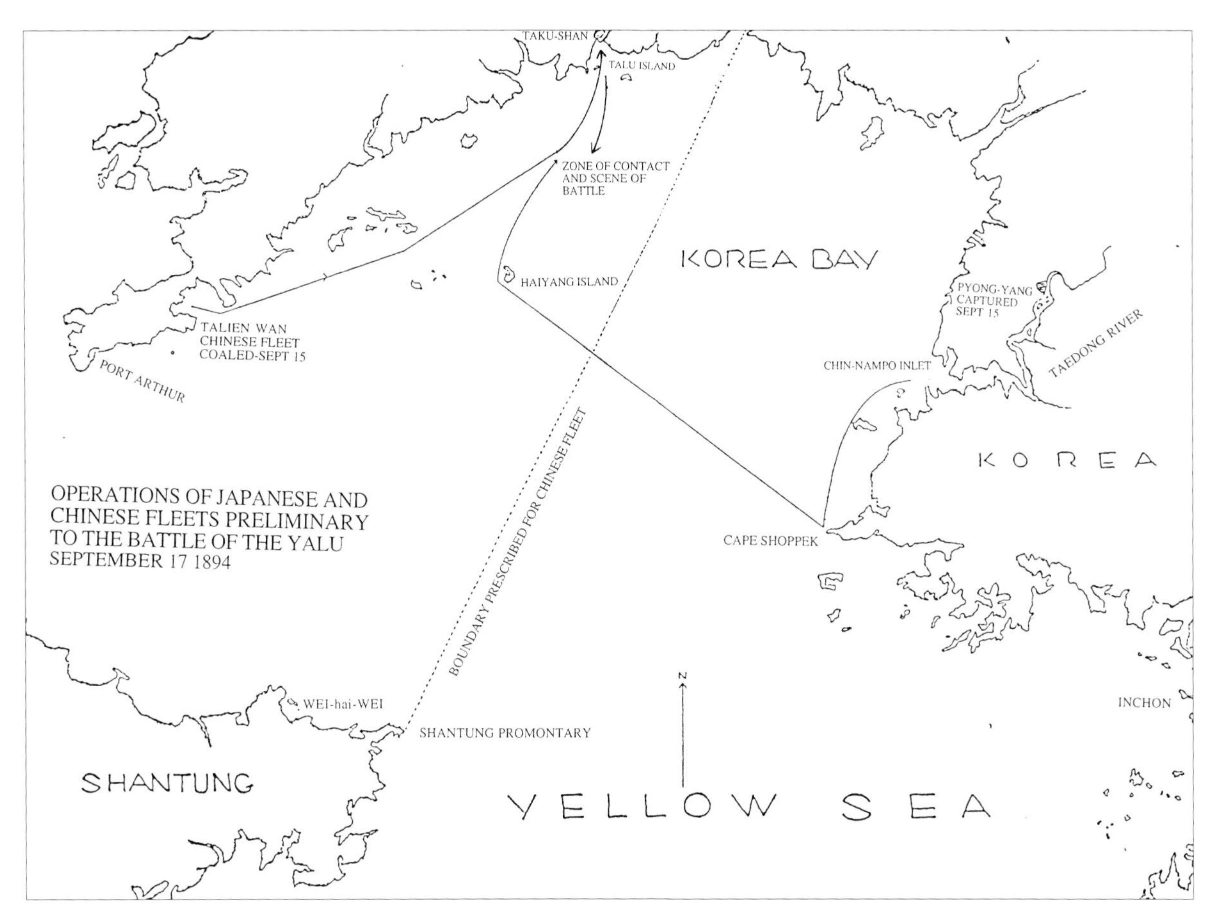

Map of operations of Japanese and Chinese fleets preliminary to the battle of the Yalu, 17 September 1894. (Author's collection)

convoy, but was delayed for a day because of a false report of two Japanese cruisers off Wei-hai-Wei. On September, while at Talienwan, Ting received an urgent message that the Chinese army had been defeated at Pyongyang; clearly reinforcements were needed as soon as possible and the convoy and fleet sailed at 1 am on 16 September arriving at the Tayang (also referred to as the Ta-tung Kau) 13 hours later. After a reconnaissance by two torpedo boats *Fo-Lung* and *Tyo Jih* and two Rendel gunboats, *Chen Nan* and *Chen Chung*, had proved the landing place clear the convoy was sent into the river with the *Ping Yuan*, *Kuang Ping*, and the two torpedo boats and two gunboats guarding the river mouth while the fleet anchored in deep water further out. The ships were already prepared for action with hammocks providing some shelter from splinters and sandbags and sacks of coal sheltering ready-use ammunition with fire hoses run out; all except one boat had been landed from each ship and excess woodwork discarded.

The Chinese ratings were highly praised by both Tyler and McGiffin for their bravery but both had little good to say about most of the officers although there were a few exceptions. Tyler was particularly scornful of Ting's second in command, Commodore Liu, who he regarded as a coward and who altered orders to save his own skin. It would seem that the original plan was for the Chinese to advance in sections, each section comprising two sister ships, the leading one obliquely in front of the other with the rear section in line ahead astern of the leading one. This was a compact formation and easily formed into line ahead or abreast. However, Liu made a signal 'starboard sectional formation in line abreast, leaders in the centre', which resulted in the weakest ships being at the vulnerable wings. Tyler and von Henneken decided that to try to countermand the order would only result in confusion and it was allowed to stand. The two fleets were now closing, each ship flying a large battle ensign, the Chinese ships painted black and the Japanese light grey.

The Battle – Main Phase

The Chinese fleet headed SW to meet the Japanese who were moving NNE across the Chinese line; this line was not straight, but was wedge shaped as the ships at each end had lagged behind (Fig 1). In his recollections, Tyler said that he advised Ting to turn the whole fleet to starboard into line ahead but that Liu disregarded the order; true or not the fleet as a whole turned a few degrees, so that while preserving the very irregular line abreast they were now heading west, steaming at 10kts. At 12.45 pm *Ting Yuan* opened fire at a range of about 6000yds. The Flying Squadron starboarded in succession (Fig 2), opening fire just after 1 pm at a range of 3000yds and with

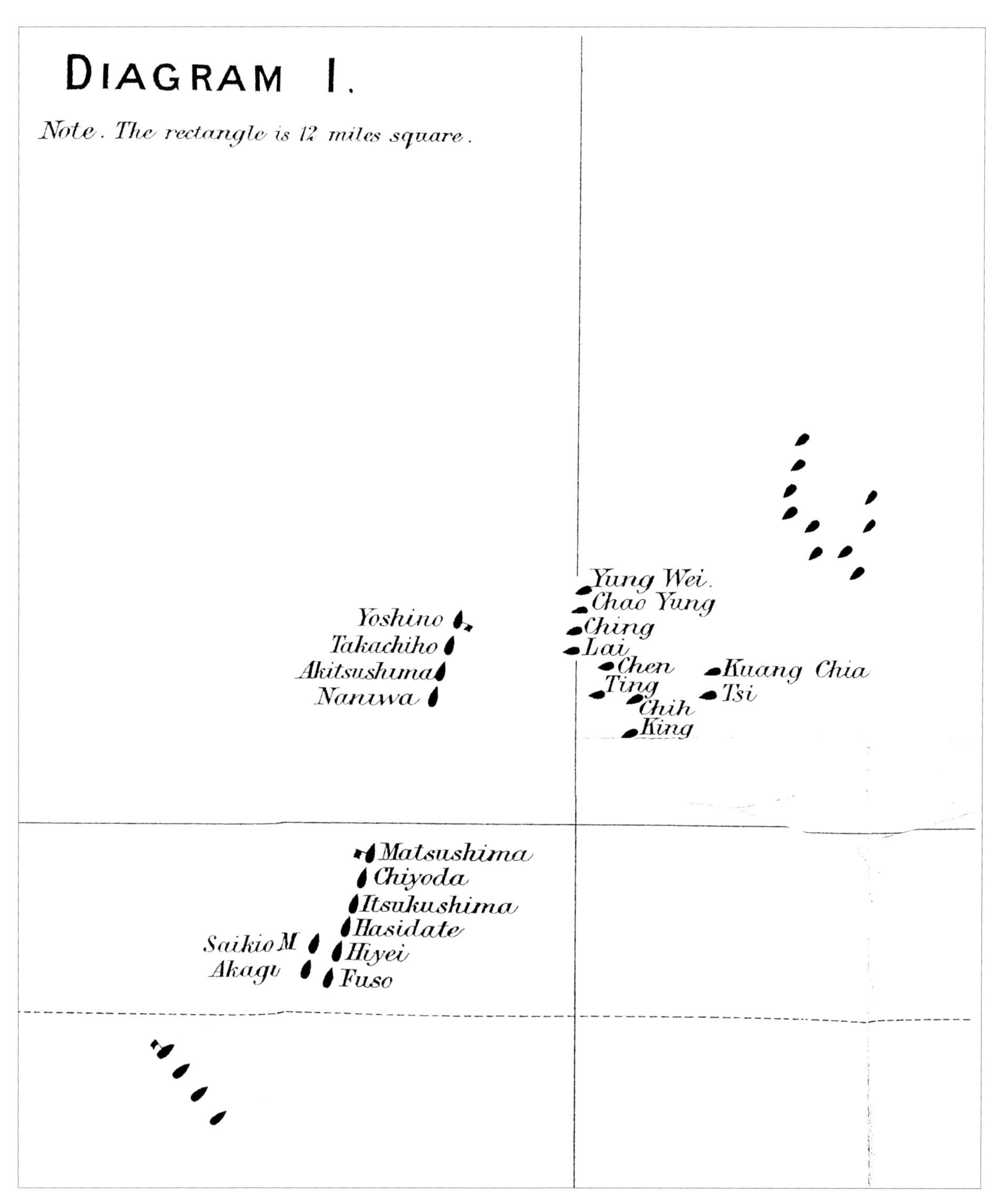

such devastating effect that the two wing ships *Ch'ao Yung* and *Yang Wei* were speedily overwhelmed, both being set ablaze but pluckily continuing to fire their big guns for a little while. *Ch'ao Yung*, engulfed in flames, sank an hour later, while *Yang Wei* was run aground with her upper deck completely burnt away. On the following day, having been abandoned by her crew, she was destroyed by the Japanese.

Early in the action the Chinese fleet had been made leaderless as Ting had been wounded by the blast of his own 12in guns, while all the flagship's signal flags had been destroyed by the rain of quick-firing shells poured in by the Japanese. The cruisers of the Flying Squadron suffered some damage but nothing serious. The main squadron followed the path of Tsuboi's division and came under fire, with *Matsushima*'s big gun temporarily disabled by shell splinters. The Flying Squadron, instead of making a full circle around the Chinese fleet, now turned to port (Fig 3) in order to drive off the inshore detachment (*Ping Yuan*, *Kuang Ping*, torpedo boats and gun-

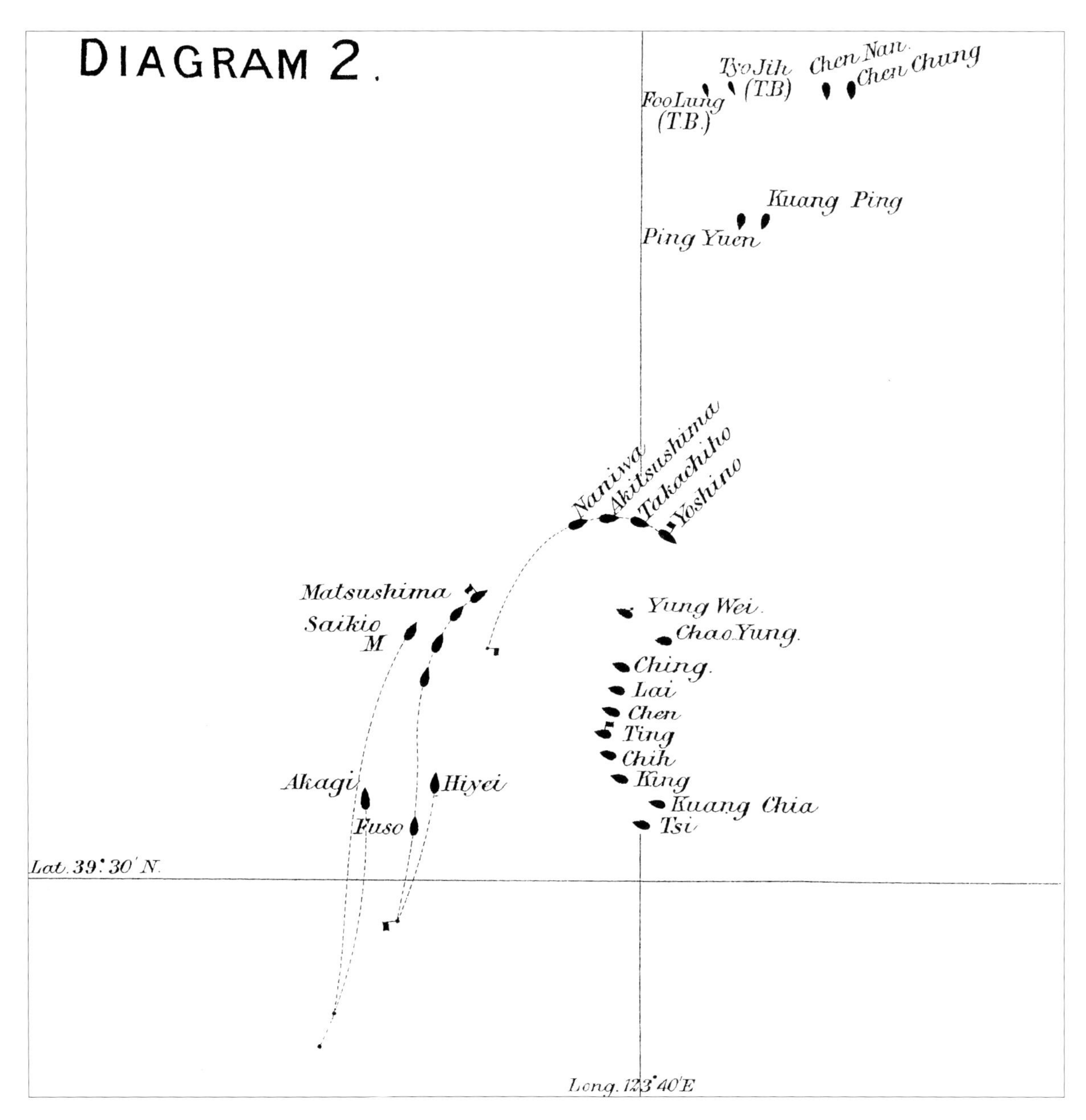

boats) which was coming up to join the main fleet (Fig 2). However, they quickly sheered off when they saw the Flying Squadron closing them (Fig 3).

Ito then signalled Tsuboi to rejoin the main body because three of his ships were in serious trouble. The *Hiei* had lagged so far behind that she took a desperate route to rejoin the main squadron – passing through the Chinese fleet where she was joined by *Akagi*; both suffered severely, the former being set ablaze and the latter losing a third of her crew killed and injured (Figs 2 and 3). *Saikyo Maru* came under fire but fortunately a shell passed straight through her thin plating without exploding; she separated from the fleet but not before someone on board had taken photographs of the battle, the first ever of a naval engagement. Doubtless under orders from Kabayama, she made off in pursuit of the disabled *Yang Wei*, but came under fire from the Chinese inshore detachment (Fig 5).The *Foo Lung* fired her bow torpedo tubes from straight ahead, both of which missed; she then fired at *Saikyo*'s beam but the torpedo ran too deep. By now the *Saikyo* had had enough and left the scene of the battle.

In the meantime the Flying Squadron had again circled to port (Fig 4), to come to the aid of *Hiei* and *Akagi*. By this time the main squadron had almost completed its circle around the Chinese left flank which had been weakened by *Chi Yuan* and *Kuang Chia* deserting the fight, both making for Port Arthur (Figs 4 and 5). The former claimed that she could no longer fight as all her guns had been disabled; the damage had been inflicted by a sledgehammer and her captain, Fong, was later beheaded for cowardice. The *Kuang Chia* ran aground near Talienwan bay. *Chih Yuan*, now at the left of the Chinese line came under heavy fire, was severely damaged and

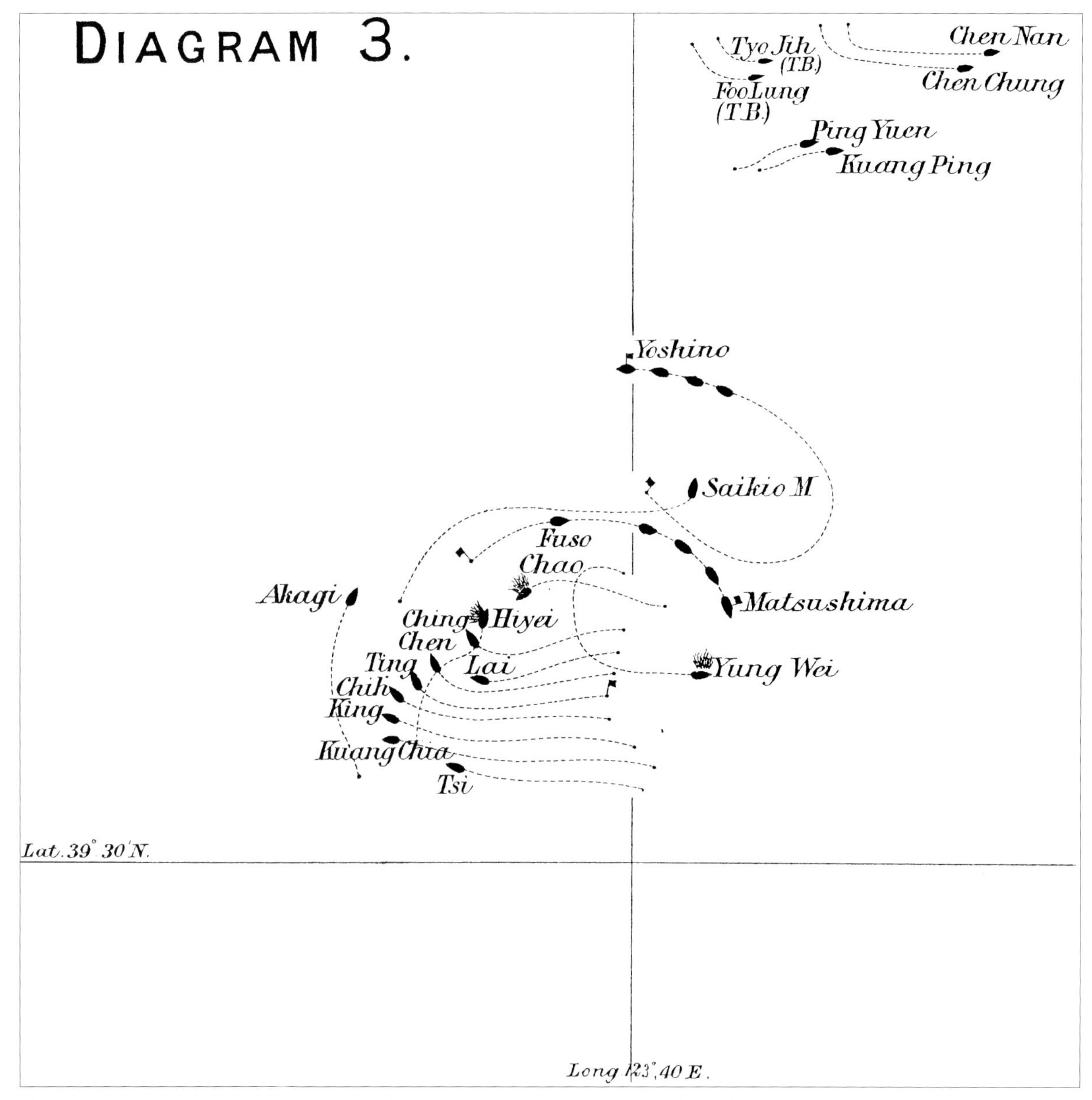

charged for the Japanese, apparently with the intention of ramming – but went down bows first, her screws still revolving. Most of the crew went down with her, including her captain and the English chief engineer, Purvis. At about the same time *King Yuan* was damaged, and made off to the SE, pursued by the whole of the Flying Squadron which, after aiding *Hiei* and *Akagi* had continued to wheel around the Chinese left wing (Fig 5). The Flying Squadron followed *King Yuan* into shallow water and sank her at a spot marked in Fig 6.

At about the same time (3.30 pm) that *Chih Yuan* sank, *Matsushima* was struck by two of the remaining Chinese shells. One striking the port bow did little damage, but the other hit the unprotected 4.7in battery setting off the ready-use ammunition. Over 100 of the 400 crew were killed or wounded. Ito was forced to shift his flag to *Hashidate* sending *Matsushima* back to Kure in Japan for repairs. The two remaining Chinese cruisers were badly damaged: *Ching Yuan* had been set on fire three times and had a large shot-hole just above the waterline 10ft from the stern, while the after part of *Lai Yuan* was almost burnt out, with the engine room like a furnace; despite this, the engine room crew kept to their posts, one of the many examples of bravery shown by the Chinese ratings.

The Final Phase

The Japanese main squadron continued to move around the two Chinese battleships at a range of 2000-3000yds; they in turn kept circling around in order to keep their bows covering the enemy. They had sustained a great deal of damage from the Japanese quick-firers; each had her superstructure riddled with over 100 hits, and the *Ting Yuan* had a serious fire towards the bow. Neither ship, however, had had her armour pierced and their big

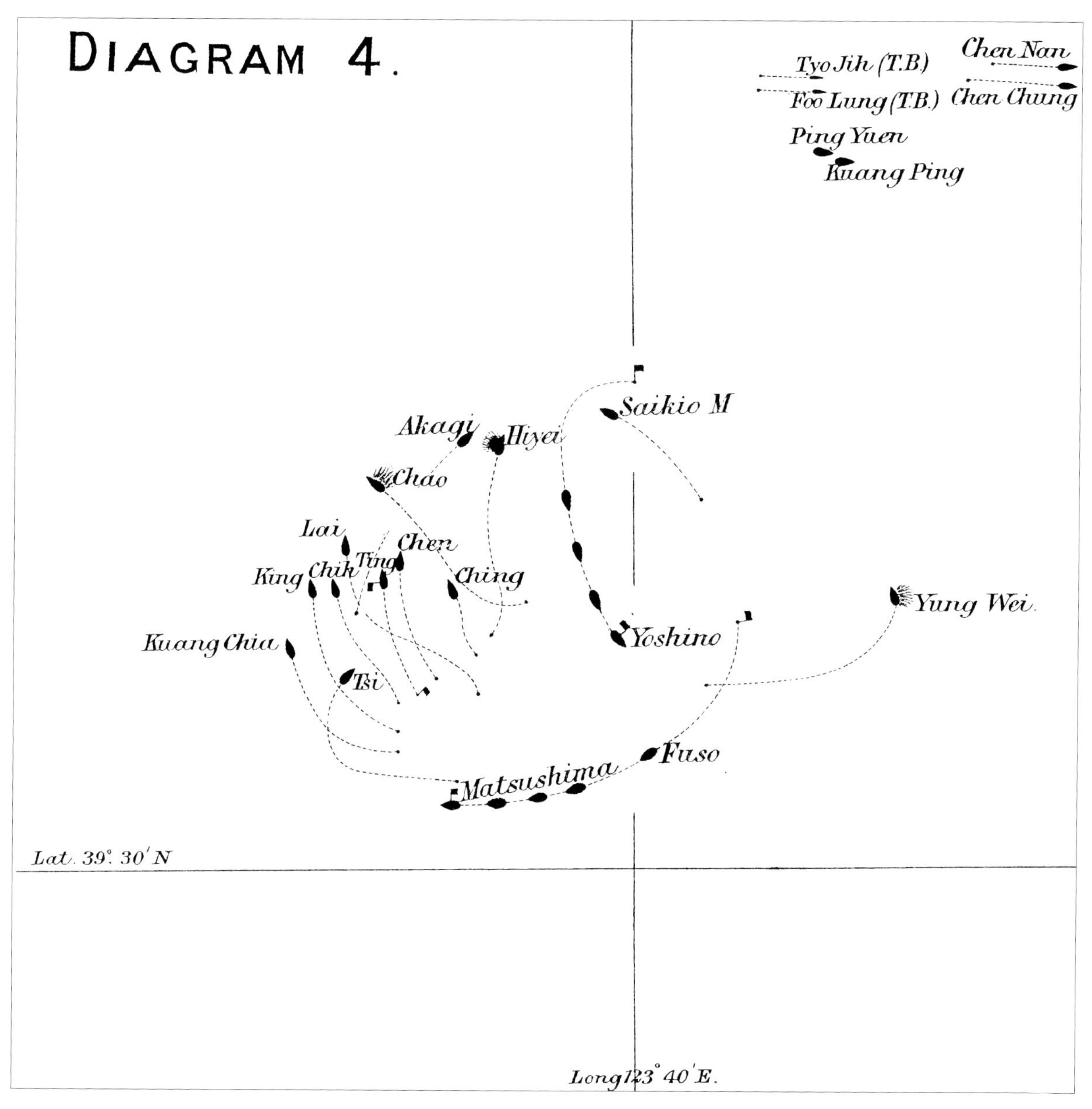

guns had only been out of action for short periods. By 5.45 pm both had expended all of their 6in ammunition and were down to their last few rounds of almost useless 12in solid shot. At 5.30 pm, Ito broke off the action, signalling the Flying Squadron to rejoin him, and formed a line parallel to the course which he thought the Chinese would be taking if they were heading for Wei-hai-Wei. There is no explanation as to why he judged that the Chinese would be heading for a base 80 miles further away than Port Arthur, and which also lacked repair and docking facilities. The next morning was again clear and sunny with a calm sea, but with no sign of the Chinese fleet. Ito returned to the scene of the battle but made no attempt to attack the Chinese transports which were still in the Tayang. Instead, he returned to the anchorage off Cape Choppek.

Throughout the battle, Ito had behaved cautiously, breaking off the action with more than half an hour of light remaining, for example. It has been suggested that he was apprehensive about the possibility of being attacked by torpedo boats. Also during the battle, he could have closed the engagement range to a few hundred yards, where the torpedoes carried by his cruisers would have been effective. While the Chinese could have made a more effective showing with better officers and sufficient explosive shell for their 12in guns, the most important factor in deciding the battle was that the Japanese had a more modern fleet, and in consequence mounted the quick-firers which proved so effective against the unarmoured Chinese ships.

The Aftermath

The surviving Chinese ships were patched up in a leisurely way at Port Arthur but, rightly apprehensive that the

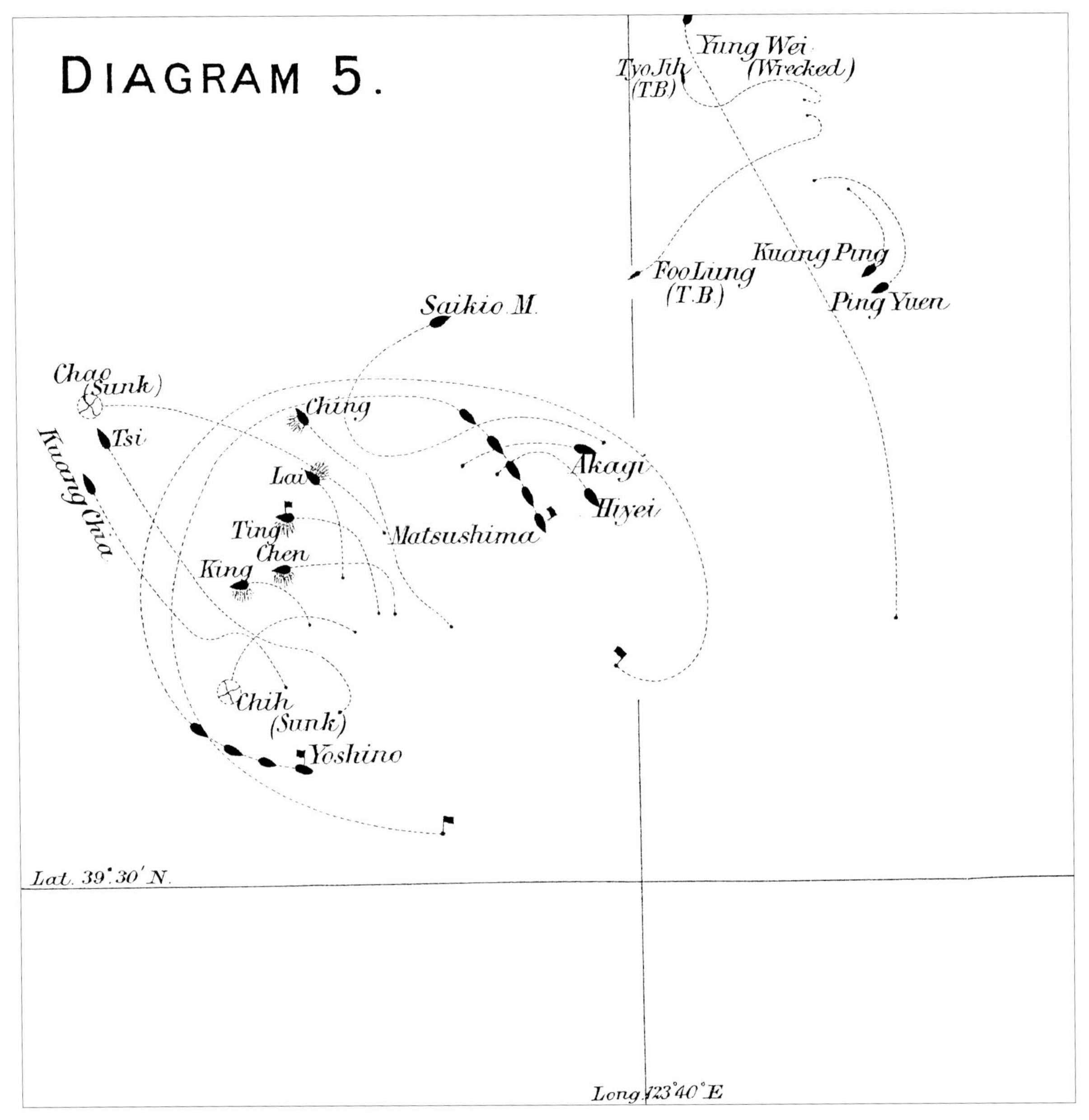

Japanese would capture that port, the fleet sailed for Wei-hai-Wei in late October, where it lay passively while the Japanese began siege operations at the end of November. *Ting Yuan* was sunk in a daring torpedo attack and when the base capitulated on 12 February, the only surviving ships were *Chen Yuan*, *Ping Yuan*, *Chi Yuan* and six Rendel gunboats, all of which were taken in to Japanese service. Ting and his senior Chinese officers, well aware of what was waiting for them at home, committed suicide. China, beaten on land and at sea, had to accept the harsh terms of the Treaty of Shimonoseki and the subsequent territorial concessions to Russia and Germany. The Japanese, humiliated by those two countries (who forced her to surrender her territorial gains), began to build a modern fleet with the indemnity paid by China. Great Britain, now seeing Japan as a first-class power, signed the first of the Anglo-Japanese treaties in 1902.

The Lessons

The most important lesson from the Yalu was the need for a well trained, professional navy. The battle exploded the myth that small, fast unarmoured ships carrying a powerful big gun armament could, by means of superior speed, defeat a battleship by choosing their own decisive range. *Ch'ao Yung*, *Yang Wei*, *Naniwa*, *Takachiho* and the three big Japanese cruisers, were all designed on this principle. The battle showed up the ineffectiveness of bow fire, the danger of excessive woodwork, the need for effective damage control and the small effect that QF guns had against armour but highlighted their deadly effect against unprotected gun crews and unarmoured structures. Finally, speed was of great value, allowing the range to be chosen and manoeuvres such as crossing the enemy's lines, to be undertaken. Speed was for the steam navy what the

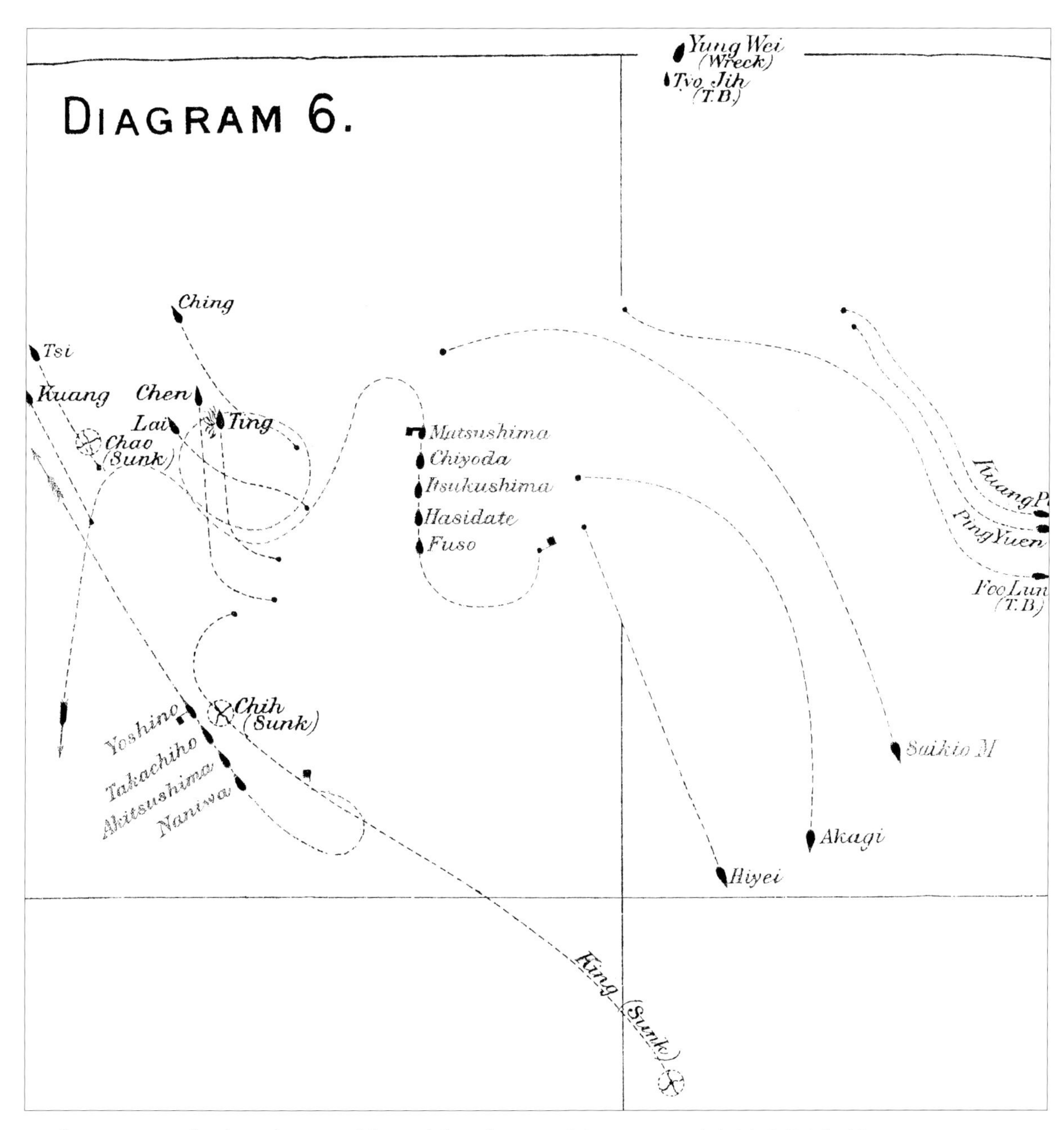

weather gauge was for the sailing one. Many of these lessons had to be re-learnt in the Russo-Japanese war.

Sources

The three most important sources are:

Perry, J C. 'The Battle off the Tayang 17 September 1894'. *Mariners Mirror* 3, pp243-249 (1964). This article is particularly useful as it has Japanese accounts otherwise inaccessible.

'The Naval Engagement Off The Yalu River September 1894'. *China-Japan War 1894-5*, pp 42 -81 (May 1901). In Modern Naval Operations Admiralty Intelligence Department No 582. The battle diagrams are drawn from this.

'The Chinese Navy: The Battle of the Yalu. By our correspondent in the East'. *Blackwoods Edinburgh Magazine* (October 1895). Invaluable as this was almost certainly Tyler's first hand account.

Other sources include McGiffin's highly suspect account in *The Century Magazine*, August 1895 (pp585-604), together with Captain Mahan's comments (pp629-632). He thought that the battle was inconclusive.

Tyler's account written many years later, *Pulling Strings in China*(1929), contains inaccuracies but gives a lot of background.

The Ship of the Line in Battle(1912) has direct quotes from Ito's official despatches.

The Influence of the Sea on the Political History of Japan (1921) gives useful general background.

Finally, *The Japan-China War* by K Ogawa has some fascinating photographs, including some of the battle taken from *Saikyo Maru* but sadly too indistinct to reproduce.

FROM *RIURIK** TO *RIURIK*:

Russia's Armoured Cruisers

The term 'armoured cruiser' has been used to describe a great many ships built in the 1890s and early 1900s, but this broad designation often conceals major differences in the intended roles of such ships. In this article **Stephen McLaughlin** explores the changing strategic and tactical rationale of Russia's armoured cruisers.

Introduction: Commerce Warfare and the Imperial Russian Navy[1]

Defeat in the Crimean War was deeply humiliating for the Russian Empire, and nowhere was that humiliation more keenly felt than under the tall spire of the Admiralty in St Petersburg. It was not merely the fact that Russia's relatively large fleet of sailing ships-of-the-line had proven useless when confronted by the steam-powered ships of Britain and France, but also that steam warships' superiority over sailing ships had been evident to many officers well before the war. The real shock was the realisation that, even had she possessed a steam-powered battlefleet, it could have done little to further Russia's cause in the war. The simple fact was that Britain and France would always be able to build *more* ships than Russia, and so in any future war with these maritime powers even a Russian steam battlefleet would have to play the inactive role of a fleet-in-being.

During the Crimean War, the navy's General-admiral, the Grand Duke Konstantin Nikolaevich, concentrated on defensive measures to prevent an Anglo-French attack on St Petersburg. Only too aware of Russia's technological backwardness, Konstantin decided to build a mosquito fleet of steam-powered gunboats that could supplement the fortresses defending the approaches to St Petersburg. He departed from this policy immediately after the war, when he began planning a fleet of steam ships-of-the-line, but Russia's weak financial condition after the war, and the rapid introduction of ironclad warships, soon called a halt to this programme. Instead, Konstantin reverted to a defensive policy not so different from the wartime mosquito fleet, only now the defending vessels would be powerful ironclad batteries and monitors, all designed to co-operate with the Kronshtadt fortresses to create a maritime defence system for the capital.

But a purely defensive policy was not enough for Konstantin; he wanted a strategy that would not only provide for Russia's maritime defence, but would also give the fleet a useful role in peacetime diplomacy. In essence, Konstantin wanted a naval strategy that could act as a deterrent should the threat of war with the western powers again arise. In the late 1850s he hit upon the strategy of commerce-raiding, and began the construction of large sea-going frigates and corvettes (called 'clippers' in the Imperial Navy) to provide what he saw as this second essential element of Russia's naval strategy.

The most important moment for this new policy came in 1863, when tensions with Britain and France again mounted over Russia's suppression of the Polish rebellion. As the situation approached the level of an international crisis, the Naval Ministry, inspired at least in part by the continuing exploits of the Confederate raider *Alabama*, dispatched two squadrons of potential commerce-raiders to American ports. These squadrons were enthusiastically welcomed in New York and San Francisco; the Union Government saw them as Russia's way of warning Britain and France to stay out of the American Civil War. But from the Russian perspective it was a warning to these same two powers to stay out of the Polish insurrection. Soon afterwards, the Polish Crisis abated, and while it has never been clear if the Russian squadrons had any real effect on British or French policy, the fact is that both Konstantin and his older brother, the Emperor, *believed* that the squadrons had exercised a restraining influence on the western powers. From this point on, commerce raiding, or more precisely, the threat of commerce raiding, became an accepted element in

* Transliteration of Russian words and names is based on the Library of Congress system. All dates in this article are given in the form Old Style/New Style; the Russian calendar was twelve days behind that of the west in the nineteenth century, and thirteen days behind in the twentieth.

Rossiia *at Yokohama, 1902. Note the 6in gun in the bow embrasure*. (US Naval Historical Center)

Russia's naval strategy.

In the late 1860s Konstantin began to replace the big wooden frigates with a series of large iron-hulled cruisers: *Minin*, *General-admiral* and *Gertsog Edinburgskii* were the first of the breed, later followed by the broadly similar *Vladimir Monomakh* and *Dmitrii Donskoi*. These ships all shared several features that would later be echoed to one degree or another in the armoured cruisers of the 1890s. They were protected by armour belts, were fully rigged and had wood-and-cooper sheathing; they also had a substantial coal capacity, generally about 1000 tons. In fact the only major ship built during the last decade of Konstantin's reign that did not share these features was the large breastwork monitor *Pëtr Velikii*, and she is the exception that proves the rule. Although often considered Russia's first sea-going battleship, she began life as a fully rigged 'cruiser-monitor' intended for long-range commerce raiding.

Russia's financial position was never very strong, and the Naval Ministry never had enough money to build ships in the numbers required for effective commerce warfare. Nevertheless, the threat of raiding was used again in 1878, when Britain made unhappy noises over Russia's war with Turkey; this time the Naval

Ministry not only sent potential raiding squadrons to American ports, but it also bought three steamers from Cramp's shipyard in Philadelphia. The 'secret' arrival of Russian crews for these ships was widely publicised, and once again the threat of war receded. In Russian eyes, it was another triumph for the deterrent effect of commerce raiders.

In the years after the Russo-Turkish War of 1877-1878 the Russian Navy not only had to contend with threats from foreign enemies, but with a threat closer to home. During the war a group of patriotic Russian merchants formed the 'Volunteer Fleet Association' and began buying steamers to use as auxiliary warships if war broke out with Britain. The president of the association was the influential conservative K P Pobedonostsev, who believed that Konstantin's political liberalism had exercised an unhealthy influence on the reputedly weak-willed Aleksandr II. The Volunteer Fleet thus became a sort of shadow naval ministry; its leading naval expert was one N M Baranov, a former naval officer who believed that artillery had become so powerful that armour was useless; he and Pobedonostsev argued that Konstantin's expensive armourclads should be replaced by swift, heavily-armed but unarmoured cruisers.

Despite the criticisms of conservatives and the threat of the Volunteer Fleet, Konstantin was able to maintain his policies, thanks to the support of his brother the Tsar. But Aleksandr II's assassination in 1881 brought his son to the throne as Aleksandr III. Not only had the new emperor and his uncle the General-admiral never liked each other but Pobedonostsev had served as the young man's tutor, further poisoning him against his uncle. It was not long before Konstantin was replaced as General-admiral by the new emperor's younger brother, the Grand Duke Aleksei Aleksandrovich.

The new reign ushered in a new era in Russian naval construction – the state's finances were more stable, and so the Navy's budget was increased. A new fleet of battleships was soon on the stocks; commerce-raiding was still seen as an important element of the navy's policy, but by this time the strategic problems of commerce-raiding were growing more complex. Neutrality laws were increasingly strict, and a repeat of *Alabama*'s cruises would be impossible – never again would raiders be able to make such free use of foreign ports for coal, supplies and repairs. Ships would have to stay at sea on their own resources for longer periods of time, a considerable challenge in an age of coal-hungry boilers and inefficient engines. The requirement for long range was also dictated by Russia's access to European waters, which was limited by both geography and climate; her commerce raiders could have freedom of action only in the broad expanses of the Pacific.

From 1882, when the new Tsar's naval policies began to take effect, until the end of the decade, the Imperial Navy laid down only two big cruisers – *Pamiat Azova* and

A grainy photograph of Riurik, *in dry dock at Vladivostok, circa 1903. Particularly evident in this picture is the sponson for the forward starboard 8in gun.* (US Naval Historical Center, Boris Drashpil collection)

the French-built *Admiral Kornilov*; a third big cruiser, *Admiral Nakhimov*, was laid down as a sea-going second-class battleship; only after her intended armament of four 9in guns in single barbettes was replaced by eight 8in twin mountings was she reclassified as a cruiser. The lack of emphasis on big cruisers did not signal an abandonment of the commerce-raiding strategy, but instead reflected the fact that there was not enough money to build both battleships and a large number of cruisers. The situation was eased somewhat by the transfer of the Volunteer Fleet to the Naval Ministry's control in 1883. While the Navy's shipbuilding resources were devoted to battleship construction, the Volunteer Fleet became the Navy's main commerce-raiding force, with fast steamers designed for rapid conversion to auxiliary cruisers in the event of war.

However, the value of the Volunteer Fleet's ships as commerce raiders was soon undercut by the growing number of British second-class cruisers; these were designed for trade-protection, and their protective decks would have given them a tremendous advantage in any encounter with an unprotected auxiliary cruiser. Thus toward the end of the 1880s thoughts once again turned toward purpose-built cruising warships for commerce raiding.

Riurik[2]

Riurik's design had its origins in a requirement for a long-range commerce-raiding cruiser sent to the state-run Baltic Works by Admiral I A Shestakov, the director of the Naval Ministry. Until the reorganisation after the Russo-Japanese War, there was no 'Naval Minister'; the navy was officially headed by the General-admiral, at this time the Tsar's younger brother, the Grand Duke Aleksei Aleksandrovich – and the Naval Ministry was run by the 'director' of the Ministry, who 'had the rights of a minister'). Although the specifications requested by Shestakov have not been published, it would seem that he wanted an enlargement of the belted cruiser *Pamiat Azova*, which was then building at the Baltic Works. Shestakov apparently wanted more emphasis placed on a large steaming range – probably to be calculated on the basis of a voyage from the Baltic to Vladivostok without coaling – and good sea-going characteristics, with protection and firepower rather lower down the list of priorities.

At first sight it seems somewhat odd that Shestakov did not assign this job to the Naval Technical Committee (*Morskoi tekhnicheskii komitet*, or MTK), which was composed of representatives from the various technical branches of the service (Shipbuilding, Artillery, Engineering, etc.) and had the resources to design ships on its own. But Shestakov had a great distrust of the MTK, whose members were largely held over from his predecessor's era. He believed that the designs produced by the committee were larger and more expensive than was necessary; throughout his tenure at the Ministry, he consistently sought ways of getting 'better' designs by circumventing the MTK. So in sending his requirements to the Baltic Works, Shestakov was following a well-established pattern.

In response to Shestakov's order, a constructor at the Baltic Works, N E Rodionov, drew up a design for a 9000-ton cruiser with 8in belt armour. The design showed many similarities to *Pamiat Azova*; it was submitted to the Ministry in July 1888, and in November it was forwarded to the Naval Technical Committee for review. At this point, things took a turn for the worse. The committee was well aware of Shestakov's distrust, and was probably still resentful of the fact that he, along with the General-admiral, had approved the French design for *Admiral Kornilov* without consulting the Committee. Rodionov's design was therefore subjected to severe criticism during the MTK's review.

Rodionov had secured relatively high sustained speed (18.5kts) and great coal capacity by adopting an unusually long and narrow hull (420ft on the waterline x 61ft), and this became the focus of the MTK's attack. Not only was the length regarded as inconvenient from the standpoint of ship-handling and docking, but the length-to-beam ratio of 6.8 was judged to be excessively fine. The representatives of the Baltic Works who attended the meeting – Rodionov himself, constructor N E Titov and M M Kazi, the director of the shipyard – countered that the length was well within the norms of commercial shipbuilding, to which the MTK replied in turn that the hull-strength of commercial vessels could not be used as a guide in designing warships, since warships were much more heavily loaded toward the ends. Kazi thereupon pointed out that Rodionov's design was in fact more similar to long commercial vessels than to warships, since it lacked heavy turrets fore and aft. These arguments, however, failed to shift the MTK from its opposition to the design.

The length was not the only issue; the MTK also expressed the opinion that the quoted 20,000 mile steaming range was optimistic, and that 15,000 miles was more likely; it also believed that Rodionov's design either underestimated some weights or left out some items altogether; to correct this would call for an additional 286 tons. Taken together, the MTK believed that a 10,000-ton displacement was a more realistic figure for the final design.

The MTK had examined the Baltic Works design on 8/20 November 1888; three weeks later, Admiral Shestakov died. His successor, Admiral N M Chikhachev, was less suspicious of the MTK, and so on the recommendation of the MTK the Baltic Works design was rejected by the general-admiral and the MTK entrusted one its members, the constructor N E Kuteinikov, with the drawing-up of a completely new design. A new set of requirements was worked out, showing somewhat more modest characteristics: speed 18kts instead of 18.5kts, range 10,000nm instead of 20,000nm. Armament was the same as in Rodionov's design – four 8in, sixteen 6in, twenty 47mm, ten 37mm and six 15in above-water torpedo tubes. Although this is not explicitly stated anywhere, it is likely that the heavy battery of quick-firing guns was intended to overwhelm small enemy cruisers quickly, before they could cause the ship any severe damage. A sailing rig was required, as was a 10in armour belt – the MTK did

Riurik *as completed, with full rig.* (Drawn by the author)
Special note on the drawings: *The drawings in this article are based on sketches in Russian publications, but these do not always agree with each other (indeed, they often show serious inconstistencies between profile and plan). Because of their scarcity and generally poor quality, photographs of these ships have proven of little help in sorting matters out. Therefore, these drawings should be regarded as provisional, until archival drawings beome available.*

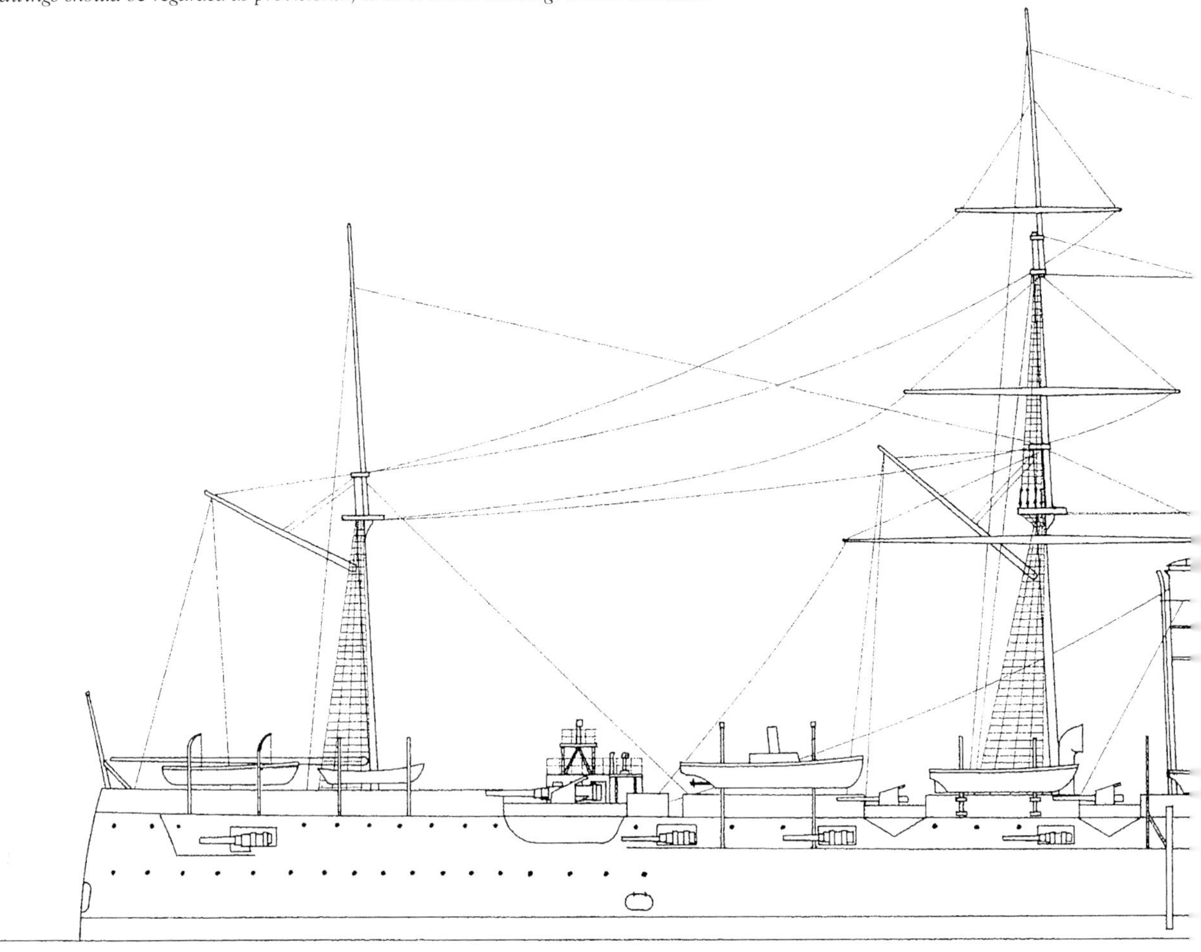

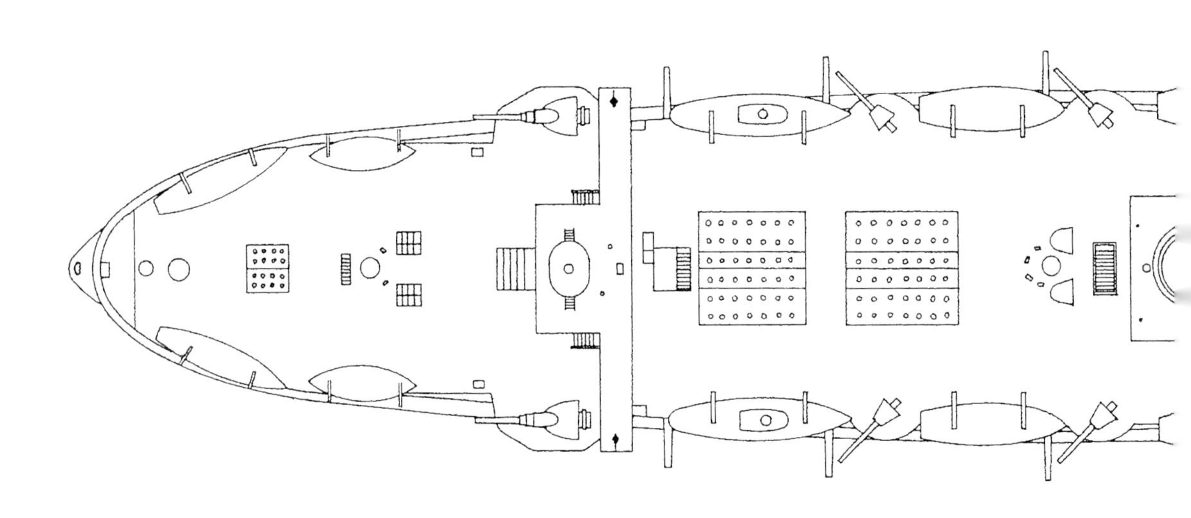

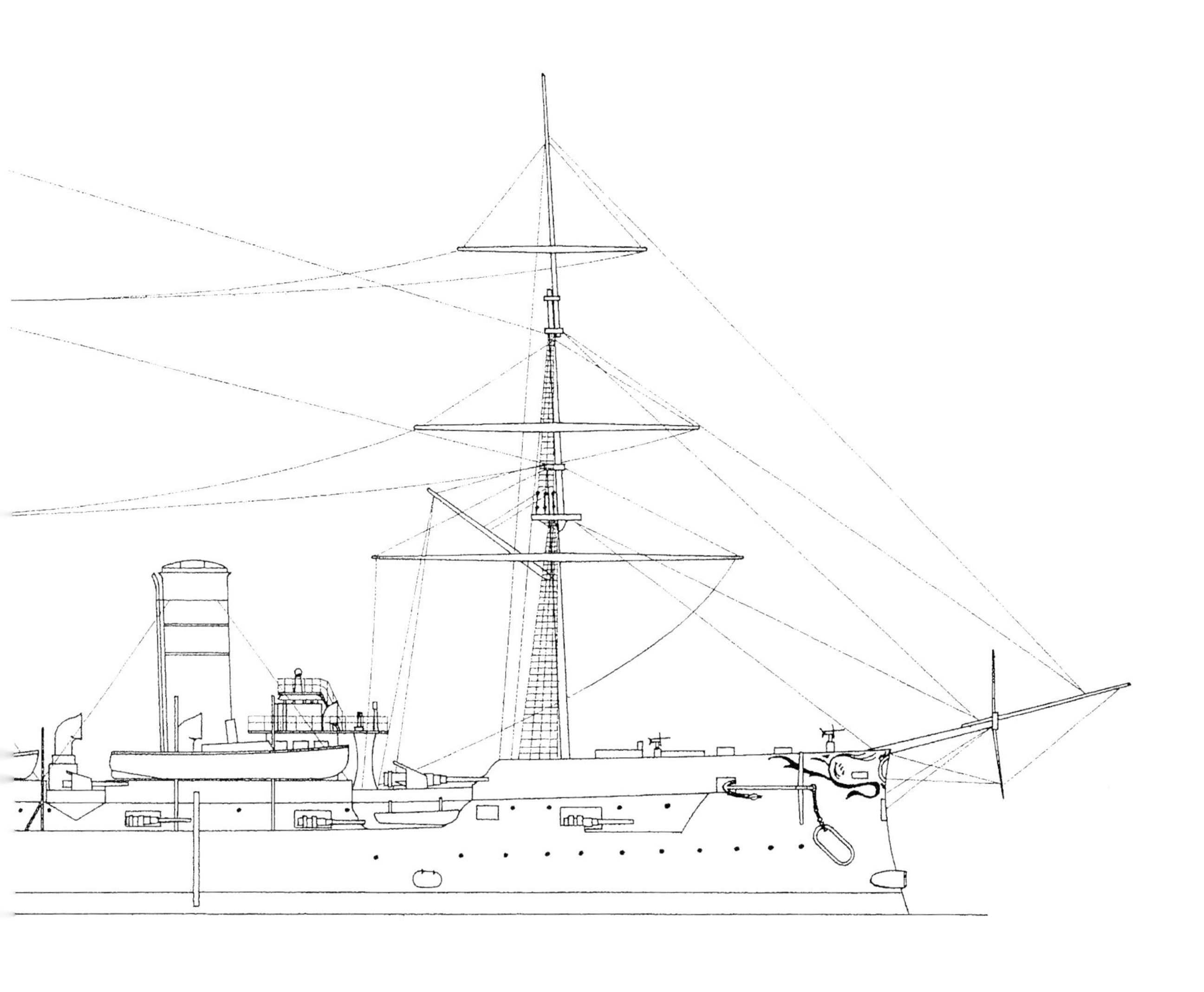

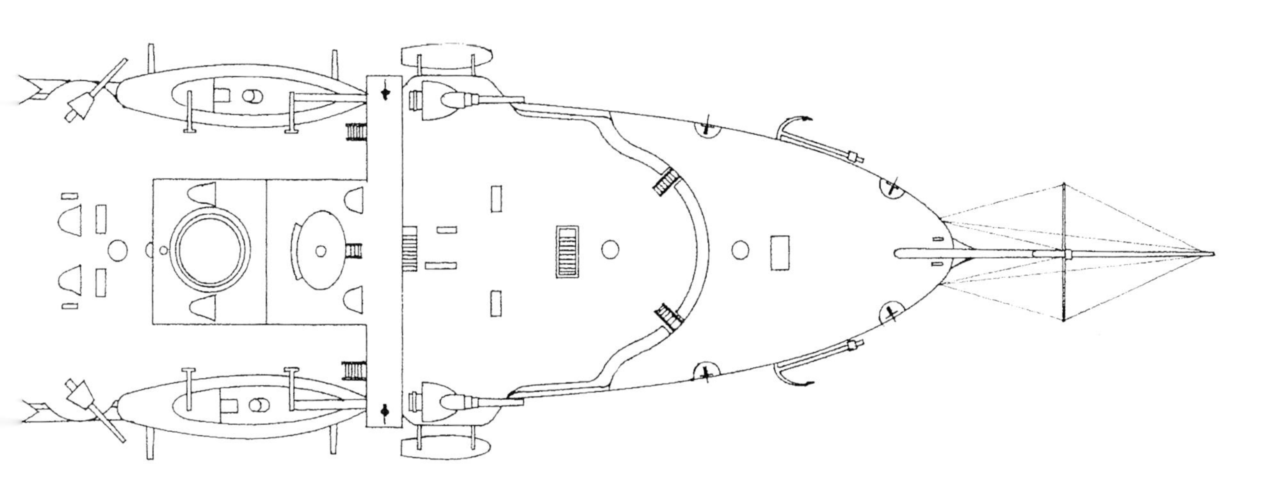

not regard a protective deck as sufficient protection for a large ship.

Kuteinikov worked out two designs, one for a 9000-ton ship, the other for a 10,000-tonner; the latter was eventually accepted as superior. The design was ready by 1/13 July 1889, despite a last-minute order from Admiral Chikhachev to replace most of the 47mm guns with six of the new 4.7in quick-firers. Kuteinikov's design showed a ship with a length of 390ft and a beam of 67ft (L:B ratio of 5.8, as opposed to Rodionov's 6.8). An order for construction was drawn up, but at the last minute there was a hitch: the design used a machinery plant based on the Napier-built engines of the Black Sea Fleet battleship *Sinop*, but these did not reach their contracted horsepower. It was therefore feared that the cruiser would not make her designed speed; Kuteinikov decided that the only way out of the mess was to install two engines on each shaft, as had recently been done in the British cruiser *Blenheim*. On the plus side, the individually smaller engines would allow the elimination of the armoured glacis over the cylinder heads, but they also meant a longer engineering space, so the design had to be lengthened by about 35ft – it was now longer than Rodionov's original design. A proposal to use Belleville watertube boilers instead of cylindrical boilers was rejected.

The final design showed a three-masted, two-funnelled ship with a high freeboard throughout, increased forward by a short forecastle deck. The hull form was unusual, with a tumble-home that curved inward sharply until it met the vertical sides of the battery deck. The 8in guns were mounted in sponsons on the upper deck forward and aft, with the 4.7in guns on smaller sponsons between them. The 6in guns were all mounted in embrasures on the deck below, one gun on either side sited well forward, six amidships and another gun well aft, for a total of eight on either side.

The hull was protected by a vertical 10in nickel-steel belt abreast the machinery compartments, reduced to 8in over the magazines; it did not extend to the bow or stern, but was sealed off fore and aft by 10in bulkheads, with a 2in flat deck above. Protection at the ends of the hull was provided by 3in protective decks below the waterline. The only other armour in the initial design was the 6in conning tower.

In addition to armour, the ship also made extensive use of coal for protection. There were coal bunkers outboard of the machinery spaces, as well as bunkers above the armour deck along the sides of the hull; these were approximately 13ft deep, and equivalent when full to about 6in of steel armour. The coal would also have limited both the explosive effect of shells and any subsequent flooding, since the coal consumed about 60% of the volume of the bunkers; furthermore, it would limit the loss of waterplane area in the event of the hull being damaged at the waterline. The bunkers were subdivided more minutely by transverse bulkheads than the ship as a whole. It is therefore fair to say that, taken overall, the stability and flotation of the ship were well-protected against shellfire; but the machinery compartments were very large and would have posed a threat in the event of underwater damage. This danger was somewhat offset by the fact that there were no centreline bulkheads in these spaces, which greatly reduced the danger of capsizing from asymmetrical flooding.

As was normal in Russian shipbuilding, the weight of the ship grew considerably during construction; the prime culprit in this was the frequent design alterations. For example, during construction it was decided to change from 6in/35 to 6in/45 guns; to protect these guns from raking fire, 4in transverse bulkheads were added at the ends of the battery deck (there were no screening bulkheads between the guns, however, so a shell exploding anywhere in the battery might have disabled several guns). Other weight increases came with the provision of two 14-ton second class torpedo boats instead of the usual steam launches, and 95 tons of additional steel was added to increase the hull strength. As a result the ship as completed was 633 tons overweight. Nevertheless, she managed an average speed of 18.84kts on four runs on the measured mile (13,326ihp vs the design figure of 12,500ihp). The basic soundness of her machinery was demonstrated by the fact that in the fall of 1902, during a 'race' from Nagasaki to Port Arthur against her squadron mates, *Riurik* was able to maintain an average speed of 17.7kts on the 38-hour voyage. She was considered an excellent sea boat, able to maintain her speed and use her guns even in rough weather.

In 1899 the commander of the Pacific Squadron, Rear-Admiral F V Dubasov, proposed the complete elimination of her sailing rig, but the Naval Ministry was not prepared to take that step; instead it was reduced from about 20,000ft^2 to 6800ft^2. As a result, the ship lost her bowsprit, her fore- and main-topgallant masts, as well as most of the yards crossed on her main- and mizzen-masts[3]. A small searchlight platform was added low on the foremast, angled slightly to starboard. A proposal to replace the cylindrical boilers with Bellevilles was ruled out due to the limited dockyard facilities available in the Far East.

Riurik has often been criticised as an obsolete design, principally due to her full sailing rig, lack of protection for the armament and side-mounted artillery, which permitted only half the heavy guns to fire on either broadside. Her long building-time contributed to this unfavourable evaluation, since by the time she entered service much later designs with superior protection were under construction or even in service. Nevertheless, it is only fair to note that the ship lived up to her designers' intentions very well. She was intended as a long-range commerce raider; in many ways she (like all commerce raiders) was not a *fighting* ship at all. Her effectiveness was dependent on her long range, high speed, and good sea-going characteristics; armament and protection were very much secondary considerations. It should also not be overlooked that the ship demonstrated considerable staying power in action with Admiral Kamimura's more modern cruisers, sinking at last only after her Kingston valves had been opened. The protection offered by her waterline belt has often been unfavourably compared to that afforded by a complete protective deck, but this assessment ignores the fact that in *Riurik* the narrow belt was combined with the same form of coal protection that was such an important element in the protective deck scheme. Thus her narrow belt-armoured deck-coal protection system was for the most part equivalent to, if not somewhat superior to, the protective deck system; its only inherent drawback was that it was considerably heavier. It is not known, however, if *Riurik*'s stability was calculated on the basis of having her lower bunkers empty and her upper bunkers full – one of the important factors in any system making extensive use of coal bunkers for protection against shellfire.

Rossiia[4]

It had originally been intended to build a second cruiser of the *Riurik* type, but on 22 August/3 September 1892 the director of the Naval Ministry, Admiral Chikhachev, ordered that the next ship have more extensive armour protection than *Riurik*. Specifically, Chikhachev wanted to reduce the belt armour from 10in to 8in in order to obtain an upper belt. The MTK set to work and came back in November 1892 with a sketch design for a ship of 12,000 tons, with the bunker capacity increased to 2246 tons, for a cruising range of 6720 miles at 9kts. The construction drawings of this design were approved in April 1893, but these drawings were extensively modified by the Baltic Works over the next year as the Naval Ministry introduced a succession of changes. Among other things, the six 4.7in guns were replaced by four more 6in guns, the 75mm guns were replaced by a new model gun of the same calibre, and the sailing rig (6,000ft^2) was eliminated.

The new ship, eventually named *Rossiia*, introduced a number of innovations. The most interesting was the use of a three-shaft propulsion plant, with a small cruising engine (2500ihp) mounted on the centre shaft. This was intended to extend her range by allowing her to steam on only one screw. Even more important was the use of French-made Belleville watertube boilers, which were more efficient than the cylindrical boilers of *Riurik*. Another unusual feature was the single enclosed 6in gun in the bow, presumably to be used as a chase piece when in pursuit, a task for which her side-mounted casemate guns were ill-suited. Study of the Sino-Japanese War of 1894-1895 led to the use of a light steel wheelhouse rather than the traditional wooden structure. Throughout her construction an effort was made to reduce the amount of wood fixtures, although the cabin furnishings were still largely made of wood (they had been ordered before the new fire-safety regulations had been approved). Like *Riurik*, she was sheathed with wood and copper.

Although Chikhachev's original intention had been to increase the vertical extent of the armour at the expense of the waterline belt's thickness, this was not achieved. Instead, the ship still had only a narrow waterline belt,

Rossiia *in May 1904, during the Vladivostok cruiser detachment's raiding cruise in the Sea of Japan. The ship is carrying a balloon on her quarterdeck; during this voyage it was used for reconnaissance – the first time an aerial device had been used by a warship at sea in time of war. The ship in the foreground is unidentified.* (Andrei Alexandrov collection, courtesy of R D Layman)

Rossiia *as completed*. (Drawn by the author)

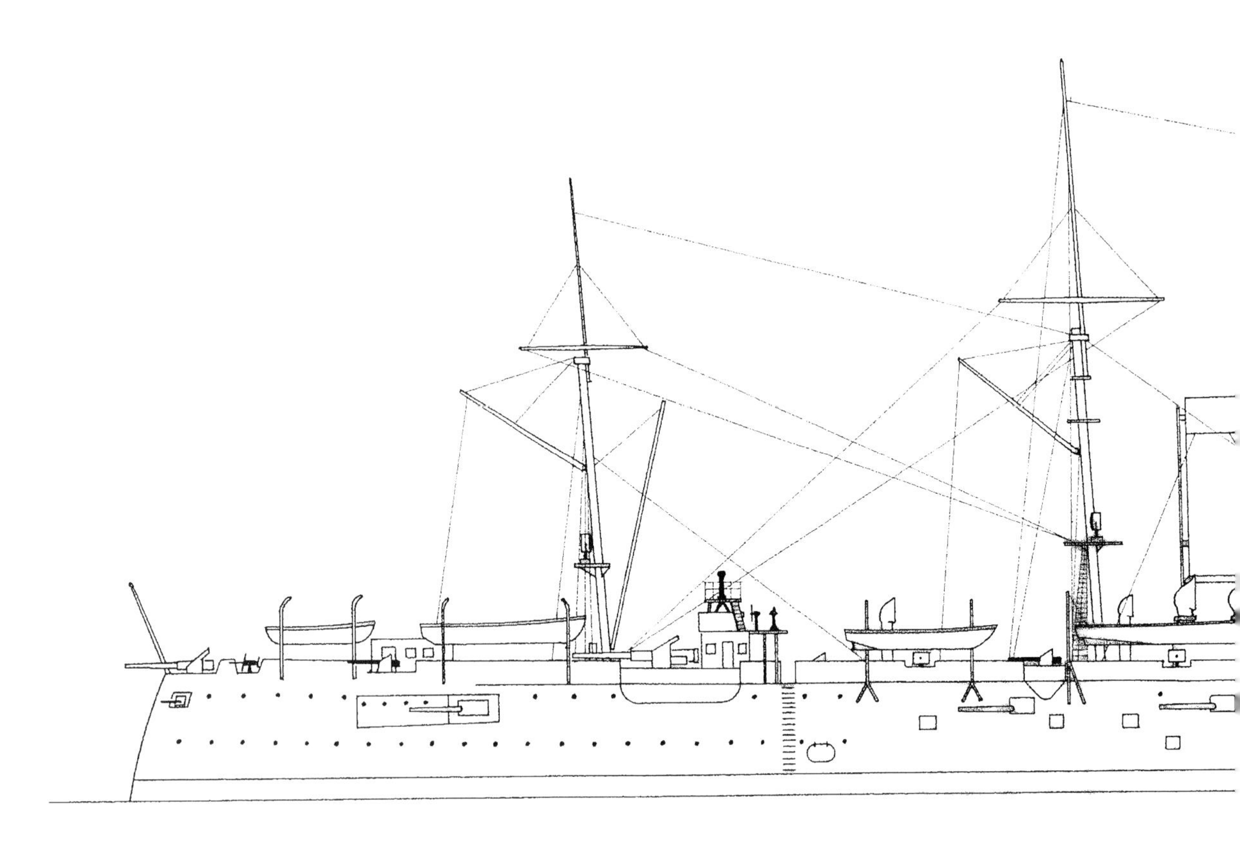

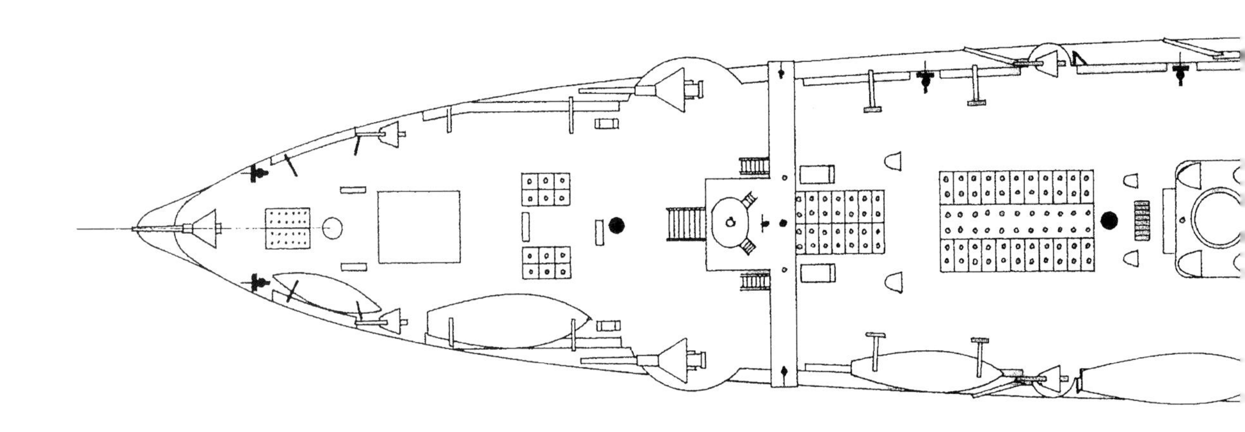

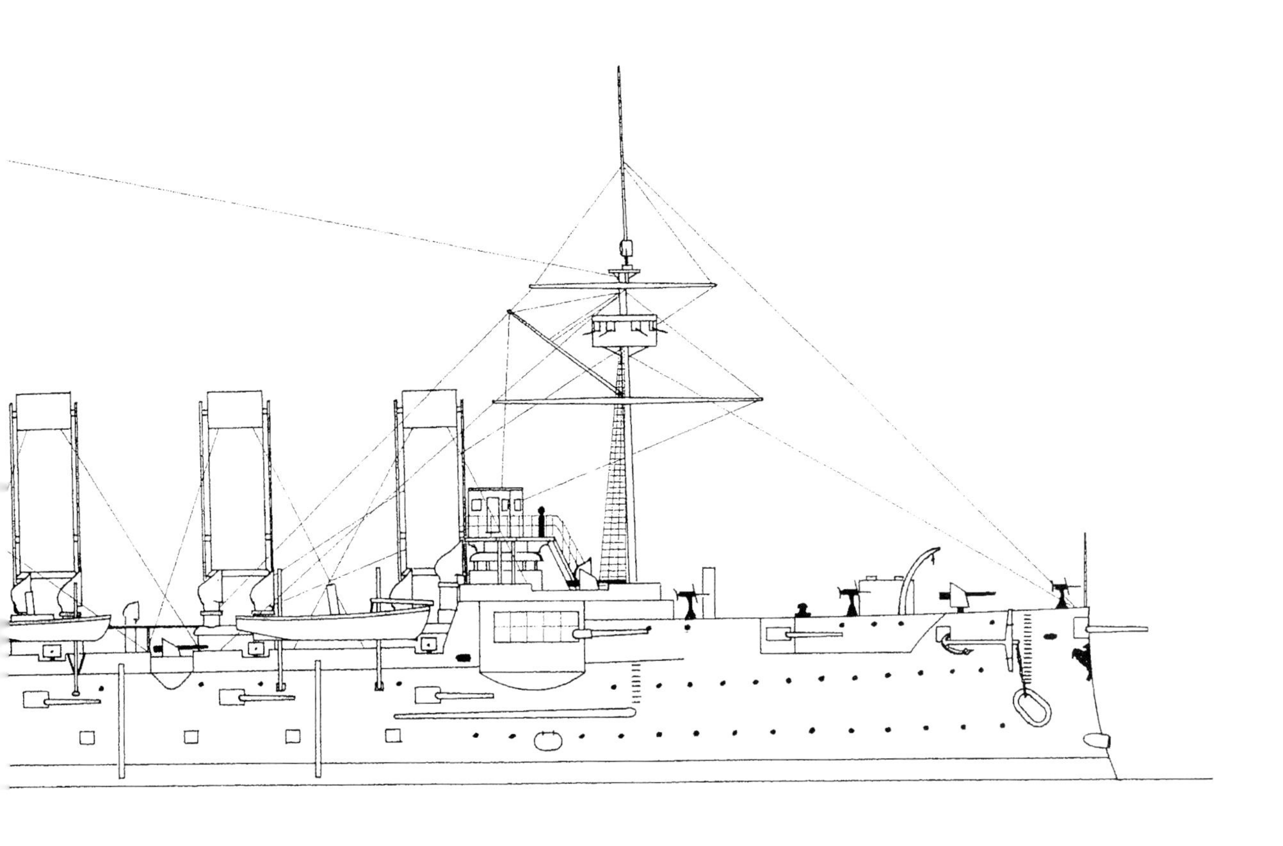

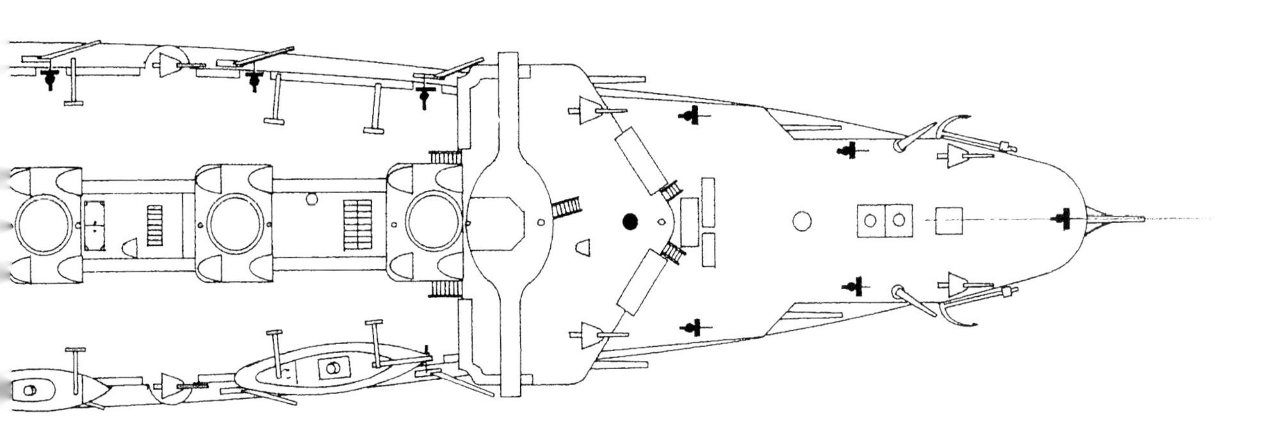

8in amidships thinned to 6in forward and abaft the machinery spaces. Harvey armour was used, so there was probably little loss of protection compared with the 10in steel belt of *Riurik*. At the bow the belt was closed off by a 7in transverse bulkhead, with an underwater protective deck (2.5-3in) extending to the bow. Aft, the belt ran right to the stern, but was reduced to 5in. The deck was 2in, with a 5in glacis projecting above it to cover the tops of the main engines' cylinders. The funnel uptakes had 3in protection between the lower and middle decks, but the armament was once again completely unprotected – although there were 5in transverse bulkheads at either end of the 6in battery to protect the guns from raking fire, as well as partial 1.5in screens between the 6in guns. The conning tower was much thicker than in *Riurik*, having 12in sides.

The ship was considered to be a good sea-boat, with a smooth roll – attributable in part to her tumble-home sides. The engines worked well, and during her official trials on 18/30 July 1897 she achieved a speed of 19.74kts on a displacement of 12,576 tons. The two main engines developed 15,523ihp, about 1000ihp more than the contracted figure.

After the Battle of Ulsan on 1/14 August 1904 the ship's armament was modified. Six more 6in guns were installed on the upper deck, three on either side in the intervals between the 6in guns on the main deck. The forward 6in gun was moved from its bow embrasure to the upper deck to increase its arc of fire. These alterations increased the broadside of the ship by four 6in guns. After the war the midships 6in guns on the upper deck were provided with lightly armoured casemates, and the mizzenmast was removed.

During the First World War the Baltic Fleet's weakness in cruisers led to the re-arming of all the existing ships. *Rossiia*'s was perhaps the most radical conversion: taken in hand at Kronshtadt in October 1915, her forecastle deck was removed and two single 8in guns were mounted on the centreline forward; another two 8in were mounted on the quarter-deck, giving her a total of eight 8in, with a broadside of six guns. Only the midships 6in guns were retained, giving her a total of fourteen guns, with a broadside of seven guns.

'Cruiser-Battleships' — the *Peresvet* Class[5]

This is not the place for a complete description of these battleships, but it is nevertheless necessary to note their role in the further development of Russia's armoured cruisers. These ships were originally inspired by the British *Centurion* class – relatively fast second-class battleships intended for operation on foreign stations; their 10in guns and good protection meant that they could easily overwhelm any armoured cruiser. The Russians therefore decided to 'stiffen' their armoured cruiser squadron with fast battleships of their own. The design documents refer to these ships as 'battleship-cruisers' (*bronenostsy-kreisery*), and their characteristics were largely determined by the dual need of countering the British second-class battleships and operating with the armoured cruisers on long raiding voyages. Thus long range and good sea-going qualities had to be merged with much improved protection and armament. This combination was made possible by the use of improved (hence thinner and lighter) armour and a new, lightweight 10in gun.

The design was approved in July 1895, and showed a ship only slightly larger than *Rossiia*'s 12,674 tons; its kinship to the armoured cruiser was furthermore shown by its relatively fine lines, its extraordinary high freeboard forward, its large 2000-ton coal supply, the 6in bow-chaser and the three-shaft machinery plant, although the battleship-cruiser featured three equally powerful engines, rather than having a low-powered cruising engine on the centre shaft.

But the new ship, soon named *Peresvet*, also differed from the armoured cruiser in many ways. She introduced several new features in Russian shipbuilding, including individual armoured casemates for the 6in guns, *à la* Sir William White's designs. Also borrowed from White's practices was the armoured deck that sloped down to meet the lower edge of the armour belt, thus greatly increasing the protection of the vitals. And of course her main battery of four turret-mounted 10in guns gave her a broadside far superior to that of the armoured cruisers.

The ship's protection was also much improved compared to what was acceptable in an armoured cruiser, with a 9in belt (thinned to 7in abreast the magazines), and a 4in upper belt amidships. The turret bases were 8in, the turrets themselves 9in, the casemates had 5in faces. A major innovation was her bilge system; in previous Russian practice a single master pipe ran the length of the major watertight compartments, and all pumps were attached to it; thus it was theoretically possible to pump water from any compartment with the combined power of all the ship's pumps. This advantage was almost entirely negated by the simple fact that the aggregate capacity of all the pumps was far greater than that of the master pipe itself; in addition, the master pipe had to be run through the bulkheads, thus forming a point of weakness. And as ships grew larger, the system of pipes and valves grew so complex that mistakes in the heat of action could easily lead to the flooding of an undamaged compartment instead of the draining of an damaged one. Therefore in *Peresvet*, and in all subsequent large Russian warships, each major watertight compartment had its own autonomous pumping system, which greatly simplified the arrangements and reduced the number of penetrations through the watertight bulkheads. This system was in considerable advance of foreign practice; the first British battleships so fitted were apparently the *Lord Nelson* class, laid down in 1905 – a full decade after the Russian ships.

The *Peresvet* class thus form an interesting off-shoot from the main line of Russia's armoured cruiser development; they were designed to support the armoured cruisers in the face of British second-class battleships, rather than fight in the line of battle. Nevertheless, the three ships of this class all found themselves facing the enemy's first-class battleships during the Russo-Japanese War – a war they were not designed to fight.

Gromoboi[6]

The construction of a third armoured cruiser was provided under a programme approved by the emperor in July 1895. The original intention was simply to build another *Rossiia*, but these plans were soon altered. A new form of armoured cruiser was beginning to emerge – a ship capable of operating beside the battleships as a sort of 'fast wing' of the battlefleet. In fact this type of ship had existed for some time in the navies of secondary powers, which could not afford large and expensive specialised ships; big ships therefore often had to act both as cruisers and as battleships, and so combined the speed of the one with the guns and armour of the other – at least to the degree allowed by the technology of the day and the ingenuity of their designers. Examples of this breed of not-quite-battleships are the US *Maine* (laid down in 1888 as an armoured cruiser, then reclassified as a second-class battleship), Spain's *Infanta Maria Teresa* (ordered in 1889) and Austria-Hungary's *Kaiserin und Königin Maria Theresa* (laid down in 1891). In the mid-1890s the introduction of improved armours such as Harvey and Krupp made such ships attractive even to the larger navies, and the Sino-Japanese War enhanced their appeal by demonstrating that even protected cruisers could stand up to ships armed with big, slow-firing guns. By 1896 Austria-Hungary, France, Italy (which kept selling hers to Argentina before they entered service), Japan and Spain all had new examples of this type on the ways; virtually every naval power joined in their construction within the next couple of years, and some authorities, such as France's Admiral François-Ernest Fournier, even proposed that such cruisers could act as 'universal' ships, replacing battleships as well as other types of cruisers. Most of these new armoured cruisers approached battleships in size, but mounted only a few guns of 8-10in calibre, with heavy batteries of quick-firers.

Aside from simply following what seemed a world-wide trend in cruiser construction, the Imperial Navy also had an immediate and compelling reason for wanting cruisers with better armour protection. Japan's naval extensive construction programme after the Sino-Japanese War meant that, for the first time, there would be a first-class fleet in the waters of the eastern Pacific, rather than the scattering of second-class battleships and cruisers maintained there by European navies. Since Russia had already earned Japan's animosity through the Triple Intervention of 1895, this new Asian power had to be considered a potential enemy – and Japan's ever-growing fleet could hardly be threatened by a few long-range commerce raiders.

The necessity of having a battle squadron in the Far East was quickly recognised in St Petersburg, and the Naval Ministry set about reviewing its construction policy. In addition to a new programme intended to provide a squadron of battleships for the Far East by 1905, the Naval Ministry quickly decided that a duplicate of *Rossiia* was not only obviously inferior to the new breed of armoured cruisers, but was likewise too weak to take part in the sort of squadron engagements likely in a war with Japan. So in June 1896 the MTK instructed the Baltic Works to work out proposals for a 'squadron' armoured cruiser, taking the hull of *Rossiia* as a basis. Other requirements included the provision of armoured deck slopes to reinforce the belt and the use of three equally powerful engines (both features used in the *Peresvet* class) instead of a low-powered cruising engine on the centre shaft. Protection to the armament was to be provided by 'individual casemates or other means.' In other words, the ship was to somehow combine the attributes of the long-range commerce raider with a ship suited for action alongside the battle fleet.

This was a tall order – to squeeze more armour and more powerful engines into an existing hull. The Baltic Works presented its sketch designs in August; displacements ranged from 12,336 to 15,385 tons – obviously the shipyard had departed some considerable way from the instruction to use *Rossiia*'s hull, and in fact the biggest design was a 20kt version of the *Peresvet* class. But the MTK preferred the smallest of the designs, which most closely matched the original specification for a *Rossiia* with improved protection for the armament.

The final design was approved by the MTK in March 1897. Although the director of the Baltic Works, S K Ratnik, complained that this ship had nothing in common with *Rossiia*, he was clearly exaggerating in order to emphasise the amount of work his constructors and draughtsmen had to contend with. The dimensions of the two ships were virtually identical, and from any distance it would have been impossible to tell the two apart. Nevertheless, there was some justice in Ratnik's remark; the new ship had a slightly larger displacement, which meant the hull lines had to be filled out slightly, and the armour protection and engines were completely altered. It had initially been hoped that the use of Krupp plate would allow a reduction in the thickness of the belt with no loss of resistance, but Russian plants had not yet mastered the new process and Harvey armour had once again to be used. Since the balance of the design hinged on thinning the belt, a reduction the belt protection had to be accepted, although this was considerably offset by the use of armoured deck slopes behind the belt. The belt was reduced from 8in to 6in and made considerably shorter than that of *Rossiia* – aft it was completely eliminated and replaced by a 2.5-3in protective deck, while the protective deck forward extended much further aft than in the earlier ship; 6in transverse bulkheads closed off the belt, and the armour deck was 1.5in on the horizontal and 2.5in on the slopes. Also eliminated was the glacis over the tops of the engine cylinders, made possible by the use of three engines of the same aggregate horse power as *Rossiia*'s two main engines. The weight saved on the belt and glacis armour was used to protect the forward 8in and twelve of the sixteen 6in guns with casemates; these had external faces of 4.7in, with 2in backs and 1in roofs – the floors were not armoured, but the coal bunkers below would have provided some protection by absorbing much of the force of shells exploding underneath the casemates. The ammunition hoists and funnel uptakes were protected by 1.5in plate, and there were 2in transverse bulkheads to protect the battery deck from raking fire. The conning tower once

A remarkably crisp photograph of Gromoboi *in the Baltic, 1911. Note the casemates added for the aft 8in guns and the upper deck 6in guns.* (Courtesy of S Vinogradov)

Gromoboi *as completed*. (Drawn by the author)

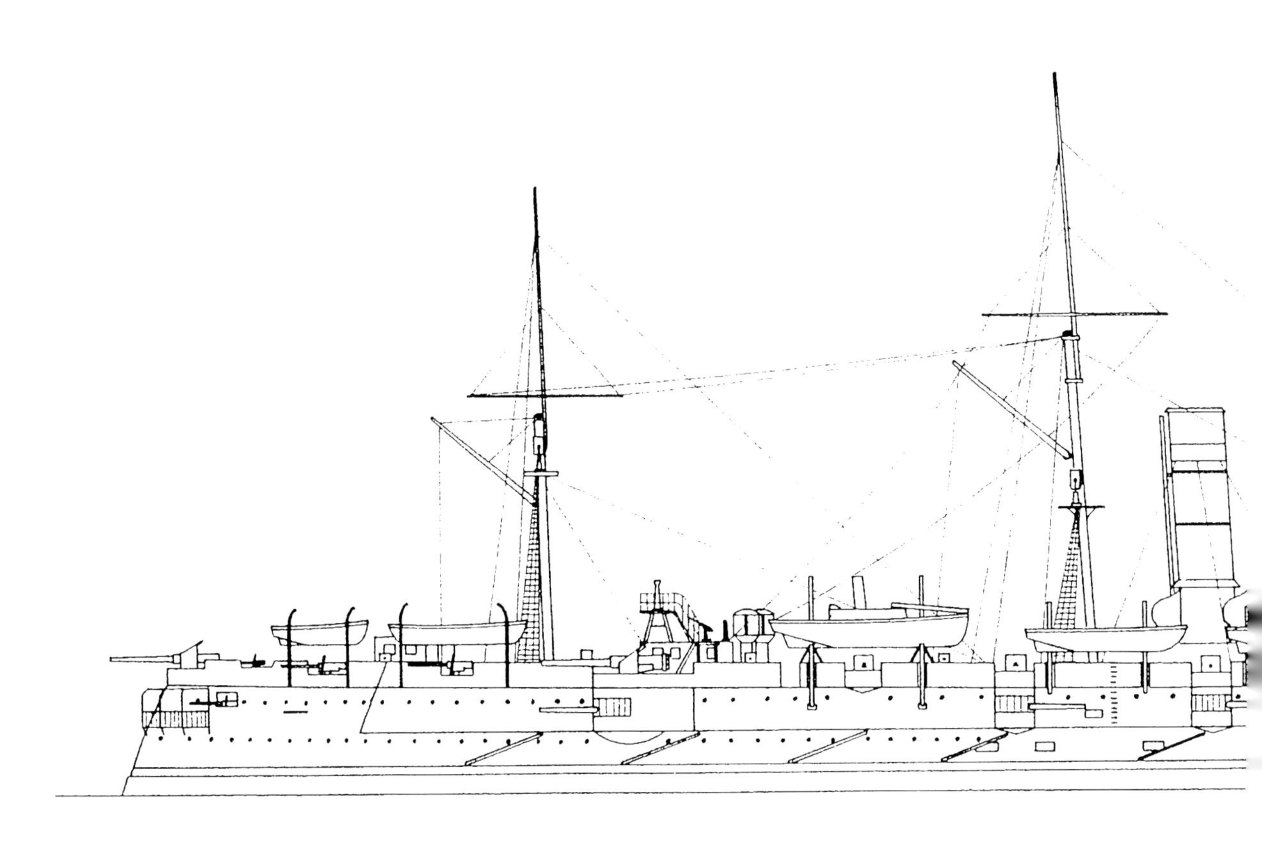

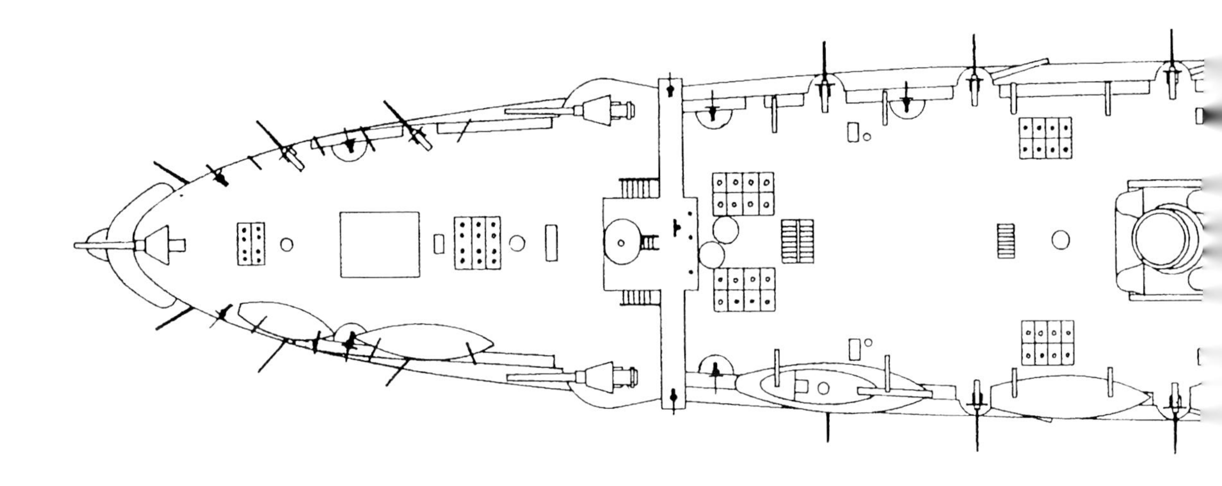

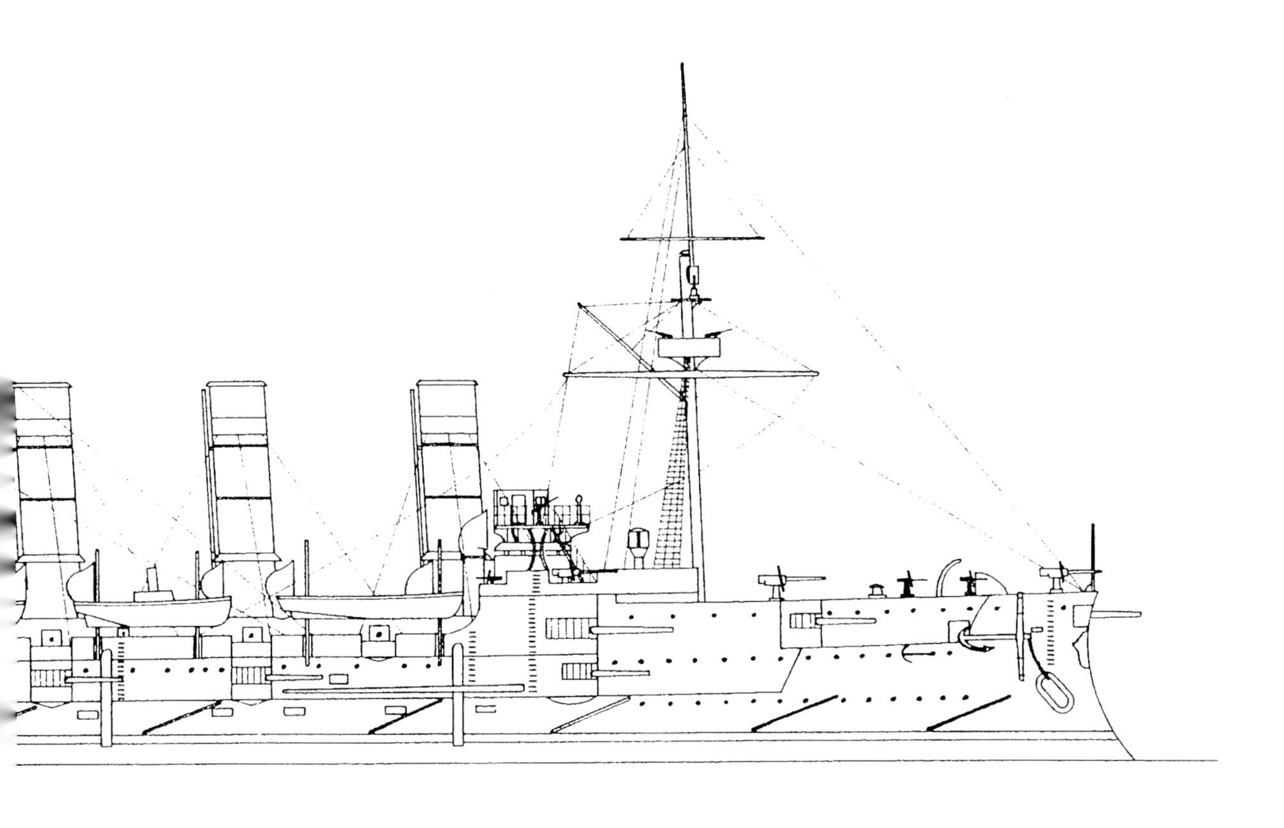

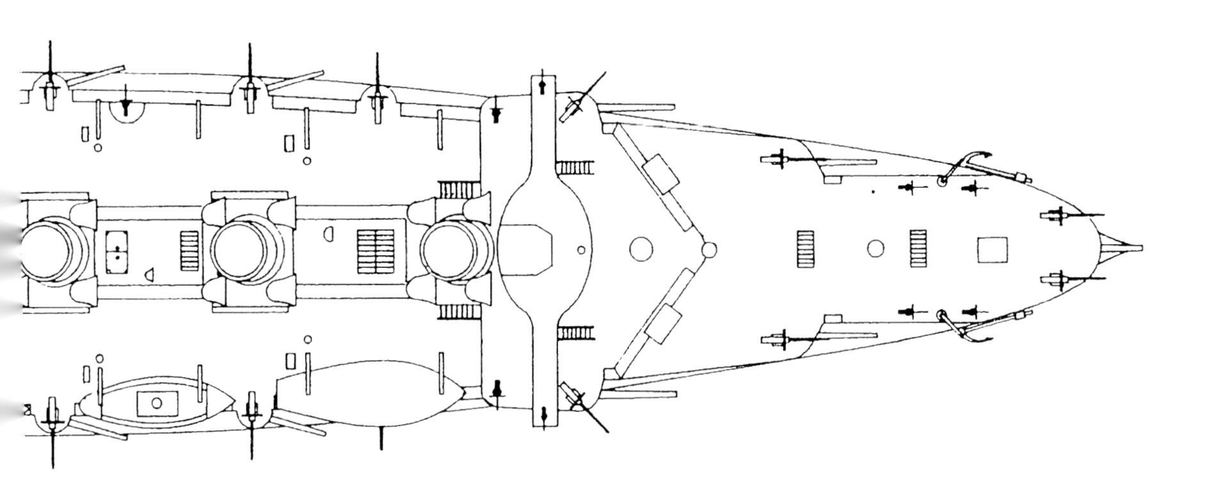

again received 12in armour, but this time Krupp plate was used, the only armour of this kind on the ship. The after 8in guns, as well as the three forward 6in and the 6in on the quarter-deck, had no armour protection. Extensive use was again made of coal bunkers for protection abreast the machinery spaces and above the armour deck amidships. The protection of the torpedo armament was also improved by the use of underwater tubes, although the arrangement of the protective decks forward and aft meant that it was not possible to fit bow and stern tubes, leaving only the four broadside tubes.

The machinery plant comprised thirty-two Russian-made Belleville boilers and three four-cylinder vertical triple-expansion engines, intended to produce a total of 14,500ihp for a speed of 19kts; on her six-hour trials (5/17 October 1900) the ship actually generated 15,496ihp for a speed of 20.1kts. The ship was wood-and-copper sheathed, like her predecessors. She also featured the new compartmentalised bilge system introduced in *Peresvet*.

The weight breakdown for the ship as completed was as follows:

Hull	4757 tons
Armour	2169.46 tons
Artillery with ammunition	832.5 tons
Torpedoes, mines, dynamos, nets	166.28 tons
Machinery with 145 tons of boiler water	1988.15 tons
Boats	57.77 tons
Crew, provisions, fresh water	85.3 tons
Anchors, masts, supplies	617.8 tons
Normal load of coal	1756 tons
Total	12,430.26 tons

As completed the ship trimmed badly by the bow, especially when fully loaded, and she suffered not only from a reduction in speed but also from considerable wetness forward. To correct this it was necessary to shift some loads as well as add ballast aft. Once this was done, however, she was regarded as a good sea boat, with an easy, if rapid, roll.

The idea of steaming on only the centre engine as a means of extending the ship's range was soon shown to be a failure. It turned out that the wing propellers would not start rotating freely ('windmilling') at speeds below 7-8kts; up to that point they were a drag on speed and actually increased coal consumption.

Like *Rossiia*, the ship was re-armed after the Battle of Ulsan. She had run aground in the fall of 1904, and during her repairs six more 6in guns were installed on the upper deck, three on either side above the main deck 6in guns, and individual lightly armoured casemates were built to protect them; 1.25in shields were added to some of the exposed guns; the aftermost 6in guns were moved forward, and the foremost 6in guns were moved up to the forecastle. Barr & Stroud rangefinders were added. The number of 75mm guns was reduced to nineteen, and only two 37mm guns were retained.

After the war *Gromoboi* returned to the Baltic and was given a more thorough refit; her boilers by this time were, according the chief of the Baltic Works' boiler shop, 'an absolute ruin,' in contrast to the French-made boilers of *Rossiia*, which were still in fair condition.

The alterations made at this time included the removal of the after 15in torpedo tubes and the replacement of the forward pair by 18in tubes; a casemate with 3in sides and a 1in roof was erected around the after 8in guns, and the after 6in guns were again shifted well aft and given protection (2in sides, 0.75in roof). Of the light artillery there remained only four of the 75mm guns and four 47mm guns. Protected towers for Barr & Stroud rangefinders were erected fore and aft, and the protection of the new upper-deck casemates for the 6in guns was increased to 2in on the sides and 0.75in on the roofs. The rig was reduced to two masts, with the mainmast moved aft and the old foremast replaced by the former mizzen-mast; 90cm searchlights were installed on both.

Trials in the fall of 1910 showed that the engines and boilers still needed work – the engines developed only 9979ihp, and even at that rate were overheating. After almost a year of adjustments and modifications, new trials were run on 14/27 July 1911. These went much better – on a displacement of 12,643 tons the engines developed 13,337.2ihp for a speed of 18.5kts.

The armament was again modified during the First World War; the 6in guns in the bow and on the quarter-deck were removed and replaced by 8in, giving the ship a total of six 8in and twenty-two 6in, with a broadside of four 8in and eleven 6in guns. All the 75mm and 47mm guns were removed at this time; later, two 2.5in and two 47mm AA guns were fitted. She could also carry 200 mines; with all these changes her full load displacement came to 13,200 tons.

'Squadron' Armoured Cruisers: The Baian *Class*[7]

In the next Russian armoured cruiser, the French-built *Baian*, the concept of the commerce-raiding cruiser was completely rejected, and a smaller cruiser, designed exclusively for work with a battle squadron, was adopted. Despite the loss of the original ship during the Russo-Japanese War, the design was considered a success, and three sister ships – *Admiral Makarov*, *Baian* (ii) and *Pallada* – were ordered before the end of the war.

Like *Gromoboi*, the prototype of this new class was provided for under the provisions of the shipbuilding programme of 1896-1902. At the time, however, Russia's shipyards were already working at capacity, and it was accepted from the start that several ships would have to be ordered abroad. At this time the French shipyard of Forges et Chantiers de la Méditerranée, Le Seyne was building the small cruiser *Svetlana*; that ship's commander, Captain First Rank A M Abaza, began negotiations with the shipyard for the construction of a new and larger cruiser. The result was that in March 1897 Abaza presented six designs worked out by the firm to the MTK.

The MTK's comments on the design are interesting, as they show with particular clarity the new cruiser policy. One design for a 'citadel cruiser' of 5500 tons was reject-

The French-built Baian *sometime prior to the Russo-Japanese War. Particularly evident in this photograph is the overhanging 'mushroom' roof of the conning tower, a feature that was to prove fatal during the war, as the overhang had a nasty tendency to deflect splinters from nearby shell hits into the conning tower.* (US Naval Historical Center)

ed because the armour was considered inadequate and the 12,000-mile cruising range was deemed twice as much as required – it would be difficult to imagine a more radical change from the design philosophy of the earlier commerce-raiding cruisers. Another design was patterned on the French armoured cruiser *Dupuy de Lôme*, but the proposed armament of two 190mm, six 160mm and six 85mm guns was considered inadequate – not to mention the fact that none of these calibres was in service with the Russian navy. There were two enlarged *Svetlanas* (4800 tons and 5800 tons), but the protection of the armament of both was judged insufficient; there was an up-dated version of the cruiser *Admiral Nakhimov*, and also a design based on the French *Pothuau*, but these were also rejected – although the final design showed several similarities to the latter ship.

This stage of the process at least helped clarify the MTK's requirements; what was wanted was a ship about the same size as the protected cruiser *Diana* (6682 tons), but with an armament equivalent to that of the British-built Chilean protected cruiser *Esmeralda* (7000 tons, two 8in guns, sixteen 6in), and with an armour belt. Speed was to be 21kts, range 7000-8000 miles. The ship's relatively small size – most foreign armoured cruisers were in the 9000-13,000-ton range – indicates that the Russians were thinking in terms of a powerful fleet scout, rather than of a ship intended to take a place in the battle line; but the 8in guns and good protection would have allowed the vessel to play a useful part in a squadron action if necessary. After these requirements had been sent to the French shipyard, other stipulations were added – the 8in guns should be in turrets, and the belt armour should be equal in height to 16% of the beam of the ship – a requirement apparently determined by the angle of roll acceptable before the lower edge of the belt emerged from the water.

It was soon clear that these requirements could not be met by a 6700-ton ship, so the MTK agreed to an increase in displacement, as well as a reduction in cruising range. By October 1897 the design had been narrowed down to a ship of about 7800 tons, but the shipyard's proposal was still not satisfactory; Forges et Chantiers returned again in March 1898 with a further re-working of the design based on the comments of the MTK. These changes, noted the designer, Antoine-Jean Amable Lagane, would increase the displacement by 200 tons; in order to preserve the 7800-ton limit, the Naval Minister, Vice-Admiral P P Tyrtov, agreed to dispense with the ship's wood-and-copper sheathing – perhaps the final nail in the coffin of the long-range commerce-raider

The first Baian *as completed.* (Drawn by the author)

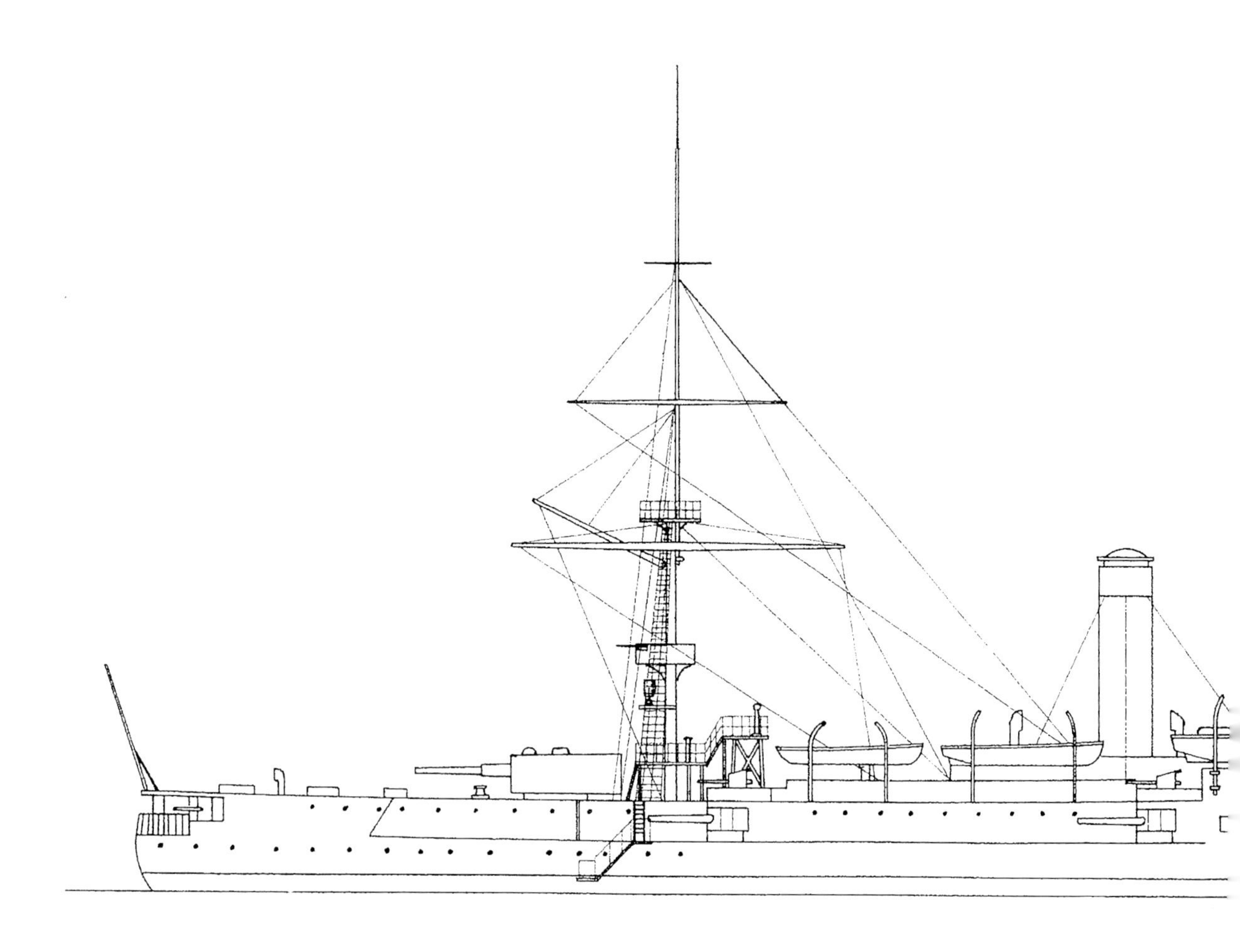

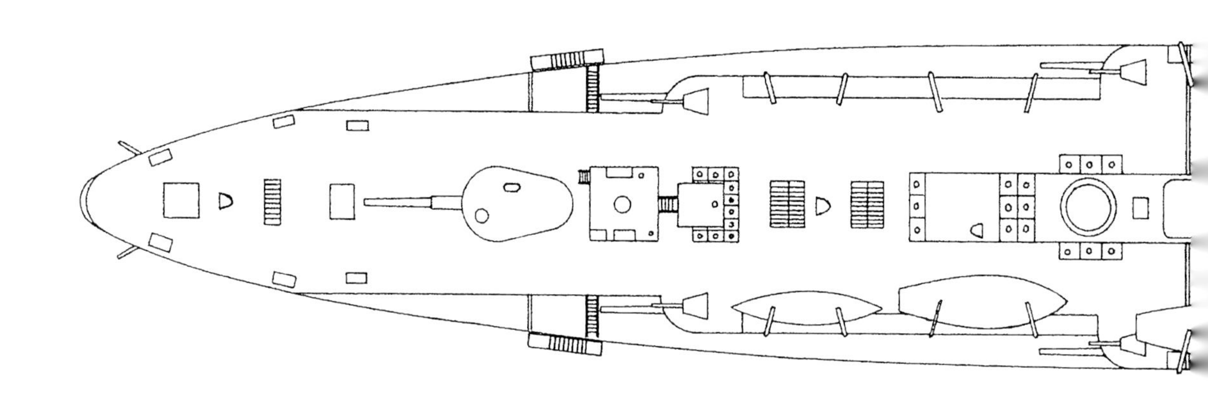

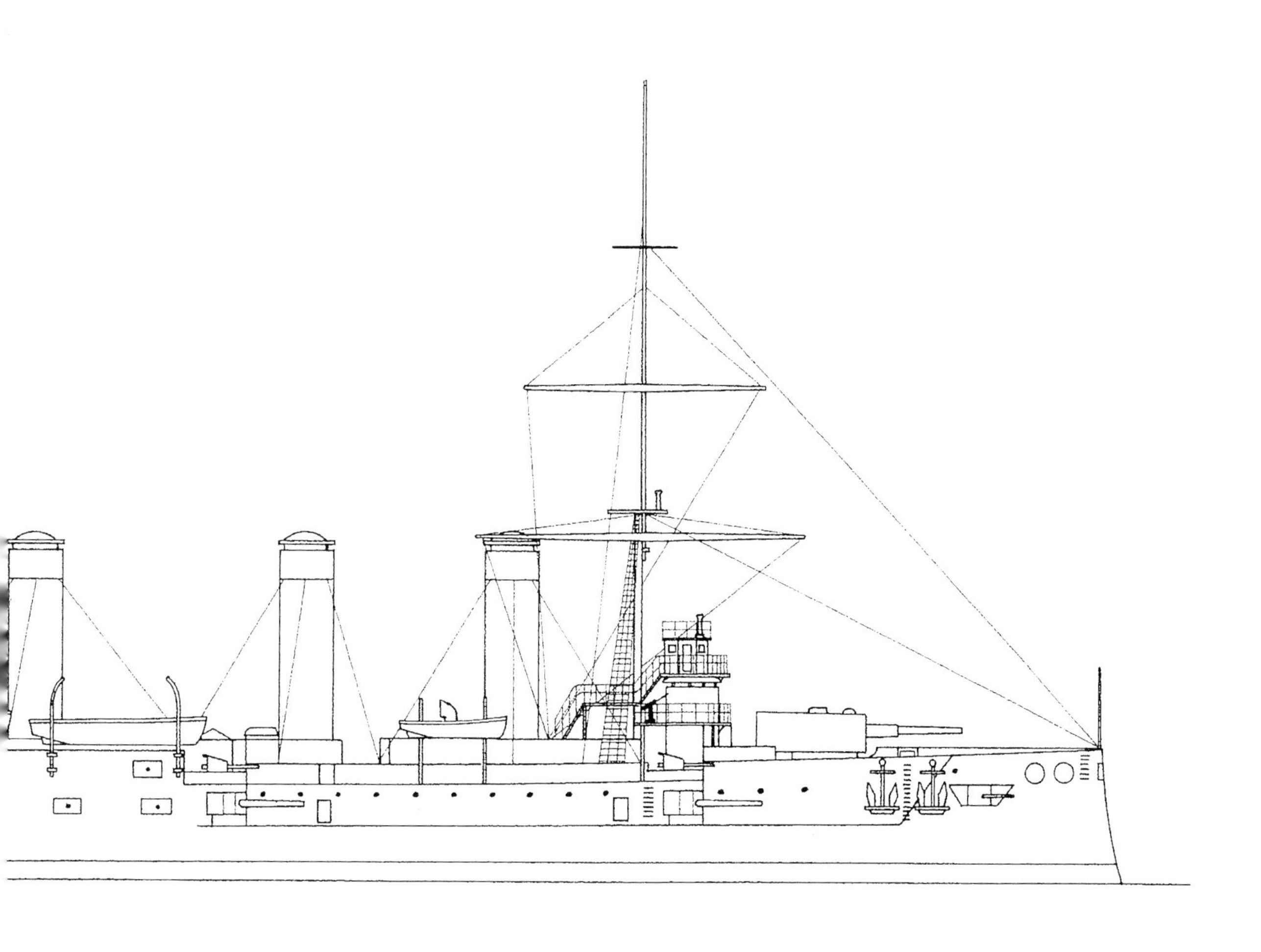

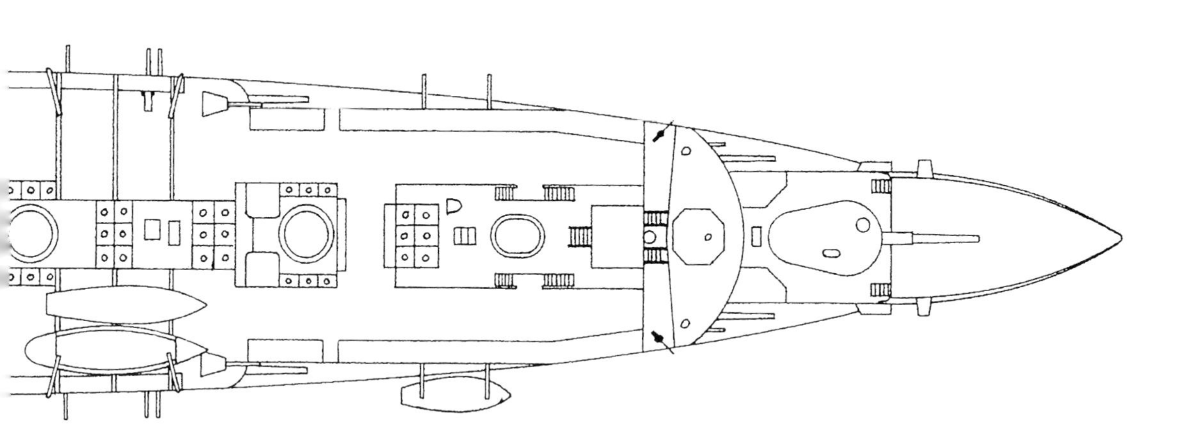

Admiral Makarov *off Revel (Tallinn) prior to World War One (Probably in 1911). She still sports her original single-masted rig.* (Courtesy of S Vinogradov)

Cruisers of the Baltic Fleet sometime before the First World War. Gromoboi *is leading* Admiral Makarov *and* Pallada. *Note that* Admiral Makarov *has been refitted with two masts.* (Courtesy of S Vinogradov)

concept. A contract with Forges et Chantiers de la Méditerranée was finally signed in May 1898 (also included in this was the construction of the battleship *Tsesarevich*), and the final design was approved in June. The ship was to be ready in thirty-six months from the date of the contract's signing; in fact, completion was somewhat delayed.

Baian carried her two 8in/45 guns in single turrets fore and aft, the forward one rather close to the bow, as was typical of contemporary French ships. Her eight 6in/45 guns were mounted in casemates on the main deck, two forward abreast the conning tower, four in an octagonal battery amidships, and two near the after turret. The sides of the hull were deeply recessed, so that all the 6in guns could bear (in theory at least) either directly ahead or astern. There were twenty 75mm guns, eight of them mounted in the central battery between the 6in guns, with four more on the deck above; the other 75mm guns were located in shielded mounts above the 6in casemates. There were two 15in submerged torpedo tubes, one on either beam.

The armour protection was far more complete than anything seen before on a Russian cruiser. The long expanse of the machinery compartments was covered by a 200mm belt (of Harvey armour, since French firms were slow to take up the production of Krupp plate), with a 100mm extension forward all the way to the stem-post; aft, there was a shorter 100mm portion over the 8in magazines, then a 50mm protective deck ran 76ft aft to the stern. Amidships above the main belt was a 60mm upper belt; the 6in casemates also had 60mm armour. The deck over the central battery was 50mm, and the unsloped deck at the top of the belt was 30mm on top of two layers of 10mm deck plating. The supporting tubes for the 8in turrets were 170mm, the turrets themselves had 150mm sides and 30mm roofs, and the conning tower was 160mm.

Coal protection was far less extensive than in the previous ships, with only narrow bunkers above and below the protective deck; it is clear that direct protection by armour plate was considered far more valuable than coal bunkers.

The ship was powered by two vertical triple-expansion engines and twenty-six Belleville boilers. Her designed power was 16,500ihp for a speed of 21kts; on trials in October 1902 the ship made 20.97kts.

Russian shipyard capacity was still overloaded with the Far Eastern construction programme when war broke out with Japan in February 1904. The Naval Ministry therefore decided to order another armoured cruiser abroad, with the intention of building another unit of the *Baian* type with minor modifications as indicated by war experience. This was in some ways an odd decision, as the design was already six years old and clearly growing obsolescent; only minor modifications would be possible if the basic design was to be retained. The explanation would seem to be that the MTK was too involved in war-related work to spend much time on a new design (in fact Ansaldo and Burmeister and Wain both submitted proposals, but these were quickly rejected). By simply repeating *Baian* it would be possible to minimise the design work load on the MTK and the naval constructors. In the end, of course, it wasn't that simple, since the alterations required by war experience eventually required a substantial amount of attention from the MTK. With hindsight, the decision to order this ship, plus two sisters in Russian yards, seems hasty and ill-advised, since by the time these ships joined the fleet far superior turbine-driven cruisers were entering service with other navies. Nevertheless, these ships gave good service during the First World War – since the Germans by and large committed only second-rank ships to the Baltic, the *Admiral Makarov* class did not suffer too badly in comparison.

Although it was decided to repeat the *Baian* design to speed up construction, the contract with Forges et Chantiers was not signed until 20 April/3 May 1905. The contract stipulated that all construction drawings would be sent to St Petersburg for use in building identical ships; their construction was apparently made possible by the fact that Admiral Z P Rozhestvenskii's Second Pacific Squadron had by this time departed for the Far East, freeing up domestic shipyard capacity. Two ships – *Pallada* and a second *Baian* – were laid down at the New Admiralty Works almost as soon as the French drawings became available.

Most of the first round of changes were in matters of detail – improvements to internal communications, ventilation and watertight integrity; it was also desired to have searchlights that could be stowed away behind armour when not in use, as these had proved vulnerable in action. To compensate for various additions in weight, the armour thicknesses were reduced, although the use of Krupp plate instead of Harvey meant that there was little loss in actual protection. The main portion of the belt was reduced from 200mm to 175mm, the forward and after portions from 100mm to 90mm, the turrets from 150mm to 132mm, and the conning tower from 160mm to 136mm; the 60mm thickness of the upper belt and casemate armour was not altered. Plans to replace the 75mm anti-torpedo boat battery with a larger calibre (presumably the 4.7in gun being adopted for other ships at this time) proved impossible due to the weights involved.

The only major problem that arose during the construction concerned the watertight bulkheads, which had to be reinforced – it turned out that similar changes had been required on the original *Baian*, but since these had not been noted on the existing design drawings, it was necessary to repeat the redesign of the bulkheads from scratch.

Other modifications included the replacement of the fore- and mainmasts with a single mast amidships, the elimination of the Temperley coal-loading booms, and the addition of a small range-finding tower aft.

Due to engine defects, *Admiral Makarov*'s official trials were not completed until early 1908. On trials on 26 December 1907/8 January 1908 she made 22.55kts at 128 revolutions, the output of her machinery amounting to 19,320ihp.

Before the First World War, *Admiral Makarov* was refitted with two masts to improve her wireless facilities; her Russian-built sisters apparently had two masts when they entered service. In December 1913 both the Baltic Fleet commander, Admiral N O Essen, and the naval minister, Admiral I K Grigorovich, approved the use of *Pallada* for experiments in the shipboard use of seaplanes, but no progress was made on this proposal before the outbreak of the First World War, and *Pallada* was soon sunk by a U-boat. In early 1916, *Admiral Makarov* and *Baian* (ii) were rearmed – the useless 75mm guns were removed, and a third 8in in a shielded mounting was added on the centreline just forward of the mainmast (frame 106); four more 6in guns were added on the upper deck, two on either beam. These additions increased the effective broadside by half again.

Full Circle: The New Riurik[8]

The Vickers-built *Riurik* was the last and largest of Russia's armoured cruisers, and can stand comparison with any of her foreign contemporaries – in fact, she has been described as 'one of the best armoured cruisers ever built.' In many ways, she was *Baian* writ large, as modified by the lessons of the Russo-Japanese War. She may also be seen as a development of the *Peresvet* class 'battleship-cruisers' – akin to the 15,000-ton design proposed by the Baltic Works during the early stages of *Gromoboi*'s design. What was wanted was essentially an armoured cruiser equivalent to the contemporary *Andrei Pervozvannyi* class battleships, with the main armament disposed in the traditional pattern of one turret forward and another aft, and the heavy intermediate battery – to be made up of twelve 8in guns in both classes – distributed in three twin turrets on either side.

An international design competition for the new armoured cruiser was announced in July 1904; the war with Japan was still in progress, but this seems to have had little influence on the design at first. As a benchmark for evaluating the foreign designs, the MTK had two constructors, I G Bubnov and D V Skvortsov, work out a 14,000-ton design of their own.

The leading contender in the competition, and its eventual winner, was the British firm of Vickers. This firm had been assiduously courting the Russian Admiralty for some time through its chief agent, the famous (or infamous) Basil Zaharoff. On 31 May/13 June 1905, just a few weeks after Tsushima, a contract was signed for the construction of one armoured cruiser.

The initial Vickers design was the work of the firm's chief naval architect, T G Owens (who later changed his name to Owens Thurston). The Thurston notebooks, now held at the National Maritime Museum, contain characteristics for an armoured cruiser prepared for 'ZZ' – Vickers' telegraphic code for Zaharoff. Designated design No. 160, it was followed after some time by the very similar designs Nos. 160A and B; unfortunately, the designs are not dated, so it is impossible to say when they were drawn up, although a 1905 date seems likely, based on the fact that the design Owens/Thurston labelled as the final version, No. 160C, is dated 7 February 1906 and is considerably farther along in the notebook. In addition to general ship characteristics, the Thurston notebooks contain detailed information on hull lines, guns and mountings, and engines; they were apparently used as a reference source by Owens/Thurston when working up new sketch designs. It is quite possible that Owens first sketched out the design No. 160 for Zaharoff to present to the Russians, then 'customised' it on the spot as the Naval Technical Committee asked for changes – a technique that had won victory for British shipbuilders in other competitions.

This ability to design ships 'on the fly' is apparent from another design in the Thurston notebooks – No. 179, noted as being 'To requirements of Admiral Dubassof.' This is the same Admiral F V Dubasov who had earlier commanded the Pacific Squadron; by this time he was chairman of the Naval Technical Committee, and his requirements were somewhat different from those finally accepted. Although otherwise similar to the other designs developed by Owens/Thurston, the main battery consists of twelve 10in/45 guns, presumably to be mounted in twin turrets on the hexagonal pattern. This would have been the most powerful armoured cruiser ever built, but for some reason it was rejected – perhaps in part because Dubasov, who was an adjutant-general in the tsar's suite and a trusted advisor to the emperor, was called away in October 1905 to help quell disturbances in Kursk, Chernigov and Poltava provinces, and in November took charge of suppressing the serious revolutionary outbreak in Moscow's Presnaia district. Thus his influence was lost at the very time when the final design decisions were being made.

There was one other proposal for an 'all-big-gun' armoured cruiser, this one submitted by the New York Shipbuilding Co of Camden, New Jersey, in May 1905, long after the competition was officially closed. New York Shipbuilding, which was at the time completing the USN's armoured cruiser *Washington*, offered to build a 10,000-ton ship with a speed of 23.5kts and an armament of no fewer than ten 10in guns – how they planned to squeeze so many big guns and the necessarily powerful machinery plant into such a small displacement is not known. Unfortunately, nothing ever came of this proposal.

The design that finally won the Naval Technical Committee's approval was for a more conventional – though still very powerful – cruiser. At this early stage the ship was to have a displacement of 13,500 tons, a speed of 21kts, and an armament of four 10in and twelve 8in guns, all mounted in twin turrets, as well as an anti-torpedo boat battery of twenty 3in guns. This design was apparently generally approved by the Naval Technical Committee, but this was but the phase of what proved to be a long design process. So far, Vickers had presented only a sketch design; under the terms of the contract, the firm now had to work out the detailed design, which also had to be examined and approved by the MTK before work could begin. By August 1905 the detailed drawings and specifications for the ship – now weighing in at 15,000 tons – were laid before the committee. For the next three or four months they were subjected to intensive discussion and criticism in the MTK. Several matters were regarded as completely unacceptable, such as the

The second Riurik *as completed. This drawing presented special difficulties, as Russian publications have only printed inboard profiles and incomplete deck plans of this ship to date. The plan view is especially uncertain.* (Drawn by the author)

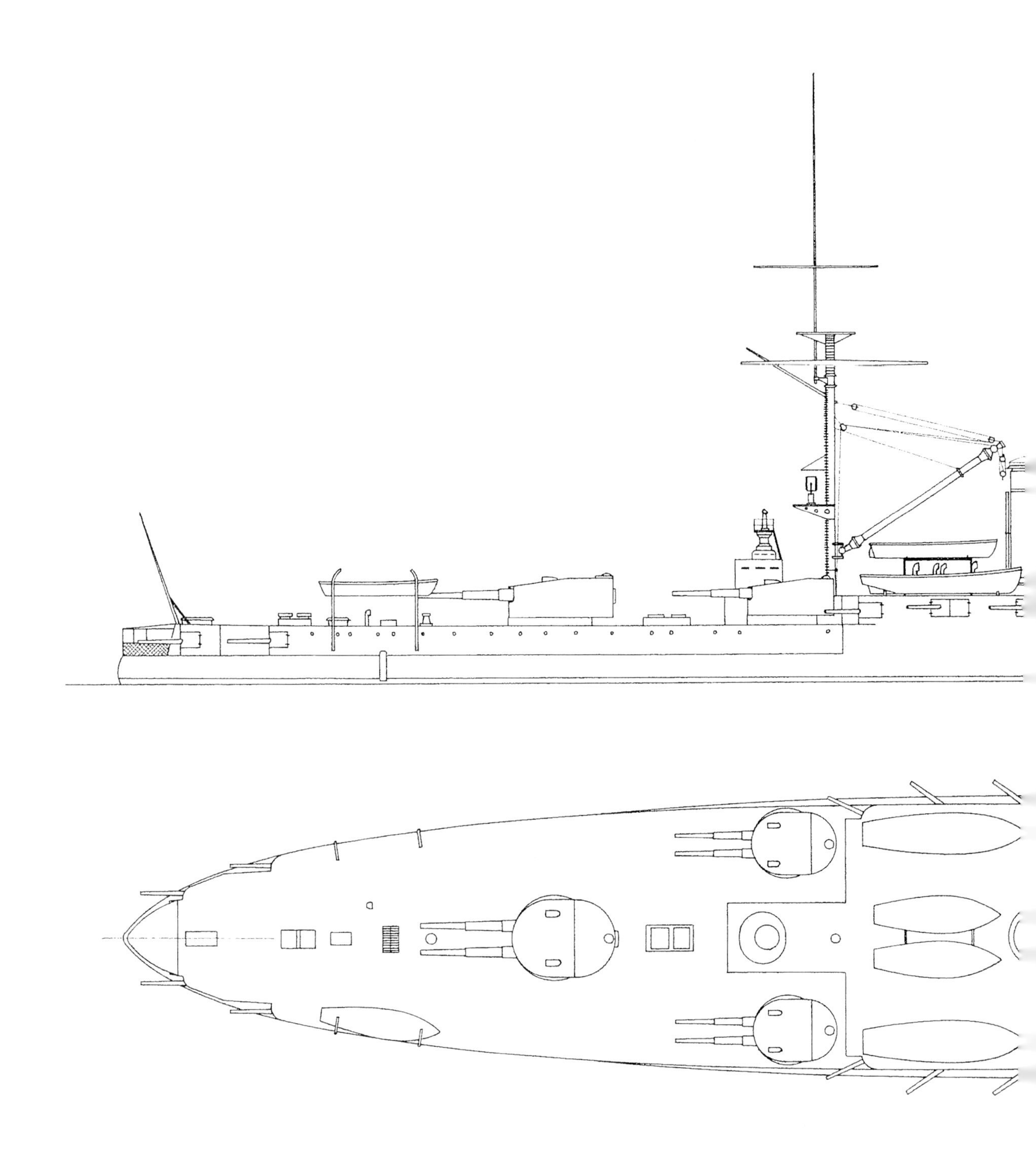

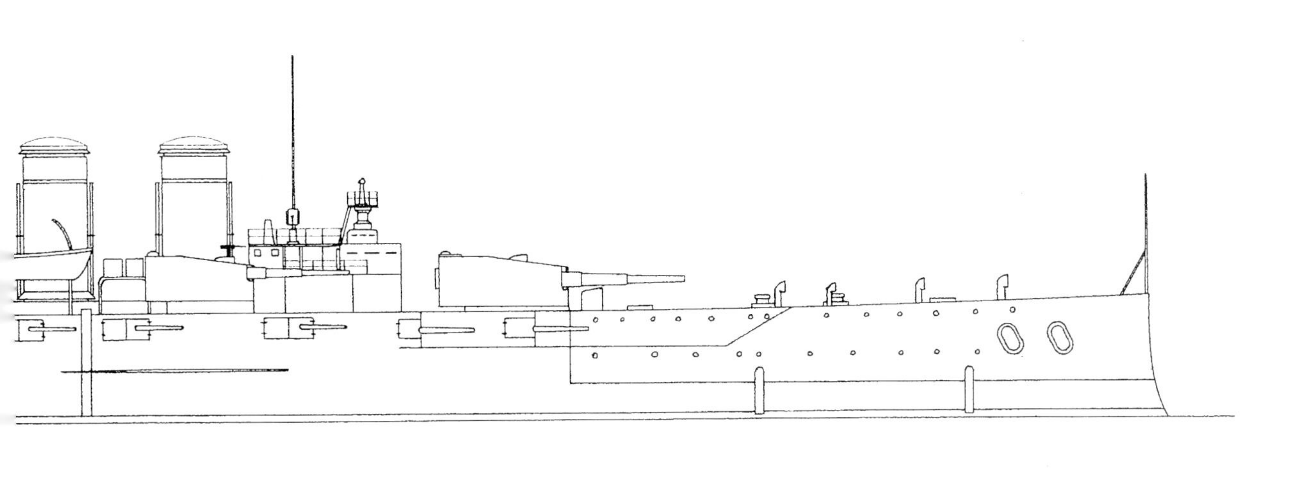

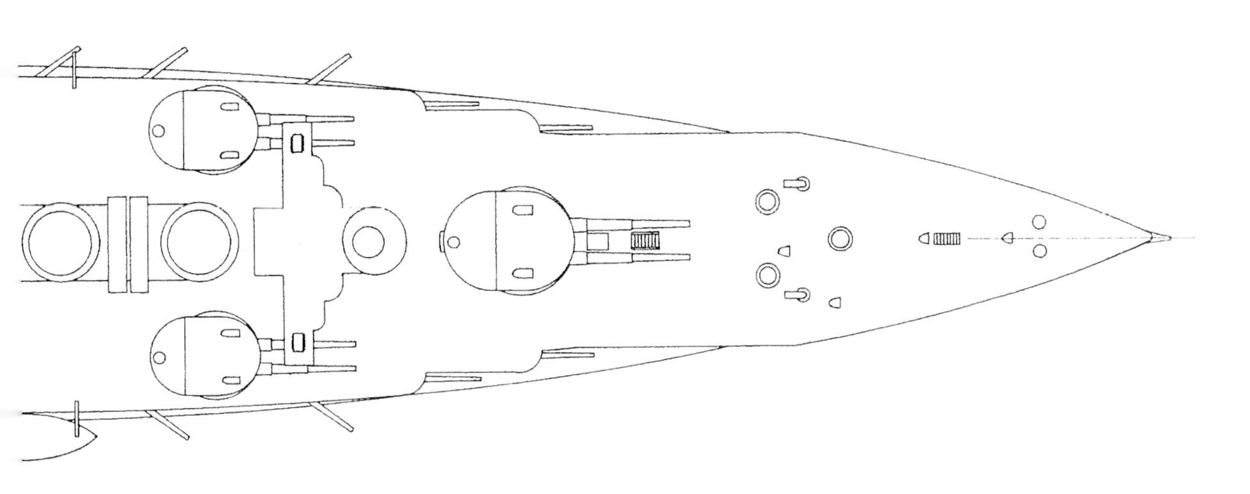

A fairly well known picture of Riurik, *taken in July 1913 off Reval (Tallinn). Just visible under the left-hand barrel of the after turret is naval minister Admiral I K Grigorovich, while Emperor Nikolai II is stooping as he starts down the companionway.* (Courtesy of S Vinogradov)

placement of the fore-mast forward of the conning tower, the relatively small area of the conning tower itself, and the inadequate means for controlling the temperatures in the magazines. Also problematic was the machinery plant, which towing tests at the Experimental Basin in St Petersburg indicated was just barely sufficient for the design speed 'without any surplus' of power.

While the Technical Committee was evaluating the Vickers' sketches, the company had moved ahead, and as early as June 1905 started laying out the ship in the mold-loft; by the time the final contract was signed in January 1906 there was already 2600 tons of steel assembled on the slipway. The work in England was monitored by a team of Russian constructors, led by K A Tennison, who

Table 1: Construction Data

	Riurik	*Rossiia*	*Gromoboi*
Construction begun:	September 1889	October 1893	14 June 1897
Laid Down:	19 May 1890	20 May 1895	7 May 1898
Launched:	22 October 1892	30 April 1896	8 May 1899
Entered service:	May 1895	Late 1896	November 1900
Builder:	Baltic Works, St Petersburg	Baltic Works, St Petersburg	Baltic Works, St Petersburg
Constructors:	N V Dolgorukov, N E Titov	N E Titov	K I Averin, V K Offenberg
	Baian (i)	*Admiral Makarov*	*Baian* (ii)
Construction begun:	late 1898	mid-1905	11 June 1905
Laid down:	mid-1899	14 March 1906?	
Launched:	May 1900	25 April 1906	2 August 1907
Entered service:	December 1902	1908	30 November 1911
Builder:	Forges et Chantiers de la Méditerranée, Le Seyne	Forges et Chantiers de la Méditerranée, Le Seyne	New Admiralty, St Petersburg
Constructors:	K P Boklevskii	V V Konstantinov	V P Lebedev
	Pallada	*Riurik* (ii)	
Construction begun:	11 June 1905	August 1905	
Laid down:	?	?	
Launched:	28 October 1906	4 November 1906	
Entered service:	8 February 1911	July 1909	
Builder:	New Admiralty, St Petersburg	Vickers Sons & Maxim, Barrow	
Constructors:	A I Mustafin	K A Tennison, A P Titov	

Notes

All dates given in the Old Style then in use in Russia, which was twelve days behind the western calendar in the nineteenth century and thirteen days behind in the twentieth.

During the Tsarist era, the laying-down date was a purely ceremonial occasion and has no significance in measuring the building time of ships; therefore a 'construction begun' date is also given; this indicates when work actually started on the slipway.

spoke English fluently. By the time the contract was signed, studies of the war with Japan indicated the need for numerous changes in the design, especially with regard to the anti-torpedo boat battery. The 3in guns had proven ineffective, so they were replaced by more powerful 4.7in guns, to be installed in two protected batteries, one amidships and the other aft. This change, as well as other detail alterations in the protection and equipment, inevitably led to weight increases, and in compensation the middle turrets on either beam were deleted. Another result of the war was the reduction of superstructures and other topside clutter.

Other alterations were more subtle, but no less important. For example, the war had revealed the dangers of asymmetrical flooding; to mitigate the effects of this, the new ship was equipped with cross-flooding ducts in the double-bottom, which would automatically transfer water from a damaged compartment to the double-bottom on the opposite side, thereby reducing the list. Another detail improvement was proposed by the ship's prospective commander, Captain First Rank N O Essen, a hero of the war; he wanted the number of transverse bulkheads at the ends of the ship increased to reduce the dangers from free surfaces of water, which had jeopardised the battleship *Peresvet* during the Battle of the Yellow Sea on 10 August 1904. This added 15 tons to the displacement, which was corrected by the reduction in various weights elsewhere – among other things, the length of the anchor chains was reduced and the foremast was deleted. The watertight bulkheads were also tested with a greater head of water pressure than was previously used.

By the end of February 1906 (New Style) the design had taken on its final form, although minor alterations would continue throughout her construction. The ship carried four 10in/50 guns and eight 8in/50 guns, the latter in twin turrets at the corners of the superstructure; all these guns had a maximum elevation of 35°. There were sixteen 4.7in/50 guns in the battery amidships and four more right aft. It was noted at the time that the magazine spraying and flooding arrangements were considerably in advance of British practice. The armament also included four 47mm and eight machine guns, as well as two 18in broadside submerged torpedo tubes.

Protection was of a much higher standard than in any previous Russian armoured cruiser; to start with, it was all Krupp plate. The main belt was 6in thick and covered the waterline from the forward to the after turret (500ft long); it extended 5ft below the design waterline. Forward and aft the belt was extended by 4in and then 3in plate right to the bow, and 3in plate aft almost to the sternpost. Above the main belt was an upper belt and above that the battery for the 4.7in guns, both with 3in sides and end bulkheads. In the battery 1in screens and

Table 2: CHARACTERISTICS:

	Riurik (i)	*Rossiia*	*Gromoboi*
Displacement			
Design:	10,933 tons	12,130 tons	12,360 tons
Actual:	11,690 tons	12,195 tons	12,455 tons
Length			
pp:	412ft	461.3ft	461.3ft
wl:	426.9ft	473.1ft	473.1ft
max:	435ft	485ft	481ft
Beam max:	67ft	68.6ft	68.6ft
Draft:	26ft	26.2ft	26ft
Armament:	4x8in/35 16x6in/45 6x4.7in/45 6x47mm/43 10x37mm/23 6x15in TT	4x8in/45 16x6in/45 12x75mm/50 20x47mm/43 18x37mm/23 5x15in TT	4x8in/45 16X6in/45 24x75mm/50 12x47mm/43 18x37mm/23 2xMG 4x15in TT
Armour	Nickel steel	Harvey	Harvey
Belt:	8-10-8in	6-8-6-5in	6in
Upper belt:	–	–	–
Turrets:	–	–	–
Barbettes:	–	–	–
Casemates:	–	–	4.76in
CT:	6in	12in	12in
CT tube:	3in	3in	3in
Prot decks:	3in F&A	2.5-3in forward	2.5-3in F&A
Arm deck:	2in over belt	2in over belt	1.5in over belt 2.5in slopes
Uptakes:	–	3in	1.5in
Machinery			
Engines:	4xVTE, 2 shafts	2xVTE, 2 shafts +1xVTE cruising	3xVTE, 3 shafts
Boilers:	8 cylindrical	32 Belleville	32 Belleville
IHP:	13,250 design 13,588 trials	14,500 2500 cruising	14,500 design 15,500 trials
Speed:	18kts design 18.84kts trials	19kts design 19.74kts trials	19kts design 20.1kts trials
Endurance			
Coal:	1933 tons max	2200 tons max.	2400 tons max.
Range:	6700nm @ 10kts	7740nm @ 10kts	8100nm @ 10kts
Crew:	719	839	874

backs separated the individual guns. The after group of 4.7in guns was also protected by 3in armour.

The 10in turrets were protected by 8in sides and faces, with 2.5in roofs; the barbettes were 7.25in, reduced to 6in-4in where screened by other armour. The 8in turrets had 7in sides and faces and 2in roofs, with 6in barbettes, reduced to 4in behind other armour. The forward conning tower had 8in sides, the small after conning tower had 5in sides. In addition to the conning towers, there was a ship control position below the waterline. Four small armoured range-finder towers, planned to be placed between the 8in turrets, were eliminated before completion to compensate for weights added elsewhere.

Deck protection consisted of a 1.5in main deck and a

	Baian (i)	*Admiral Makarov** *Baian* (ii) *Pallada*	*Riurik* (ii)
Displacement			
Design:	7725 tons	7750 tons	15,170 tons
Actual:	7802 tons	7750 tons	15,130 tons
Length pp:	443ft	?	490ft
wl:	?	443ft	517ft
max:	449.6ft	449.6ft	529ft
Beam max:	57.5ft	57.5ft	75ft
Draft:	22ft	22ft	26ft
Armament:	2x8in/45	2x8in/45	4x10in/50
	8x6in/45	8x6in/45	8x8in/50
	20x75mm/50	20x75mm/50	20x4.7in/50
	8x47mm/43	4x47mm/43	4x47mm/43
	2x37mm/23	2x18in TT	2x18in TT
	2x15in TT		
Armour	Harvey	Krupp	Krupp
Belt:	100-200-100mm	90-175-90mm	3-4-6-3in
Upper belt:	60mm	60mm	3in
Turrets:	150mm	132mm	8in (10in turrets)
			7in (8in turrets)
Barbettes:	170mm	?	8in/6in
Casemates:	60mm	60mm	3in
CT:	160mm	136mm	8in
CT tube:	?	?	?
Prot decks:	30+10+10mm Aft	30+10+10mm Aft	
Arm deck:	30+10+10mm	30+10+10mm	1.5in above casemates
	–	–	1.5in upper deck
	–	–	1in main deck, 1.5in slope
Uptakes:	?	?	N/A
Machinery			
Engines:	2xVTE, 2 shafts	2xVTE, 2 shafts	2xVTE, 2 shafts
Boilers:	26 Belleville	26 Belleville	28 Belleville
IHP:	16,500 design	16,500	19,700
	17,400 trials	19,320	20,675
Speed:	21kts design	21kts design	21kts design
	20.9kts trials	22.55kts trials	21.4kts trials
Endurance			
Coal:	1200 tons max.	1100 tons	1920 tons
Oil:	–	–	200 tons
Range:	3900nm @ 10kts	?	?
Crew:	573	568	899

***Note:** Some characteristics of *Admiral Makarov* and her sisters are uncertain.

1in lower deck with 1.5in slopes. The deck above the 4.7in battery was also protected by 1in plate. The deck protection was made with high-tensile steel rather than the normal mild steel, which gave resistance similar to nickel-steel plate, but at a considerably reduced cost. The processing – in particular the shaping – of this steel proved difficult, as it had not been used for this purpose (and probably not in such thicknesses) in Britain before. The Russians had worked out the necessary techniques for manipulating the material, but it took some time for these to be mastered. In the end the attempt proved successful, and similar steel was apparently later used for deck protection in the British battlecruiser *Queen Mary*.

Underwater protection consisted in an internal 1.5in longitudinal bulkhead abreast the machinery and magazines; this bulkhead was about 12ft inboard of the ship's side amidships.

The machinery consisted of two four-cylinder triple-expansion engines and twenty-eight Belleville watertube boilers; the contract specified that the ship had to achieve her full speed with only 75% of her boilers in operation, which allowed for some boilers to be damaged or under repair at all times. Trials revealed that the engines and boilers worked well, although a 30-hour trial at 19kts revealed some knocking and vibration. On 8/21 July 1907 the ship made 21.43kts on the Skelmorlie mile, the engines developing 20,580ihp (compared with the contract figure of 19,700ihp).

The 1907 trials were run without the armament aboard, since there had been delays in its manufacture. Even bigger problems followed its delivery, however, as gunnery trials revealed that the fastenings of the 10in and 8in turret barbettes were insufficiently strong, leading to their deformation. Vickers was forced to reinforce the barbettes, the work being carried out at Kronshtadt after the ship's delivery.

The ship was also the occasion of a political controversy; the Naval Ministry's critics in the State Duma (the new Russian legislature) argued that the Navy had revealed state secrets in passing on to Vickers Russian drawings and specifications for the guns and deck armour. These accusations were part of a broad effort by members of both the right and centre parties to force reforms on a reluctant ministry, and seem to have had no lasting effects on policy – aside from a residual distrust of Vickers in some circles when dreadnought designs were later being considered.

As was the case with *Admiral Makarov*, the Naval Ministry originally intended to build two ships in Russian yards to the same drawings as *Riurik*, but these plans were eventually cancelled, since budgets were limited and a major redesign would have been necessary to equip the ships with turbines, which were now seen as essential for high-speed vessels. In fact Vickers did prepare a 17,000-ton, turbine-driven version of *Riurik* (design No. 217 in the Thurston notebooks, dated 5/18 May 1906), but her mixed-calibre armament and 23kt speed could not compare to the recently laid-down *Invincible* class 'armoured cruisers,' although her protection would have been somewhat superior to the new British ships.

Riurik underwent relatively few changes during her service. Completed with a single mast, she had a foremast added before the First World War (presumably to improve her wireless and/or long-range spotting facilities). During docking for repairs after her mine damage in November 1916 she was equipped with a tripod foremast.

Conclusion

With the second *Riurik* the Imperial Navy at last took up the world-wide trend of big armoured cruisers – too late, as it turned out, since by the time she entered service the Royal Navy had already introduced a new type of armoured cruiser, eventually dubbed the 'battlecruiser.' In early 1907, before the battlecruiser was generally accepted by the world's navies, Vickers prepared a final armoured cruiser design for Russia; as can be seen from the table, design No. 284 was very much a transitional type, a sort of semi-battlecruiser; she was intended for service as a fleet scout.

Displacement:	10,200 tons
Dimensions:	535ft pp x 61ft x 20ft 5in
Armament:	four 12in, twelve 4.7in in 'dwarf barbettes' (small turrets?)
Protection:	
complete waterline belt	4in-4in-6in-4in-3in
upper belt	4in citadel, 3in forward
conning tower	12in
observation tower	6in
Machinery:	Reciprocating; 36,000ihp
Speed:	27kts
Coal:	350 tons normal, 1200 tons full load

Nothing came of the proposal, probably because the Naval Ministry was still faced with very tight budgets at this time; it would be several years before the increasingly unstable international situation forced the State Duma to vote large sums for new naval construction.

In some ways, the type of ship envisaged by design No. 284 was an aberration in Russian capital ship policy; a scout of this type could not long have survived in the line of battle. When Russia again began to design big cruisers, the Naval Ministry returned to the 'squadron armoured cruiser' concept of *Baian* and *Riurik*, designing the powerful and well protected battlecruisers of the *Izmail* or *Borodino* class, which were intended to take their place in the line of battle as the fleet's fast wing.

Service Histories

Riurik (i) – The semi-legendary founder of first Kievan dynasty in the ninth century.
The ship was sent to represent Russia at the Kiel Canal ceremonies in June 1895 despite the fact that she had yet to run her acceptance trials; she was officially accepted only in November after her return from Kiel. By this time she had already left for the Far East in company with the

cruiser *Dmitrii Donskoi*. She arrived at Vladivostok on 12/24 May 1896. She spent the rest of her career in Pacific waters, never returning to European Russia.

The ship underwent a refit at Vladivostok from the winter of 1900 until June 1901. At this time her rig was much reduced and her bowsprit removed completely.

Riurik served with the Vladivostok Cruiser Detachment during the Russo-Japanese War, participating in six raiding forays against Japanese shipping between February and July 1904.

Riurik's seventh and final voyage of the war was an attempt to assist the Port Arthur squadron's escape from the besieged port. On 27 July/10 August 1904 the squadron set course for Vladivostok, but was turned back and partially scattered by the Japanese. In the meantime the Vladivostok cruisers had sailed out to support it before news of the defeat had been received. Instead of meeting the Port Arthur squadron, the cruisers *Rossiia* (flag), *Gromoboi* and *Riurik* ran into Admiral Kamimura's powerful armoured cruiser squadron on 1/14 August; in the action that followed, known as the Battle of Ulsan, *Riurik*'s steering was damaged and she fell behind the other ships. Her squadron mates' attempts to rescue her were beaten off by the superior Japanese squadron, and *Riurik* was left to her fate. The ship sustained severe damage and had most of her guns put out of action; her senior officers were killed or wounded. The order was finally given to open the Kingston valves, and she sank on an even keel. Of her crew of 763, 204 were lost in the action.

Rossiia – 'Russia'.
In October 1898, after *Rossiia*'s launch – she was at the time the largest ship ever launched by the Baltic Works – she was taken to Kronshtadt for completion; while there she was run onto a sandbar by a storm and it took a month to free her. She left Kronshtadt on 28 May/9 June 1897 to attend Queen Victoria's Diamond Jubilee Review at Spithead, returning to Kronshtadt for trials. These were considered 'more than satisfactory,' the engines working smoothly with very little vibration even at high speeds.

She left for the Far East in October 1897, arriving at Nagasaki on 26 February/10 March 1898. She remained in the Pacific until the outbreak of the Russo-Japanese War; by that time she was the flagship of the Vladivostok cruiser squadron. As such she led the squadron on several raiding voyages against Japanese shipping to Korea; on one such voyage, in May 1904, the Vladivostok cruisers steamed in the Sea of Japan looking for enemy shipping; despite the use of an observation balloon – the first operational use of an aerial device from a warship on the high seas in time of war – only a few small craft were found. During another cruise, on 2/15 June 1904, the ships encountered several Japanese transports; among them was *Hitachi Maru*, carrying more than 1000 soldiers bound for Korea. The ship refused to surrender and was sunk by the Russians with great loss of life.

In the Battle of Ulsan on 1/14 August 1904 *Rossiia* received considerable damage at the hands of Admiral Kamimura's armoured cruisers, with 48 men killed and 165 wounded.

After the end of the war *Rossiia* returned to Kronshtadt, arriving on 26 March/8 April 1906, at which time she was taken in hand for a refit. She emerged in 1909 with reconditioned engines and boilers. She represented Russia at King George V's Coronation Review on 11/24 June 1911. In September 1912 she steamed to the Canaries and the Virgin Islands as part of a training cruise, returning to the Baltic the next spring. In March 1913 *Rossiia*, *Oleg* and *Avrora* visited Copenhagen, then returned to Kronshtadt for the ceremonial unveiling of a monument to Admiral S O Makarov. She departed in September 1913 for another Atlantic training cruise, calling at the Azores, and in March 1914 cruised in the Mediterranean.

During the First World War *Rossiia* served as the flagship of the Baltic Fleet's Second Cruiser Brigade, and was used on occasion as a fast minelayer. In January 1915 she carried out a mine-laying mission between Kiel and Mecklenburg harbours along with the cruisers *Bogatyr'* and *Oleg*; the German cruisers *Augsburg* and *Gazelle* ran foul of these mines several days later and both were damaged.

The ship's armament was augmented in October 1915, with four more 8in guns added at the expense of her lighter weapons. The crew took an active part in the revolutionary events of 1917; in 1918 she took part in the 'Ice Voyage' from Helsingfors to Kronshtadt, where she was then placed in reserve. In 1922 she was sold to a German firm and subsequently broken up.

Gromoboi – 'Thunderer'.
The ship departed the shipyard for completing at Kronshtadt on 12/24 November 1899; however she soon encountered ice, and was gradually forced first toward the southern side of the Sea Channel, and then out of the channel altogether, running aground. She was freed on 15/27 November and finally reached Kronshtadt, where her sheathing required repair.

After final preparation in Libau, where *Gromoboi* had been transferred to avoid being trapped in the winter ice at Kronshtadt, the ship left on 28 November/10 December 1900 for the Far East. She stopped briefly at Kiel, where she was inspected by Prince Henry of Prussia; she transited the Suez Canal and visited Melbourne and Sydney in April-May 1901 to join in the celebrations attendant upon the grant of a constitution to the newly federated Australian colonies. *Gromoboi* finally arrived at Port Arthur on 17/29 July 1901.

Gromoboi participated in the various sorties of the Vladivostok Cruiser Detachment, including the Battle of Ulsan on 1/14 August 1904. During the action she sustained heavy casualties – 94 men killed and 182 wounded – despite her improved protection. This was apparently due to the fact that her commander kept the crews by the unprotected small-calibre guns throughout the action, despite the fact that these weapons were useless in the long-range (5000-9000yds) battle. Almost two months were required for repairs after the battle; on her next trip to sea (30 September/13 October 1904) the ship ran hard aground in Posiet Gulf and damaged her bottom severely; repairs were completed in February 1905. During her period of repair the ship's armament and protection were improved, and six new 6in guns were shipped on the upper deck.

On 11/24 May 1905, while testing her new Telefunken wireless gear, the ship fouled a mine; it exploded on her port side near the forward boiler room. The ship was able to return to Vladivostok under her own power but took no further part in wartime operations. After the war *Gromoboi* returned to the Baltic and was taken in hand for a major refit; she was returned to service only in 1911.

During the First World War the ship was a unit of the Second Cruiser Brigade. She was transferred from Helsingfors to Kronshtadt on 1 February 1918 and placed in reserve. She was sold to a German firm in 1922 for scrap, but while under tow a storm blew up and drove the ship ashore near Liepaja, Latvia. The hulk was subsequently scrapped.

Baian (i) – An ancient Slavic bard.
The ship's construction was supervised by Captain First Rank I K Grigorovich, who was also the prospective commanding officer of the battleship *Tsesarevich*, which was under construction at the same yard. The first underway trials were run in October 1902; after her acceptance the ship visited several ports in the Mediterranean (Poros, Athens, Brindisi, Naples), then sailed for Kronshtadt, where she arrived in April 1903. On 25 July/7 August *Baian* sailed for the Far East.

The ship served with the Port Arthur Squadron during the Russo-Japanese War; she struck a mine on 14/27 July 1904. Repairs lasted until September, and so the ship missed the Battle of the Yellow Sea on 28 July/10 August 1904. She was sunk in the harbour by shells from Japanese 11in siege guns on 25 November/8 December 1904. After the surrender of the fortress, she was raised by the Japanese and refitted. She entered service with the IJN in 1908 under the name *Aso*. In 1920 she was converted into a mine-layer, and in 1930 she was stricken. She was sunk as a target on 3 August 1932.

Admiral Makarov – The famous admiral, killed during the Russo-Japanese War.
Upon completion of her trials, the ship left the Mediterranean for the Baltic on 14/27 May 1908; she arrived at Revel on 29 May/11 June and then joined the Baltic Fleet. She returned to the Mediterranean in the fall of 1908. In December she, along with other Russian and foreign warships, rendered assistance to earthquake victims at Messina, Sicily. Admiral Makarov then returned to the Baltic; she again sailed to the Mediterranean in 1910 as a unit of the international squadron in Cretan waters. She visited Montenegro that year in company with the battleship *Tsesarevich* and the cruisers *Riurik* (ii) and *Bogatyr* on the occasion of King Nicholas' coronation. She spent 1911 in Baltic waters; at this time her single mast was replaced by two new ones. In 1912 she visited Copenhagen, and in 1913 joined a cruiser detachment that visited Portland, Brest and Stavanger.

During the First World War *Admiral Makarov* was a unit of the First Cruiser Brigade and participated in numerous mine-laying sorties, acting as either a minelayer herself or in the covering forces. She took part in the action with German cruisers off Gotland Island on 19 June/2 July 1915, and in the defence of the Moonzund in October 1917; on the latter occasion the ship was given a list of 5° to increase the elevation of her guns.

In 1918 the ship participated in the Ice Voyage from Helsingfors to Kronshtadt; she was in the first detachment, which included the *Sevastopol* class dreadnoughts, as well as *Riurik* and *Bogatyr*. The group reached Kronshtadt on 17/30 March with the assistance of ice-breakers. *Admiral Makarov* was placed in reserve soon after and was sold for scrap in 1922; she was broken up in Stettin.

Baian (ii)
The ship entered service in 1911 and apparently spent her entire career in the Baltic. Like her sister, *Admiral Makarov*, she was a unit of the First Cruiser Brigade, taking part in various offensive minelaying operations. During the battle off Gotland Island on 19 June/2 July 1915 she engaged the German armoured cruiser *Roon*, scoring at least one hit, but was herself hit by the German ship.

Baian took an active part in the defence of the Moonzund in 1917; on 4/17 October she, along with the battleships *Grazhdanin* (ex-*Tsesarevich*) and *Slava* engaged the German dreadnoughts *König* and *Kronprinz*. *Baian* received one hit, but was able to stay in action; *Slava* was more seriously hit, and the Russian ships were forced to withdraw. *Slava* was later scuttled. The *Baian* was sold for scrap in 1922; like her sister, she was dismantled at Stettin.

Pallada – A form of Pallas Athena.
Pallada joined the fleet in 1911, and appears to have spent her entire pre-war service in the Baltic. At the outbreak of war she, along with other cruisers, was detailed to patrol the entrance to the Gulf of Finland to give warning of a German approach. It was while on this duty that *Pallada* was torpedoed by U-26 on 28 September/11 October 1914. She suffered a magazine explosion and sank immediately; there were no survivors.

Riurik (ii)
On 3/16 September 1906, the day before her intended launch, there was an accident aboard the ship – while cleaning, there was a small explosion and fire caused by the ignition of benzine and turpentine vapour; about two weeks were required for repairs.

The ship ran trials without her armament (which was delayed in manufacture) on 8/21 July 1907; these were by and large successful, the vessel reaching an average speed of 21.43kts on four runs on the Skelmorlie mile.

The guns were finally installed in the spring of 1908. Subsequent trials were successful, except for the gunnery trials, which revealed that the barbettes of both the 10in and 8in guns were insufficiently rigid; also, the ammunition supply to the 8in guns was too slow. Vickers had to reinforce the barbettes at its own expense.

The ship finally hoisted the Russian ensign in August

1908 and set sail for the Baltic. Further gunnery trials were carried out after her arrival; these were also unsatisfactory, particularly with regard to the forward 10in turret and the starboard forward 8in turret, where some rivets sheered during firing. The ship was further modified by Vickers personnel during the winter lay-up of 1908-1909, and in July of that year she finally entered service with the Baltic Fleet.

In July 1910 *Riurik*, in company with the battleships *Tsesarevich* and *Slava* and the cruiser *Bogatyr* left the Baltic for a cruise to the Mediterranean; *Slava* had boiler problems and had to be left behind at Gibraltar, while the other ships sailed on to attend the coronation festivities of King Nicholas of Montenegro.

Admiral N O Essen, commander of the Baltic Fleet, selected *Riurik* as his flagship, and in September 1913 she led a squadron consisting of most of the Baltic Fleet's major warships on a cruise to Portland and Cherbourg.

During the First World War the ship was active in minelaying operations. She was damaged by grounding on 31 January/13 February 1915, taking on 2400 tons of water but was able to return to harbour under her own power; repairs were carried out at Kronshtadt and required three months.

In June 1915, the ship took part in the battle off Gotland Island with German cruisers; she briefly engaged *Roon*, but did not hit the German ship. In November 1915 there was a minor mutiny aboard the ship caused by the arrest of sailors who had earlier caused a disturbance in the dreadnought *Gangut*.

Riurik struck a mine on 6/19 November 1916 near Gogland Island; she was damaged in the region of frames 0-20. She was able to retire to Kronshtadt under her own power, but repairs required five months.

The ship took part in the 'Ice Voyage' of March 1918 from Helsingfors to Kronshtadt; she was in the first detachment of ships, and served as an escort for the icebreakers that assisted the next detachment. Later that year she was placed in reserve. She was sold for scrapping in 1922.

Bibliographical Notes

1. This section is based on the following works:
Robert F Byrnes, *Pobedonostsev: His Life and Times* (Bloomington, Indiana. Indiana University Press, 1968).
F A Golder, 'The Russian Fleet and the Civil War' (*American Historical Review*, vol. XX, no. 4, pp 801-812 [July 1915]).
John E Jessup, 'Alliance or Deterrence: The Case of the Russian Fleet Visit to America' (*New Aspects of Naval History: Selected Papers Presented at the Fourth Naval History Symposium, United States Naval Academy*, 25-26 October 1979, edited by Craig L Symonds *et al.* Naval Institute Press, 1981, pp 238-252).
Jacob W Kipp, 'Consequences of Defeat: Modernizing the Russian Navy, 1856-1863' (*Jahrbücher für Geschchte Osteuropas*, XX, pp 210-225 [June 1972]).
Jacob W Kipp, 'Tsarist Politics and the Naval Ministry, 1876-81: Balanced Fleet or Cruiser Navy?' (*Canadian American Slavic Studies*, vol. 17, no. 2, pp 151-179[Summer 1983]).
Leonid I Strakhovsky, 'Russia's Privateering Projects of 1878: A Page in the History of Russian-American Relations' (*Journal of Modern History*, vol. VII, no. 1, pp 22-40[March 1935]).
2. See I P Spasskii (editor), *Istoriia otechestvennogo sudostroeniia* (five volumes; Sudostroenie, 1994-1996), vol. II, pp 346-358 and R M Melnikov, 'Kreiser 1 ranga "Riurik"' (*Sudostroenie*, no. 12, 1979, pp. 57-60).
For the value of coal protection, see David K Brown, *Warrior to Dreadnought: Warship Development 1860-1905* (Chatham Publishing, 1997), pp 132-135. For the general appearance of the ship and the armour arrangements of *Riurik*, *Rossiia*, *Gromoboi* and *Baian*, I have relied heavily on Sergei Vasilevich Suliga, *Korabli Russko-Kiaponskoi voiny* (Askold, 1993).
3. The question of *Riurik*'s rig presents a problem. Photographs of the ship early in her career show a barque rig, with no mizzen topgallant mast. A photograph (reproduced in this article) shows her with reduced rig following her 1900/1901 refit. Yet a photograph published in J N Westwood, *Russia Against Japan, 1904-1905: A New Look at the Russo-Japanese War* (State University Press of New York, 1986, plate 11a), which is captioned as 'The last seconds of the cruiser *Rurik* (photographed by a Japanese officer)', shows the masts of a fully rigged ship, with a topgallant mizzen-mast as well as yards crossed on the mizzen-mast , sticking out of the water, which doesn't seem to match *Riurik* at any stage of her career. It seems extraordinarily unlikely that her rig would have been re-introduced (and, indeed, elaborated) after it had been cut down, so the only reasonable explanation is that this photograph has been incorrectly identified, and actually shows the sinking of another ship entirely. The rig, however, doesn't seem to match that of any other ship lost in the Russo-Japanese War.
4. Spasskii, *Istoriia otechestvennogo sudostroeniia, op. cit.*, vol. II, pp 359-363; R M Melnikov, 'Kreiser "Rossiia"' (*Sudostroenie*, no. 1, 1980, pp 63-65). For the re-arming of *Rossiia* (and the other surviving cruisers) during after the Russo-Japanese War, see I I Chernikov, 'Perevooruzhenie kreiserov 1906-1916' (*Sudostroenie*, no. 3, 1983, pp 60-63).
5. On the *Peresvet* class, see R M Melnikov, 'Eskadrennyi bronenosets "Osliabia"' (*Sudostroenie*, nos. 5-6, 1995, pp. 52-58). The pumping arrangements of the *Lord Nelson* class are described in J H Narbeth, 'Three Steps in Naval Construction: *King Edward VII., Lord Nelson, Dreadnought*' (*Transactions of the Institution of Naval Architects*, vol. 63, pp 23-62 [1922]).
6. See L A Kuznetsov, 'Kreiser I ranga "Gromoboi"' (*Sudostroenie*, no. 12, 1989, pp 43-48) and Spasskii, *Istoriia otechestvennogo sudostroeniia, op. cit.*, vol. II, pp 363-368.
7. See Spasskii, *Istoriia otechestvennogo sudostroeniia, op. cit.*, vol. II, pp 368-372; A V Fedechkin, 'Kreiser dlia eskadrennykh srazhenii' (*Tsitadel*, no. 1, 1997, pp 45-54); R M Melnikov, 'Kreiser "Admiral Makarov"' (*Sudostroenie*, no. 10, 1980, pp 67-70); *Admiralteiskie verfi: Korabli i gody 1704-1925* (Gangut, 1994).
8. See R M Melnikov, 'Bronenosnyi kreiser "Riurik"' (*Sudostroenie*, no, 11, 1980, pp 67-71); Spasskii, *Istoriia otechestvennogo sudostroeniia, op. cit.*, vol. III, pp 56-63; 'The Russian Armoured Cruiser "Rurik"' (*Engineering*, vol. LXXXII, pp 656-658[16 November 1906]); and the Thurston notebooks (National Maritime Museum, Greenwich).

THE JAPANESE EXPERIMENTAL LIGHT CRUISER *YÛBARI*

Frido G Kip describes the design and history of this innovative Japanese light cruiser. Many of the original ideas used on *Yûbari* eventually found their way into battleships, cruisers, destroyers and other combatants. In the long run, *Yûbari* had a profound influence on the development of warship design in Japan and can therefore be regarded to be one of the most influential Japanese warships of her time.

Even before the Washington Naval Treaty, the Japanese Naval General Staff (*Gunreibu*) was aware of the fact that the Imperial Japanese Navy (IJN) would probably have to fight the next conflict with inferior numbers because of Japan's limited resources. Although it was firmly believed that Japanese spirit and training would compensate for the smaller number of warships, as had been so convincingly demonstrated during the wars against China and Russia, it was also recognised that something more was required.

Therefore, special measures were adopted in order to defeat a powerful enemy like Russia or the United States, both of which were considered to be Japan's most likely future antagonists.[1] Emphasis was placed on warlike training, including the notorious night battle tactics, on the development of advanced weapons such as the Type 93 oxygen-propelled Long Lance torpedo and on the superiority of individual ships. As Japan could never hope to out-build her most likely opponents, she opted for quality out of necessity. This resulted in the continuing Japanese quest for the installation of the heaviest possible armament, creating impressive ships such as the *Fubuki* class Special Type destroyers.

The light cruiser *Yûbari* was ordered specifically for this purpose, being built to new design concepts, which would make it possible to obtain heavy armament, adequate protection and high speed on a much smaller hull than had previously been possible. If successful, the Japanese designers would be able to built powerful large cruisers which would outclass their opponents and give the IJN a significant advantage in battle.

Table 1: *SCOUT CRUISER DESIGNS*

	1916 design	1918 design	1921 Hiraga design
Characteristics			
Displacement (normal):	7200-ton s	8000-ton s	7500-ton s
Armament*:	4 twin and 4 or more single 5.5in/50	5 or 6 twin 5.5in/50	6 single 7.9in/50
	4 twin 24in fixed TT	4 twin 24in fixed TT	4 triple 24in fixed TT
Broadside:	304kg or more	380-456kg	690kg
	4 24in torpedoes	4 24in torpedoes	6 24in torpedoes
Protection:	3in (76mm) HT belt	armoured belt	3in (76mm) NVNC belt**
	armoured deck	armoured deck	1.4in (35mm) NVNC deck**
Speed:	36kts	35.5kts	35kts
Range:	6000 to 8000nm at 14kts	more than 6000nm at 14kts	ca. 7000nm at 14kts**

* The new 7.9in/50 (200mm) gun was also considered for the 1916 and 1918 designs but because it was not yet ready the designs used the standard 5.5in/50 (140mm) cruiser gun instead.

** Data based on the final *Furutaka* class design.

Origin

The first proposals for a new type of large scout cruiser (*Teisatsu Junyôkan*) were put forward by the Naval General Staff in 1910. Planned to serve as the eyes of the fleet, they were to be fast, heavily armed, well protected and have sufficient range. From the beginning, the Naval General Staff wanted these valuable cruisers to be more powerful than those of their antagonists so as to be able to push aside any opposition they might encounter in order to fulfil their primary mission.

Programme planning proved to be rather difficult. The first three 7200-ton scout cruisers were only authorised under the 8-4 Fleet Completion Programme (*Hachi-Shi Kantai Kansei Keikaku*) of 1917, together with six small 3500-ton cruisers, repeats of the *Tenryû* class destroyer leaders.[2] Initially, this shipbuilding programme had been presented to the 38th Diet Session (27 December 1916 - 25 January 1917), but was then postponed to next year's session because the Diet was dissolved before a decision was reached. However, a special meeting, the 39th Diet Session (23 June - 15 July 1917), was held when details of the large American 1916 programme became known. The 8-4 programme was adopted on 14 July 1917 and shipbuilding funds were provided for under the Warship Construction Expenditures (*Gunkan Seizô Hi*) of FY 6 (1917-18) to FY 12 (1923-24).[3]

By this time, the Naval General Staff realised that with the rapid development of cruiser designs abroad (caused by the war), the new 7200-ton scout cruiser was no longer adequate. It was therefore decided to postpone its construction and to further improve the design. At the same time, they realised that the current 3500-ton leader was both too small and too weak to perform its job adequately. Consequently, they shifted to an enlarged medium type, the 5500-ton cruiser, that could serve both as a leader and a scout. In late 1917, building orders were changed to eight of these new 5500-ton cruisers: five *Kuma* and three improved *Natori* class light cruisers were built. The originally authorised ninth cruiser was now to become a small cruiser to test experimental machinery. This experimental ship was not regarded as a top priority and her construction was therefore postponed for the time being, although the name *Ayase* was allocated on 20 September 1919.

Three additional 5500-ton *Natori* class cruisers were authorised under the 8-6 Fleet Completion Programme (*Hachi-Roku Kantai Kansei Keikaku*) of 1918, but no scout cruisers were requested. They re-emerged under the next shipbuilding programme, the 8-8 Fleet Completion Programme (*Hachi-Hachi Kantai Kansei Keikaku*) of 1920. It authorised the construction of eight improved 5500-ton *Jintsû* class cruisers, five of which were eventually cancelled, and four scout cruisers of a revised 8000-ton design. However, even this large cruiser design did not compare favourably with new powerful foreign cruisers such as the *Omaha* and *Hawkins* classes,[4] resulting in the continued postponement of building orders.

At this time, Yuzuru Hiraga, Head of the Basic Design (*Kihon Keikaku*) bureau of the Shipbuilding (*Zôsen*) section of the Navy Technical Department (*Kaigun Kansei Honbu*), took the opportunity to propose the use of radical new construction techniques to create the powerful scout cruisers sought. He suggested that hull weight could be reduced using the horizontal and vertical armour as part of the hull's longitudinal strength. The weight saved could then be used to mount a heavier armament without loss of speed or range. Hiraga believed that the new system would neither weaken the hull nor the protection scheme.

The Naval General Staff approved Hiraga's novel and revolutionary ideas in August 1921 and ordered the construction of an experimental ship to test them in October 1921. The small cruiser *Ayase* of the 8-4 programme was chosen for this purpose as she had already been officially authorised. In order not to lose any more valuable time, the building order was placed under the FY 11 (1922-23) estimates. It was also decided to change the cruiser's name and on 5 November 1921 proposals were made for names such as *Kamo*, *Kitsu* and *Nayoro*. Finally, on 23

Table 2: *YÛBARI*

Name	Builder	Laid down	Launched	Commissioned
Yûbari	Sasebo Naval Arsenal	5 June 1922	5 March 1923	31 July 1923

Characteristics (as designed)

Displacement:	2890 tons standard; 3141 tons normal
Length:	435ft (132.59m) pp; 447ft 10in (136.50m) wl; 455ft 8in (138.90m) oa
Beam:	39ft 6in (12.04m)
Draught:	11ft 9in (3.58m) mean
Armament:	six 5.5in/50 (140mm) LA guns in two twin and two single mountings; one 3in/40 (76mm) HA gun; two 7.7mm AA machineguns in single mountings; four 24in (610mm) torpedo tubes in two twin mountings; 8 torpedoes; 48 mines
Protection:	Belt 1.5in (38mm) NVNC; deck 1in (25mm) NVNC
Machinery:	three sets *Kanpon* single geared turbines; two mixed-fired and six oil-fired *Kanpon Ro-gô* boilers; 57,750shp; 35.5kts
Fuel and range:	830-tons of oil and 100-tons of coal; 5000nm at 14kts
Complement:	340 officers and men

December 1921, the name *Yûbari* was chosen, the name of a river in Hokkaidô, in accordance with regulations specifying that second class cruisers (*Nitô Junyôkan*), i.e. cruisers of less than 7000 tons displacement, should be named after rivers.

Design and construction

The design was immediately drawn up under Hiraga's guidance by his assistant Lt-Cdr Kikuô Fujimoto in late 1921. To test Hiraga's innovative construction techniques, *Yûbari* was to have the same broadside, speed, range and degree of protection as the 5500-ton cruiser on the lowest possible displacement, without loss of hull-strength or seaworthiness.

Apart from the integration of the horizontal and vertical armour into the hull structure, several other ideas were tried to further reduce weight. For instance, all guns and torpedo tubes were placed on the centreline. This gave the experimental cruiser the same broadside as the larger 5500-ton ship while the number of guns and torpedo tubes could be reduced. In order to fit all armament on the centreline of the relatively short hull, twin gun mounting were used for part of the main armament. New machinery was also installed, based on destroyer practice, weighting less than the current cruiser type machinery. These measures allowed the requirements to be met on a designed displacement of 3100-tons.

A comparison with the first 5500-ton light cruiser *Kuma* clearly shows the benefits of the new construction techniques (see tables 3 and 4). On a displacement of only 56% of the 5500-ton cruiser, the same broadside, speed, range and an improved protection scheme were obtained, a remarkable achievement. When compared with the 3500-ton light cruiser *Tenryû*, *Yûbari* was unmistakably superior, carrying two more 5.5in/50 (140mm) guns, the heavier 24in (610mm) torpedo and being more than 2kts faster while displacing 400 tons less.

Yûbari was laid down at Sasebo Naval Arsenal (*Sasebo Kaigun Kôshô*) on 5 June 1922. This was a logical choice as Sasebo specialised in cruiser and destroyer size warships. In fact, a large number of the latest cruisers, including several of the 5500-ton type, were built at Sasebo.[5] As *Yûbari* was an experimental cruiser, the contract was deliberately placed with a navy yard. The new cruiser was completed in little more than a year, on 31 July 1923.

Yûbari introduced an entirely new look to Japanese warships. The many new features gave her a fast and powerful appearance that contrasted sharply with earlier Japanese cruisers. She had a large forecastle and a straight weather deck, known in Japan respectively as the uppermost and upper decks. The forecastle was given a considerable flare forward to improve seakeeping conditions. A new bow shape was introduced, the so-called swan neck bow. It was similar to the current spoon-shaped bow, but it had an outward flare on top to prevent water from coming over the bow, a distinct failure of the spoon-shape. It proved to be very successful and was used for most warships thereafter. Two anchors were carried and a gilded Imperial Crest (*Gomonsho*) was placed at the bow, as was the custom for major Japanese warships.

The hull was largely constructed of high tensile (HT) structural steel, being stronger than mild steel. It contained, among others, carbon, manganese and silicium. Tensile strength was 767-852psi (54-60kg/cm^2), with an elongation of more than 20% and an elastic limit higher than 454psi (32kg/cm^2). It was used extensively, both for structural purposes and light armour plating. *Yûbari* was given a continuous double bottom from bow to stern. Bilge keels were fitted on both sides of the hull, measuring 137ft 10in (42.00m) in length and 3ft 10in (1.17m) in width.

A large bridge covered nearly half of the uppermost deck. This tower-like structure was based on the novel idea of centralised command that would eventually result in the typical Japanese pagoda masts, particularly prominent in battleships. All command, navigation, communication and fire control was to be exercised from this centralised area to improve effectiveness and combat response. An armoured conning tower as in the *Tenryû* and *Kuma* classes was not provided. This was probably done to save top weight forward, where the large bridge was already quite a burden. To give the centreline torpedo tubes large enough firing arcs, the upper deck was kept quite clear with only two deckhouses, a low one at the base of the funnel and a short one aft to carry the rear twin gun mounting.

Two masts were fitted. A tripod foremast was used to reduce vibrations on the open director platform at its top. This mast was largely enclosed by the bridge and had a pole topmast behind the director platform. A pole mainmast was placed in front of the rear deckhouse. For night engagements, two 35.4in (90cm) searchlights were installed in centreline positions. These were Type SU Searchlights (*Superii Shiki Tanshôtô*), introduced in 1918, producing a 97,000 candles/ft^2 (9,000 candles/m^2) beam up to a range of 3850-4400yds (3500-4000m). They elevated to 100° and depressed to -30° and were not limited in their rotation. One was placed behind the funnel on a raised platform and the other on top of the bridge in front and below the director platform. This resulted in a wide arc for both searchlights, although they were both 'wooded' straight aft. A radio direction-finder antenna was fitted on the small deckhouse in front of the rear twin gun mounting. Four boats were carried on davits alongside the funnel, two cutters (*Katta*) in front and two motor boats (*Naikatei*) behind them.

Because of the adoption of centralised command, a change was made in the usual accommodation arrangements. Sleeping and working areas for the captain and several of his officers were situated in the lower part of the bridge near their battle stations. The remaining officers were accommodated at the upper deck level underneath the bridge. Officers were therefore no longer berthed in the rear part of the ship as had been standard practice up till now. Crew accommodation was forward and aft. As the berths above the hot boiler rooms in *Kuma* had proven to be unhabitable, this layout was not repeated in *Yûbari*. Instead, the fore part of the ship had crew accommodation as low as the store deck, resulting in three rows of scuttles forward. Although a crew of 340

Table 3: Comparison weight distribution Yûbari and Kuma as completed

	Yûbari		*Kuma*	
Hull:	1276 tons	31.3%	2510 tons	38.3%
Protection:	349 tons	8.6%	221 tons	3.4%
Fittings and equipment:	375 tons	9.2%	527 tons	8.0%
Machinery:	1057 tons	25.9%	1630 tons	24.9%
Armament:	330 tons	8.1%	444 tons	6.8%
Standard displacement:	3387 tons		5332 tons	
Fuel and lubrication oil (2/3):	642 tons	15.8%	1140 tons	17.4%
RFW (2/3):	46 tons	1.1%	78 tons	1.2%
Trial displacement:	4075 tons	100.0%	6550 tons	100.0%

Table 4: Comparison Yûbari and Kuma as completed

	Yûbari	*Kuma*
Normal displacement:	3560 tons	5580 tons
Waterline length:	449ft 11in (137.14m)	518ft 6in (158.03m)
Beam:	39ft 6in (12.04m)	46ft 6in (14.17m)
Draught:	12ft 8in (3.86m)	15ft 10in (4.83m)
Machinery:	three single geared turbines two mixed and six oil-fired boilers 57,750shp	four single geared turbines two mixed and ten oil-fired boilers 90,000shp
Maximum speed:	35.5kts	36kts
Range:	5000nm at 14kts	5000nm at 14kts
Armament:	two twin and two single 5.5in/50 one single 3in/40 HA two twin 24in TT (8 torpedoes) two single 7.7mm AA machineguns 48 mines	seven single 5.5in/50 two single 3in/40 HA four twin 21in TT (16 torpedoes) two single 7.7mm AA machineguns 48 mines
Broadside:	six 5.5in, one 3in and four 24in TT	six 5.5in, one 3in and four 21in TT
Armour:	1.5in (38mm) NVNC belt* 1in (25mm) NVNC deck	1.5+1in (38+25mm) HT belt 1.15in (29mm) HT deck (partial)
Complement:	328 officers and men	430-455 officers and men

* *Yûbari* lacked the 1in (25mm) backing behind the armour belt that was used in *Kuma*. Instead the belt was placed inboard behind 0.75in (19mm) HT shell-plating which added to the protection.

officers and men had been contemplated, actual complement when commissioned was 328.

Protection

The most interesting part of the new cruiser was the protection scheme. Based on Hiraga's ideas, the armour was used as an integral part of the hull structure. It thus contributed both to the longitudinal strength of the vessel and protection. The usual backing to support the armour was no longer required, saving a considerable amount of weight. As a result of the innovative design, hull weight was only 31.3% of the trial displacement in *Yûbari* compared to 38.3% in the 5500-ton cruisers.

In *Yûbari* new and tougher NVNC armour was used to replace the HT steel of the earlier light cruisers. NVNC is short for New Vickers Non-Cemented armour, also referred to in Japan as Hardened Chrome Steel (*Nitsukeru Kurômu Kô*). It was developed at the end of the First World War from Vickers Hardened (VH) steel and was intended to be used for protective plating and thin armour. The new armour contained nickel, chrome, carbon, manganese and copper and had a elastic limit higher than 568-710psi (40-50kg/cm^2), depending on thickness. Elongation was more than 18-20%, also depending on thickness, and tensile strength was about 1065-1207psi (75-85kg/cm^2). These features made the new armour superior to HT steel.

Yûbari had an internal 1.5in (38mm) NVNC armour belt. It was placed on top of the inner shell of the double bottom at a 10° inboard slope and ran up to the upper

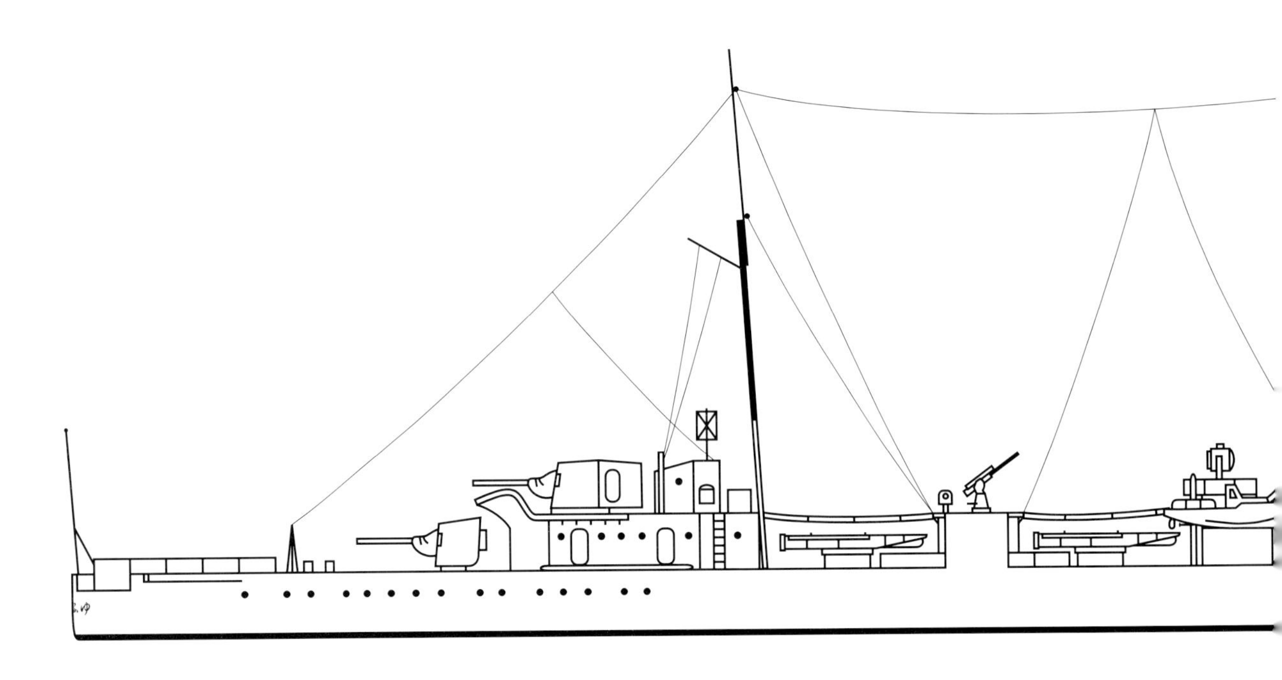

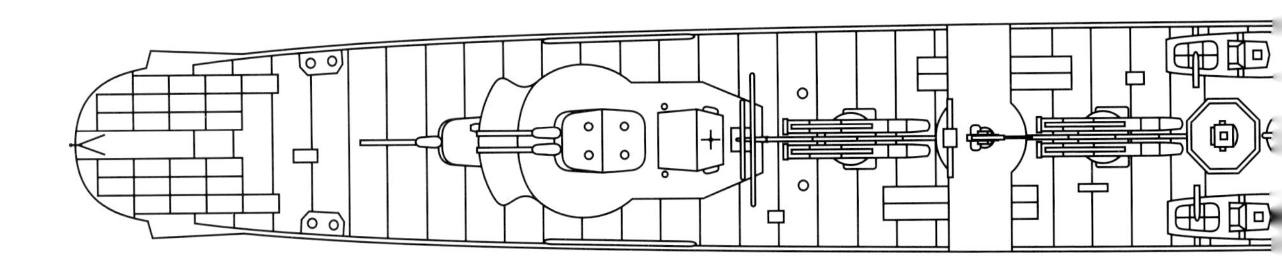

Profile and plan of the light cruiser Yûbari *as completed in 1923. Scale 1/400.* (Drawn by the author)

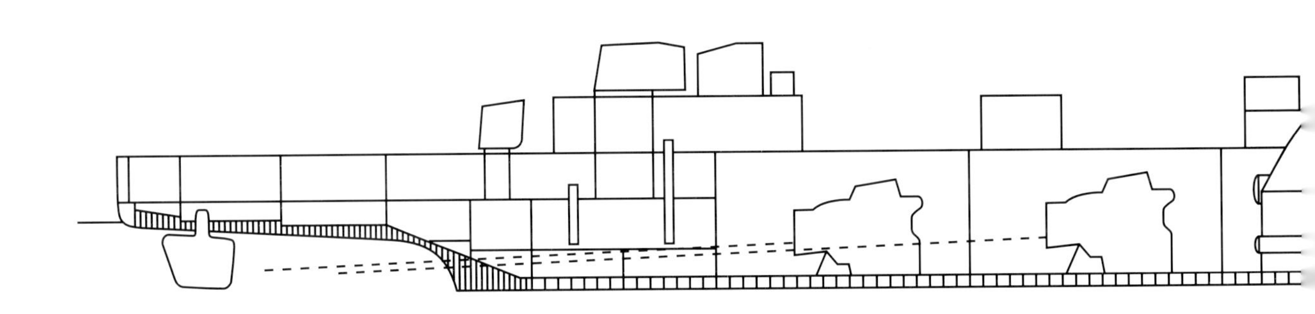

Inboard profile of Yûbari *as completed. Scale 1/400.* (Drawn by the author)

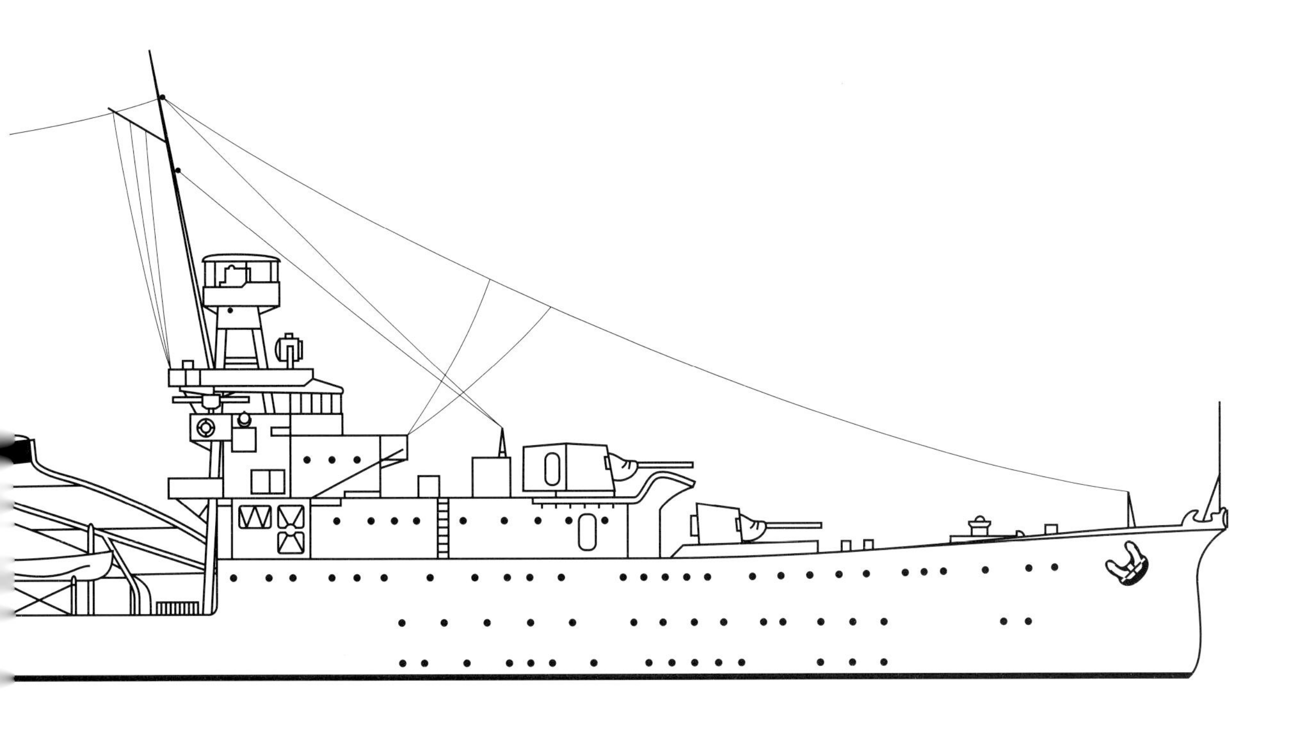

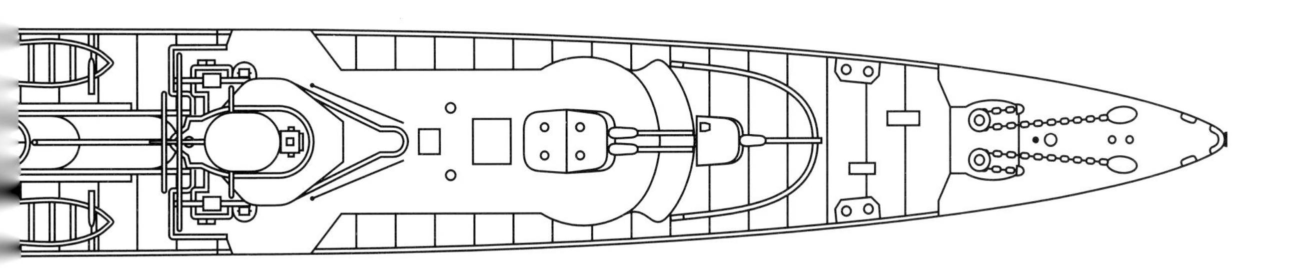

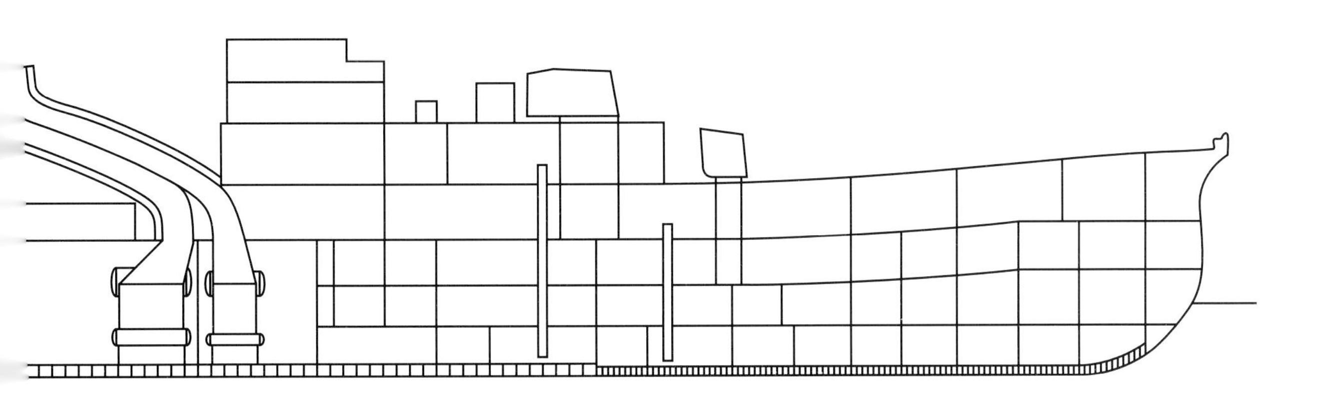

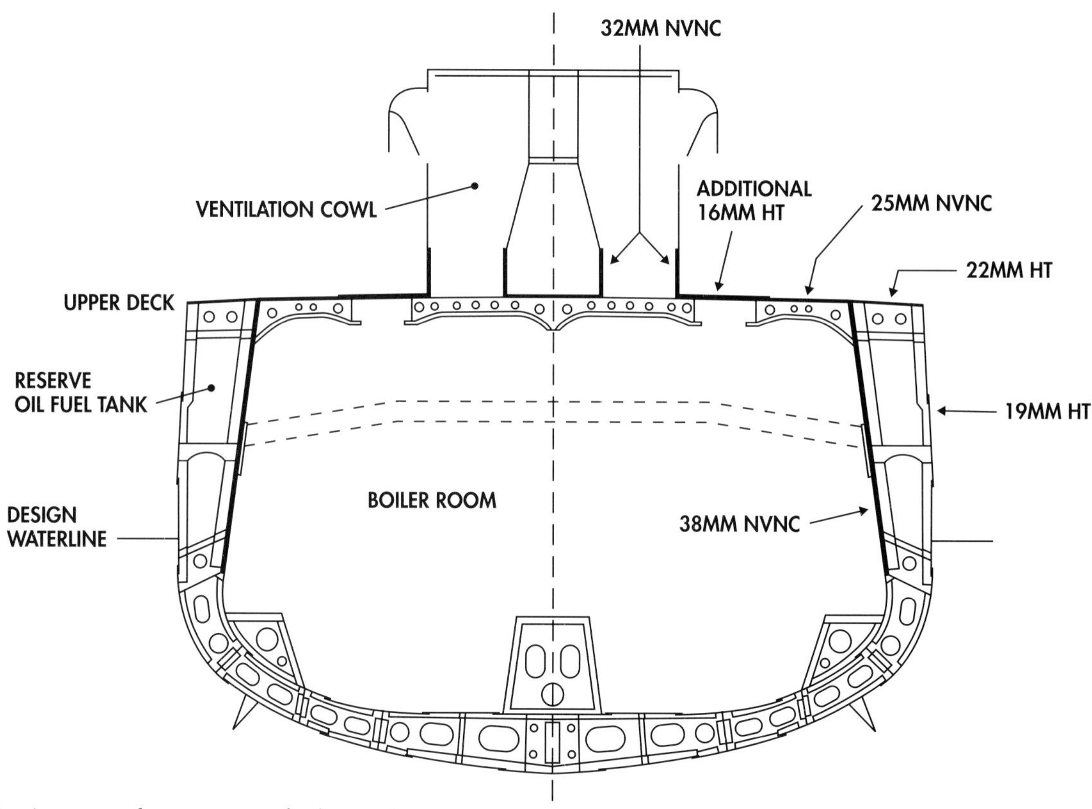

Yûbari's *armour scheme. Not to scale.* (Drawn by the author)

deck where it was connected to the outer edge of the 1in (25mm) NVNC flat armour deck. The belt had a height of 13ft 7in (4.15m). The space between the belt and the outer hull shell, which was made of 0.75in (19mm) HT steel, was used for reserve oil fuel tanks. The armour deck completely covered the deck area between the belts. This was not the case in the 5500-ton cruisers, which only featured partial deck protection. The upper deck area between the belt and the outer hull shell was not armoured, but constructed of slightly stronger 0.85in (22mm) HT steel plates instead.

Apart from the armour belt and deck, specific areas were also strengthened with armour plates. Vertical 1.25in (32mm) NVNC armour plates were fitted alongside the bases of the funnel uptakes and ventilation cowls up to a height of 2ft 1in (0.63m) above the armour deck. Horizontal 0.6in (16mm) HT plates were placed on the armour deck abreast the funnel uptakes and ventilation cowls to strengthen these relatively weak areas. This was a novel feature for light cruisers that greatly increased the resistance to enemy gunfire.

The armoured area in *Yûbari* amounted to a length of 191ft 11in (58.50m), about 42% of the ship's overall length. It covered all machinery spaces and was extended approximately 9ft 10in (3.00m) to the front to protect the fire control room below the bridge. In the 5500-ton cruisers the armour barely covered the machinery. Because of this, and because of the adoption of the new NVNC armour and the additional plates to reinforce weak areas, *Yûbari*'s protection scheme was quite superior. This showed in the percentage of weight allocated to armour in both designs, 8.6% in *Yûbari* compared to only 3.4% in *Kuma*. In fact, the weight of the armour carried by *Yûbari* was 128-tons higher than the armour in the much larger *Kuma*.

Main armament

The main armament consisted of six 3rd Year Type 5.5in/50 (140mm) LA guns. As already mentioned, all six guns were placed on the centreline to achieve the same broadside as the 5500-ton cruisers. Two guns were carried on the standard single pedestal mounting, but the other four were installed in two twin mounting to save centreline space, a new feature for light cruisers. The twins were placed in superimposed positions on deckhouses behind the single mounts. This new layout had the additional advantage of having three guns bearing both fore and aft, while the 5500-ton cruisers had only one, the guns abreast their bridges not really being available for dead ahead fire because of blast damage to the bridge. Large deck extensions were fitted in front of the twin mounts to protect the exposed crews operating the open single mounts below them from the blast effects of the twins. A large bulwark was fitted in front of the forward single mounting to protect it against spray.

The 5.5in/50 gun was designed before the First World

Table 5: GUN ARMAMENT

	5.5in/50 (140mm) LA gun	3in/40 (76mm) HA gun	4.7in/45 (120mm) HA gun
Adopted:	24 April 1914	4 February 1916	1926
Gun Data			
Barrel weight (incl. Breech)	5.5 tons	0.6 tons	2.9 tons
Barrel length:	23ft 9in (7.235m)	10ft 6in (3.203m)	18ft 5in (5.604m)
Bore length:	23ft 0in (7.000m)	10ft 0in (3.048m)	17ft 9in (5.400m)
Muzzle velocity:	2789fps (850m/s)	2198fps (670m/s)	2707fps (825m/s)
Round weight:	-	20.8-22.5lbs(9.4-10.2kg)	71.6-74.9lbs (32.5-34.0kg)
Round length:	-	2ft 4in (0.711m)	3ft 6in (1.068m)
Projectile weight:	83.7lbs (38.0kg)	13.2lbs (6.0kg)	45.0lbs (20.5kg)
Propellant charge weight:	22.8-24.2lbs (10.3-11.0kg)	2.1lbs (0.9kg)	11.5lbs (5.2kg)
Maximum range:	20,900yds (19,100m) at 30°	11,800yds (10,800m) at 45°	17,050yds (15,600m) at 45°
Maximum altitude:	-	22,300ft (6800m) at 75°	32,950ft (10,050m) at 75°
Effective altitude:	-	17,400ft (5300m) at 75°	27,700ft (8400m) at 75°
Barrel life:	500-600 rounds	1200-2000 rounds	700-1000 rounds
Rate of fire:	6-10rpm	13-18rpm	10-11rpm
Mounting Data			
Weight of mounting:	36.5 tons (twin mount)	3.4 tons	10 tons
Training speed:	4°/sec (twin mount)	11°/sec	10°/sec
Elevation speed:	6°/sec (twin mount)	7°/sec	6.5°/sec
Maximum elevation:	30°	75°	75°
Maximum depression:	-7°	-5°	-10°

War, originally intended for use as secondary armament on board battleships, but soon adopted for light cruisers. The gun was introduced because the weight of the standard 6in (152mm) shell was found to be too heavy for the average Japanese sailor. The new gun was officially adopted on 24 April 1914 as the 50cal 3rd Year Type 5.5in Gun (*50 Kôkei 3 Nendo Shiki 5.5in Hô*) and was first installed on the battleship *Ise*. It was renamed 50cal 3rd Year Type 14cm Gun (*50 Kôkei 3 Nendo Shiki 14cm Hô*) on 5 October 1917.

The gun was semi-wire wound and had a Welin screw breech block. Shells and charges were loaded and rammed by hand at any angle. Fire rate was 6-10rpm, but this could be seriously affected by the rate of supply of both shells and charges. In *Yûbari*, the guns elevated to 30°, compared to 25° in the *Kuma* class. With the higher elevation the 5.5in/50 guns could reach a maximum range of 20,900yds (19,100m) instead of the 19,150yds (17,500m) for the earlier version. Depression was the same at -7°.

The ammunition consisted of capped common (high-explosive) shells, incendiary shells, illuminating star shells and anti-submarine shells, weighting about 83.7lbs (38.0kg) each. The capped common shells were fitted with base percussion fuzes and the star shells used double-action fuzes. All shells were fired by a single silk powder bag with a black powder igniter. Reduced charges were used for exercise shells and light charges for star shells.

Yûbari's single mountings were of the standard hand-operated open shielded pedestal type, used on earlier light cruisers. The twin mountings were of a new design with a fully enclosed gunhouse (*Hôshitsu*), intended to improve the operational availability of the guns by reducing the effects of weather conditions on the gun crew. These so-called Type A (*Kô Gata*) mountings had originally been projected for the planned 1916 scout cruisers and were by now available. The shields of the twin mountings were thin, only 0.4in (10mm) thick, and therefore only gave protection against splinters. The mountings were not yet turrets but a central shell and charge hoist was fitted that reached to the deck below the mount, so no handling of ammunition in the open was required, improving the rate of fire. The twin mountings were power-operated by hydraulic gear and could be operated manually in case of emergency.

The magazines were placed directly below the two groups of mountings to reduce transfer distances. In fact, the close grouping of the mountings was a great advantage as the shell and charge supply route from the magazines was kept as short as possible, resulting in an adequate supply of ammunition to maintain the rate of fire. Both charges and shells were transferred from the magazines by bucket chain hoists to the deck below the mountings in the vicinity of the guns. Separate hoists were available for the single and twin mounts. From there they were manhandled to the single mountings as in the earlier cruisers. The central dredger hoist of the twin mountings hauled the shells and charges from below the mounting to within the gunshields near the guns, allowing a more rapid supply. All handling between hoists and between hoists and guns was by hand.

Fire control

As already mentioned, a fire control director was installed on an open platform on top of the foremast. This location gave it almost complete all round view, being only wooded dead aft by the masts. The system was the new Type 13 Director Aiming Installation (*13 Shiki Hoiban Shôjun Sôchi*), adopted on 2 May 1916 as the Imperial Japanese Navy's first director. It was installed in battleships and battlecruisers from 1916 and in all new cruisers from 1918. It was capable of surface (LA) fire only. The Type 13 director was developed on the basis of data obtained on the British Vickers director in the early part of the First World War. It was a simple instrument that used 2.5in (64mm) telescopes for both laying and training on the target and it directed the gunmounts in both elevation and training by follow-the-pointer gear. The Type 13 was effective up to a range of 20,800yds (19,000m), virtually identical to the maximum range of the 5.5in/50 guns on board *Yûbari*. Removable 8ft 2in (2.5m) range finders were provided which could be installed in the bridge wings or in the fore part of the bridge.

Anti-aircraft weapons

A single 3rd Year Type 3in/40 (76mm) HA gun was placed on the small platform between the torpedo tube mounts. This gave the unshielded gun reasonable arcs of fire although it was wooded dead ahead and astern. Since it was placed on the centreline, only one mount was needed compared to the two carried by *Kuma*.

The 3in/40 HA gun was the first anti-aircraft gun of the Imperial Japanese Navy, being adopted on 4 February 1916 as the 40cal 3in High Elevation Gun (*40 Kôkei 3in Dai Gyôkaku Hô*). Shortly after, on 5 October 1917, it was renamed 40cal 8cm HA Gun (*40 Kôkei 8cm Kôkaku Hô*) and finally, on 29 March 1922, 40cal 3rd Year Type 8cm HA Gun (*40 Kôkei 3 Nendo Shiki 8cm Kôkaku Hô*). Initially, it was installed in battleships, soon followed by cruisers and other combatants.

The gun was modified in 1914-15 from the existing 3in/40 surface gun by increasing its elevation to 75°. Several improvements had to be made to adjust the gun to its new role. Extra weight was attached to the breech to balance the gun at high elevation, and the aiming telescopes used by the operators for training and elevation, were modified. The gun had a built-up construction with a vertical sliding breech, placed at an upward angle of 45°. Recoil was absorbed by a single oil-hydraulic cylinder and run-out was by spring mechanism. Rounds were provided in fixed brass cases for quick loading. The gun was entirely hand-operated. First, fuzes were set by hand. Then, the rounds were loaded at any angle and rammed by hand. The firing rate of the gun depended on the supply of rounds which had to be manhandled from the magazine to the mount. The gun was fitted on an unshielded Type C (*Hei Gata*) pedestal mounting. A small platform was fitted at the base of the mount to allow the operators to rotate with the weapon.

Several types of shells were available. The standard AA round was the common (high-explosive) shell with a head fuze, replaced by a double action fuze later on that allowed for time-settings. Exercise shells and, later on, timed exercise shells with the same double-action fuzes were provided for training. Also produced were tracer, shrapnel and marker or target shells, the latter two with double-action fuzes. Shells weighted about 13.2lbs (6.0kg).

For close range defence, two single 7.7mm Lewis AA machine guns were installed abreast the 3in/40 HA gun. These machine guns, more commonly known as 0.303in weapons, were imported from Britain. They were gas-operated air-cooled guns, fed by disk magazines placed on their top. They were fitted on free-swinging pedestal mountings and fired at a rate of 550rpm, although magazine changes must have had a profound effect on the effective firing-rate. Effective range was about 1100yds (1000m). Gunners had to aim on sight as no telescopes or eyesights were fitted.

Table 6: AA MACHINEGUN

	7.7mm Lewis
Adoption:	1925
Gun Data	
Barrel weight:	26.0lbs (11.8kg)
Barrel length:	4ft 3in (1.283m)
Muzzle velocity:	2444fps (745m/s)
Effective range:	1100yds (1000m)
Rate of fire:	550rpm
Mounting:	free swinging single pedestal

Underwater weapons

The torpedo armament consisted of two unshielded twin 24in (610mm) 8th Year Type Torpedo Tube Mountings (*8 Nendo Shiki Hasshakan*), placed amidship on the centreline. *Yûbari* thus achieved the same broadside as the larger 5500-ton cruisers with only half the number of tubes. Moreover, the new 24in torpedo was a much more formidable weapon than the standard 21in (533mm) used in the *Kuma* class. The heavy torpedoes were fired by compressed air. The mountings were not limited in training and could be rotated a full 360° if necessary. Training of the mounting was electric but could be done manually in emergencies.

Yûbari carried ten 8th Year Type 61cm Torpedoes (*8 Nendo Shiki 61cm Gyôrai*). This was not the notorious Long Lance oxygen-propelled torpedo of the late 1930s, but, in essence, an enlarged version of the current 6th Year Type 53cm Torpedo (*6 Nendo Shiki 53cm Gyôrai*) used in the *Kuma* class and other Japanese warships. The

Table 7: *TORPEDO ARMAMENT*

	24in (610mm) No. 1 torpedo	**24in (610mm) No. 2 torpedo**
Adoption:	1920	1921
Torpedo Data		
Length:	27ft 7in (8415mm)	27ft 7in (8415mm)
Weight:	4,879lbs (2215kg)	5,203lbs (2362kg)
Warhead:	661lbs (300kg) Shimose	762lbs (346kg) Shimose
Range:	10,900yds (10,000m) at 37kts	10,900yds (10,000m) at 38kts
	19,700yds (18,000m) at 27kts	16,400yds (15,000m) at 32kts
	–	21,900yds (20,000m) at 27kts

larger size made it possible to increase the torpedo's range and allowed for a heavier warhead, which was considered necessary by the Japanese to sink the better protected modern battleships. The machinery and other components were simply adjusted to the new size. The engine was a wet-heater type Schwartzkopf four-cylinder radial, driven by compressed natural air and kerosene and using water as a coolant. Two versions of the 8th Year Type torpedo were produced. The No. 1 (*1 Gô*) was adopted in 1920 as the first Japanese 24in torpedo. Its production was, however, soon overtaken by the improved No. 2 (*2 Gô*) of 1921. The latter featured a larger warhead, had a slightly larger range and was provided with an intermediate range-setting. Both torpedoes had *Shimose* picric acid warheads. *Yûbari* probably still carried the 8th Year Type No. 2 torpedoes during the Pacific War as did several destroyers of similar age.

Yûbari was not equipped with the elaborate rapid reloading system that proved to be so devastating during the Pacific War. The four reserve torpedoes were simply carried in two large canisters on deck. These canisters were placed alongside the mounting which rotated over them. Note that the canister on the port side was placed abreast the forward mount and the starboard canister abreast the rear mounting. For reloading, an electric motor was available, but hand operation was also possible.

Apart from torpedoes, *Yûbari* could also carry mines. In 1914 the Japanese had realised that they had been neglecting mine warfare, despite its heavy influence in the Russo-Japanese War, when they encountered German mines at Tsingtao. Therefore, a special mine policy was drawn up that was to provide the Navy with an adequate number of minesweepers and minelayers. To create sufficient minelaying capacity, the policy stated that new destroyers and light cruisers were to be fitted with minelaying equipment. *Yûbari* was no exception to this rule and carried 48 No 1B mines on her quarter-deck. To protect these mines from the blast effects of the 5.5in guns special sheds were erected. These consisted of six rows of four compartments that could each hold two mines.

Propulsion

Because *Yûbari* was smaller than the 5500-ton cruisers, she needed less powerful machinery to reach the same maximum speed. Moreover, in an effort to save weight, light but powerful destroyer machinery was used for the first time in a cruiser, instead of a reduced 5500-ton cruiser plant. The new machinery was virtually identical to that installed in the *Minekaze* class destroyers. These fast destroyers carried four oil-fired *Kanpon* boilers and two sets of *Kanpon* geared turbines, each capable of 19,250shp for a total output of 38,500shp.

Yûbari received three sets of these *Kanpon* impulse reaction single geared turbines to drive three shafts at a total output of 57,750shp. Designed maximum speed was 35.5kts, actually slightly below the 36kts of the *Kuma* class. Each turbine set consisted of a HP and a LP turbine geared in parallel to a single shaft. No separate cruising turbine was provided. Instead a cruising stage was built into the front part of the HP turbine, based on Parsons' design. In Japan, these turbines were called the Cruising Stage Type (*Junkô Danraku Shiki*). In the *Minekaze* class destroyers one stage (*Ichi Dan*) was used, but the design was improved to a two stage (*Ni Dan*) type in *Yûbari*. During cruising, steam first past through the cruising stages and then through the HP and LP turbines. When steaming at high speed, the cruising stages were bypassed. Two turbine sets were installed in the forward engine room and the other one in the after engine room in between the two shafts of the forward turbines.

Steam was provided by eight *Kanpon Ro-gô* small-tube boilers, six large oil-fired types and two small mixed-fired types. Operating temperature was 260psi (18.3kg/cm^2) at 138°C, which was higher than in the *Kuma* class cruisers, obtained by superheating. Three boiler rooms were provided in which the boilers were placed side by side. The two small mixed-fired boilers were placed in the forward room, four large models in the middle room and the other two in the after room. The two engine rooms were located directly behind the boiler rooms. The length of the machinery spaces in *Yûbari* was 182ft 1in (55.50m) compared to 223ft 1in (68.00m) in the *Kuma* class, although both occupied about 40% of the ship's overall length.

The boiler uptakes were trunked into a single funnel. Originally, it had been planned to fit two funnels, one for four boilers each, but upon the insistence of Lt-Cdr Fujimoto the forward uptakes were curved backwards and attached to the rear uptakes during construction. Fujimoto hoped that this would reduce smoke interference on the bridge and on the important fire control director, a profound problem that plagued several of the

Table 8: *AA* MACHINEGUNS

	13.2mm Type 93	25mm Type 96
Adopted:	1935	6 August 1936
Gun Data		
Barrel weight:	43.7lbs (19.8kg)	94.8lbs (43.0kg)
Barrel length:	3ft 3in (1.000m)	4ft 11in (1.500m)
Total weight:	92.2lbs (41.8kg)	253lbs (115.0kg)
Overall length:	4ft 7in (1.400m)	7ft 10in (2.400m)
Muzzle velocity:	2641fps (805m/s)	2953fps (900m/s)
Round weight:	0.25-0.26lb (112.6-118.5g)	1.5lbs (680g)
Round length:	5.29-5.38in (134.4-136.6mm)	9in (0.233m)
Maximum range:	7000yds (6400m) at 50°	8200yds (7500m) at 50°
Maximum altitude:	14,750ft (4500m) at 85°	17,200ft (5250m) at 80°
Effective range:	750-1650yds (700-1500m)	1650-3300yds (1500-3000m)
Barrel life:	–	3000-15,000 rounds
Rate of fire:	425-475rpm (setting) 250rpm (effective)	200-260rpm (setting) 110-120rpm (effective)
Mounting Data		
Weight of mounting:	690lbs (313kg) twin mount	2425lbs (1100kg) twin mount 3965lbs (1800kg) triple mount
Training speed:	–	18°/sec
Elevation speed:	–	12°/sec
Maximum elevation:	85°	80°
Maximum depression:	-15°	-10°

Japanese battleships that had recently been provided with fire control equipment. The large curved funnel created a very distinctive appearance that was to become a characteristic Japanese feature.

A single balanced centreline rudder was fitted behind the three propellers with an effective area of 105.2ft^2 (9.77m^2). Maximum fuel stowage was 830 tons of oil and 100 tons of coal. Apparently, coal was still used because the Japanese feared an oil shortage during wartime, since Japan had very few oil resources of its own. Designed range was 5000nm at 14kts cruising speed.

History up to 1941

When *Yûbari* was completed, she exceeded her designed displacement by no less than 419 tons, about 13.5% of the normal displacement. This was a direct result of the

Light cruiser Yûbari *after her 1934-35 refits. Note the large shields of the torpedo tubes amidship and the reserve torpedo canisters between them.* (Maritime History RNN)

many new features for which not enough weight had been reserved in the design. Consequently, her draught rose by 1ft (0.30m), immersing the transom and making it impossible for *Yûbari* to reach her designed maximum speed. During trials off Koshikijima on 5 July 1923 she made 34.786kts with 61,336shp on 3463 tons. Moreover, the additional drag reduced the effective range to only 3300nm at 14kts. The originally designed freeboard of 12ft (3.66m) was reduced to about 10ft (3.05m) in the new and heavier trial displacement.[6] As a result, the lower row of forward scuttles came dangerously close to the water level.

Table 9: YÛBARI *AS COMPLETED*

Characteristics (as completed)

Standard displacement:	3387 tons
Normal displacement:	3560 tons
Normal waterline length:	449ft 11in (137.14m)
Normal draught:	12ft 8in (3.86m)
Trial displacement:	4075 tons
Trial waterline length:	450ft 0in (137.16m)
Trial draught:	13ft 9in (4.19m)

Despite being overweight, *Yûbari* proved an unqualified success. During her trials she performed very well, showing that she was a strong and seaworthy ship. *Yûbari* thus proved that Hiraga's basic design concepts were correct, although the design had been too optimistic in its weight calculations. Many of the innovative features soon appeared on new Japanese warships.

When it was discovered that smoke interference was still a problem at high speed, *Yûbari*'s funnel was raised 6ft 7in (2.00m) at Sasebo in 1924, shortly after her completion. This modification seems to have been satisfactory as no further changes were made to the funnel or the fire control platform on top of the foremast.

Yûbari's first assignment was to the third squadron (*Sentai 3*) with the light cruisers *Tama* and *Isuzu* in 1924. The next year she visited Australia. From 1926 onwards she performed duties as flagship of destroyer divisions or as a training ship. In 1932, *Yûbari* was part of the naval presence sent to Shanghai during the Shanghai incident.

Yûbari was refitted twice in 1934-35. The first time she was taken in hand between 17 May and 20 July 1934 at Sasebo Naval Arsenal, followed by a second refit between 9 July and 15 November 1935 at Yokosuka Naval Arsenal. A total of 124 tons of ballast was added to improve stability, found wanting after the *Tomozuru* incident. The two torpedo tube mountings received shields for all-weather operations. The platform between the torpedo tubes was remodelled with open sides, probably a weight-saving measure to compensate for increased top weight. Because of its closeness to the waterline, the lower row of forward scuttles was plated in. The mine sheds were removed and the associated openings in the stern were plated over. The platforms at the rear end of

Yûbari *in 1936 on the Musi River in Sumatra during her visit to the Netherlands East Indies. This photo clearly shows the elaborate bridge structure. Note the director top with canvas cover and the two range finders fitted in the sponsons at the sides of the bridge.* (BD van der Zwan)

the bridge were altered. The 3in/40 (76mm) HA gun was replaced by a Type 93 twin 13.2mm AA machinegun, which was installed in the same position.

The 13.2mm AA machinegun was based on a French Hotchkiss design, of which small quantities were imported from France. Domestic production of a slightly modified type was started in 1935 as the Type 93 13mm Machinegun (*93 Shiki 13mm Kijû*). The new machine guns were gas-operated and air-cooled. Construction was mostly monobloc with some reinforcement. A large 76 calibres barrel was used with high muzzle velocity. The barrels could be replaced very quickly by simply screwing them on or off. The ammunition was supplied in 30-round magazines and consisted of armour-piercing, incendiary common (high-explosive), tracer and exercise shells. Twin, quadruple and single mountings were provided, all of which were operated entirely by hand. The trainer and elevator had seats attached to the mounting so that they rotated with it.

In 1936, after the refits, *Yûbari* paid an official visit to the Netherlands East Indies and the next year she was again sent to Shanghai. She was placed in reserve from 1938 to 1940. In the spring of 1940 the twin 13.2mm

Profile and plan of Yûbari *in 1935, after her refits. Scale 1/400.* (Drawn by the author)

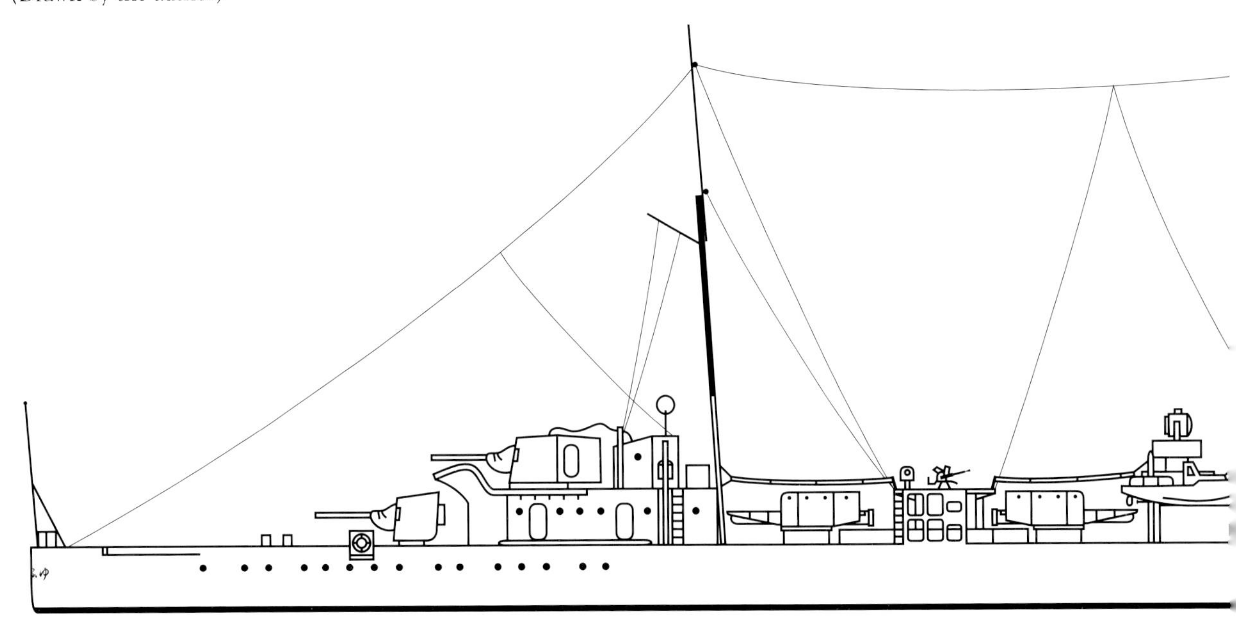

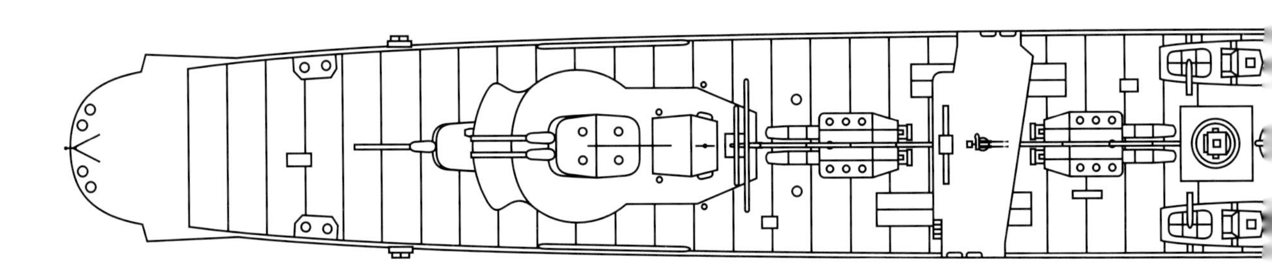

machinegun was replaced by two twin 25mm AA machine guns. The new 25mm AA machinegun was also a French Hotchkiss weapon developed in the early 30s. A number of these guns were imported from France for evaluation. As from 1936, modified guns of Japanese manufacture became available for operational service and received the designation Type 96 25mm Machinegun (96 *Shiki 25mm Kijû*) on 6 August 1936.

The 25mm machine gun was essentially a gas-operated forged monobloc weapon. It featured a 60cal air-cooled barrel which could easily be screwed on or off the breech mechanism. The rate of fire could be adjusted between 200 to 260rpm, the usual Japanese setting being 220rpm. The machine gun used magazines with a capacity of only fifteen rounds which had to be replaced frequently, reducing the effective rate of fire. The ammunition consisted of armour-piercing, common (high-explosive), incendiary common and tracer rounds. Shells were fuzed and weighed on average 8.8oz (250g) while a complete round weighted 24oz (680g).

The first machine guns were installed in twin mountings of French or Japanese design. These mounts were operated manually in both training and elevation. Seats were provided for the trainer and pointer so that they moved with the mounting. Both were provided with eyesights for aiming. Later on, triple and single mounts of Japanese manufacture appeared. The 25mm machine gun proved to be a good and reliable weapon that required little or no maintenance. Unfortunately, it proved to be ineffective in the later part of the war because of its relatively small calibre.

In the autumn of 1941, the Japanese fleet was reorganised to prepare for war. *Yûbari* was assigned to the Fourth Fleet (*Kantai 4*), referred to as the South Sea Force (*Nanyô Butai*). This fleet was given responsibility for the Mandate area under command of V-Adm Shigeyoshi Inouye on board the light cruiser flagship *Kashima*, stationed at the forward base on Truk, Caroline Islands. *Yûbari* was assigned to be the leader of the 6th Destroyer Squadron (*Suiraisentai 6*), consisting of the 29th and 30th Destroyer Divisions (*Kuchikutai 29 and 30*). The former was made up of the *Kamikaze* class destroyers *Oite*, *Hayate*, *Asanagi* and *Yûnagi* and the latter of the *Mutsuki* class destroyers *Mutsuki*, *Kisaragi*, *Yayoi* and *Mochizuki*.

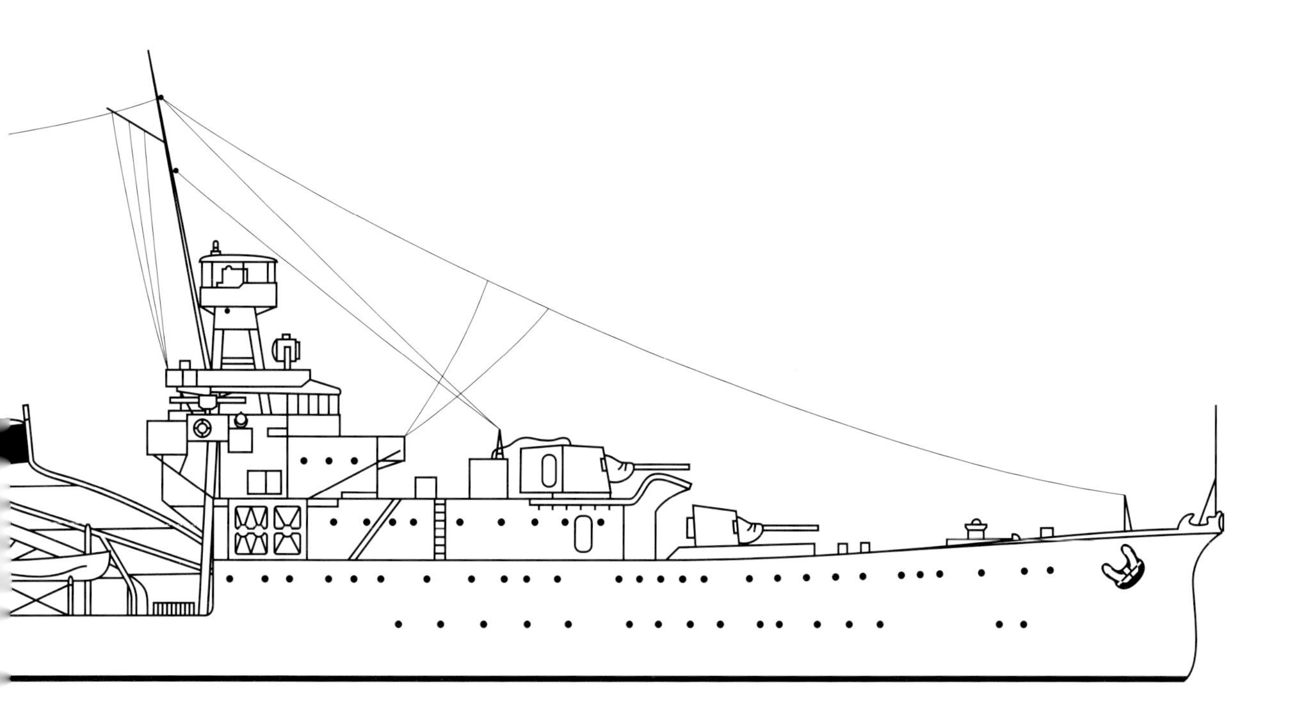

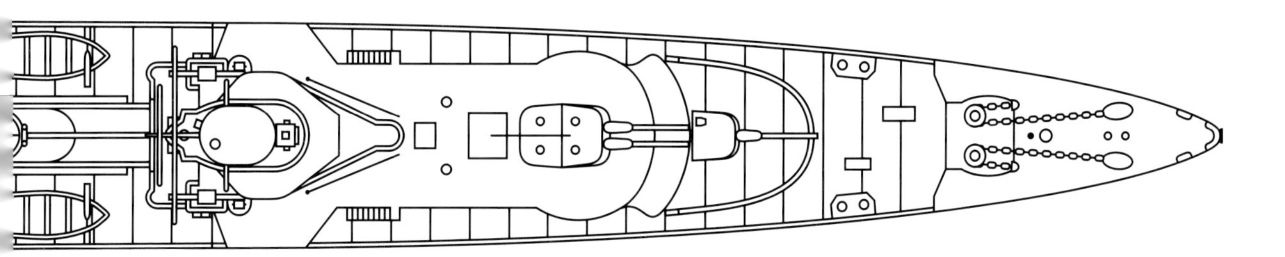

War operations 1941 - 1943

At the outbreak of the Pacific War in December 1941, the Fourth Fleet was, among other things, responsible for the capture of Wake Island. For this purpose a small attack force had been gathered at Kwajalein, Marshall Islands, on 3 December 1941. *Yûbari* served as the flagship of R-Adm Sadamichi Kajioka, who commanded the force. She led the 6th destroyer squadron consisting of the above mentioned 29th and 30th destroyer divisions, with the exception of the destroyers *Asanagi* and *Yûnagi* which were assigned to the force that was to capture Tarawa and Makin, Gilbert Islands. The attack force further included a number of transports and was supported by two light cruisers. V-Adm Inouye aboard his flagship *Kashima* at Truk was in overall command of the operation.

On 8 December 1941, the attack force left Kwajalein to arrive at Wake Island during the night of 10-11 December. Unfortunately for the Japanese, the defenders still had some fighters and the coastal batteries had not been destroyed during the air raids of the previous days, so the defenders were able to repulse the attack, sinking the destroyers *Kisaragi* and *Hayate*. The invasion force had to retreat and returned empty-handed to Kwajalein on 13 December.

A second attack with larger forces was immediately planned. More transports were made available and heavier cruiser support was provided. Moreover, after the Pearl Harbor attack a carrier group was sent to Wake with its own escorts. *Yûbari* and her destroyers were assigned to escort and support the invasion force. The 29th destroyer division now consisted of *Asanagi*, *Oite* and *Yûnagi*, while the 30th destroyer division was made up of *Mochizuki*, *Mutsuki* and *Yayoi*. R-Adm Kajioka was still on board, but after his initial failure he was only given responsibility for the invasion force. Prior to the landing, carrier and land-based aircraft softened the defences. The attack force arrived at Wake on 22 December and the first landings were carried out in the early hours of 23 December, securing the atoll in the morning. After the successful completion of this operation, the invasion force arrived at Kwajalein on 29 December, after

Also taken in 1936 on the Musi river in Sumatra, this photograph shows the small platforms of the new minelaying equipment in the left lower corner. (BD van der Zwan)

which *Yûbari* and her consorts returned to Truk on 3 January 1942.

The next operation in which *Yûbari* played a part was the move into the Bismarck Archipelago in January 1942. The objective was the capture of the excellent harbour at Rabaul in New Britain, intended to be used as a forward base. At the same time, the occupation of Kavieng in New Ireland was planned. Support was provided by aircraft carriers, cruisers, destroyers and many other vessels. *Yûbari* and her six destroyers of the 29th and 30th divisions were assigned to the protective screen of the Rabaul landing force. The attack forces left Truk on 17 January 1942 and the landings were carried out in the night of 22-23 January, Rabaul being secured on 23 January. In early February the warships returned to Truk, while the work to convert Rabaul into a fortified forward base was immediately started.

With the conclusion of the Rabaul operation, attention shifted to New Guinea. This large island was to be captured to keep Australia out of the war by cutting her lifelines. In late February the Fourth Fleet, still under command of V-Adm Inouye, left Truk for the new base at Rabaul. A landing force was assembled there for the first assault on New Guinea, consisting of transports, minecraft and smaller vessels. On 5 March it left Rabaul escorted by the 6th destroyer squadron, once again consisting of *Yûbari* and the six destroyers of the 29th and 30th divisions, and under distant cover of heavy and light cruisers. Landings were made at Salamua and Lae in New Guinea on 8 March. Two days later, aircraft from the American aircraft carriers *Yorktown* and *Lexington* surprised the landing forces by flying over the Owen Stanley mountains from the other side of New Guinea. Four transports were sunk and *Yûbari* and the destroyers *Asanagi* and *Yûnagi* were among the ships damaged. Nevertheless, Salamaua and Lae were taken and the support forces returned to Rabaul on 14 March. *Yûbari* sailed for Truk on 22 March to repair her damage, the work being completed on 10 April.

The next objective was the capture of Port Moresby on the other side of New Guinea. As usual, *Yûbari*'s 6th destroyer squadron was assigned to escort and support the invasion force. Since the destroyer *Yûnagi* could not join her division as a result of damage sustained during the previous operation, her place was temporarily taken by *Uzuki* of the 23rd division. The invasion force left Rabaul on 4 May for a planned attack on 10 May, but was recalled on 8 May because the Battle of the Coral Sea left the invasion force without aircraft support. The operation was postponed for the time being and was eventually cancelled. *Yûbari* left for Yokosuka for a long-needed overhaul and returned to Truk on 23 June.

After the Midway disaster in early June, the Combined Fleet (*Rengo Kantai*) was reorganised on 14 July 1942. The South Sea Force was divided in two separate forces, the Inner South Sea Force or Fourth Fleet and the Outer

South Sea Force or Eighth Fleet. The Fourth Fleet was given responsibility for the former Mandate area under command of V-Adm Inouye in his cruiser flagship *Kashima*, again stationed at Truk. The Eighth Fleet was made responsible for the forward area of the Japanese assault in the South Pacific, including the Solomon Islands and New Guinea. It was commanded by V-Adm Gunichi Mikawa aboard the heavy cruiser *Chôkai*, based at Rabaul. *Yûbari* was allocated to the Fourth Fleet along with the 29th destroyer division, while the 30th destroyer division was assigned to the Eighth Fleet. At this time, the 29th division consisted of the destroyers *Yûnagi*, *Oite*, *Asanagi* and *Yûzuki*. The latter was a reinforcement from the abolished 23rd division. Although officially allocated to the Fourth Fleet, *Yûbari* and her four destroyers were sent to Rabaul to support further New Guinea operations. On 29 June 1942, *Yûbari* and the destroyer *Uzuki* escorted three transports to the little known island of Guadalcanal in the Solomon Islands. They returned to Rabaul on 10 July.

On 7 August 1942, American troops landed at Guadalcanal and captured the newly built Japanese airfield at that location. V-Adm Mikawa immediately responded by launching air strikes and by collecting all available warships for a surface night attack. He took to sea in his flagship *Chôkai* together with the heavy cruisers *Kako*, *Furutaka*, *Aoba* and *Kinugasa* and the light cruiser *Tenryû*. Since *Yûbari* and the destroyer *Yûnagi* were at Rabaul at the time, they accompanied the attack force too. *Yûnagi* was the only destroyer in the force because the rest was otherwise engaged.

During the resulting Battle of Savo Island in the night of 8-9 August, this force succeeded in surprising the Allied warships guarding the transports, and virtually annihilated them. The American heavy cruisers *Astoria*, *Quincy* and *Vincennes* and the Australian heavy cruiser *Canberra* were sunk and the American heavy cruiser *Chicago* and the destroyers *Patterson* and *Ralph Talbot* were damaged. *Yûbari* expended ninety-six 5.5in shells and four 24in torpedoes during the engagement and received one hit, but there were no casualties. *Yûbari* and Yûnagi returned to Rabaul on 10 August and with the other three destroyers of the 29th division returned to Truk shortly afterwards.

On 26 August 1942, *Yûbari* and the destroyer *Yûnagi* set out of Truk to escort a landing force, occupying Naura Island on 30 August and Ocean Island on 31 August. They returned to Truk on 5 September. The remainder of the year were spent in the Mandate area, mainly on escort duties, operating from Truk. In December, *Yûbari* was once again sent to Yokosuka for a refit, returning to Truk on 28 March 1943.

In April 1943, *Yûbari* was transferred to the Eighth Fleet and returned to Rabaul, leaving her destroyers behind. When the Americans landed on Rendova, Solomon Islands on 30 June 1943, *Yûbari* and nine destroyers were sent to disrupt the advance. They shelled the island during the night of 2-3 July, but with little effect. On 5 July, *Yûbari* hit an air-laid mine at Buin, Bougainville. Although the damage was not severe she had to leave for Japan to receive full repairs and she did not return to Rabaul until 3 November 1943. There, she was slightly damaged by near misses during the American air raid on 11 November 1943, executed by the aircraft carriers *Essex*, *Bunker Hill* and *Independence*. As Rabaul was no longer considered safe, *Yûbari* left for Truk on 3 December 1943, towing the immobilised destroyer *Naganami* all the way.

1944 refit

Between 19 December 1943 and 9 March 1944, *Yûbari* was taken in hand at Yokosuka to augment her AA armament, necessary to counter Allied air superiority. The two single 5.5in/50 mountings were removed. They were replaced by a single Type 10 4.7in/45 (120mm) HA gun in the forward position and a triple 25mm AA machine-gun aft. Two more triple, two twin and eight single 25mm mountings were added to reach a total of twenty-five 25mm machine guns. The triples were placed on side platforms in front of the rear 5.5in/50 twin mounting. The two twins were situated on side platforms behind the forward 5.5in/50 mounting.[7]

The 4.7in/45 gun was Japan's second HA gun converted from a standard surface weapon, in this case the 3rd Year Type 4.7in/45 surface gun used on destroyers. It was designed in 1921 to obtain a more effective AA gun than the 3in/40 HA gun. The weapon was finally adopted in 1926 as the 45cal 10th Year Type 12cm HA Gun (*45 Kôkei 10 Nendo Shiki 12cm Kôkaku Hô*).

The gun was of built-up construction and had a semi-automatic horizontal sliding breech block. Later models, produced during the Pacific War, were of radially expanded monobloc construction. The HA gun used fixed rounds, which had to be loaded and rammed manually. Cartridge-ejection was automatic. The fuze was set by hand before ramming. Ammunition was probably supplied by the bucket chain hoist originally used for the single 5.5in/50 gun and had to be manhandled from there to the mount. Rate of fire was about 10-11rpm, depending on the supply of ammunition. The gun was fitted in a Type E single pedestal mounting with electro-hydraulic power. An open shield protected the gun crew against spray coming over the bow. Elevation was 75° and depression -10°.

Five types of shells were available for the 4.7in/45 HA gun, notably common (high-explosive), exercise, timed exercise, marker and star shells. The fixed rounds weighted 75lbs (34kg) on average and were 37in (940mm) long. Common shells carried a 3.7lbs (1.7kg) *Shimose* picric acid charge and a head percussion fuze, later replaced by a time fuze. The timed exercise and marker shells initially had double-action fuzes, but later on they were provided with time fuzes. Star shells used time fuzes, but had no parachutes and, as a consequence, they had a rather short illumination life.

A No 22 search radar was fitted above the bridge, replacing the searchlight on the same location. This radar was officially designated No 2 Electric Wave Detector Model 2 Modification 4 (*2 Gô Denpa Tanshingi 2 Gata Kai 4*), abbreviated as No 22 (*22 Gô*). No 2 indi-

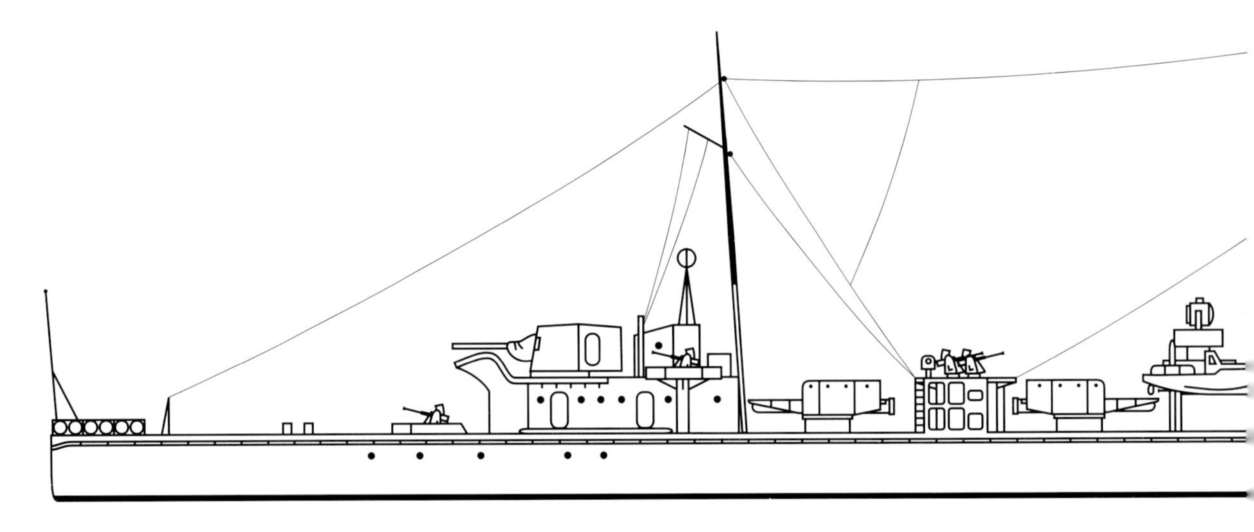

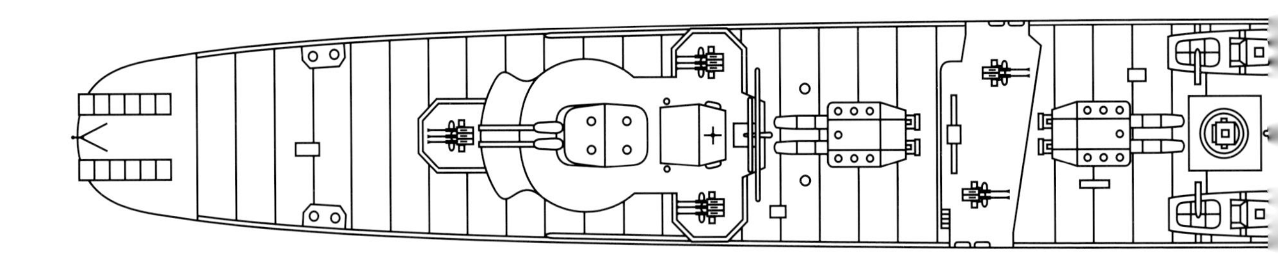

Profile and plan of Yûbari *as she appeared in 1944 after her AA upgrade. Note the absence of the torpedo canisters and the large number of 25mm machineguns. A Type 22 radar is fitted on top of the bridge. Scale 1/400.* (Drawn by the author)

cated a shipboard search (*Kantei Kenchô*) radar, Model 2 the second model of this specific type of radar and Modification 4 the fourth version adopted. This specific version was designed between December 1942 and December 1943 for use on board large surface ships. The No 22 radar was developed for surface search, operating on the 3.9in (10cm) wave length. It featured two electromagnetic horns with a 15.7in (40cm) diameter. They were placed one above the other, receiver on top and transmitter below. The fourth version had a power output of 2kW and had a minimum detection range of 1650yds (1500m). Maximum detection range was 38,300yds (35,000m) for large surface ships and approximately 18,600yds (17,000m) for smaller vessels such as destroyers. Because of a range error of ± 765yds (700m), the radar could not be used for fire control. The installation weighted 1320kg and was operated by 4-6 men.[8]

Two depth charge rails were installed at the stern, each containing six depth charges. A large number of *Yûbari*'s remaining scuttles were plated in to improve damage control, with only a few aft and several of the upper row forward remaining. Both masts were shortened. To compensate for added topweight, the four reserve torpedoes and their canisters were removed, as well as the minelaying equipment. The displacement rose to 3780 tons and maximum speed dropped to 32kts with 58,943shp, still an impressive speed at this age.

Fate

On her return to the front, *Yûbari* escorted a convoy to Palau by way of Saipan. Near the Bonin Islands, this small force was attacked by the American submarine *Pollack* (SS-180), which sank the submarine chaser *Ch 54* on 25 March 1944. Afterwards, *Yûbari* returned to Saipan, where she was allocated to transport reinforcements to Sonsorol Islands, a small group of islands southwest of Palau. It was to be her last mission. *Yûbari* left Saipan on 23 April and arrived at Palau on 25 April Continuing her journey, in company with the light cruiser *Kinu*, the destroyers *Samidare* and *Yûzuki* and the transport *T149*, she arrived off Sonsorol Islands on 27 April where she landed 365 men and 50-tons of material.

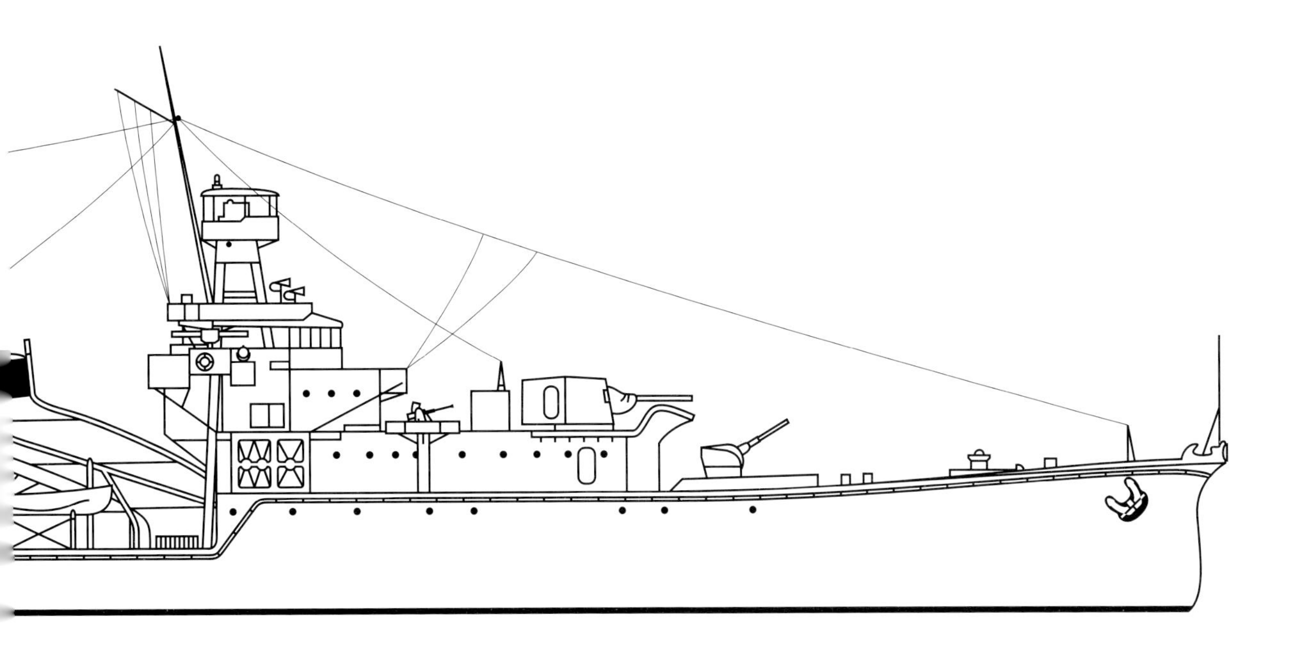

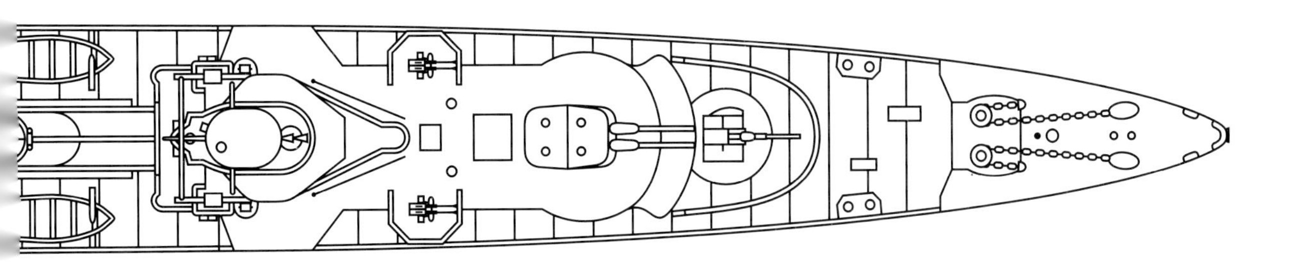

The American submarine *Bluegill* (SS-242) was directed to Sonsorol Islands after communication intelligence had revealed that landings were about to be made. On 27 April, she encountered the small landing force there, but was forced down by aircraft and the escorting warships. Nevertheless, the submarine was able to get into a firing position and she fired a full spread of six torpedoes at *Yûbari* at a range of 2600yds (2400m).

At 10.04 in the position 05-20N 132-16E, while she was just getting underway, *Yûbari* was hit by one torpedo on the starboard side abreast the No 1 boiler room. The two forward boiler rooms immediately flooded, causing the loss of six out of eight boilers. The old cruiser stopped and started to list to starboard. At 10.11, an oil fuel fire broke out, caused by the ruptured fuel tanks, and only four minutes later the flooding reached the engine room. Unable to sail under her own power, the destroyer *Samidare* took *Yûbari* in tow at 16.50 at a speed of 3kts, heading for Palau. However, at 04.15 the next day, the upper deck went awash and the cruiser lay dead in the water. Since nothing could be done at that moment to save the cruiser, the order to abandon ship was given at 05.41. The crew was taken off by the destroyer *Yûzuki*, fewer than nineteen men being killed. *Yûbari* finally disappeared below the waves at 10.15, 28 April 1944, in the position 05-28N 131-45E. She was stricken from the Navy List (*Kanseki*) on 10 June 1944, marking the end of an extraordinary vessel.

Conclusions

Yûbari clearly proved that Hiraga's innovative construction technique was sound and could be used for the planned large cruisers. In fact, it had already been incorporated into the design of the *Furutaka* class, the first heavy cruisers built in Japan. These two and the sixteen that eventually followed all combined high speed, heavy armament and adequate protection on displacements that astonished Western nations, even if one keeps in mind that they were also overweight, because of over optimistic weight calculations. They featured most of the ideas tried in *Yûbari*, such as integrated armour, swan-neck bows, large towerlike bridges, new crew arrangements, enclosed gunhouses and trunked funnels. Only the unorthodox Japanese wavy deck line had not been tried in *Yûbari*, although she had considerable flare forward.

Many of the ideas tried for the first time in *Yûbari*, found their way to battleships, cruisers, destroyers and other combatants. As such, *Yûbari* had a profound influence on the development of warship design in Japan, resulting in the appearance of fast and powerful looking warships. Therefore, *Yûbari* can be regarded to be one of the most influential Japanese warships of her time.

Principle sources

Anonymous. *Warships of the Imperial Japanese Navy, Volume 13: Light Cruisers Tenryu Class, Kuma Class, Yubari*. Kojinsha, Japan, 1997.

John Campbell. *Naval Weapons of World War Two*. Conway Maritime Press, London, 1985.

Paul S Dull. *A Battle History of the Imperial Japanese Navy* (1941-1945). Naval Institute Press, Annapolis, 1978.

Robert Gardiner (ed). *Conway's All the World's Fighting Ships 1922-1946*. Conway Maritime Press, London, 1987.

Hansgeorg Jentschura, Dieter Jung and Peter Mickel. *Warships of the Imperial Japanese Navy 1869-1945*. Arms and Armour Press, London, 1986.

E Lacroix. 'The Development of the "A Class" Cruisers in the Imperial Japanese Navy', *Warship International*, 1977-1984.

E Lacroix. 'The Imperial Japanese Navy', *The Belgian Shiplover*, 1959-1975.

Eric Lacroix and Linton Wells II. *Japanese Cruisers of the Pacific War*. Naval Institute Press, Annapolis, 1997.

Yukikazu Okada. 'Stories of the Old and New Combatants Named Yubari', *Ships of the World*, 1983.

J. Rohwer and G Hummelchen. *Chronology of the War at Sea 1939-1945*. Greenhill Books, London, 1992.

Anthony J Watts and Brian G Gordon. *The Imperial Japanese Navy*. Macdonald, London, 1971.

Notes

1 The Japanese Imperial Defence Policy (*Teikoku Kokubo Hoshin*) of 29 June 1918 stated that Russia should be regarded as Japan's most likely future opponent, followed immediately by the United States. This secret document was modified on 28 February 1923, when the United States replaced Russia as the most likely future enemy.

2 The 8-4 Fleet Completion Programme also authorised three battleships (*Mutsu* and two *Tosa* class), two battlecruisers (*Amagi* class), 28 destroyers (*Tanikaze*, nine *Minekaze* and eighteen *Momi* class), eighteen submarines (three *No 22*, six *No 25*, three *No 31* and six *No 34* class) and three oil supply ships (*Noma* and two *Shiretoko* class) which made, together with the nine light cruisers eventually ordered (*Yûbari*, five *Kuma* and three *Natori* class), a total of 63 warships.

3 The fiscal year (FY) in Japan was numbered according to the year of the current Emperor's era. The fiscal year of 1917 corresponded to the sixth year of *Taishô* and was therefore called FY 6. The Japanese fiscal year lasted from 1 April to 31 March the next year; thus, FY 6 started on 1 April 1917 and ended on 31 March 1918.

4 The American *Omaha* class cruisers displaced 7050-tons and had a length of 555ft 6in (169.32m). They carried an armament of twelve 6in/53 (152mm) guns, two 3in/50 (76mm) HA guns and ten 21in (533mm) torpedo tubes. They featured a 3in (76mm) belt and a 1.5in (38mm) deck and were capable of 34kts. The British *Hawkins* class displaced considerably more, 9750-ton s, and had a length of 605ft (184.40m). They had a 1.5-3in (40-75mm) belt and a 1-1.5in (25-40mm) deck and reached a maximum speed of 30kts. The armament consisted of seven 7.5in/45 (191mm) guns, six 3in/50 (76mm) guns, four 3in (76mm) HA guns and six 21in (533mm) torpedo tubes.

5 At Sasebo Naval Arsenal were built, among others, the light cruisers *Tone* and *Chikuma*, the *Tenryû* class light cruiser *Tatsuta*, the *Kuma* class light cruisers *Kuma* and *Kitakami* and the *Natori* class light cruisers *Nagara* and *Yura*. Construction of the *Jintsû* class light cruiser *Kako* was started, but this ship was cancelled in 1922. Because of their size none of the Japanese heavy cruisers were built at Sasebo. However, when new light cruisers were ordered to replace the ageing 5500-ton ships, Sasebo built three of the four *Agano* class cruisers.

6 Trial displacement was introduced in the early 1920s because it was closer to reality than the lighter normal displacement used until then. Trial displacement meant that the ship was ready for sea with ⅔ fuel, ammunition, stores, lubrication oil and RFW on board. Normal displacement meant that the ship was ready for sea with ¼ fuel, ¾ ammunition and ⅓-⅔ stores and lubrication oil on board, but without RFW. *Yûbari* was designed when normal displacement was still used, but was completed after trial displacement was introduced, clearly showing that normal displacement figures had been too optimistic to correspond to average conditions.

7 The changes to the AA armament are based on Japanese sources. However, most Western sources state that the close range armament consisted of four triple 25mm and four twin 13.2mm machineguns without the 4.7in/45 HA gun, to have taken place in 1943, probably during the mine damage repairs. It is possible, however unlikely, that this refit was carried out in 1943, followed in 1944 by a further upgrade of the AA armament, so urgently required for vessels operating in forward areas.

8 It is possible that, because of her small size, *Yûbari* carried the Modification 2 version of the No 22 radar instead of the fourth version. This radar was intended for coast defence ships (*Kaibôkan*) and submarine chasers (*Kusentei*) and had been designed between June and December 1942. However, it is more likely that the more recent Modification 4 was installed.

THE ORIGINS OF *DUNKERQUE* AND *STRASBOURG*

Dunkerque and *Strasbourg* were the first of the new generation of fast battleships built during the 1930s. **John Jordan** traces their development from the Washington Conference of 1921-22 until their completion shortly before the Second World War.

The *Marine Nationale* ended the First World War with seven modern battleships of the *Courbet* and *Bretagne* classes, and a larger number of elderly pre-dreadnoughts of dubious military value. In addition to the seven modern ships there were five uncompleted battleships of the *Normandie* class, designed and laid down pre-war; four of the latter had been launched during 1914-16 while the fifth, *Béarn*, was still on the slipway. With the outbreak of war and the introduction of large-scale conscription, work on these ships had been abandoned. Some of their machinery was utilised in other ships, and their main and secondary artillery was placed at the disposal of the army and distributed among the various fronts.

Following the Armistice, serious consideration was given as to whether the *Normandie* class should be completed. Arguments in favour included the major investment already made in the hulls, the shortage of modern battleships (the Naval Statute of 1912 had envisaged no fewer than twenty-eight by 1920), and the impossibility of building new ships comparable in size and power to the latest foreign construction due to infrastructure constraints.

There were, however, significant arguments against their completion. The *Normandie* class had been designed prior to the First World War. Horizontal and underwater protection was therefore totally inadequate by post-Jutland standards, and these defects would be virtually impossible to remedy given that the hulls of the ships were essentially complete. They were 21kt coal-burners, and their hybrid mix of reciprocating engines and direct-action turbines was obsolescent even at its time of conception. Other retrograde features included the absence of director fire control, which was well-established in the British Royal Navy prior to 1914, and the low angle of elevation of the 340mm guns, which effectively precluded engagements at the longer ranges then envisaged.

The studies conducted post-war concluded that these ships would be expensive to modify and to complete, and that even if this course of action was followed, they would remain inferior to contemporary foreign construction. The programme was therefore abandoned and the hulls broken up, save that of the fifth ship, *Béarn*, which was to be completed as an aircraft carrier.

The Washington Conference

In late 1921 France was invited, together with the other major naval powers, to attend a conference on naval arms limitation in Washington. Whilst there can be no doubting the very genuine concerns of the United States and Britain regarding the potential threat posed by current naval construction programmes to world peace, each of the major powers approached the conference with its own national agenda. The British were anxious to preserve their status as the world's premier naval power, and to prevent a naval arms race which would be beyond their financial capabilities. The Americans were equally concerned by the potential cost of the new naval programmes, and were also anxious to secure agreed constraints on the naval ambitions of the Japanese, which threatened their political and economic interests in the Pacific. The Japanese would fight for everything they could get, including recognition by Britain and the USA that Japan was now a major world power with legitimate maritime interests.

The arms race which developed during the immediate post-war period was characterised not only by the large number of capital ships planned or under construction by the three major naval powers, but by the rapidly escalating size and power of these warships. The British and the Americans quickly grasped that the only equitable way out of this situation was to freeze new construction, to place an overall ceiling on the total displacement allocation allowed to each of the participating countries based on current strengths, and to prescribe limits on the size and power of future capital ships.

The base coinage for overall tonnage allocation was a

Table 1: *THE FRENCH BATTLEFLEET IN 1921*

Name	Built	Displacement	Main armament	Fate
Condorcet	1907-11	18,500 tons	2 x 2 305mm	stricken 1931
Voltaire			6 x 2 240mm	stricken 1936
Diderot				stricken 1935
Courbet	1910-14	22,500 tons	6 x 2 305mm	extant 1939
France				foundered 1922
Jean Bart				T.S. 1935
Paris				extant 1939
Bretagne	1912-16	23,500 tons	5 x 2 340mm	extant 1939
Lorraine				extant 1939
Provence				extant 1939

Table 2: *THE ITALIAN BATTLEFLEET IN 1921*

Name	Built	Displacement	Main armament	Fate
Regina Elena	1904-11	13,500 tons	2 x 1 305mm	stricken 1923
Vittorio Emanuele			6 x 2 203mm	stricken 1923
Napoli				stricken 1926
Roma				stricken 1927
Dante Alighieri	1909-13	19,500 tons	4 x 3 305mm	stricken 1928
Giulio Cesare	1910-15	23,000 tons	3 x 3, 2 x 2 305mm	rebuilt 1933-37
Leonardo da Vinci				stricken 1923
Conte di Cavour				rebuilt 1933-37
Andrea Doria	1912-16	23,000 tons	3 x 3, 2 x 2 305mm	rebuilt 1937-40
Caio Duilio				rebuilt 1937-40

capital ship of 35,000 tons maximum, which corresponded to the displacement of the latest US battleships of the *Tennessee* and *Maryland* classes. Taking into account the existing size of the respective fleets, the British and the Americans were to be allowed 525,000 tons of capital ships (equivalent to fifteen battleships of the new standard), the Japanese 315,000 tons (equivalent to nine battleships), and the French and the Italians each 175,000 tons (five battleships).

Whilst the other four participants were able to accept these governing principles, the French delegation, which was headed by the Minister for the Colonies, Albert Sarraut, was profoundly unhappy with the outcome, and felt marginalised by the unwillingness of the other participants to respond to its concerns. By contrast, as a newly-emerging naval power Italy had grounds for satisfaction, being granted parity with her Mediterranean rival. Attempts to apply the 5:3:1.75 ratio to other categories of warship met with considerable resistance from the French delegation, anxious to reserve the right to compensate for its meagre allocation of capital ship tonnage by the construction of large numbers of submarines and flotilla craft. France's claims for a significantly larger tonnage allocation were based on the following arguments:

- the strength of the *Marine Nationale* of 1921 was artificially low because of the nature of the conflict which had just ended, and its calamitous effects on French naval construction;
- the French empire was second in size and scale only to that of Britain, and the protection of French overseas interests ranging from the Atlantic to the Pacific required a fleet structure comparable to that of the other major world naval powers; Italy, on the other hand, was a newly-established national entity with no colonial responsibilities;
- besides maintaining a substantial presence overseas, the Marine Nationale had to be divided between the Atlantic and the Mediterranean (France continued to regard Germany as a potentially hostile power, but could not disregard Italian political ambitions with regard to North Africa).

The Washington Treaty was duly signed on 6 January 1922. A number of special clauses had to be included to satisfy the participating delegations that the constraints on new construction were being applied fairly. The British were permitted to build two new battleships of 35,000 tons to compensate for the cancellation of the much larger G3s; the Americans and the Japanese were permitted to complete two and one respectively of the 16in gun battleships currently building; and the French and the Italians were authorised to begin the construction of two new capital ships of 35,000 tons in 1927 and 1929 respectively. The rationale for the latter clause was that whereas the three major powers all had 16in gun battleships authorised or building in late 1921, some of which they would be permitted to complete, the latest French and Italian battleships (the French *Lorraine* and the Italian *Andrea Doria*) had been completed in 1916. Neither type was in any way comparable with the latest ships building for Britain, the USA, or Japan. So while the ten-year 'battleship holiday' agreed at the Conference would run from 1921 until 1931 for the major naval powers, for France and Italy it would effectively be 'back-dated' to 1916, a compromise which weakened the common stance prohibiting new construction, and which was to have some interesting consequences explored in this article.

The results of the Washington Conference were not well received by the French Parliament, the *Chambre des Députés*, and the Treaty was ratified only in July 1923 following fierce and acrimonious debate. In the event economic circumstances did not permit the *Marine Nationale* to build up to the limits with which it had expressed so much dissatisfaction. France was not alone in this, but the irony has not been lost on historians; the limitations proposed at the Washington Conference were readily agreed because none of the governments concerned could finance the new generation of 45/50,000-ton capital ships dreamed up by the naval staffs and their constructors, and even the 8in gun 10,000-ton cruiser which temporarily filled the gap in battleship construction, following its invention by the participants, proved ultimately to be unaffordable in the numbers anticipated.

French battleship projects 1926-31

In 1926, the French began studies for the new battleships they would be permitted to lay down from 1927. It was recognised that a completely new design would be required, incorporating a modern geared-turbine propulsion system, improved horizontal and underwater protection, and an effective modern fire control system which would make it possible to engage other ships at long range.

In theory the French were permitted to build two ships of 35,000 tons armed with 16in (406mm) guns, but there are no indications that this option was even considered at this time. In part this was because the French simply could not have built or maintained ships of this size without a considerable investment in infrastructure; the existing slipways, fitting-out basins and docking facilities at the naval dockyards would have required major modifications to accommodate the hulls. However, it is equally clear that the naval staff wished to use their 70,000-ton allocation in a more imaginative way. French naval thinking of the period was shifting away from the traditional concept of relatively slow, heavily-armed and well-protected ships fighting in a battle line towards a fleet of fast, lightly-armoured, hard-hitting vessels capable of 'hit-and-run' raids. The Western Mediterranean was seen as ideally suited to such operations and the Italian Navy, to judge from its latest building programmes, appeared to have reached similar conclusions.

The *Marine Nationale* was particularly concerned at the threat to the sea lines of communication with the North African colonies posed by the new Italian 10,000-ton cruisers of the *Trento* class, which had been laid down in 1925 and had a designed speed of 35kts. Thus in 1926 Admiral Salaün, Chief of the French Naval Staff (CEMG), requested the study of a *croiseur de combat* ('battle cruiser') of 17,500 tons capable of hunting down and overpowering fast 10,000-ton cruisers. Specifications included eight 305mm/55 guns, a speed of 35kts, and protection sufficient to resist shells of 203mm (8in) calibre. The main armament was to be capable of engaging targets out to a maximum range of 43,000m, and was to be disposed in two quadruple turrets forward ('*en chasse*') in part to assist pursuit but also to reduce the length of the armoured citadel (an extension of the latest British theories). Besides being able to hunt down Treaty cruisers, it was envisaged that the new ships would be able to attack merchant shipping defended by slow battleships, and could act as a scouting force for a combined Allied fleet.

The choice of 17,500 tons is significant in that for every battleship of 35,000 tons France was permitted under the Washington Treaty two of these smaller units could be built. Thus the 70,000 tons allocated for the first *tranche* of new construction would permit a class of four *croiseurs de combat*. This would still leave 105,000 tons of France's capital ship allocation for the construction of either three battleships of 35,000 tons or, more probable in view of the infrastructure issue, four ships of 26,250 tons.

The STCN studies for these ships remained on the drawing board. Neither Italy nor France laid down a new battleship in 1927 or 1928, and in December 1928 publication of the details of the new German *panzerschiff Deutschland* effectively rendered the earlier French studies obsolete. It had previously been considered unthinkable that the Germans, who were working under the even more stringent constraints of the Treaty of Versailles, could design a ship with the displacement of a cruiser and the armament of a battleship. Although the projected *croiseur de combat* would have the speed and the hitting power to hunt down such a ship, its protection would be totally inadequate against 28cm (11in) shell.

This led the *Marine Nationale* to reassess the mathematics of its situation, the *Conseil Supérieur* having stipulated in December 1927 that the displacement of any new ship must be a precise fraction of 175,000 tons. During 1928 the new CEMG, Admiral Violette, ordered the study of a battleship of 29,600 tons with a speed of 27kts (six ships). Studies of a battleship of 35,000 tons (five ships) were also undertaken, but in March 1929 the *Service Technique des Constructions Navales* (STCN) reported that whilst a ship of 215m length with a speed of 25kts was technically feasible, infrastructure remained a problem. The latter conclusion led the *Conseil Supérieur* to advise the French Government to back a

British proposal to reduce the maximum displacement permitted for new construction at the forthcoming London Conference (the figure of 25,000 tons was touted prior to the Conference). In the interim no new battleship was ordered.

In the event, the British were unsuccessful in their attempts to secure a reduction from the 35,000-ton maximum displacement agreed at the Washington Conference, as the Americans were insistent that a ship of this size was necessary for long-range operations in the Pacific. However, it was agreed that the 'holiday' in new battleship construction would be extended for a further five years, until the end of 1936. France and Italy, which had not yet taken advantage of the special concessions agreed in 1922, would again be permitted to complete new ships up to a maximum displacement of 70,000 tons. This tonnage could be allocated to two ships of 35,000 tons, or a larger number of smaller ships (this latter concession being at the insistence of the French delegation).

The 17,500-ton *croiseur de combat* proposal was by now dead in the water, as it was generally recognised that a ship of this size could not be adequately protected. Even the pre-war British battlecruisers of the *Lion* class had a displacement of 26,000 tons (normal load), and their horizontal protection was considered to be totally inadequate by post-war standards. The CEMG therefore asked the STCN to prepare plans for three battleships of a maximum 25,000 tons displacement (the preferred figure was 23,333 tons standard, but there was little confidence that a ship with the required specifications could be designed to this limit). In June 1930, the *Conseil Supérieur* approved an STCN preliminary study of a fast *croiseur de bataille* of 25,000 tons, armed with eight 330mm guns in two quad turrets forward, with a dual-purpose secondary armament, and with protection capable of resisting 280mm (11in) shell at normal battle ranges. Horizontal protection would be sufficient to resist 500kg (1000lb) bombs dropped from 3,000m (10,000ft), and there would be a deep underwater protection system capable of resisting an explosive charge of 300kg (660lb). In October of the same year the CEMG ordered the preparation of a first *project de loi* for a battlecruiser to replace the battleship *France*, which had foundered in 1922, for approval by the Navy Minister, Jean-Luc Dumesnil.

The latter, concerned that France should have the best ships permitted by the Treaty, was initially unconvinced by the proposal. In a note of December 1930 the CEMG, Admiral Violette, was asked to justify the Navy's preference for a ship of 23,333 tons, and was requested to provide detailed costings for the construction of two ships of 35,000 tons. In his reply the CEMG stated that France did not currently have the facilities to build the 35,000-ton ship, studies of which suggested a length of up to 245m for a ship with a speed approaching 30kts. Infrastructure costs alone would total 130 million francs. The only realistic alternative to two 35,000-ton ships was three of 23,333 tons, for which preliminary studies had been satisfactorily completed.

The proposal was re-submitted to the new Navy Minister, Albert Sarraut, in mid-December of the same year, and the latter agreed to propose the construction of the first of the new ships to Parliament. From January to March 1931, attempts were made to secure agreement with Italy on the construction of two battleships of 23,333 tons, but the Italians were unwilling to make this commitment. A project dating from 1928-29 for a small fast battleship of similar displacement with a speed of 29kts, a main armament of six 381mm (15in) guns, and protection on a par with the contemporary STCN studies had been considered but rejected. In the event the Italians would embark on a major reconstruction of their ageing dreadnoughts, and await developments.

For the *Marine Nationale*, time was more pressing. The first of the *Deutschland* class was due for launch in May 1931, and a sister would be laid down in June. The first of the new French battleships was therefore included in the Naval Programme to be debated in June and July, and a heated debate ensued over the 23,333-ton proposed displacement, in which the Minister conspicuously failed to satisfy critics of the project. When it was finally approved on 10 July it was on condition that further studies be undertaken, and submitted to the National Assembly for further approval.

The STCN now undertook a detailed study of the characteristics of the new ships, taking into account the latest Naval Staff directive which stipulated that 26,000 tons was the minimum displacement to ensure adequate protection, and made a number of changes to the initial proposal (see table). The new design was only slightly longer, but beam was increased by fully 3.5m to provide the necessary stability to accommodate a heavier armament (330mm versus 305mm main armament, plus an additional pair of twin 130mm DP guns) and a major upgrading of the horizontal protection. The increase in

Table 3: *STUDIES FOR DUNKERQUE 1930-32*

	December 1930	Final design (April 1932)
Displacement:	23,333 tons standard	26,500 tons standard
Length:	213m	215m
Beam:	27.5m	31.08m
Speed:	30kts	29.5kts
Armament:	2 x IV 305mm/55	2 x IV 330mm/52
	3 x IV 130mm/45	3 x IV, 2 x II 130mm/45
Protection:	230-215mm belt	250mm belt
	130-100mm deck	140-130mm + 45mm decks

Dunkerque *as completed in early 1938, with her original funnel cap. It would be modified in March/May of the same year to prevent the funnel gases fouling the forward range-finders atop the tower.* Dunkerque *entered service on 1 September 1938, becoming the flagship of the* Escadre de l'Atlantique *(Vice-Adm Gensoul).* (Marius Bar)

beam also provided the necessary depth for an effective system of underwater protection. The cost of these improvements was an increase in the displacement to 26,500 tons standard.

This left the *Marine Nationale* on the horns of a dilemma. If two ships each of 26,500 tons were built, this would leave only 17,000 tons of the 1931-36 Treaty allocation for new capital ships unaccounted for. A third ship of 26,500 tons would bring France 9500 tons over the Treaty limits – unthinkable in political terms – while 17,000 tons had already been deemed inadequate for an effective vessel. The end result was that the new ships had been 'designed down' to an artificial limit to little purpose. Moreover, even before the world's 'battleship holiday' finally ended in 1936, France would have to confront the infrastructure issue. In June 1934, Italy announced that it would begin construction of two battleships of 35,000 tons, and there was never any question that this would have to be met by an equivalent French response.

The first of the new ships, to be named *Dunkerque*, was finally approved in March 1932 and laid down on 26 October of the same year. The type was now officially designated *bâtiment de ligne* ('battleship'). A sister-ship was to be included in the 1934 Programme. The latter decision would subsequently be thrown into question by the announcement of the two new Italian battleships. However, the delays in beginning the construction of 35,000-ton battleships for the *Marine Nationale*, which would require new plans and heavier artillery, were estimated at 15-18 months. It was therefore decided to proceed with the construction of the second ship, *Strasbourg*, and to incorporate whatever enhancements to her protection might be feasible within the overall constraints of the design. After all, these ships would still be an effective counter to the German *panzerschiffe*, of which a further two had been laid down in 1931-32.

General Configuration

In her general configuration and layout, *Dunkerque* was essentially a scaled-down version of the battlecruiser designs projected for the Royal Navy in the wake of the First World War, with the main armament all forward, the secondary armament aft, and a prominent tower structure housing the control spaces and carrying the giant rangefinders for an elaborate director fire control system. The major difference was that whereas the British designs generally featured three triple turrets, of which two were positioned forward and one abaft the tower, the French opted for two quadruple turrets, which eliminated the mounting abaft the tower, thereby reducing the length of the armoured citadel. A further effect was to enable the boiler rooms to be placed more centrally, at the point of maximum beam, which enhanced underwater protection arrangements and gave the ships a more 'balanced' appearance, with a single broad funnel midway between the tower structure and a heavy pole mainmast, around which the after rangefinders were seated, and a quarterdeck available for aircraft operation.

Quadruple turrets had been considered first for the

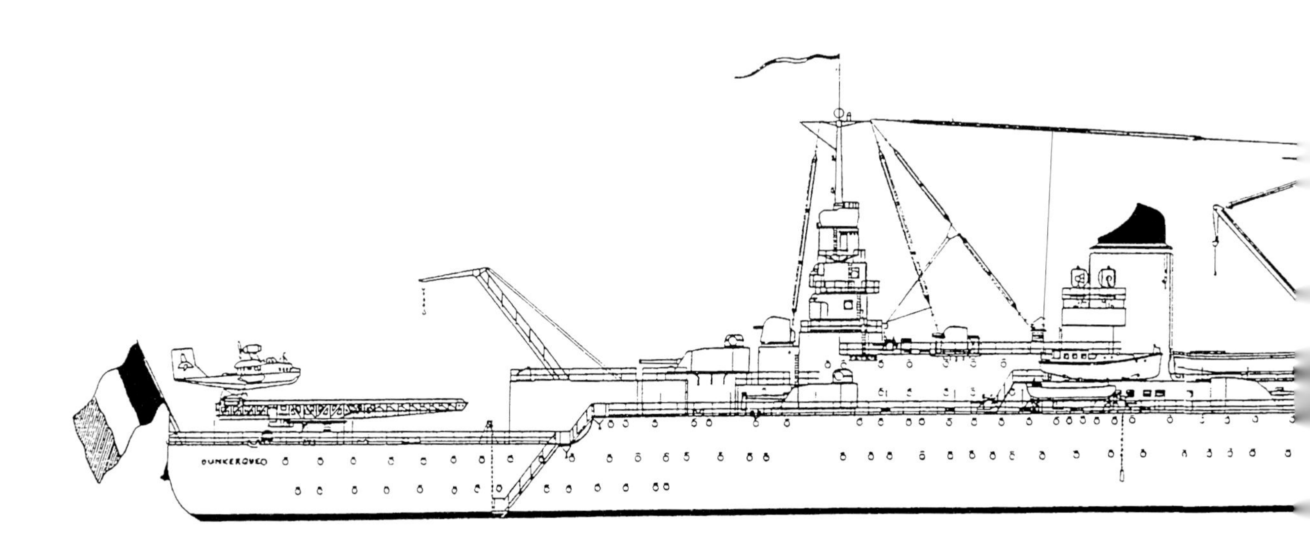

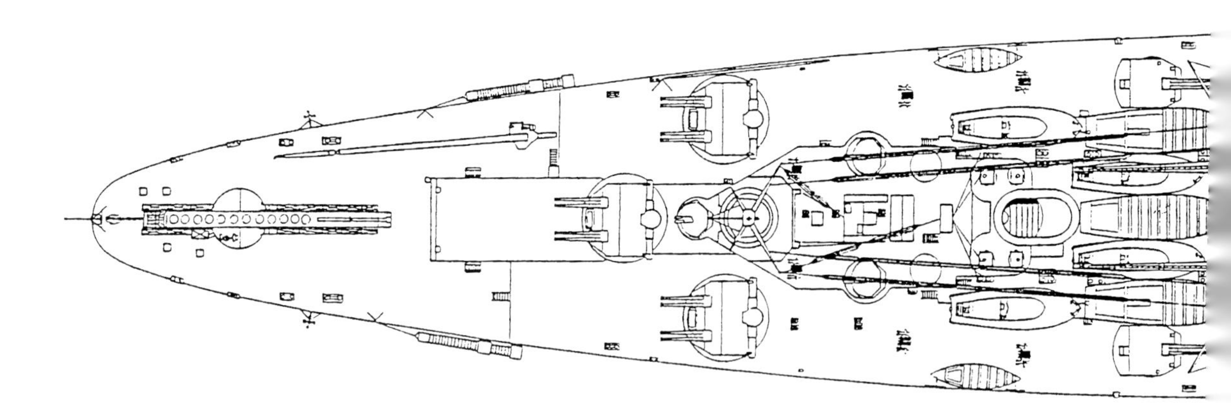

Dunkerque 1939: *profile and plan views.*
The profile and plan view are based on official plans dated Brest 1 March 1939. They show Dunkerque *with her designed tertiary anti-aircraft armament of ten 37mm Model 1935 and thirty two 13mm Hotchkiss MG. The enclosed fully-automatic twin 37mm mountings are disposed at forecastle deck level abeam 'B' turret, and atop the after superstructure. Development of this weapon had to be abandonned, and the less advanced Model 1933 was eventually fiited in its place. Six of the quad Hotchkiss MG are mounted on the upper deck abeam the tower and the single funnel (see plan view), with the other two atop the after superstructure. The modified funnel cap is in evidence, as is the double-storey hangar for the Loire 130 reconnaissance aircraft.* (Drawn by the author)

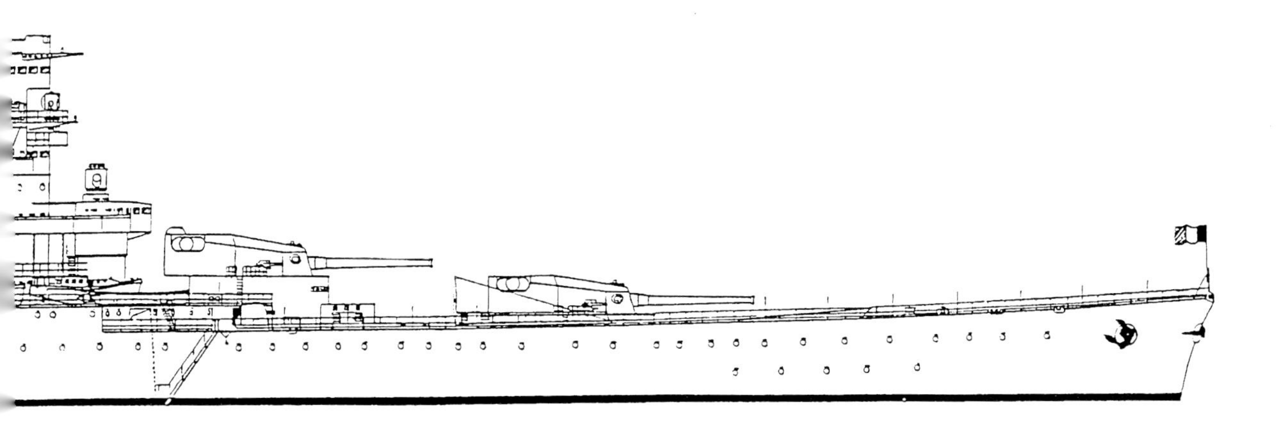

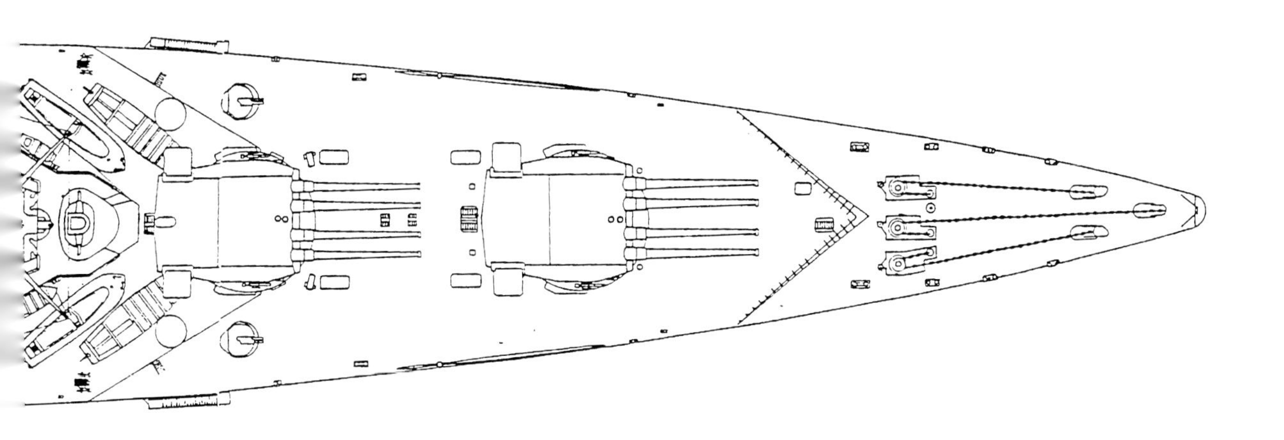

Table 4: CHARACTERISTICS OF ARTILLERY

	330mm/52 Model 1931	130mm/45 Model 1932 (quad mounting)
Gun Data		
weight of gun	68.5 tonnes	3.7 tonnes
muzzle velocity	850m/s	800m/s (OPf) 840m/s (OEA)
max. range	41,500m	20,800m
weight of projectile	570kg (OPf)	32.5kg (OPf) 29.5kg (OEA)
projectiles	OPf Mod.?	OPf Mod.? OEA Mod.1934 /34-5
Mounting Data		
weight of turret	1,497 tonnes	200 tonnes
protection	(see separate table)	(see separate table)
elevation of guns	-5°/+35°	-10°/+75°
max. elevating speed	6°/s	8°/s
max. training speed	5°/s	12°/s
firing cycle	2rpm per gun	10rpm per gun

uncompleted super-dreadnoughts of the *Normandie* class, and for their successors, the *Lyon* class, which were never laid down. The quadruple turret was adopted primarily to save weight, studies for the *Normandie* having shown that her three quadruple turrets and their associated armour weighed marginally less than the five twin turrets of the *Bretagne* class, and enabled two additional 340mm guns to be carried. Concerns expressed included the vulnerability of the turrets to being disabled by mechanical breakdown or a single unlucky hit, eventualities which were more acceptable in a ship with a larger number of twin turrets. However, the restrictions on displacement imposed by the Washington Treaty made multi-gun turrets inevitable, and the French were anxious to save as much weight as possible in the *Dunkerque* design in order to secure the high speed required.

In order to minimise the risk of both quadruple turrets being disabled by a single shell or torpedo they were well spaced, being separated by a distance of 28.5m (in the latest British battleships of the *Rodney* class, which mounted three triple turrets, the distance between the respective centres of 'A' and 'B' barbettes was only 19.5m, whilst that between 'B' and 'C' barbettes was 23m). The guns were paired and the turret partitioned by a 40mm bulkhead which extended down into the working chamber at a reduced thickness (25mm), so that damage from shellfire could be isolated to one-half of the turret. This arrangement was replicated in the quadruple 130mm turrets of the secondary armament.

Armament and Fire Control

The construction of the 330mm/52 Model 1931 gun, which was a new calibre for the *Marine Nationale*, was a mixture of modern and traditional methods. It fired a 570kg shell with an initial velocity of 850m/s, and was fitted with a traditional Welin screw breech block, hydro-pneumatically powered and balanced by counterweights, which opened upwards as the gun ran out after firing.

The quadruple turret was designed by Saint Chamond. Although each gun was in a separate cradle the relative movement of the guns in each pair was limited. The maximum angle of elevation was 35°, at which the 330mm Model 1931 had a theoretical range of 41,500m. The magazines and shell rooms for each pair of guns were on the same deck on opposite sides of the barbette and there were two levels, the upper level serving the port-side guns and the lower level the starboard pair. A total of 456 AP and HE shells (228 on each level) were provided for 'A' turret, and 440 shells (220 per level) for 'B' turret. The propellant charges were in quarters. Ammunition was fed by a shell and cartridge ring to a dredger hoist, one for each pair, and transferred in the working chamber to the gun loading cages of the upper hoists, of which there was one for each gun. The cages had three compartments, the lower for the shell and the upper two for two quarter-charges each. An electric chain rammer was carried on an extension from each cradle and loading was at any elevation, although in practice the guns were generally reloaded at 15° elevation to avoid the shell becoming jammed in the breech when the other guns were fired.

The secondary armament comprised sixteen 130mm/45 Model 1932 guns, the three quadruple turrets mounted aft being supplemented by two twin mountings amidships to cover the forward arcs. These were the first French dual-purpose mountings; they had a vertical-sliding breech and a maximum elevation of 75°. In anti-surface mode they fired a 32.5kg AP shell with an initial velocity of 800m/s to a maximum range of 20,800m; against aircraft they fired a 29.5kg time-fuzed HE shell with an initial velocity of 840m/s. The cartridges weighed 53kg, a figure close to the maximum for fixed ammunition in the Second World War. Magazine capac-

Strasbourg *at Toulon on 16 October 1940, shortly after her escape from Mers-el-Kebir. On 25 Sptember, under the reorganisation imposed by the Armistice, she became flagship of the* Forces de Haute-Mer, *flying the flag of Admiral de Laborde.* (Marius Bar)

ity was 2000 AP and 4150 HE rounds.

Like the quadruple turrets of the main armament, the quadruple 130mm mounting was developed by Saint Chamond. The guns were paired in cast steel cradles, and there was a 20mm steel bulkhead dividing the turret into two independent halves.

Each pair of guns was served by a double pusher hoist (one for anti-aircraft, the other for anti-surface rounds). The hoists for the centre-line quad turret rose vertically from its two-level magazine, whereas the hoists for the beam quads were broken at the upper armoured deck. The hoists came up by the outer cradle trunnions of each pair of guns. A ready-use platform with a capacity of 48 rounds (32 AA and 16 anti-surface) was fixed to the upper section of the hoist, the rounds being stowed vertically by hand. The rounds were then passed to loading trays by a combination of hydraulically-powered tilting and rotating trays and slide racks. Pneumatic rammers were employed to ram the cartridges home, following which the breech closed automatically.

The twin mounting resembled the quadruple half-mounting in layout, although the gun barrels were mounted farther apart. Whereas the quad mountings were fully armoured, the twins had only light 20mm plating. The mountings were 23m abaft their magazines, so that ammunition had to be transferred horizontally between the upper and lower armoured decks.

The *Dunkerque* was the first French battleship with a purpose-designed director control system for both the main and the secondary armament, the first such system having been tried in the battleship *Bretagne* in 1920. Arrangements were particularly elaborate. The five main directors, each fitted with a multiple OPL stereoscopic range-finder, were mounted one above the other atop the forward tower structure and at the base of the pole mainmast. For the main armament there was a triple 12-metre range-finder (replaced in 1940 by a 14-metre model) in the lower director of the forward tower, a double 8-metre R/F in the lower director of the after tower, and a double 12-metre R/F in each of the two main turrets. For the secondary armament there were 6-metre (middle) and 5-metre (upper) R/F on the forward tower, a 6-metre R/F on the after tower, and 6-metre R/F in each of the three quad turrets.

The location of the main directors atop towers favoured accurate target discrimination at long range without smoke interference, and their position was deemed to give them virtual immunity to direct hits and shell bursts. The advantages were clearly considered sufficient to outweigh the heavy cost in topweight; the main FC director, which was 30m above the waterline, weighed 40 tonnes, the lower of the two 130mm directors 25 tonnes and the upper director 20 tonnes. The directors were gas-tight, and were fitted with light steel plating to protect them from the machine guns of strafing aircraft.

The directors provided distance, bearing and angle of target to computer-equipped calculating positions located beneath the armoured decks, with continuous transmission to both the director and the guns. The main

Table 5: PROTECTION

	Dunkerque	Strasbourg
Vertical protection		
Main belt (11°50)	225mm	283mm
Forward bulkhead	180mm	210mm
After bulkhead	210mm	260mm
Horizontal protection		
Main deck (PBS)	115-125mm	115-125mm
Lower (PBI)	40mm	40mm
Steering gear/shafts	100-150mm	150mm
Conning tower		
Face and sides	270mm	(as *Dunkerque*)
Rear	220mm	
Roof	130-150mm	
Communications tube	160mm	
330mm turrets		
Barbette above PBS	310mm	340mm
Barbette below PBS	50mm	50mm
Turret face (30°)	330mm	360mm
Turret sides	250mm	250mm
Turret rear ('A')	345mm	352mm
Turret rear ('B')	335mm	342mm
Turret roof	150mm	160mm
130mm quad turrets		
Barbette	120mm	(as *Dunkerque*)
Turret face (58°30)	135mm	
Turret sides	90mm	
Turret rear	80mm	
Turret roof	90mm	

calculating position had facilities for firing at a target over the horizon with data supplied by another unit. Range clocks (carried until removed in 1940) enabled the ship to use target data supplied by another vessel in formation in the event of her own director control system being disabled.

In addition to the main gunnery directors a stereoscopic OPL 5-metre rangefinder was located atop the conning tower (in *Strasbourg* it was relocated atop the forward edge of the tower), and four stereoscopic SOM 3-metre R/F were mounted on the sides of the tower (two for night fire, two for navigation).

Dunkerque was the first French battleship to have remote power control (RPC) for training and for elevation. The turrets for the main and the secondary armament were powered by Léonard electric servo-motors with hydraulic drive. However, the Sautter-Harlé-Blondel RPC training gear proved unreliable; synchronisation between the turrets and the directors was poor, and manual intervention was needed for fine adjustment. Moreover, the training mechanisms had insufficient power to cope with turrets of this weight and size, resulting in slow tracking speeds and frequent breakdowns. Major problems were experienced on trials, and even following modification the system never worked properly.

For night firing there were seven 120cm searchlight projectors: three grouped around the tower structure (two only in *Strasbourg*), and a further four on a raised platform around the after base of the single funnel. All were fitted with RPC, and could be directed either from the 130mm fire control system or from four positions on the tower.

For close-in air defence, *Dunkerque* was originally to have had five of the automatic twin 37mm Model 1935 guns then under development, together with eight quadruple 13.2mm Hotchkiss Model 1929 machine gun mountings; major delays were experienced in the development and production of both these items of equipment. *Dunkerque* was fitted on completion with eight single 37mm guns Model 1925 as a temporary measure, replaced in early 1939 by the twin 37mm Model 1933, the advanced Model 1935 having been abandoned. The 37mm guns were disposed in two groups fore and aft for control purposes, four 1-metre rangefinders being provided. The 37mm magazines housed 3500 rounds plus 1200 tracer; as with the forward 130mm mountings, the forward 37mm guns were some way abaft their magazines, and the hoists were broken at the main deck, the

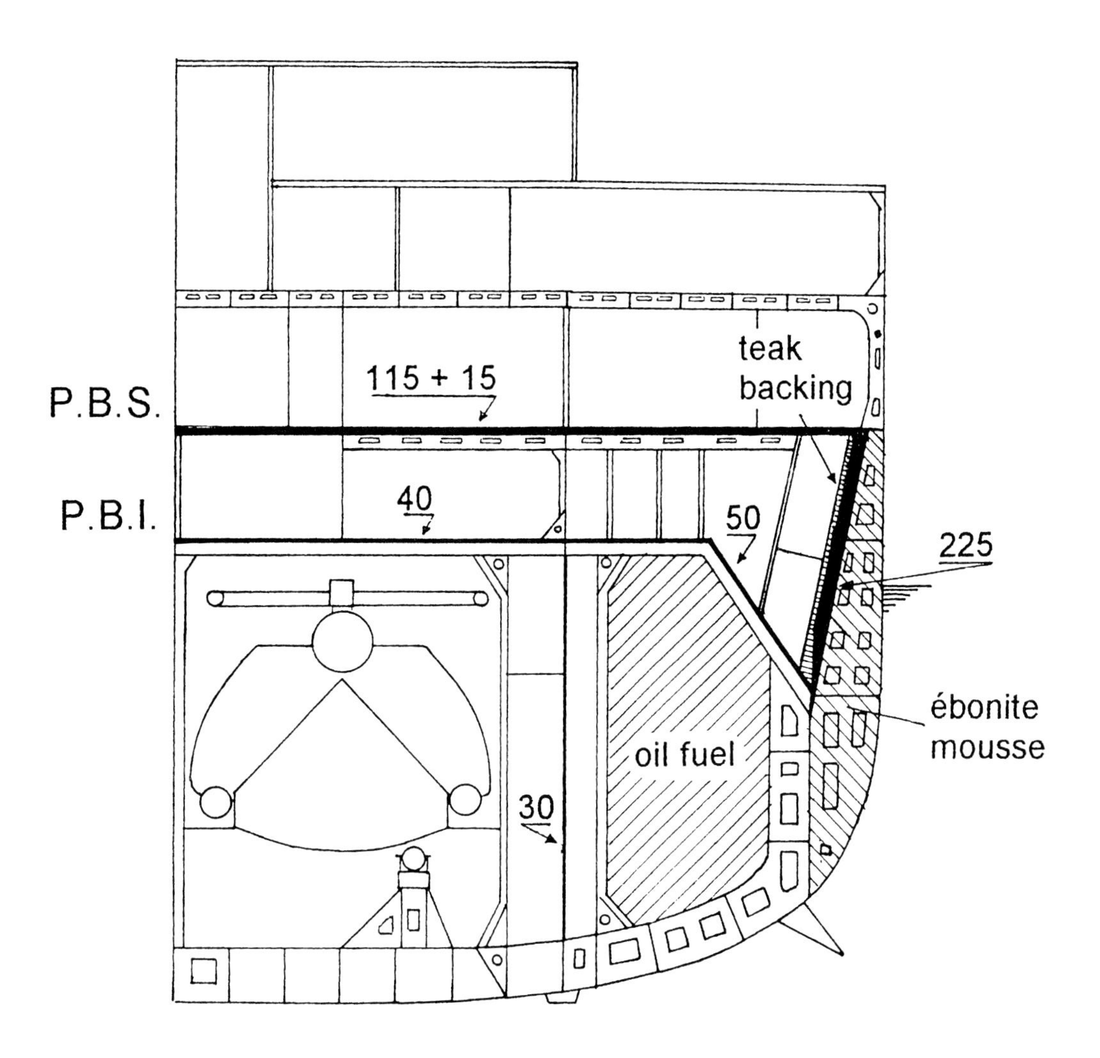

Protection system of Dunkerque. *The cutaway is of frame 85.70, abeam Boiler Room no.2. It shows clearly the internal belt angles inboard at 11°50, and the 40mm lower armoured deck (or 'splinter deck'), with its 50mm sloped sections outboard. The underwater protection system was based on an outer compartment filled with a rubber-excluding compound* (ébonite mousse)*, void compartments flanking a partially-filled oil fuel bunker, and an inner 30mm torpedo bulkhead.* (Drawn by the author)

ammunition cases being transferred horizontally. The 13.2mm MG were divided into three groups: after, amidships, and forward.

Protection

The system of protection adopted for the *Dunkerque* marked an acceptance of the 'all-or-nothing' principle introduced by the Americans in the *Nevada* class of 1912. This was all the more remarkable in that the French had persisted with attempts to protect the entire hull of their battleships with armour of medium thickness long after this practice began to be questioned in other major navies (the weight of bow armour in the *Paris* and *Bretagne* classes proved so detrimental to seakeeping that a 10-metre length had to be removed). Recognition that engagements between capital ships would now take place at much longer ranges than had been thought possible in 1912 led the French to accept that future battleships would have to be protected against plunging shell (together with the new threat of aerial bombs). The additional weight of horizontal armour could be compensated for only by the restriction of vertical armour to the ship's vitals (i.e. the area covering the magazines and propulsion machinery, together with the steering gear).

French concerns to save weight wherever possible resulted in the adoption of a system of protection remarkably similar to that of the British *Nelson* and *Rodney*, with an internal belt of 225mm thickness (283mm in *Strasbourg*) secured to a 60mm teak backing and inclined inwards at 11°50, extending downwards from the main armoured deck. It was closed at its fore and after ends by transverse bulkheads with a thickness of 180mm and 210mm respectively (in *Strasbourg* these were increased to 210mm and 260mm).

The inclined belt had the advantage of increased resistance to shell for a given thickness of armour.

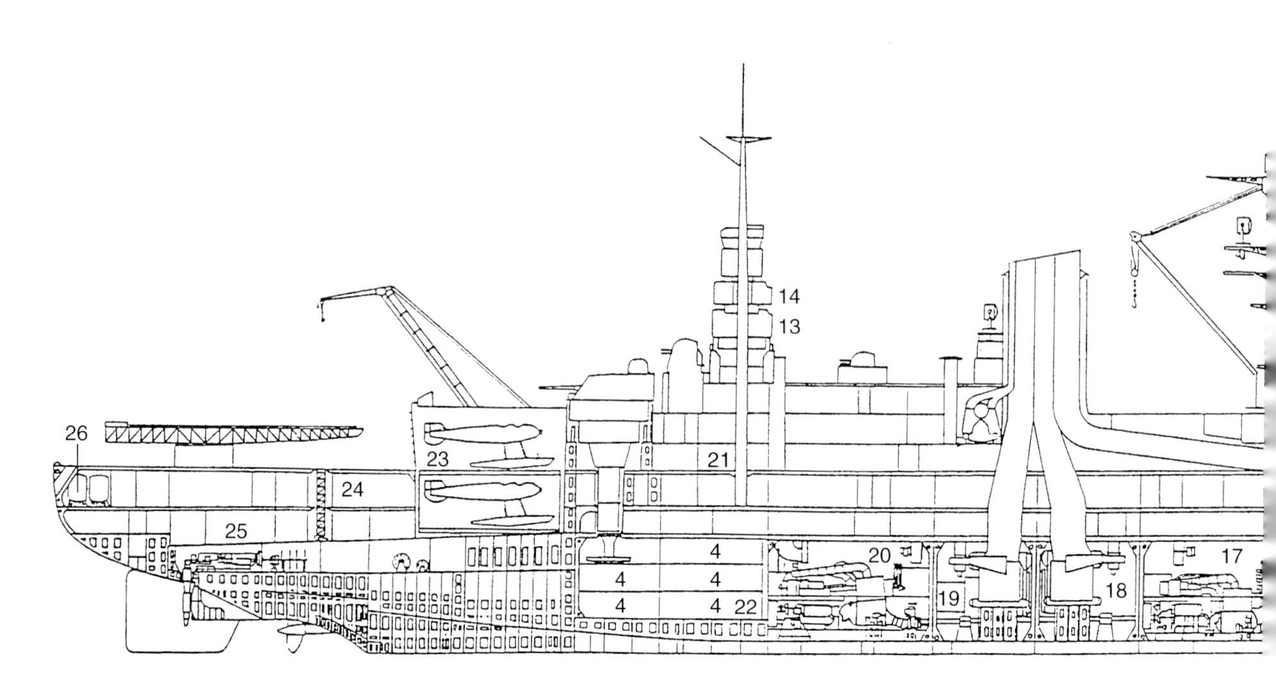

Dunkerque: *Inboard Profile.* *The inboard profile shows clearly the 'unit' machinery layout, with the forward engine room (wing shafts) between the forward and midships boiler rooms, and the after engine room (centre shafts) abaft Boiler Room no.3. Note the long, unprotected trunking between the forward boiler room and the single funnel, and the double-storey hangar with its 'box-lift' arrangement. Seating the fire control directors around the masts resulted in unforeseen problems in action, torpedo hits causing a whiplash effect which unseated the directors from their bearings.*

However, there were concerns that a steeply diving shell might pass beneath the armour belt and attack the ship's vitals. The inclined belts fitted in the *Dunkerque* and her successors of the *Richelieu* class were therefore extended farther beneath the waterline than in their British counterparts, albeit at a reduced thickness (*Dunkerque*'s main belt was 5.75m high as compared with 4m for the British *Nelson*'s). A further departure from contemporary British practice was the inclusion of a 'splinter deck' based on the American model beneath the main armoured deck, covering the ship's vitals. This was designed to resist splinters from shells striking the armoured deck above. The British preferred to maximise the thickness of the main armoured deck, which was 6 ¼ inches (161mm) in the *Nelson* class as compared with 115mm (125mm over the 330mm magazines) in the *Dunkerque*. The splinter deck, or 'lower armoured deck' (PBI) in French parlance, was of 40mm thickness on the flat, and was angled down on both sides to meet the bottom edge of the inclined armoured belt, the thickness on the slope being 50mm.

The protection of the armoured conning tower, the quadruple turrets of the main and secondary armament and their respective barbettes was a match for any battleship built during the 1930s (see table).

The underwater protection system of *Dunkerque* was in line with the latest thinking, employing a combination of voids, light bulkheads and liquid loading to absorb the explosion of a torpedo warhead. The major innovation was the filling of the compartment outboard of the inclined armour belt, which had a maximum depth of 1.5m, with a rubber-based water-excluding compound (*ébonite mousse*) to absorb the initial impact and to prevent uncontrolled flooding of the side compartments, which in other systems threatened stability. Inboard of this compartment there was a void compartment 0.9m deep, followed by an oil fuel bunker 3.9m deep, followed by a void compartment 0.7m deep, backed by a 30mm torpedo bulkhead. The

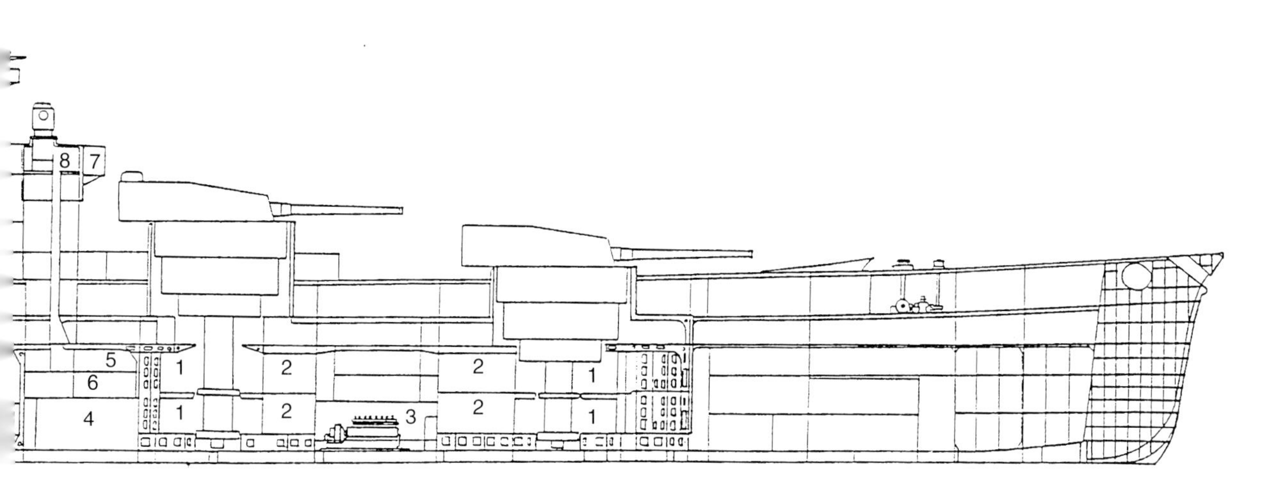

Key to Inboard Profile:
1. *330mm shell rooms*
2. *330mm magazines*
3. *diesel generators*
4. *130mm magazines*
5. *transmitting station*
6. *damage control centre*
7. *compass bridge*
8. *conning tower*
9. *emergency diesel room*
10. *W/T office (reception)*
11. *Admiral's bridge*
12. *combat bridge*
13. *chart room*
14. *main FC directors*
15. *secondary FC directors*
16. *no.1 boiler room*
17. *fwd engine room*
18. *no.2 boiler room*
19. *no.3 boiler room*
20. *aft engine room*
21. *W/T office (transmission)*
22. *37mm magazine*
23. *two-tier aircraft hangar*
24. *elevating turntable*
25. *steering gear compartment*
26. *aviation fuel tanks*

(Drawn by the author)

total depth of the underwater protection system from the outer skin to the inner face of the torpedo bulkhead was 7.66m, an impressive figure by any standards (most contemporary foreign systems had a depth of around 5m).

The underwater protection system covered the same area as the main armoured belt. Outside the armoured citadel the thickness of the torpedo bulkhead was increased to 40-50mm to compensate for the loss of absorbent protection. There was also a double bottom with a 30mm floor to protect the 330mm and 130mm magazines from the effect of mines exploding beneath the hull.

Hull protection in *Dunkerque* accounted for fully 27.2% of normal displacement (28.2% in *Strasbourg*), while the protection of the main and secondary armament accounted for a further 8.7% (9.1% in *Strasbourg*). The total of 36% was claimed to be higher than in any earlier battleship.

Propulsion

The propulsion machinery, in which the latest high-pressure boilers were combined with lightweight geared steam turbines, was remarkably compact for its power rating, and accounted for 7.2% of displacement, with oil fuel (¼ load) accounting for a further 9.3%.

Six Indret small-tube boilers with superheating were paired in three boiler rooms: the first was located directly beneath the tower, which necessitated substantial angled uptake trunking above the armoured deck; the other two boiler rooms were adjacent, directly beneath the funnel. Between the forward and after boiler rooms was the forward engine room, containing the turbine sets for the two wing shafts. The after engine room, with the turbines for the centre shafts, was directly abaft the after boiler rooms. The 'unit machinery' layout, effectively dividing the machinery into two independent systems, was in line with the latest cruiser practice, being consid-

Strasbourg on 23 May 1942. (Marius Bar)

ered essential for these lightly-armoured ships to enable them to continue operating following action damage. *Dunkerque* was the first battleship to incorporate this layout; all the most recent British and American battleships, including the post-war *Nelson* class, had their boilers grouped together, with the turbine machinery abaft the boiler rooms.

The Indret small-tube boilers operated at a pressure of 27kg/cm^2 (350°). Those for *Dunkerque* were built by Indret, while those for *Strasbourg* were manufactured under license by the shipbuilder, Penhoët. They were located side by side in each of the three boiler rooms: nos.11 and 12 were in the forward boiler room, nos.21 and 22 in the centre boiler room, and nos.31 and 32 in the after boiler room.

There were four independent sets of Parsons geared turbines, each driving a three-bladed propeller with a diameter of 4.2m (four-bladed 4.045m in *Strasbourg*). Each set comprised two HP (27kg/cm^2) turbines, one MP (8.5kg/cm^2) turbine, and LP forward and reverse turbines, which were linked in series with HP1 as a cruise turbine. The ships could steam 15.5kts on two shafts and 20kts on four, HP2 being engaged at between 0.34 and 0.5 maximum power. Designed horsepower was 107,000shp for 29.5kts, but *Dunkerque* attained 31.06kts with 135,585shp on trials.

The maximum fuel load for peace-time cruising was 4500-5000 tonnes, but this figure was reduced to 3700 tonnes in wartime in order to maximise the effectiveness of the underwater protection system (filling the liquid loading compartments to the brim meant that instead of the fuel oil absorbing the pressure of the explosion it created additional pressure on the internal bulkheads). The lower figure gave an estimated range of 2450nm at 28.5kts, 6300nm at 20kts, and 7850nm at 15kts.

To provide the ship with the necessary electrical power there were four turbo-generators each of 900kW distributed between the machinery rooms, and three diesel generators each of 400kW located low in the ship, for a total of 4800kW. This was a remarkable figure for the period (the British *Hood* had a total generating capacity of 1400kW, while the *Nelsons* had a capacity of 1800kW), and reflected the increasing demands on electrical power of modern battleships equipped with power-operated control systems. Two emergency diesel generators mounted high in the ship directly beneath the tower each could provide 100kW in an emergency.

Aviation facilities

A major advantage of the all-forward layout adopted for the main armament was that it freed the quarterdeck for the operation of aircraft. Aircraft were increasingly seen as important both for scouting in broad expanses on ocean (a particular advantage when searching for commerce raiders), and for spotting fall of shot at the longer ranges now anticipated for engagement. However, they were vulnerable to damage by the firing of the big guns, and the stowage of aviation fuel adjacent to their catapults presented a major fire hazard. Ideally they needed to be accommodated in a hangar when not in use to protect them from blast damage and from corrosion.

For ships with a conventional arrangement of the main

Table 6: DUNKERQUE CLASS

Name	Builder	Laid down	Launched	In service
1931 Programme				
Dunkerque	Arsenal de Brest	24 Dec 1932	2 Oct 1935	1 Sept 1938
1934 Programme				
Strasbourg	Penhoët	25 Nov 1934	12 Dec 1936	24 April 1939

Characteristics (as completed)

Displacement:	26,500(D)/27,300(S) tonnes standard 30,750(D)/31,570(S) tonnes normal 35,500(D)/36,380(S) tonnes full load
Length:	209m pp, 215.14(D)/215.50(S)m oa
Beam:	31.10m
Draught:	8.57(D)/8.73(S)m
Machinery:	Six Indret boilers, 27kg/cm^2 (350°); four-shaft Parsons geared steam turbines for 107,000shp; speed 29.5kts (designed)
Oil fuel:	3,700 tonnes; radius 7,850nm at 15kts, 2,450nm at 28kts
Armament:	Eight 330mm/52 Model 1931 in quadruple mountings (896 rounds); sixteen 130mm/45 Model 1932 in three quadruple and two twin mountings (1996 AP rounds + 4148 HE rounds); ten(D)/eight(S) 37mm/50 Model 1933 in twin mountings (8015 rounds); thirty-two 13.2mm/76 Model 1929 Hotchkiss MG in quad mountings Model 1931 (102,090 rounds)
Aircraft:	Three Loire 130 seaplanes
Protection:	belt: 225(D)/283(S)mm deck: 115mm + 40mm CT: 270mm-130mm main turrets: 345mm-150mm(D)/360mm-160mm(S) 130mm quad turrets: 135mm-80mm
Complement:	*Dunkerque* (as flagship): 81 officers + 1300 men *Strasbourg*: 32 officers + 1270 men

armament aircraft presented a problem. The British and the Germans opted for location of the hangar and catapult amidships for their 1930s battleships and cruisers, but many of the ships' commanders were unhappy with this arrangement, feeling that aircraft operation was ideally left to specialist vessels such as carriers (hence the British preference for deploying a single carrier in company with the battlefleet, in contrast to Japanese and American practice).

There can be little doubt that the aviation arrangements in *Dunkerque* and her battleship successors of the *Richelieu* class were superior in every respect. They comprised a trainable catapult 22m long, operating by compressed air and with a capacity of 3300kg. The two-tier hangar incorporated its own workshop, and was served by a system of deck rails and trolleys on which the aircraft were manoeuvred. A lift with a circular turntable set into the quarterdeck raised the aircraft to the level of the catapult, and to port of the hangar there was a crane with a capacity of 4.5 tonnes for lifting the aircraft aboard. The bomb magazine and the fuel tank, divided into three drums with a total capacity of 11,400 litres of aviation fuel, were located beneath the quarterdeck. The fuel tank was directly beneath the stern, and incorporated a number of safety features, including the replacement of used fuel by an inert gas, and refrigeration and sprinkler systems. The fuel could quickly be pumped over the side by remote control if threatened by a fire in or on the quarterdeck.

Conclusions

Given the innovative nature of their design, which broke completely with established French design practices, it is not surprising that there were delays in bringing *Dunkerque* and *Strasbourg* to full operational effectiveness, and some defects were to plague them throughout their all-too-brief careers.

North Atlantic operations during the winter of 1939-40 revealed that the long, unprotected bow had insufficient sheer and flare, and tended to bury itself in a seaway (similar problems were experienced by the German Navy with the *Scharnhorst* and *Gneisenau*, which were subsequently refitted with an 'Atlantic' bow). This meant that speed had to be substantially reduced in heavy weather conditions to prevent the forward quadruple turret being submerged. The lightly-constructed stern section also suffered from vibration, which frequently disabled one or other of the motors for the steering gear, powering a single counter-balanced rudder.

The propulsion system, on the other hand, proved reliable and economical. This is all the more remarkable given that this was the first French geared steam turbine plant installed in a battleship, and provides testimony to the experience gained with the 10,000-tonne cruisers built post-war. The reduction to only six boilers (HMS *Hood* had twenty-four, and *Nelson*, with less than half the installed horsepower, eight) was made possible by the high steam conditions adopted, and had considerable benefits for the layout of the machinery. However, the unit arrangement proved less effective than had been hoped at Mers-el-Kébir, due to the loss of electrical power throughout the ship and the spread of acrid smoke to the undamaged boiler rooms via the ventilation trunking.

Despite the experience of Mers-el-Kébir, during which two consecutive 15in shells fired by the British squadron penetrated the 225mm main belt of *Dunkerque* amidships, the system of protection was regarded as satisfactory for a ship of this size. It was designed, after all, to protect against German 28cm (11in) shell, and it was unsurprising that the main belt should have been penetrated by a shell more than twice as heavy.

The principal weakness of the protection system was that watertight integrity was threatened by the bulkhead seals around the tunnels for the electrical cabling, which tended to leak when damaged by underwater explosion. This led to extensive flooding of adjacent 'watertight' compartments both in *Dunkerque* and in *Richelieu*. The electrical cabling also proved to be a fire hazard, the insulating material producing the acrid fumes which were ultimately responsible for the evacuation of the boiler rooms in *Dunkerque* at Mers-el-Kébir.

The major weakness of these ships was undoubtedly their artillery, which like that of other contemporary French warships was over-complex in operation and liable to frequent break-downs. Despite modification the RPC never worked properly. The accuracy of the main armament was further reduced by a dispersion of 200-1000m experienced when firing salvoes. This was later found to be due to the effect of firing large shells simultaneously from the closely-paired barrels of the quad mountings, and the problem was eventually resolved in *Richelieu* by modifying the electrical firing circuits so that there was an interval of a fraction of a second between the firing of the paired guns. However, this solution would have to wait until 1948, when the pressures of wartime operations had subsided.

Interestingly, the partitioning of the turrets proved its worth at Mers-el-Kébir, where a 15in shell striking the starboard side of 'B' turret dislodged the armour plating and caused flash damage which effectively disabled the starboard pair of guns. The port-side pair remained intact, and the turret remained operational until all power was lost.

The dual-purpose secondary armament proved to be effective neither in the anti-surface rôle, for which it was too light-weight, nor in the anti-aircraft rôle, for which it was too cumbersome. Although the *Marine Nationale* would continue to follow the dual-purpose path with the triple 152mm mountings of the *Richelieu* class, the latter – although more effective in the anti-surface rôle – proved even less suited to anti-aircraft fire, and were supplemented by the purpose-designed 100mm AA twin mounting installed in the later 10,000-tonne cruisers.

Sources

Robert Dumas, *Les cuirassés Dunkerque & Strasbourg*, Marines (Bourg-en-Bresse 1993).

Official plans of *Dunkerque*, Centre d'Archives de l'Armement.

John Campbell, *Naval Weapons of World War Two*, Conway Maritime Press (London 1988).

Norman Friedman, *Battleship Design and Development 1905-1945*, Conway Maritime Press (London 1978).

DIRE STRAITS:

The Transit of the Lombok Strait, September 1964

When the newly independent Malaysia was threatened with destruction by its powerful neighbour Indonesia in 1964, it precipitated the limited military action known as Confrontation. As a guarantor of Malaysia's external defence, the United Kingdom sent powerful forces to the area, including the aircraft carrier HMS *Victorious*. When she was sent through the Lombok Strait, there were fears that Indonesia might have been provoked to mount an attack by air or by sea, using Soviet-supplied weapons. **Paul French** describes this exercise in sea control.

Introduction

The transit of HMS *Victorious* and her escorts through the Lombok Strait in 1964 is frequently cited as a classic 'Freedom of Navigation' exercise. But the circumstances that brought it about, and accounts of the actual event are usually vague. This is unfortunate on two counts. Firstly, little recognition is given to the operations of the RN during the Indonesian Confrontation, despite the fact that this was its longest and largest post-war operational deployment to date. Secondly, by virtue of its success the potential hazards and consequences of failure are forgotten.

Background

'Confrontation' was the title used to describe the guerrilla war between Indonesia and Malaya, supported by Britain and Commonwealth countries (particularly Australia and New Zealand). It was the result of Indonesian opposition to the creation of the Federation of Malaysia (the inclusion of Sarawak, Brunei and Sabah with Malaya). Its roots lay in Indonesia's outstanding territorial claims in Borneo and the perception that Malaysia was a 'neo-colonial' state designed to check Indonesian aspirations in the region. The revolt in Brunei in December 1962 gave President Sukarno the opportunity to intervene. Despite its failure, in mid-1963 Indonesia embarked upon a formal policy of 'confrontation', the objective being the break-up of Malaysia and persuading the British to leave the area. Despite the secession of Singapore in 1965, the Federation held and the Confrontation ensured an active British presence in the region for much longer than originally intended.

The key to the Confrontation was the maximum use of diplomacy backed by the minimum use of force. Political control on both sides was paramount, and it was as good an example of 'a continuation of politics by other means' as anyone is likely to find in the post-1945 period. The limited nature of the war in no way detracts from this; indeed, it can be argued that it accentuated the link and emphasised the fact that military activity could be responded to diplomatically and *vice versa*. Thus escalation could be either military or diplomatic, or a combination with no clear division between them.

In its early stages the Confrontation was largely contained in Sarawak, where the common border and jungle terrain made an ideal location for a guerrilla war. Most of the indigenous residents of the area (the Iban and Dayak tribes) were indifferent to the Indonesians and responded to the British 'hearts and minds' campaign. Following large-scale reinforcements throughout 1963 and 1964, Commonwealth forces established clear military superiority in the area. This led the Indonesians to change the emphasis to the mainland.

The climax occurred in August-September 1964, with a large seaborne landing at Pontian followed by a parachute raid at Labis. Despite the fact that these incursions were rapidly mopped up, there was great concern that they were precursors of serious escalation, and it was decided that further large-scale incidents would be met by punitive action against suitable Indonesian targets. However, before such operations could be seriously contemplated the military capability in and around Malaya needed to be upgraded. First, to improve the air defences and second, to ensure suitable capacity to respond decisively in the event of escalation occurring. It was taken for granted that the Indonesians would retaliate, although it was felt that their response would be commensurate with the sensitivity of targets attacked. At highest risk were the Embassy and other installations in Java, the airfields in East Malaysia (Borneo) and small warships acting as guardships or carrying out patrols. Consequently, the Commander in Chief Far East (CinCFE, Vice Admiral Sir Varyl Begg) made a formal request on 7 September for reinforcements, which resulted in the following units being placed at notice to move:

22nd Light Air Defence Regiment (BAOR)
A further infantry battalion
A Javelin squadron (it would take at least eleven days for

this unit to become operational)

A medium bomber squadron to be based at Gan

Three Canberra PRs and two Shackleton MRs from the UK

Three fast escorts and another ship with an air warning radar (these would take fourteen days to move from the Mediterranean). In the interim, greater use was to be made of the Sea Vixen aircraft embarked in HMS *Victorious* and HMS *Centaur*. CinCFE was directed to carry out 'unprovocative' reconnaissance and to draw up a list of suitable targets.

Diplomatic support was also sought from the United Nations (UN). The Foreign Office recommended that major reinforcements should not be despatched prior to the UN Security Council meeting on 8 September, as this might be considered provocative. However, by 10 September the reinforcements listed above were underway. Meanwhile discussions took place with the Australian and New Zealand governments over the use of their forces in offensive operations. The strong possibility that the Confrontation might escalate into 'limited war' was accepted. Some concern was expressed by the Foreign Office that Britain might find herself at war when the general public were barely aware of the existing conflict.

Decisions

Against this background, the transit of HMS *Victorious* and her escorts from Fremantle to Singapore had significant military and political overtones. On the trip south the Indonesians had been advised routinely of their passage through the Sunda Strait. Early indications that a crisis was beginning appeared when the Chargé d'Affaires in Djakarta was advised that more formal notice was required. This signalled the beginning of a effort by the Indonesians to substantiate their claims that the Sunda and Lombok Straits were entrances to an inland sea, i.e. Java Sea, and therefore territorial waters. Suffice to say the British did not recognise this claim, and neither for that matter did international maritime law. While it was agreed that the straits were undoubtedly within territorial waters it was maintained they were international waterways.

This was followed up on 3 September by complaints that an aircraft carrier had traversed the Sunda Strait without notice. These reports were without substance and were initially viewed as part of the Indonesian diplomatic offensive, as they were later played down, it was considered that they were the result of a genuine error. Subsequently the Indonesian Foreign Minister suggested that permission for the passage north would be refused and it was implied that any attempt would be opposed. This was confirmed by a communication stating that it would indeed be inconvenient for HMS *Victorious* to transit the Strait because naval exercises were being carried out in the area. If the inferred threat of force, combined with the refusal to grant permission for the use of the Sunda Strait, had compelled the *Victorious* to use an alternative route, in the context of the Confrontation it would be a clear political defeat. This was unacceptable, particularly in the light of the recent raids.

This was considered by the Chiefs of Staff Committee (COS), under Lord Mountbatten. After some discussion it recommended that *Victorious* should pass through the Sunda Strait, despite the reservations of CinCFE. This decision was later ratified at the Defence and Foreign Affairs Committee on 7 September, notwithstanding

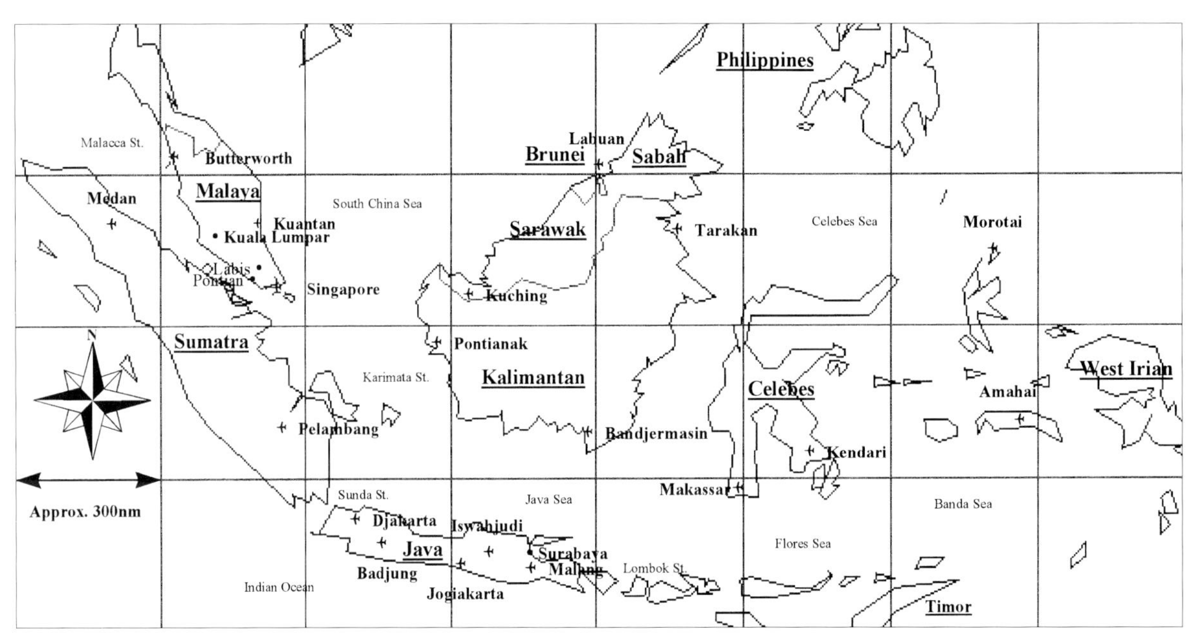

Indonesia-Malaya: Principal Airfields. Djakarta also represents Halim and Kemajoram, Singapore includes Changi, Tengah and Selatar. (Drawn by the author)

HMS Victorious *in July 1963*. (Wright & Logan)

misgivings regarding her safety expressed by the Foreign Secretary, R A Butler.

It was, however, considered prudent to delay two to three days to allow the escort to be augmented and to avoid 'provocative' actions while Indonesian aggression was being discussed at the UN. For this reason the additional escorts were directed through the Malacca Strait, and then round the NW tip of Sumatra to join the carrier in the Indian Ocean. In support, the smaller carrier HMS *Centaur* with suitable escort would be placed approximately 100 miles to the north of the Strait to keep a radar watch on the airfields around Djakarta. With regard to the Indonesian exercises, they were to be informed of RN exercises involving both carriers and were to be assured that any Indonesian vessels would be avoided.

This option was considered too provocative by the Government, which instead proposed that the destroyers *Caesar* and *Cavendish* make the transit supported by *Centaur* and *Victorious* from the north and south respectively. It was accepted unequivocally that any attack upon warships would be met by immediate retaliation. 'We must recognise that, if these [destroyers] were attacked, it would be an act of war and we should have to retaliate in force, not merely against the attacking forces but also against the bases from which they came, including the airfield at Djakarta'.

Forestalling the British notice of intent to use the Sunda Strait, on 10 September a telegram was received from Djakarta confirming the naval exercises in the vicinity of the Sunda Strait and requesting that *Victorious* use the Lombok Strait as an alternative. At their meeting later in the day the COS agreed that this was a reasonable alternative and recommended its adoption. COS considered that the use of the Lombok Strait did not involve conceding a point of principle and in addition provided a greater demonstration than that of two escorts. Furthermore, the long passage through the Java Sea allowed significant opportunities for intelligence-gathering. They were also in receipt of an intelligence report which observed that Indonesian forces were 'in a high state of alert' and concluded that 'in their present truculent state of mind the Indonesians had decided to refuse and resist passage of the Sunda Strait to HMS *Victorious*, and that they were prepared for any naval clash and retaliatory British and Malaysian air attacks, which, in Indonesian eyes, would have no conclusive military effect'.

How much influence upon the decision this report had is debatable, as it was considered rather gloomy. However, the intelligence view was later bolstered by a leak from the CIA via the Canadians, suggesting that the Indonesians intended attacking a naval force with the aim of provoking a counterattack, which they would exploit in negotiations with the UN.

At Sea

HMS *Victorious*, with Flag Officer Aircraft Carriers (FOAC), Rear Admiral H Janvrin onboard accompanied by HMS *Cavendish* and HMS *Caesar* sailed on the morn-

HMS *Hampshire in May 1963.* (Wright & Logan)

HMS *Cavendish in July 1956.* (Wright & Logan)

HMS Berwick *in November 1962.* (Wright & Logan)

ing of 8 September. *Victorious* was ordered to remain in the vicinity of Western Australia to work up her air group but the destroyers pressed on to join RFA *Tidespring* and took the opportunity to carry out close-range surface and anti-aircraft (AA) exercises. During the afternoon of 10 September Wessex HAS.1 helicopters of 814 Squadron co-operated in anti-submarine warfare (ASW) exercises and simulated attacks by fast attack craft (FACs). They rejoined *Victorious* briefly that evening, and all three replenished from the *Tidespring*.

The air work-up was curtailed at midday on 9 September by steering gear failure, which caused *Victorious* to 'snake' while attempting to land on aircraft. This led to the diversion to RAAF Pearce of the CO of 801 Squadron Lt Cdr Perks and a Sea Vixen of 893 Squadron. The same problem next day called a halt to the fixed-wing programme and, despite the efforts of her engineers, it was not until the following day that uninterrupted flying, uninterrupted was possible. The programme was abruptly terminated at 12.00 when orders were received to recall all aircraft and re-embark the diversion party from RAAF Pearce. *Victorious* was to proceed to the Cocos Islands to embark additional aircrew.

The COS telegram on 10 September to CinCFE set in train preliminary movements. To augment the escort the destroyer HMS *Hampshire* was released from patrolling the Malacca Strait, while the frigates *Berwick* and *Dido* were detached from exercises with HMS *Centaur* SE of Singapore. It is clear that preparations were being made for extended operations because of the frequency of replenishment. They rendezvoused at 14.10 on 12 September, and with final topping-off from RFA *Wave Sovereign*, headed north through the Malacca Strait.

Meanwhile, *Victorious* took the opportunity to exercise emergency and action stations, closing temporarily with *Tidespring* and her devoted escort to carry out a replenishment at sea (RAS). Rear Admiral Janvrin took the opportunity to brief the Captain and crew of *Cavendish* when he was flown over. The only flying carried out was by Wessex helicopters and Gannet AEW aircraft on routine patrols. On reaching the Cocos Islands on 14 September the extra aircrew were flown on and stores taken onboard from RFA *Reliant*.

15 September brought the various groups together, with the ammunition ship RFA *Resurgent* joining at 05.00, *Hampshire*, *Dido* and *Berwick* at 07.00, and *Tidespring*, *Cavendish* and *Caesar* shortly after. The rest of the day was taken up with RAS, during the course of which a bomb being transferred from *Resurgent* to *Victorious* was lost over the side. RFAs *Resurgent* and *Reliant* were detached later in the day, while the rest of the task group set a course for the Lombok Strait. The following day a conference took place on board the *Victorious* attended by the captains of all ships in company.

The remaining two days on transit to the Lombok Strait were taken up by air exercises. Buccaneers prac-

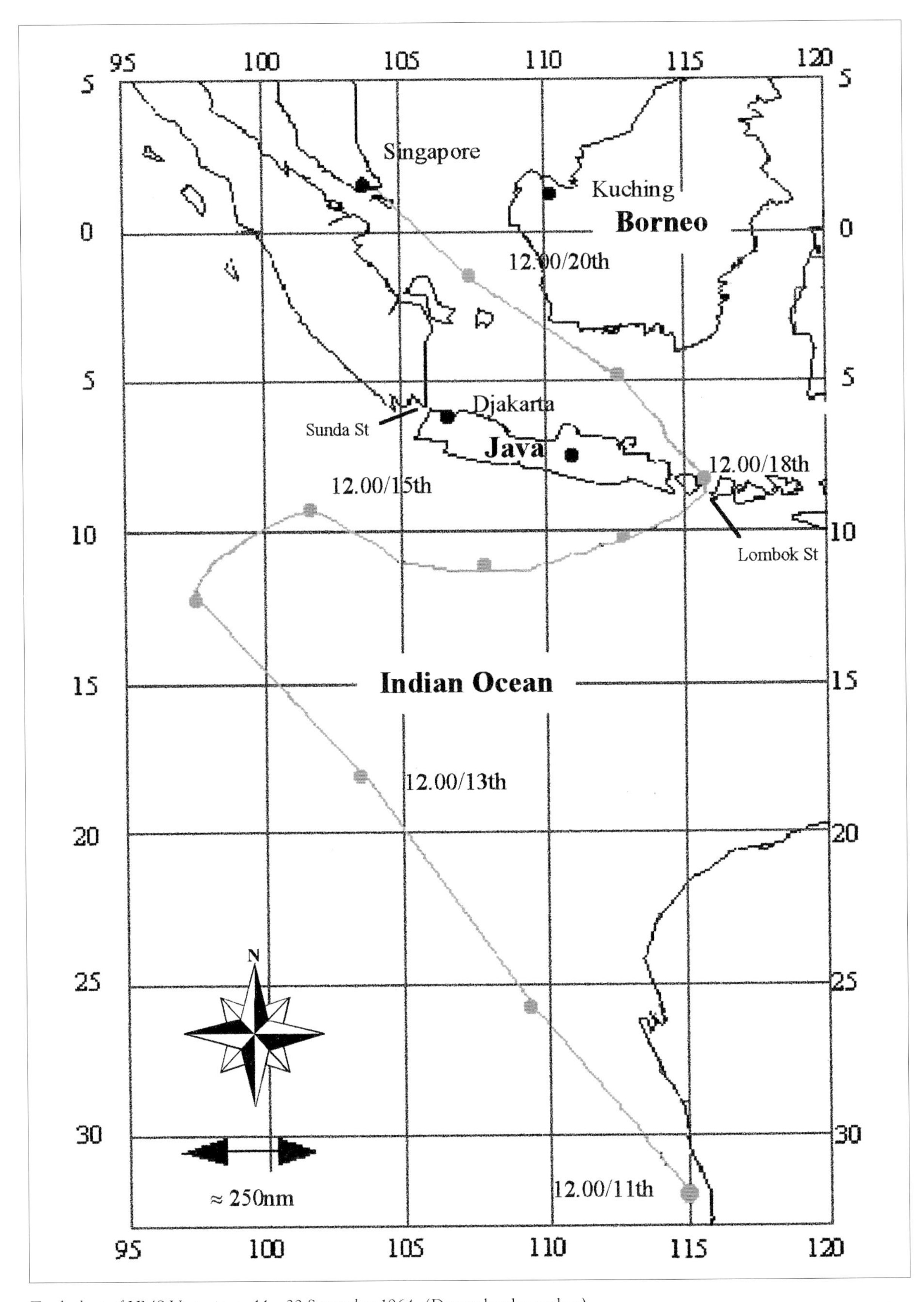

Track chart of HMS Victorious, *11 - 20 September 1964*. (Drawn by the author)

tised low-level attacks on ships in the task group and simulated 'Kennel' attacks, with one aircraft acting as the Tu-16 'Badger' bomber while others played the role of its missiles. Interceptions were carried out by Sea Vixens and *Hampshire's* Seaslug missile system. The results were clearly satisfactory, for the squadron diary records, 'the Vixens and Seaslugs would have had little difficulty in disposing of them'. Sea Vixens supported by Gannets carried out high- and low-level combat air patrol (CAP) exercises, while two fully-armed aircraft were held at Condition 2 (ready for launch with the crew aboard) This was later relaxed, crews being allowed to wait in the ready room. They were scrambled twice to investigate approaching aircraft, identified as Indonesian Tu-16 'Badgers' some 40nm to the north, but, as they remained within their Air Defence Identification Zone (ADIZ), they were merely shadowed. Meanwhile the Wessexes of 814 Squadron carried out routine screening and simulated FAC attacks.

To the north of Java other precautions were being carried out to ensure the safety of the task group, should the Indonesians take exception to its activities. There was a very high state of alert, with RAF and Commonwealth units prepared for immediate defensive and offensive missions. Furthermore, a second carrier task group was formed on 18 September around HMS *Centaur*, with the Second in Command Far Eastern Fleet (FO2 FEF), Rear Admiral Peter Hill-Norton, on board. Screened by HMS *Kent*, HMS *Ajax*, HMAS *Vendetta* and HMAS *Vampire*, this group had a dual role, firstly to cover the approaches to Singapore and secondly, to support *Victorious* in the latter part of her voyage through the Karimata Strait between Sumatra and Borneo. This group remained NE of Singapore until 20 September, when it moved SE during the night to avoid detection, taking up a position to support *Victorious* at the end of her transit of the Java Sea and in closest proximity to Djakarta.

The level of alert can be judged by the fact that *Centaur* maintained at least one crew at Condition 2 during the day and Condition 4 at night from 17.00 on 19 September to 22.20 the following night. Eight Sea Vixens were armed throughout the period with four 2in rocket pods or Firestreak air-to-air missiles, according to their role (CAP or anti-FAC). In addition to the CAP maintained for much of 19 September, other exercises included low-level rockets and AA tracking with ships in the screen. Despite the close proximity of Singapore, underway replenishment was carried out from RFAs *Tidesurge* and *Fort Duquesne* .

To the south of Java, *Victorious* and her consorts proceeded on their passage to the Lombok Strait, remaining 100nm off the coast. There was no contact with Indonesian forces on 17 September, although constant air patrols were maintained. One Gannet and two Sea Vixens were held at Condition 2, armed with two 2in rocket pods and two Firestreak missiles, while Buccaneers carried out dummy Bullpup missile and low-angle rocket attacks. The ships adopted wartime routines with respirators and anti-flash gear carried by all crew. Of note was the frequency of replenishment from *Tidespring* to ensure that the escort was never likely to be short of fuel.

It was intended that the task group should pass through the Strait during the evening of 17 September, but this was deferred to the following morning to allow better identification of contacts. Two aircraft detected at 09.35 were later identified as Indonesian Gannets; they made a close visual inspection in the morning and then shadowed. To reassure the visitors (and perhaps the ship's company) it was decided to present '... a less tense countenance ...', and as a consequence the crews of the aircraft at Condition 2 vacated their cockpits and the deck was utilised for hockey. At around 11.00 a submarine was spotted on the surface approximately 8nm away moving in the opposite direction. This turned out to be an Indonesian 'Whisky' class, *No.* 406, which passed within two miles to port of the carrier before signalling 'Bon Voyage' and disappearing astern. This was followed by a radar contact by *Victorious* of ten vessels apparently in convoy moving west. To avoid unnecessary complications the task group altered course to avoid them, and at sunset the shadowers broke off and the ready aircrew stood down.

The following day the task group moved through the Java Sea. Perhaps the most significant change was the substitution of a tug-of-war competition for hockey. The high level of alert was maintained and aircraft were held at Condition 2, although the crews did not remain in their cockpits. Because of the proximity of territorial waters there was no flying. At midday *Dido* investigated a sonar contact and *Cavendish* was briefly detached to follow up a radar contact, although the only confirmed sighting occurred late in the evening, when an Indonesian patrol vessel was identified 10nm away. As RFA *Tidespring* had been detached early the previous day *Victorious* replenished the more needy members of her screen.

The next day saw the resumption of normal peacetime routine. 'Action Stations' were sounded at dawn for the passage of the Karimata Strait and maintained for much of the morning, but the level of alert was reduced. For the first time in two days flying was resumed, although on a restricted basis, with a number of sorties by Wessexes. Two Gannets were sent to Tengah to pick up mail and two naval constructors to assist in repairs to the rudder. Interaction with the Indonesians was limited to the brief appearance of a patrol at 15.40. The task group dispersed at 22.00, when the screen was detached under the command of *Hampshire*. The end of the operation was formally recognised with the resumption of peacetime steaming. *Centaur*, joined by *Hampshire*, *Dido*, *Vendetta* and supported by *Tidesurge*, proceeded to Hong Kong. Of the others, *Kent* accompanied by *Vampire* returned to Singapore separately and arrived shortly after the remaining members of the screen. *Victorious* arrived late on 21 September and after her aircraft, minus two Wessexes which had flown ashore and the unserviceable Buccaneer, which was ignominiously towed to RAF Changi, and a Sea Vixen transferred to *Centaur*). On their arrival the aircraft were armed and placed at two hours' notice. *Victorious* herself entered dock on 23 September for repairs to her rudder.

Conclusions

The lack of British response to the initial refusal of passage through the Sunda Strait, followed by the arrival and despatch of significant reinforcements to the region, convinced the Indonesians that an attack was imminent. This conclusion is supported by the dispersal of shipping and redeployment of aircraft to the east. In an effort to forestall an attack they looked for other options, and it is therefore probably no coincidence that the telegram suggesting the Lombok Strait route arrived soon after *Victorious* had left Fremantle.

From the British point of view, the use of an aircraft carrier to make a symbolic transit of a narrow strait seems presumptuous. The views of CinCFE were unequivocal in recommending that *Victorious* should not be brought through the Sunda Strait, considering 'that it would be militarily unsound in present circumstances for *Victorious*, even if her escort were reinforced, to be sent through the Sunda and Gaspar Straits if there is a high probability her passage will be opposed'. He went on to say, 'I appreciate, however, that the passage might not be opposed particularly if *Victorious*' escort had been reinforced with, say, a DLG ['County' class destroyer] and two or three Frigates or Destroyers'. The COS, more aware of the political climate, recommended the passage largely to avoid a significant political defeat following the landings in Malaya, exacerbated by the pressing need to bring *Victorious* back to Singapore to enhance the island's defence against further raids.

Few alternative options were feasible in the time available – the movements of *Victorious* were widely reported and the date of her return to Singapore was known within a day or two. It was made clear that *Caesar* and *Cavendish* would have been at risk if they made the transit alone, as they would have been unable to handle either the potential air or surface attacks that could be made against them. The Cabinet Conclusions of 10 September records, stationing *Victorious* 100 miles south of the Sunda Strait would not ensure air cover for the destroyers before an attack was launched, with the stark warning, 'this could not guarantee in all circumstances that the destroyers might not be sunk', but would be available to assist in their defence.

Under the circumstances, exposing the two destroyers could have increased the chances of an incident. An attack on them could be considered 'minor' and be blamed on over-zealous local commanders. Furthermore, parallels could be drawn between their presence in the Sunda Strait and the Gulf of Tonkin Incident, thus making full-scale retaliation very difficult politically. Even the Australian and New Zealand governments were slightly circumspect and reluctant to allow use of their forces in the theatre for anything but defensive operations. An attack upon *Victorious* and her escorts would have been an undertaking of much greater magnitude both politically and militarily. It is likely that the preferred option would have been the transit of a significant surface group supported by aircraft carriers outside the confines of territorial waters.

The potential risk to *Victorious* and her escorts is difficult to quantify. The Joint Planners' assessment of the Indonesian Air Force's (AURI) capability estimated that it had between seventy and ninety jet fighters (MiG 17, 19 and 21), of which between thirty and forty were operational, twenty-two Il-28 light bombers and twenty-five Tu-16 'Badgers', some of which were equipped with AS-1 missiles. These were backed up by P-51 Mustang fighters and B-25 Mitchell bombers, and in addition there was a naval unit of Gannet ASW aircraft. Most of the modern aircraft were usually based at Kemajoram (near Djakarta) and Iswahjudi. In response the rising tension it seems those from Kemajoram were relocated to Iswahjudi and Abdulrachman/Saleh. There were relatively few airfields capable of operating Il-28s and Tu-16s, although the use of minor airfields for staging other types was possible.

Operationally, the AURI could mount limited attacks without preparation, although a major effort would require preparation and give between two and seven days' warning. Due to its poor logistic and support structure it was unable to sustain more than a small number of effective operations. Even this ability would decline in the event of dispersal to smaller airfields and in the face of any form of retaliatory action. It was considered that the most likely form of attack was conventional bombing from medium altitude, although missile strikes with AS-1 'Kennels' could not be completely excluded. With their poor night training and limited blind bombing capability nocturnal attacks were considered most unlikely.

During the early 1960s the Indonesian Navy had been expanded to match RN forces deployed in the region. In numbers the fleet looked impressive, but the elderly Soviet designs lacked modern weapons, so overall capability and serviceability was poor. The most effective units were the FACs (torpedo- and missile-armed) particularly in coastal waters. It is noteworthy that the preferred escorts were the two RAN *Daring* class destroyers *Vendetta* and *Vampire*, with their heavy gun armament. Australian susceptibilities meant they could not be used to escort *Victorious*. The 'Komar' FACs were the most potent threat and contemporary documents give some indication of the emphasis put upon countering them. This led to the development of RN doctrine that has been vindicated in recent years. The only other credible naval threat lay in the submarines although they were relatively poorly trained.

On balance it was considered that in most circumstances the two carriers and their escorts could handle anything the Indonesians could mount against them. Conflicting with this assessment, however, is the composition of the air groups – the COS briefings noted full squadron strengths but both carriers had fewer aircraft embarked than attributed to them. The RN had its own serviceability problems!

Possibly the greatest weakness lay in the rules of engagement, which were issued in two parts. Firstly, general notes for the CinCFE, who in anticipation of the COS decision to proceed had asked for activation of Operation 'Althorp' with delegated authority to implement 'Althorp Red' – i.e. active retaliation:

> If attacked, *Victorious* and her escorts have the right of self-defence to shoot down or sink any attacking air or naval forces after a hostile act has been committed. A hostile act does not include buzzing by aircraft or a near approach on a collision course by ships. In the event of only one ship or aircraft making an attack from a formation, the whole formation and any other Indonesian forces subsequently approaching our forces become fair game. In these circumstances action is to be confirmed to air and sea attacking forces and no, repeat no, retaliatory action maybe carried out against Indonesian territory without further authorisation from us. You should ensure that with the forces available ... you are in a posture to take out Indonesian air bases should you then be instructed to do so.

Secondly, the rules of conduct issued to *Victorious* when passing through the Lombok and Karimata Straits:

a The aim must be to avoid any action inconsistent with an innocent passage
b Normal courtesies to be observed
c Aircraft should not be flown
d Aircraft may be kept at readiness on deck but preparation for immediate flying should be as unobtrusive as possible
e Speed should be normal
f Ships should not zigzag except in the face of an overt threat or detection of a submarine
g Ship's companies may be at action stations but unobtrusively. Guns are to be fore and aft
h In the event of threatened attacks or buzzing, HM Ships should not fire first
i Helicopters should not be used to supplement the screen because this might be considered provocative.
j When on high seas between Kangean and Karimata Straits flying may take place so long as aircraft keep well clear of Indonesian territory and avoid any act that might be considered provocative.

This was worsened by the width of the Lombok Strait (twelve miles) which precluded manoeuvre and impaired screening. Later, a notice advising against flying and gunnery practice between the Kangean and Karimata Strait was issued. Despite the fact that two Sea Vixens and two Buccaneers were held armed at Condition 2, with no early warning and impaired ship-borne radar cover (due to the proximity of land) the RN force would have been hard-pressed to defend itself from a surprise attack or to respond effectively had it occurred. Direct assistance from aircraft based at Singapore or Australia would have been problematic. Air strikes from Singapore would only be able to reach targets in the west and initial strikes would only have involved RAF units. Attacks to the East would need to be staged from Darwin or by the Victor bombers at Gan or Tengah, but both options would have taken some considerable time.

The substitution of the Lombok Strait seems to be a win-win scenario. The Indonesians had defused a perceived threat and despite the transit of 'territorial waters' had kept a powerful symbolic force away from Djakarta. Their concern was emphasised by the meeting between the Chargé d'Affaires in Djakarta and Mr Suwito, the Indonesian Deputy Foreign Minister. On confirmation that *Victorious* would use the Lombok Strait he was apparently visibly relieved. Significantly, the Indonesians requested that the Lombok Strait option should not be attributed to them to avoid embarrassment to their government.

For the British, no principle had been conceded and subsequent reports of consternation in Djakarta were undoubtedly encouraging. Overall, the response was muted, as it was agreed that no publicity would be made regarding the change. In response to any enquiries, however a statement would be issued along the lines of :

'The Indonesians had requested us to avoid the Sunda Strait owing to naval exercises in the area, and as a matter of normal courtesy we had agreed to do so', stressing the fact that 'we claim the right to innocent passage of both the Sunda and Lombok Strait, and that in neither case do we consider it necessary to seek Indonesian permission to sail through them. We do, however, as a matter of courtesy, normally inform them of the intended passages of these straits by HM ships'. On the precise instructions of the Foreign Office, notification of the passage had been handed in on the afternoon of 15 September by the Naval Attaché in Djakarta on plain paper (i.e. non- headed), to emphasis the informal nature of the communication. It was agreed that at the earliest opportunity RN warships would transit the Sunda Strait on legitimate business. They were, however, somewhat perturbed by an Indonesian press release:

> The Indonesian Government had permitted a flotilla of the British Fleet to pass through the Lombok Strait on 18 September after it had received an official request from the British Government.

While irksome from the British viewpoint, it was not surprising as Indonesian public opinion was inflamed by the presence of HMS *Victorious* and her escorts off their coasts.

The long-term impact of the transit of the Lombok Strait is difficult to assess. If the British had backed down it is probable that it would have been interpreted as a lack of resolve and the Indonesians would have stepped up the tempo of the Confrontation, making open conflict more likely. Ultimately, it became a symbolic 'freedom of navigation' exercise as a result of negotiation between the respective governments. Whether it fits the traditional model is questionable. That the operation was extemporised is clear from the initial lack of escorts, the rather weak air group embarked, and probably by the presence of *Victorious* herself. It is notable that throughout the crisis the Indonesians had maintained they would refuse 'permission', but not 'passage', the difference being that the former implies that force 'may be' used, whereas the latter implies that force 'will' be used. Such subtleties were lost in the public's mind, and perception always increases the risk of escalation. However, it was undoubtedly successful from the British and Malayan point of view, and not without some benefit for the

Indonesians. That escalation did not occur and a 'Sunda Strait Incident' did not find its way into the history books is at least part of its success – and worth a closer look for that reason alone.

Order of Battle

Royal Navy

Victorious - fleet carrier, flagship of RAdm Janvrin (FOAC)
801 Squadron - six Buccaneer S.1s (one unserviceable)
814 Squadron - seven Wessex HAS.1s s
893 Squadron - nine Sea Vixen FAW.1s (six capable of carrying 500lb bombs)
849A flight - four Gannet AEW.3s and one Gannet COD
Hampshire - air defence destroyer (DLG), one Wessex HAS.1
Caesar and *Cavendish* - destroyers
Dido and *Berwick* - frigates, one Wasp HAS.1

Centaur - fleet carrier, flagship of RAdm Hill-Norton (FO2 FEF)
814 Squadron - six Wessex HAS.1s (one lost in crash)
892 Squadron - nine Sea Vixen FAW.1s
849B - four Gannet AEW.3s (estimated)
Kent - DLG, one Wessex HAS.1
Ajax - frigate, one Wasp HAS.1

Royal Australian Navy

Vendetta and *Vampire* - destroyers

Royal Fleet Auxiliaries

Tidespring and *Tidesurge* - fleet oilers
Reliant - aviation support ship
Resurgent - ammunition stores ship
Fort Duquesne

The above list includes only those RN and RFA ships involved between 8-20 September. At this time nearly fifty ships (including auxiliaries) were under the command of FO FEF Vice Admiral Dreyer. However, when the numbers absorbed by refits, patrols and deployment to Hong Kong and Aden are taken into consideration, it can be seen that the RN presence could be sparse.

Sources and References

Calvocoressi, P. *World Politics since 1945*. Longmans.
Mackie, J A C. *Konfrontasi*. OUP.
Squadrons of the FAA. Air-Britain.
Fundamentals of British Maritime Doctrine. HMSO 1995.
RAF Squadrons. Air-Britain.
Flintman, V. *Air Wars and Aircraft*. Arms and Armour Press.
Lee, D. *Eastward*. HMSO 1984.

Public Record Office (London)
ADM53/161444; ADM53/161152; ADM53/162259; ADM53/162462;
ADM53/162704; ADM53/161349; ADM53/161611; ADM53/162623;
ADM53/162484; DEFE4/174; DEFE6/92; DEFE11/364; DEFE13/271; DEFE13/419; FO371/175296; F0371/181524; DEFE4/173; DEFE24/105.

Fleet Air Arm Museum (Yeovilton)
Diaries and Logs 801, 814, 815, 849A, 892, 893 Squadrons.

With particular thanks to Mr J Shore of the Research Dept.

THE STEAM GUNBOATS

George L Moore describes the Royal Navy's steam gunboats – a response to the threat of German E-boats and MTBs. The proposal battled against various design obstacles, ranging from the lack of shipyards willing to build them to the problems of finding available engines and armaments. Despite building setbacks leading to a nine-month delay, the steam gunboats eventually proved to be powerful antagonists for the German E-boats.

Origins

In May 1940 the Royal Navy was facing an increasing threat from German motor torpedo boats (E-boats or MTBs) and a countermeasure, which was more effective than the existing resources available to the coastal forces, was becoming a necessity. A certain Mr Reid had at this time submitted his proposals for a 'diesel-driven torpedo boat and anti submarine chaser' to the Admiralty. On 10 May, the Admiralty departments were asked by the Director of Scientific Research to consider a proposed design of what was described as a motor torpedo boat. Unfortunately, details of Mr Reid's ideas have not been found, but a note made on 1 June indicated that machinery of 6000shp was needed to gain a margin of 5kts over German motor torpedo boats. One can deduce that the idea was for a craft of around 100 tons with dual-purpose capabilities. The first reaction to this request came from the Director of Training and Staff Duties (DTSD) on 22 May, stating that an answer to German motor torpedo boats was an immediate requirement. He did not believe that another vessel of a similar type would provide a satisfactory solution unless it was a steadier gun platform than the existing 70ft boats.

The situation developed rapidly under the pressure of war, and by 10 June the requirements of the Naval Staff ambitiously demanded a boat with a speed of 40kts, an endurance of 400 miles at full speed, and good close range weapons. The response of the Director of Naval Construction (DNC) was to look at two options. Steam-powered machinery was considered first, but questions about the weight problem of this power emerged. The Engineer in Chief (EinC) was asked what power could be obtained with an available weight of 50 tons for both machinery and fuel. No definite answer was received, indicating an element of caution, but it was stated that only about 6000shp could be obtained with the ship having two shafts, a length of about 120ft and a beam of about 20ft. A steel hull was expected to be weigh about 48 tons with the weight available for armament about 11 tons. Anticipated displacement was 109 tons when all equipment and fuel were included. Speed was only expected to be 32.5kts, but with composite construction this could rise to 34kts with a saving of about 8 tons in weight. To rise to 40kts it was believed that about 8200shp was required – with the weight of machinery and fuel rising to 70 tons. The steel-hulled boat with 6000shp machinery proved to be the precursor of what became the anti-E-boat, the original description for the steam gunboat. At the time, the idea clearly did not meet the Staff Requirement because of the considerable shortfall in the operational speed requirement. The use of steam therefore seemed to be ruled out unless the Engineer in Chief could produce something better.

A possible answer to the machinery problem was to use diesels, the second line of approach. There were said to be a number of 900hp Paxman diesel engines available and the EinC was asked if a four shaft arrangement could be considered with two engines on each shaft. Again there was a cautious reply, but the idea died as the Engineer in Chief did not feel confident about fitting eight diesels in one boat. The 'way ahead' now clearly lay only with steam turbine power, as no practical alternative existed and the requirement was urgent.

Machinery Design

On 6 July, representatives from the DNC and the EinC departments discussed the outline for these vessels. A two shaft arrangement was being investigated with one boiler and two turbines, which would develop 8000shp at 900 revolutions per minute. Metropolitan Vickers were already becoming involved with the machinery specification whilst Lamont were involved with the boiler designs. Both firms were said to be exceedingly keen to try to develop suitable answers to the testing requirements. A modification of the Foster Wheeler D-type boiler was also selected for development. The basis of the warship design was clearly being driven at this point by the propulsion needs, which were going to be the main influence on the size of the ships. At this stage, it was

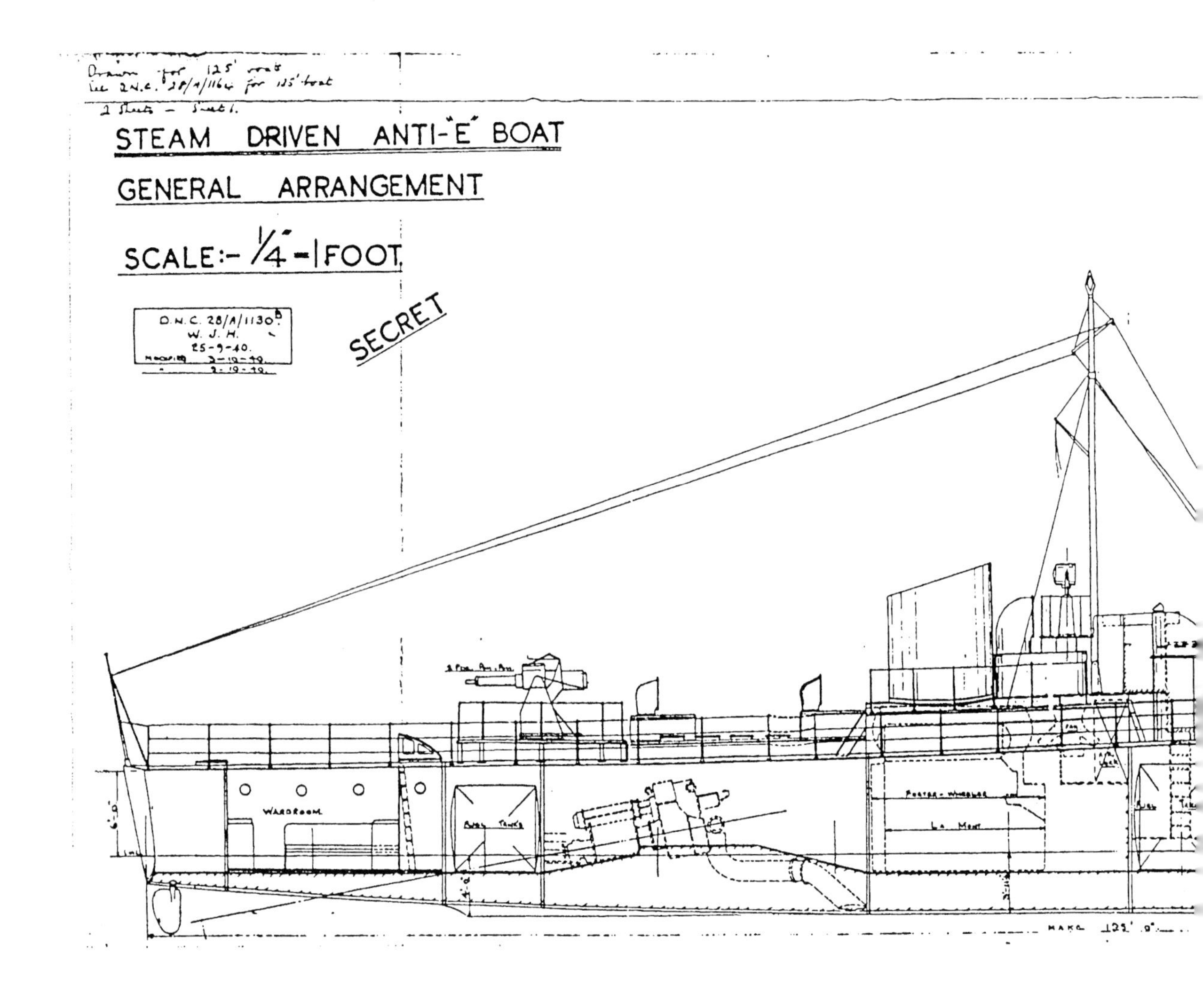

expected that the engine room would have a length of 23ft, a depth of 12ft, whilst the beam was going to be between 19ft and 20ft. This was slightly smaller than expected. The hull weight was anticipated to be about 45 tons, machinery 70 tons (including fuel), whilst the armament would be 11 tons, giving a displacement of 126 tons. The estimated full speed was 33kts, which rose to 35kts when running in half oil condition. It was optimistically said that the first set of machinery would be ready in six months with delivery of subsequent sets being made every six weeks.[1]

The technical demands made, bearing in mind the machinery requirements, were considerable and in order to obtain the required performance, a weight limit was set which many engineers thought impossible with steam machinery. A policy was laid down stating that design stresses in excess of those known to have given satisfactory results could not in general be exceeded, and that owing to the supply position no light alloys could be used. It was anticipated that the vessels would only have a working life of five years, so allowances for wastage of material by corrosion were reduced or omitted. Castings were eliminated wherever possible, and parts were fabricated by welding which proved a major source of weight saving. There were no spare auxiliaries of any sort; the omission of a feed pump was a feature which caused some difficulties in service. The weight allowance for the complete machinery installation in an anti-E-boat was 14lb/shp, an objective just achieved. The corresponding figure for the emergency destroyers (Q and CR classes) was 31lb/shp, which illustrates the demands placed upon the design team.[2]

The Anti-E-Boat Evolves

The DNC, Sir Stanley Goodall, first became involved with the anti-E-boat on 15 August.[3] A minute dated 17 August with his signature set out a 'Summary of the position to date':

> A vessel of good sea keeping qualities and high speed is essential. Owing to the necessity of keeping weight to a minimum for high speed the consequent low weight

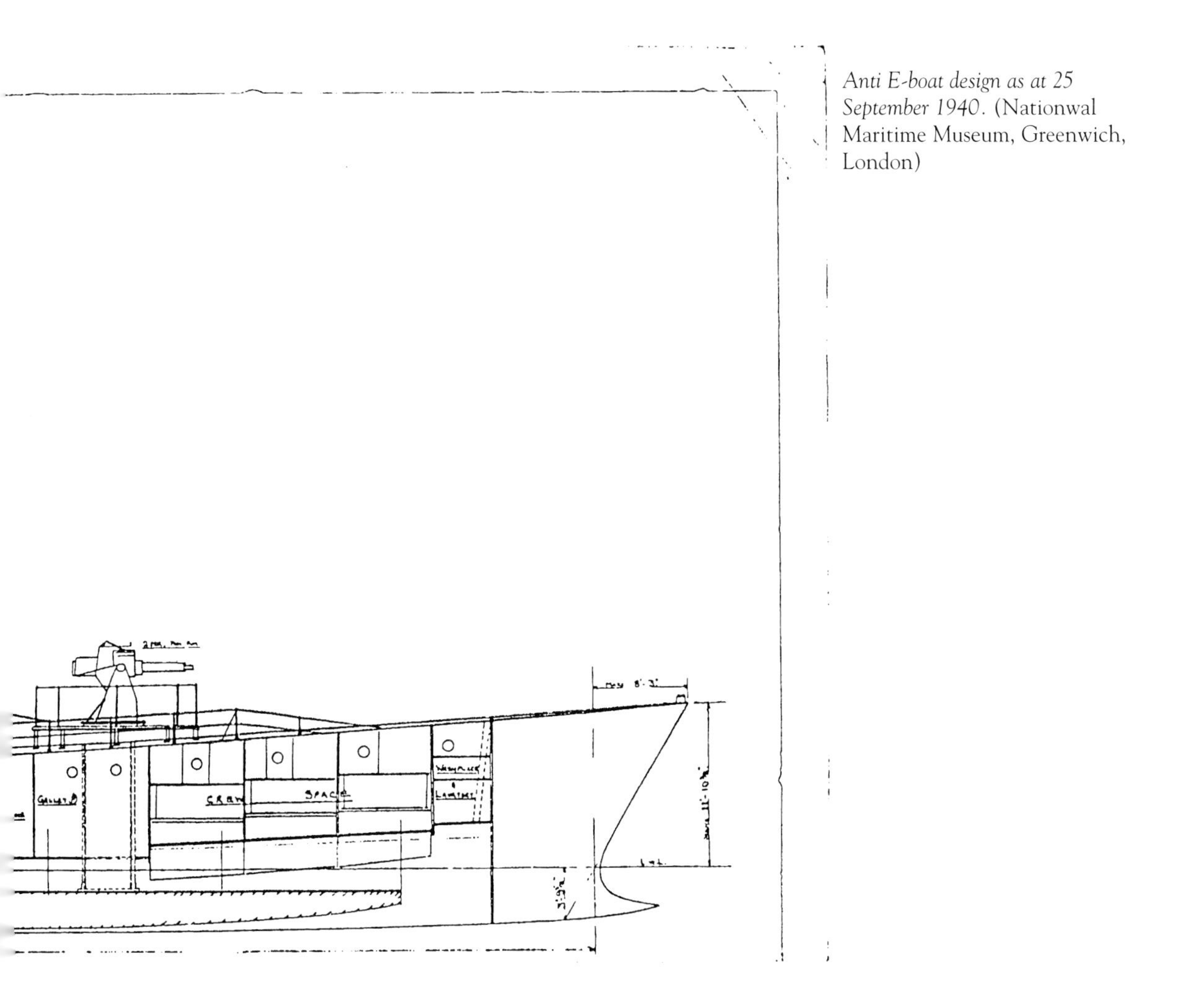

Anti E-boat design as at 25 September 1940. (Nationwal Maritime Museum, Greenwich, London)

> available for machinery has necessitated a somewhat detailed investigation into machinery arrangements. The arrangement now appears to offer considerable promise. Approximate details of a vessel fitted with steam machinery are length 115ft, beam 20ft, depth 12ft. Displacement loaded with 16 tons of oil fuel is 120 tons, 8000shp. A weight of 12 tons has been allowed for armament and protection. Endurance 200 miles at full power, 480 miles at 20kts. If a higher endurance is required some reduction in speed fully loaded would result. This could be investigated when Staff (The Naval Staff) state the necessary endurance. Speed 34kts, half oil condition = 36kts. There is no machinery limitation on the period for which full power can be obtained.
>
> Production – First three or four sets of machinery within six months, subsequent sets – two sets at three week intervals. Machinery proposed does not include new or untried features nor have reduced factors of safety been embodied. Such machinery can be produced by a number of firms who now have capacity available. Extensive use of aluminium or special alloy steel is not called for. Advantage of steam over internal combustion engines are quietness, greatly improved reliability and much reduced maintenance are considerable such as to warrant full consideration being given to the production of a few such craft. It is considered steam should be available within thirty minutes from cold. The hulls could be produced in time for the machinery sets. With reference to Mr Reids' proposal it is proposed to thank him for his letter and inform him that it is not desired to utilise his design.[4]

The first indication of the proposed armament of the anti-E-boats was made at a meeting in Bath held on 27 August when the subject was the 'Tentative Programme of New Construction up to 31 March 1941'. The basic details of the craft now included an armament of 0.5in quadruple mountings, one Oerlikon gun, and one mortar. With the boat having a steel hull, it was felt that 'it might be best to put the work with firms building destroyers'. Production was clearly not going to be a straightforward matter for it was stated that 'capacity for building these craft requires further investigation'. Another problem was apparent with the DNC commenting that 'the armament may be difficult'. The estimated time to build was said to be four to five months.[5]

Views of the Naval Staff

Sir Stanley Goodall's minute started the process under which members of the Naval Staff were able to propose their ideas and give opinions on the evolution of the anti-E-boat project. This formality commenced on 24 August with the contribution from the Director of Anti Submarine Warfare (DASW). Although clearly disappointed with the speed of the class, he highlighted the advantages of reliability, quietness and ease of maintenance. From an anti-E-boat point of view, possible drawbacks were said to be their deep draught (someone put a question mark against this comment – depth may have been confused with draught) and comparatively low endurance. 'We might be buying a pig in a poke but if they do not come up to expectations they can always be turned into asdic fitted minelayers'. He wanted to order two flotillas, totalling eighteen craft, straight away.

The Assistant Chief of Naval Staff (ACNS) said that the new type appeared to be a great advance on any craft yet obtainable which was capable of destroying E-boats. He reiterated the advantages outlined by his colleague, adding good seakeeping as a positive feature. Speed at 34kts (full load) and 36.5kts (half fuel) was considered adequate. Guns should be effective at a range at which an E-boat was visible on a dark night; this was said to be approximately the effective range of an E-boat torpedo. He also emphasised that an 'end on approach was the best chance of closing range, and weapons were to give maximum fire on forward bearings'. Weak areas were the lack of weight left for defensive armament and protection and the endurance figures which were said to be 'most disappointing'. A 30% increase in endurance was suggested, even at the expense of defensive armament and protection. No opinion was forthcoming from the ACNS on the make up of the armament; he asked DTSD for his suggestions.

The DTSD's response took a week to produce. He suggested an armament of twin Oerlikon HA/LA power-turrets forward, two power-operated 0.5in guns either side further aft, with each able to right ahead. This armament was said to be on the light side, but it was felt that some weight would have to be utilised to protect personnel and power control gear. As an alternative, twin Oerlikon guns could be mounted fore and aft. He ruled out superfiring guns, an open hand worked pom-pom, a semi-automatic Rolls Royce gun, and a single Mark VIII pom-pom. These last two were disregarded on weight grounds.

The Sea Lords held a meeting on Saturday 31 August, when amongst other matters the anti-E-boat was discussed; it was decided that further consideration of the design was necessary before the craft could be built. One theoretically helpful piece of news came from the EinC on 3 September when he minuted that 'a small saving in machinery weight can be achieved which if wholly devoted to increased fuel capacity, would increase endurance quoted by 18-20%'.

The Deputy Controller now referred the papers to the Director of Naval Ordnance. The DNO, who wanted further matters examined, such as the time it would take to build the boats inclusive of the availability of armament. Another question regarded numbers, and here he asked that if twenty boats were ordered, could they all be built at the same time, and if twenty was too many then just how many could be built? He referred to suggestions being made that the vessels could be built in four to five months (made by the DNC department); they were described as 'indeed optimistic'!

Ideas on the armament had developed by the time the DNO produced his contribution on 7 September. The question of providing a 2pdr automatic gun for the forward position was now under consideration, which had a greater hitting power than a twin Oerlikon. One problem was availability of production – the Oerlikon was more likely to be available. If the 2pdr scheme was not accepted then it was felt that the Oerlikons could be provided in time to meet the boats. It was also felt to be 'probable' that two power operated 0.5in turrets could be provided, but again the allocation of such a scarce resource would need to be given careful consideration. Another suggestion was the provision of two small-calibre (0.303in) shoulder-shooting guns.

On 10 September, Sir Stanley minuted that the proposed design of the anti-E-boat was now being worked out in detail. There had been some modifications in the principal dimensions: the waterline length was now 125ft, beam 22ft, and depth 11ft 7in. Displacement was 130 tons, with 10 tons of oil, speed in half oil condition was 36kts. Armament was one 2pdr power-operated gun, two 0.5in twin powered anti aircraft turrets, and two stripped Lewis guns. Accommodation was provided for two officers, three petty officers and twelve ratings. Some bullet-proof protection was to be provided for a lookout hut, the bridge and the wheelhouse. The vessel's sparseness was such that the words 'stoop down protection' were used to describe the armour on the bridge. The aim was to provide some cover against aircraft and bomb splinters. The design was passed to the Controller on the last day of September.[6]

Enthusiasm for the anti-E-boat project was not universal, for in mid September, Sir Stanley Goodall had to persuade an official named Tower not to scrap the anti-E-boat for more Fairmiles.[7] The Controller, Vice Admiral Sir Bruce Fraser, also seemed far from enthusiastic when he sent a minute to the Naval Staff on 28 September. 'The only advantages I can see over the MTB type are more reliability and better sea keeping qualities'.[8] As early as 4 September, the Controller clearly had his doubts about the project, for in a memorandum to The Board of Admiralty he suggested: 'MTBs armed as a gunboat for which a release of Merlin engines and development of Sabre engines for marine work will be necessary. Otherwise turbine machinery and a fairly large type of vessel taking eighteen months to build are involved'.[9]

The Controller's minute initiated a joint and detailed response from the Director of Plans and the DTSD on 2 October. All the positive attributes of the craft were stressed, including the advantages over existing motor gunboat (MGB) designs. The boats were to be organised into flotillas of eight giving two operating divisions of three boats. This left two for refitting, replacing casualties, etc. The twin-powered Oerlikon was preferred to a single 2pdr in view of its reduced flash, which was considered a vital factor at night, its greater output during a fleeting engagement (120 rounds produced in eight seconds compared with 16 rounds) although the weight of metal delivered was almost identical, and some saving in weight was anticipated by choosing the Oerlikon. The Controller had suggested mounting a third 0.5in gun; although the idea was described as attractive, it came up against weight additions and also a bottleneck in the production of the gun. Small sponsons on each side of the bridge were suggested for stripped Lewis guns, whilst some double plating was suggested for protection. The VCNS generally concurred with these views, but preferred the 2pdr gun as it was harder hitting. On 7 October, the Controller minuted: 'Please consider 2pdr to be retained. We must now finish discussion and propose to place orders for ten in the first instance'.[10] Sir Stanley Goodall recorded this event in his diary.[11] The future of the anti-E-boat was assured.

The 1940 Supplementary Programme

The inclusion of the anti-E-boat in the building programme was, as we have seen, first discussed on 27 August, but at this stage no thought was given to the number proposed.[12] Two days later, the Plans Division were considering the resumption of the new construction programme. The main constraint was said to be the difficulty in increasing 0.5in production. Regarding numbers, it was suggested that a first order for twenty would be desirable to get the programme underway. One good question was raised: 'will they cut across other production?'[13] With the programme still very much in its formative stage fifty anti-E-boats were included in the 1940 Supplementary Programme. The memorandum prepared for discussion in the Cabinet was dated 9 September under the signature of the First Lord of the Admiralty, A V Alexander. The boats were described as 'steel vessels of about 120 tons with turbine machinery capable of 35kts and carrying Oerlikon guns'. The total estimated cost was £2.5 million in 1940 and £2.5 million in 1941 (£100,000 per vessel).[14] By 15 September the Prime Minister had seen the suggested programme. He minuted: 'Surprised only fifty Anti-E-boats wanted. Unless this is the utmost of capacity, one hundred would be more appropriate'.[15] The War Cabinet discussed the 1940 Supplementary New Construction Programme on 25 October 1940. There was no specific discussion about the anti-E-boat programme, and general approval was given to the proposals with no constraint that would be likely to effect the plans (other than the possibility that shortages of steel and other necessary materials might mean completion dates being delayed). In practice, this provision was directed at the aircraft carrier and the cruisers in the programme.[16]

Development Proceeds

With the Anti-E-boat firmly in the projected 1940 Supplementary Programme, a decision was made on 10 October to order ten vessels as soon as building facilities had been found for them.[17] This figure was rather less than the estimate provided to the Controller on 30 September, when it had been indicated by the Director of Naval Construction that twenty four could be placed by giving two boats to each of the Destroyer firms.[18] The boats' particulars at this date are set out in Appendix One. The design process proved difficult to implement, and by 18 October Sir Stanley Goodall recorded 'difficulties over anti-E' in his diary.[19] A few days earlier, there was another indication of problems; on 10 October letters were sent to the shipbuilders Yarrow, White, Denny, Thornycroft, Swan Hunter, Vickers-Barrow, Cammell Laird and Hawthorn Leslie, giving basic particulars of the design and new features particularly the machinery arrangements. The benefit of their experience was sought and a meeting arranged. Responses were mixed. Hawthorn Leslie said that they had built HMS *Viper* (1899); they clearly lacked interest. Swan Hunter said that they had no experience and that all of their berths were full. If boats were placed with them there would be a severe effect on ten 'Hunt' class escort destroyers and three month delays on their second and third Emergency Destroyers. They went on to say that the best sources of assistance would be Thornycroft, Yarrow and White. Unlike the builders of the larger warships the response from the specialist destroyer yards was positive, with Thornycroft and Denny giving more committed replies. Thornycroft even submitted their own outline design. The next move was a conference at Bath attended by representatives of the shipbuilders. Here it was decided that the first ten boats would be placed with firms experienced in light construction. The effect of placing orders with the smaller firms would also cause difficulties and the problem is best illustrated by the analysis produced by the representative of Whites. Each anti-E was expected to set back the four latest 'Hunt' class ships by a month. The best delivery expected was the first pair eight months after construction started and the last pair in twelve months – but only if contracts were given the highest priority. The Director of Contract Works proposed that orders for the first ten gunboats might be chosen from White (one or three), Thornycroft (two), Yarrow (two), Hawthorn Leslie (two), Swan Hunter (two), and Denny (two). Swan Hunter were to investigate the possibility of contracts being taken by Wallsend Slipway. It was decided that one firm would do all of the drawings including machinery and order all of the necessary materials. The difficulty in finding builders resulted in Camper & Nicholsons being considered. This yard was ruled out on 24 October, because of the likely difficulties they would experience with the installation of the machinery.[20] Ultimately, only nine boats could be placed and on 8 November, orders were given for two ships each at Thornycroft, Yarrow, Hawthorn Leslie (in spite of their earlier reticence) and Denny. White's yard could only take one boat.[21] Development of the design still

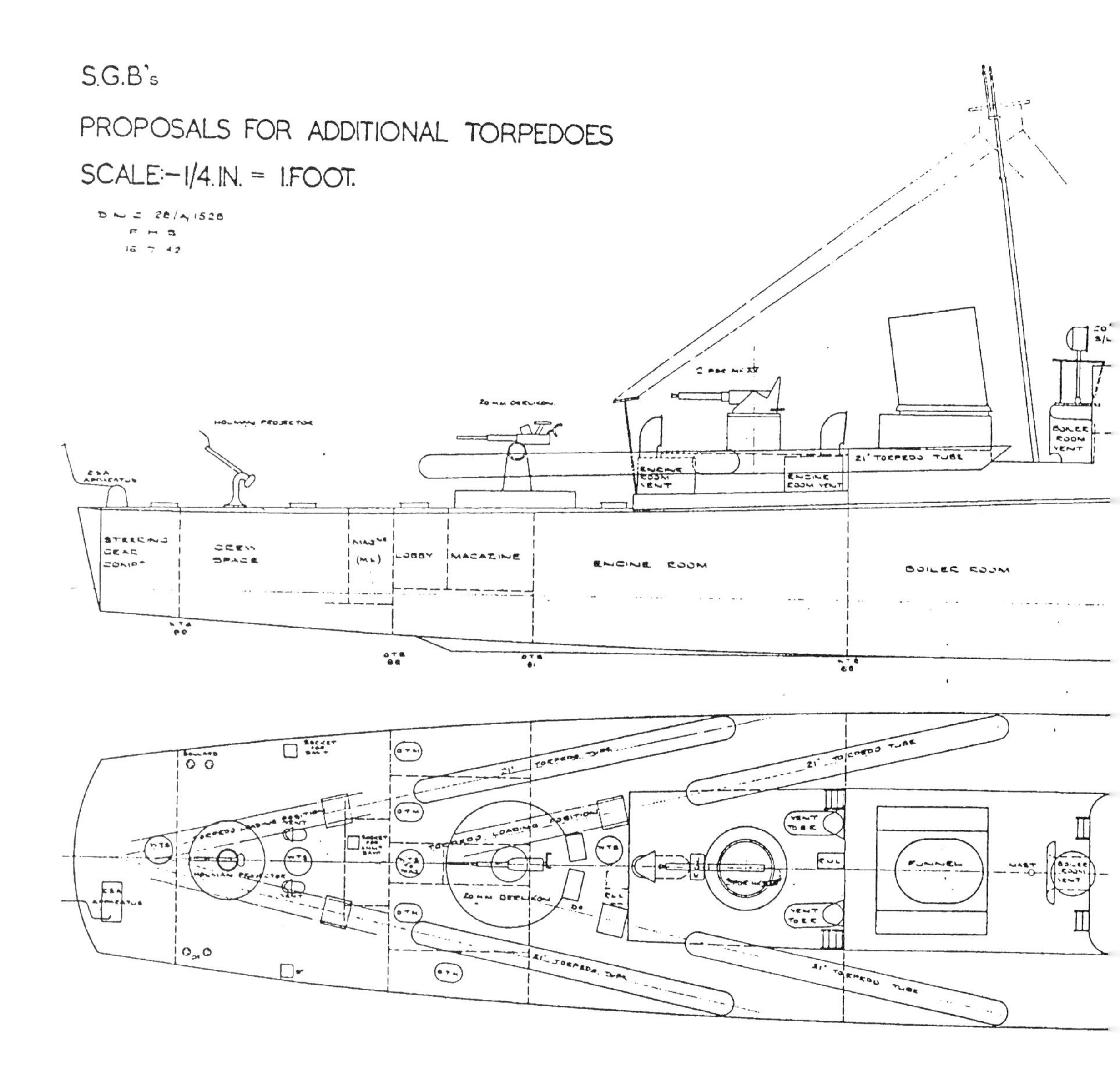

proved difficult, for there were frequent references to the project in Sir Stanley Goodall's diary. At one time or another, three of the best Constructors in the DNC's department, A P Cole, W J (Bill) Holt and M C Dunston were involved.[22] The size of the boat was clearly too constrained for all of the requirements, for by 4 November the length had increased by 10ft to 135ft, whilst the beam had risen from 22ft to 23ft. Displacement with 20 tons of oil fuel had risen to 157 tons, whilst with an overload fuel load of 50 tons on board the maximum speed was 33kts. Another major change was an increase in the main armament to two 2pdr guns (750 rounds per gun) with the two 0.5in machine guns (2400 rounds per gun) retained. It was decided in early November that both Yarrow and Denny would produce the drawings. By mid November, the description of this class had changed from anti-E-boat to steam gunboat.[23] The decision to increase the 2pdr armament still awaited ratification when a general description of the class was prepared in early December. The second 2pdr gun was not a feature, although provision for fitting had been made in the design. The number of rounds carried for the single weapon had been increased to 1150 rounds per gun.

By early December, the design was sufficiently advanced and effectively frozen to enable the 'Legend of Particulars' to be prepared, together with a general description of the steam gunboat for submission to the Board of Admiralty. The details are set out in Appendix Two.[24] The design was submitted to the Board of Admiralty on 3 January 1941, and duly approved.[25]

Even before the design had been approved by the Board of Admiralty, plans for the building of what would effectively be the prototype of the class were progressing

Steam Gun Boat as at 16 July 1942, mounting the proposed 4in gun and four torpedo tubes. (National Maritime Museum, Greenwich, London)

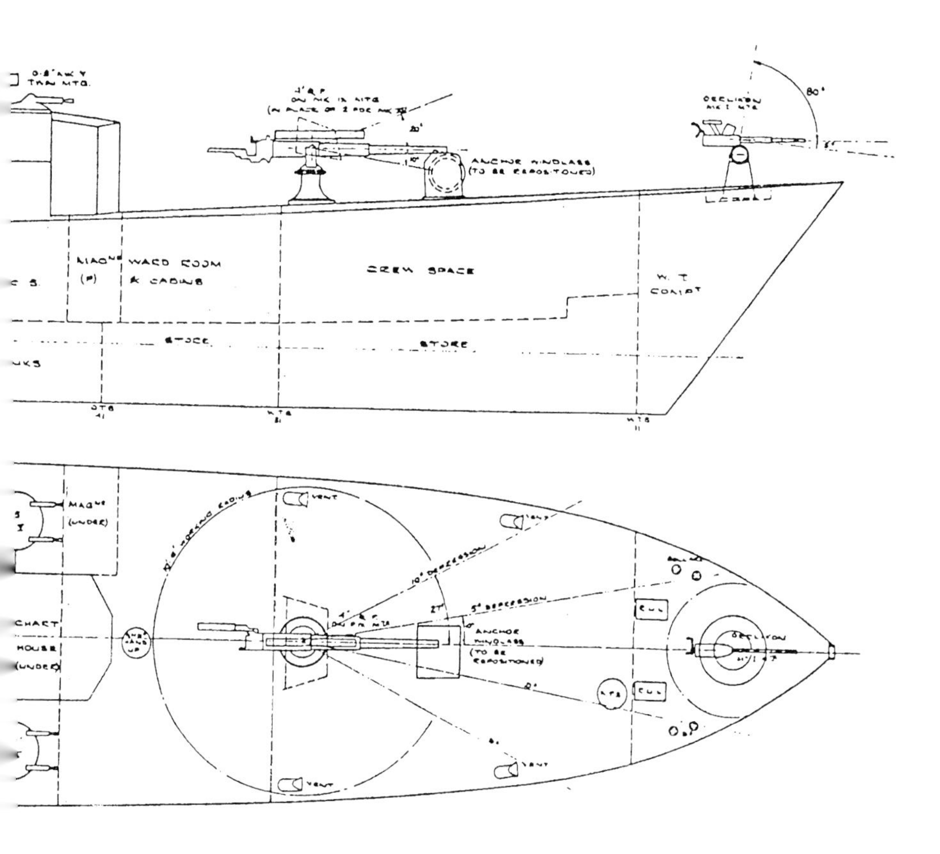

at Denny's, who were effectively the lead yard. The building schedule was set out on the 7th December as follows:

Start setting frames	4 December 1940
Start erecting frames	4 January 1941
Start shell	4 February 1941
Finish shell	4 April 1941
Launch	2 May 1941
Complete	4 June 1941

All Admiralty-supplied items, such as the guns and auxiliaries, were to be delivered by the end of April or early in May at the latest, with equipment for the second Denny boat following one month later. The schedule seems to have dropped behind schedule by a month at the start of construction and after this, progress was clearly very difficult. The launch date slipped by over four months, and the completion date by nine months; the total building time eventually became thirteen months – a far cry from the four to five months being heralded earlier in the project's life. The scepticism expressed by the Controller was proving to be well founded. A blow to the programme was the bombing of Thornycroft's yard at Southampton at the beginning of January 1941, where the destroyer *Norseman* was badly damaged on the slipway. She had to be virtually rebuilt, which resulted in inevitable delays to other ships. The start of the two steam gunboats would have had to be put back until November and December 1941, so another builder was sought. After a search, the only yard capable of accepting the vessels was found to be White's, but only at the price of starting work in October and December 1941 – hardly a better prospect. There would also be delays of

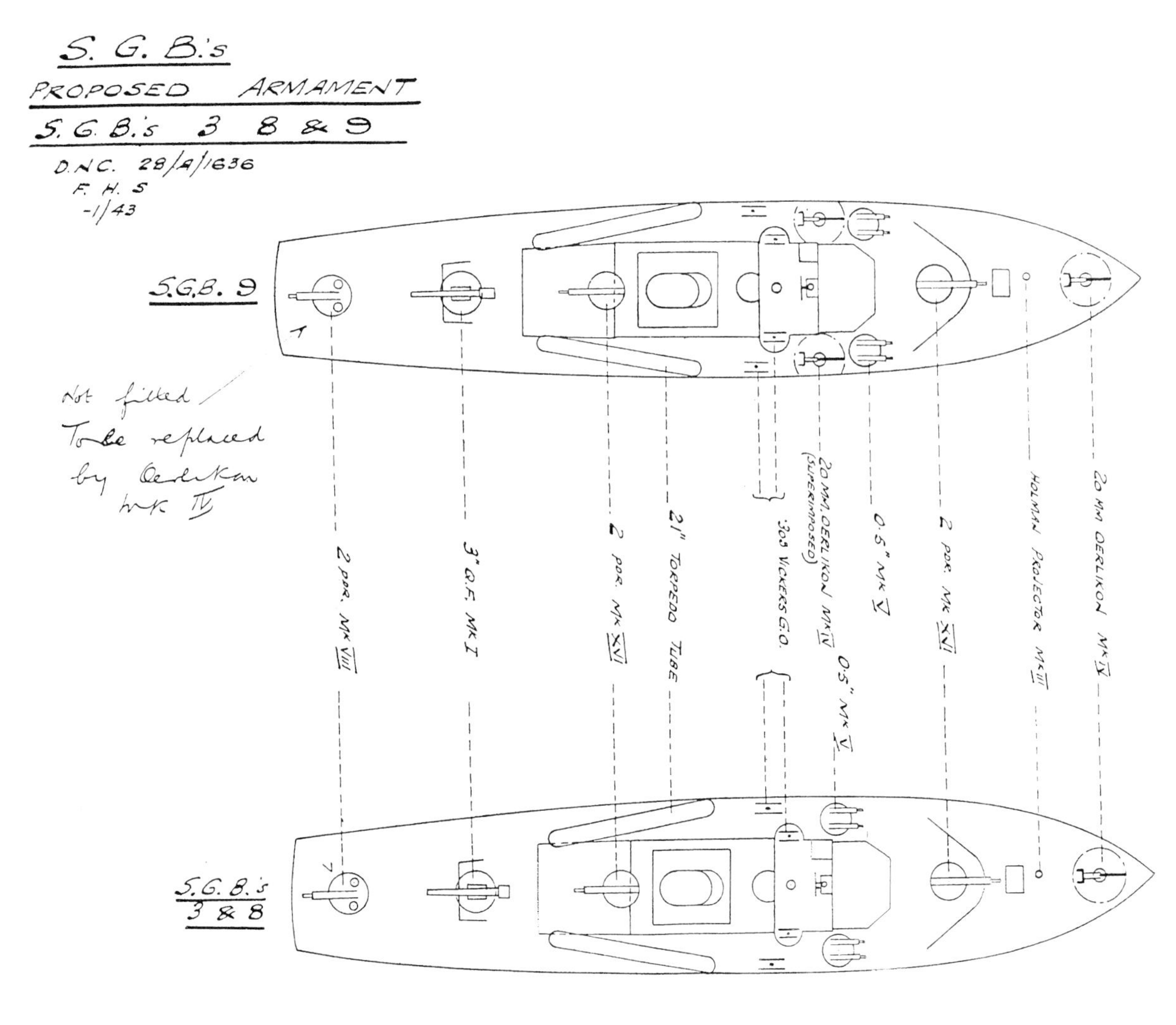

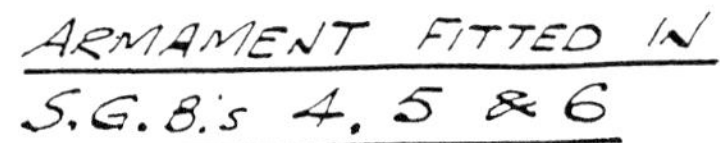

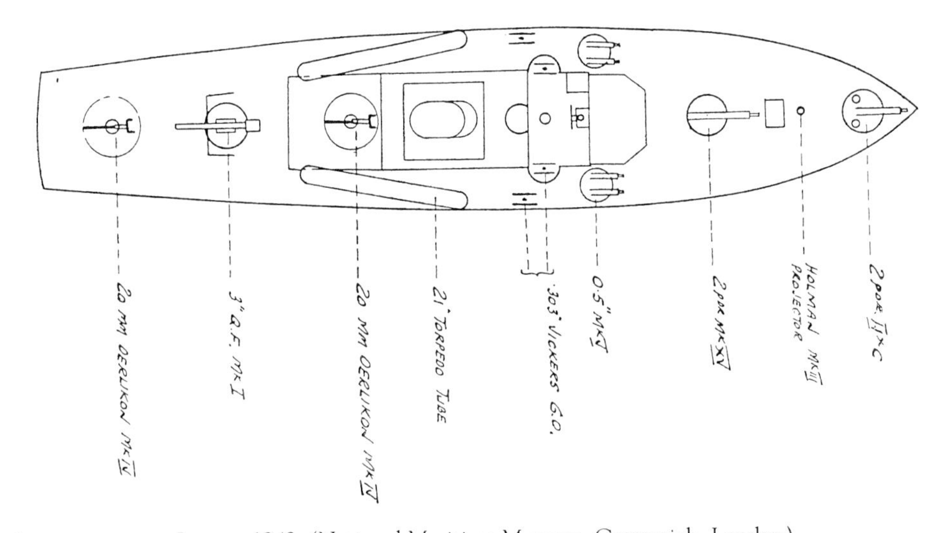

Proposed armaments as at January 1943. (National Maritime Museum, Greenwich, London)

three months to four 'Hunt' class escort destroyers. The Controller could not face this prospect, so the ships were cancelled but work continued on the machinery as there still remained a requirement for fifty boats. All the main machinery was being manufactured by Metropolitan Vickers whilst Lamont and Foster Wheeler boilers were for the most part manufactured by John Thompson of Wolverhampton (although the shipyards were responsible for some parts of the Foster Wheeler model).[26]

Further New Construction Plans

The provision of ship building facilities to enable the unordered steam gunboats to be built was clearly going to be difficult. The experience with Thornycroft and White clearly illustrated the conflict between building this new class and the construction of destroyers, escort destroyers and sloops. The 1941 New Construction Programme was being considered in December 1940, and Sir Stanley Goodall inserted fifty boats which presumably were the vessels financed by the 1940 Supplementary New Construction Programme. He was, however, experiencing opposition in the form of what he described as a 'tiresome paper by Staff' (Naval Staff) on the subject. By the end of February, his diary was recording the possibility of building steam gunboats in the United States.[27] The 1941 New Construction Programme mentioned only two more steam gunboats for building in the United Kingdom (presumably replacements for the two abandoned Thornycroft boats), in addition to the seven laid down. The question of building a further sixteen in the United States was under investigation, and it was decided that the remaining twenty five would be replaced by the same number of a modified version of the 110ft motor launch. These boats cost £70,000 per vessel; this was a favourable comparison against £100,000 per vessel for a steam gunboat. The programme was approved by the Cabinet without comment on 24 April 1941.[28]

By March, the proposal to build steam gunboats in the United States was described as 'promising' and there were thoughts of using one of two types of diesel engine under development. A month later the use of diesel engines was ruled out, as they were not yet sufficiently developed to enable a firm promise of availability to be made. Full sets of drawings were sent to America so that the project could be developed. By 25 July, the number of boats to be built in the United States had been reduced to eight. Four sets of boilers and four sets of machinery had already been ordered from John Thompson and Metropolitan Vickers for the United States, but it was agreed that they would be used in the United Kingdom if the American project failed to materialise. A matter of days later the project was abandoned as there were difficulties in translating the design to American standards. It was suggested that the machinery and boiler orders should be cancelled as there were unlikely to be any further steam gunboats built. However, the work continued. The quest for shipbuilding berths was not yet over; in September there were thoughts of building two in Malta Dockyard – which was ruled out, no doubt, because of the island's perilous situation. White's were also approached but the predicted effect on the existing programme of destroyer building again ruled out this initiative. Then in November, Vospers were considered because 70ft MTB orders were expected to diminish. This suggestion was ruled out just as the earlier idea of using Camper & Nicholsons had been. By the end of the month, eleven sets of machinery were in various states of completion , but the Staff Requirement still remained twenty-five boats. The good news was that the first craft were now nearing completion.[29]

Difficult Times

The first trials of the Denny and Yarrow boats took place in December 1941 and January 1942. The results were very disappointing with *SGB 3* only achieving 29 to 31kts over the measured mile on 13 January 1942; the best performance was 33.2kts on Run 39 when the fuel load would have been very low. The highest power output was 7265shp, a substantial shortfall against design expectations. The problems were diagnosed as the Lamont boiler which failed to produce the steam required, and the propeller design.[30] The boiler problem was caused by bad combustion and impure feed water. This was solved with the insertion of inlet nozzles in each element of the boiler to improve combustion and the impure feed water difficulty was dealt with by using the United States system of cleaning which used a boiler compound.[31] Another factor which influenced the trials was the very heavy load of fuel, the full 50 tons being carried where as the intention had been to use this facility on an 'overload' basis only. There were also far more personnel on board than would be normal – which on a small ship had a noticeable effect. Sir Stanley Goodall felt the results to be 'quite good' from a propulsive standpoint. By the time that the last boat (*SGB 9*, the future *Grey Goose*) was completed, she had the benefit of the accumulated experience of her sisters. In trials held on 11 June 1942 her mean average speed over a measured mile was 35.4kts, at 894rpm and 8345shp, with a displacement of 172 tons. The boat had a Foster Wheeler boiler, a new propeller design and a 3in gun, a major departure from the original design. The results were reported by Sir Stanley Goodall, no doubt with an element of relief.

One week later another problem came to the fore, when what turned out to be 'the Achilles heel' became evident. *SGB 7*, which had only been completed three months previously, was in action in the Seine Bay when she received damage in the boiler room, which resulted in her loss. The Commodore controlling the coastal reacted rapidly to the vulnerability problem. He wrote:

> It is agreed that experience although very limited has shown them [the steam gunboats] to be vulnerable in that, unlike a motor torpedo boat with its three independent engine units, they are rapidly stopped by a single hit. Some measure of armour may reduce this vulnerability but I do not feel qualified to remark but I regret a consequent loss of speed.

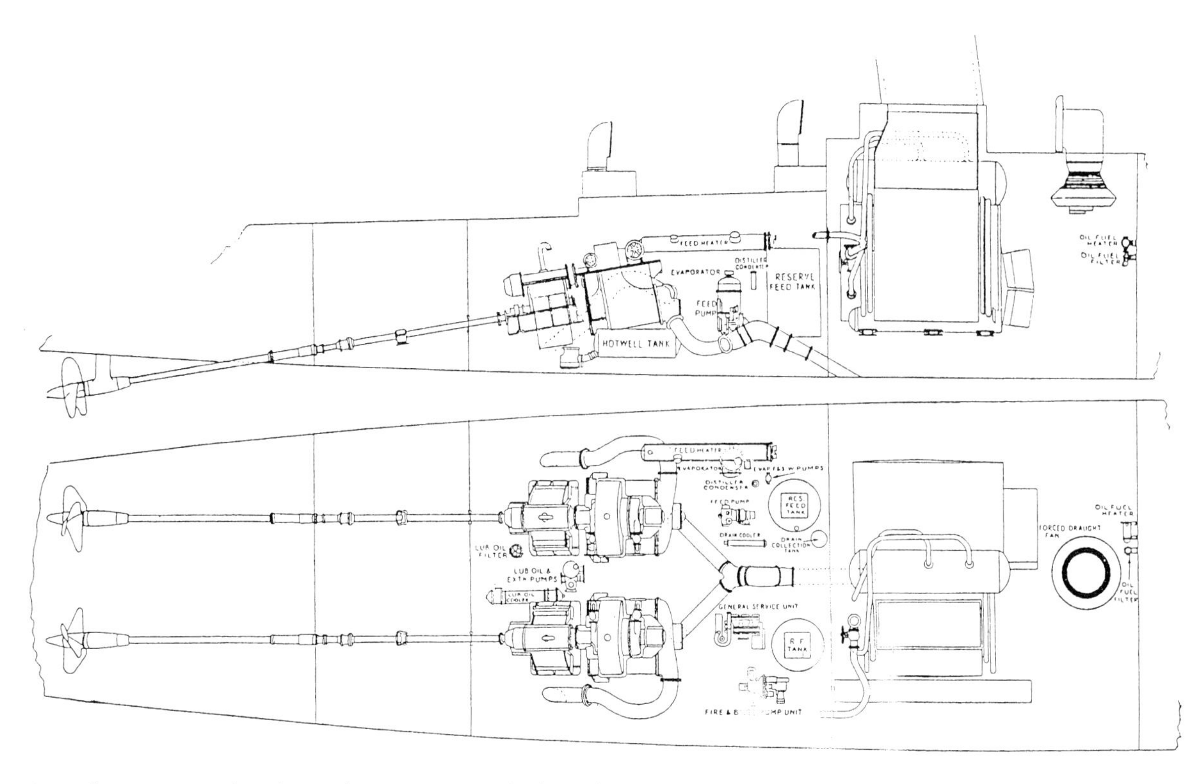

General arrangement of machinery showing a Foster Wheeler Boiler. (Royal Institution of Naval Architects)

He also made the suggestion that the boats could be converted to minelayers – an option quickly ruled out as the steam gunboats were considered too valuable. Within four days the decision had been taken for protection to be fitted around the boiler, when the craft were due to undertake their next repair period. The armour utilised was supplied by the United States and consisted of 30lb DIHT plating. Also to be considered at this time were the fitting of 3in or 4in guns with a 2pdr and two Oerlikons. Additional torpedoes were also considered, the number now rising to four carried in four tubes, an option seemingly not followed up.[32] The armament of the steam gunboats evolved into a multitude of variations, but it seems unlikely that a 4in gun was ever fitted. The torpedo armament was an addition to the original design.

Further Plans and Evolutions

The intensity of the war meant that there was a continuing demand for light forces which would attack enemy coastal shipping in the Channel and North Sea and counter E-boat activity. When the 1941 Supplementary New Construction Programme was compiled it was confirmed that the Fairmile 'D' class was to be the main constituent of the anti-E-boat forces. Eight 71ft motor gunboats were also authorised.[33] By February 1942, Plans Division were producing the 1942 New Construction Programme. A combination of steam gun boats and Fairmile 'D' class were wanted. The latter were described as 'the most powerful high speed craft we can produce in the motor driven type'. There was still clearly considerable faith in the steam gunboat. They were said to have 'undergone trials successfully' and it was 'hoped that we have produced in this country a type of vessel which can be useful in attacking enemy shipping in the North Sea and Channel and which will be more than a match for the E-boat'. Ten were proposed in the Programme.[34] These boats were effectively replacements for the two cancelled Thornycroft units and the residual eight planned for construction in North America. The programme presented to the Cabinet on 27 April 1942, included the ten steam gunboats each still said to cost £100,000, forty-eight Fairmile D class at £75,000 per vessel, and eight motor gunboats at £60,000 each.[35] The inclusion of the steam gunboats seems surprising but there were now ten sets of turbines either manufactured or nearing completion and this factor may have influenced the decision. The first of this batch were intended for the ex-Thornycroft boats and in May 1941 they were listed as scheduled to complete on 1 and 15 November.[36]

Problems again came when homes had to be found for the new boats; this search started in May 1942. Both Denny and White said that if more were ordered then other warships would be delayed, and no one else offered to build the boats. One anonymous firm said 'the last two caused considerable dislocation in our programme'; another 'that they proved most unbalancing in the production programme, for although they were hulls only (we) had to fit up the machinery, the erection of which

SGB 6, later Grey Shark*, as completed 30 April 1942.* (GM Hudson collection)

Grey Fox *(SGB 4) in December 1942.* (GM Hudson collection)

was then a bottleneck.' By 20 July, the Vice Controller said that a decision to build the steam gunboats would await a comparison of the operational value with that of the Fairmile 'D' class. Virtually the final blow to the programme was the increase in the Intermediate (Light Fleet) Carrier Programme which caused considerable dislocation to warship building plans. The last port of call was the Royal Dockyards, which were asked to consider building steam gunboats instead of sloops. They too declined on the grounds that considerable material was already assembled for the sloops, and that in any case they had no experience of building small ships of destroyer type. On 24 August the proposals were held in abeyance by the Director of Naval Construction and seemingly never raised again.[37]

The surviving six steam gunboats were very active in the Channel from mid 1942 until September 1944 serving in the 1st SGB Flotilla. The use of bases was flexible; Portsmouth, Newhaven, Dover and Portland were utilised. They were then converted into fast minesweepers to deal with German pressure mines, all being fitted with a 75kw pulse generator and 'LL' magnetic sweep gear. They were then commissioned into the 1st SGB Minesweeping Flotilla by December 1944. Operational use in the new role seems to have been light, and with the end of the war all were quickly placed into reserve. By 1949, all had been sold with the exception of *SGB 9 Grey Goose*, which served as a trial-ship for Rolls Royce RM60 gas turbines from 1954 to 1956. She was finally sold in 1958 and later named *Anserava*. Her hull is said to still exist at the time of writing at Hoo near Rochester on the River Medway.[38]

Perspective

Should the steam gunboats have been built? First of all, the war when the concept was initiated must be considered. An answer was needed to the German E-boats, no diesel engine existed which was suitable for use in a fast coastal craft and Rolls Royce Merlin engines were all needed by the Royal Air Force. Inevitably steam power was the only alternative. The concept was good, but as we have seen, building the boats proved far more difficult, lengthy and probably more costly than anticipated. There were also considerable teething troubles when the first craft went to sea. They also proved very vulnerable until armour was fitted to overcome the weak protection around the boiler and attachments. Once in service they proved to be powerful antagonists for the German E-boats, and after the war it became clear that German commanders had a particular dislike of them.[39] The best answers proved to be the Fairmile 'D' and the 71ft 6in British Power Boat, which did not interfere with the main warship building programmes but were not available when the steam gunboat was first conceived. It was right to build the seven boats completed, but perhaps it was as well that the remaining forty-three boats of the main programme did not proceed. The steam gunboats have one claim to fame; they were the last true torpedo boat destroyers

References

1 ADM 138 643. Ship's Cover – The Steam Gun Boats. (National Maritime Museum).
2 'Steam Gunboat Machinery – A Light-Weight Steam Plant' by Commander E H K Lay and Commander L Baker, DSC, Royal Navy. (*Transactions of the Institution of Naval Architects*, Volume 91, March 1949).
3 Diary of Sir Stanley Goodall (via D K Brown, RCNC). The diary is held in the British Library.
4 The Anti-E-boat is the original type name for the SGB. The diary reference seems to be the earliest record of this nomenclature.
5 ADM 138 643.
6 ADM 229 25. DNC file, March 1941-March 1942 (Public Record Office) . Note: The file contains material from dates earlier than March 1941.
7 ADM 138 643. Tower is believed to be the Director of Naval Equipment.
8 Diary of Sir Stanley Goodall. The official probably referred to was Admiral Sir F T B Tower, KBE who was Vice Controller or Director of Naval Equipment between 1936 and 1944.
9 ADM 138 643.
10 ADM 167 109. 1940 Board Minutes and Memoranda (Public Record Office). The Sabre engine was manufactured by Napier and used in aircraft such as the Hawker Typhoon. American-built Packard Merlin engines were not being produced at this time. The first engines from this source for Coastal Forces were fitted in May 1941.
11 ADM 138 643.
12 Diary of Sir Stanley Goodall.
13 ADM 229 25.
14 ADM 1 10850. 1940 New Construction Programme (Public Record Office).
15 CAB 66 5. New Construction Programme (Ref WP(40)349 Public Record Office).
16 CAB 120 281. Secretariat files – Navy, 1940 June-1945 June: Shipbuilding and Repairs.
17 CAB 65 9. Cabinet Minutes (Ref WM 277 (40)).
18 ADM 229 25.
19 ADM 138 643.
20 Diary of Sir Stanley Goodall.
21 ADM 138 643. Swan Hunter were included because of their experience with the experimental motor launch Tarret. This 80 ton vessel fitted with a diesel engine had a designed speed of 30kts but only made 23.5kts on trials. She was rapidly scrapped. (*The Design of British Warships 1939-1945* Part Two; *Warships Supplement 76* (Spring 1984); *The Steam Gun Boats of 1942* World Ship Society).
22 Diary of Sir Stanley Goodall.
23 ADM 138 643.
24 ADM 167 109.
25 ibid.
26 ADM 138 643.
27 Diary of Sir Stanley Goodall.
28 CAB 66 16. New Construction Programme 1941 (Ref: WP(41)88). The modified 110ft motor launch became the Fairmile D class. Cabinet approval is in CAB 65 18 (Ref: WM (41)43).
29 ADM 138 643.
30 *ibid*.
31 *Steam Gunboat Machinery* (Institution of Naval Architects).

[32] ADM 138 643.
[33] CAB 66 20. Supplementary New Construction Programme 1941 (Ref WP(41)280). Cabinet approval is in CAB 65 20 (Ref: WM(41)118).
[34] ADM 116 4601. 1942 New Construction Programme (Ref: PD0789/42).
[35] CAB 66 24. New Construction Programme 1942 (Ref: WP(42)173). Cabinet approval is in CAB 65 26 (Ref: WM(53)42).
[36] ADM 138 643. In May 1943 when a small monitor was being considered as a support craft for the invasion of Europe, there were ten sets of SGB machinery available (*Work Book* by M K Purvis, held at National Maritime Museum, via D K Brown, RCNC).
[37] ADM 138 643.
[38] Operational and disposal details were published by the World Ship Society in *Warships Supplement 76*. Details of the conversion to fast minesweepers are set out in the last part of 'Steam Gunboats of the Royal Navy' by John Lambert, which was published in *Model Boats* between May and November 1979.
[39] Paper 'Coastal Force Design' read by W J Holt, RCNC to the Institute of Naval Architects on the 27th March 1947. (Reprinted in *Selected papers on British Warship Design in World War Two* 1983).

Acknowledgements
My thanks are due to David K Brown RCNC and Geoffrey Hudson for producing background information from their records and for providing ideas which I incorporated in the text. I would also like to thank the Royal Institute of Naval Architects and the National Maritime Museum for allowing use of their drawings; also the staff of the Public Record Office and Bob Todd and his team at the National Maritime Museum.

Appendices

Appendix One

The Anti-E Boat. 10 October 1940

Length on waterline	125ft
Breadth extreme	22ft
Depth amidships	11ft 7in
Approximate Draughts (half oil condition):	
Forward	4ft
Aft at Propellers	7ft
Displacement (half oil condition):	130 tons
Displacement (load condition):	140 tons
Shaft Horsepower of Engines	8000 (twin screw)
Boilers	One, either Lamont or Foster Wheeler
Armament	One 2pdr automatic gun in power mounting
	Two power twin 0.5in turrets
	Two Lewis shoulder shooting guns
	Two Star Shell Mortars
Protection	Non magnetic protective plating ⅜in thick to wheelhouse and control position abaft it.
R/D/F	To signal School requirements.
Searchlight	20 degree placed off middle line to obtain clear view forward and aft. Will be wooded by funnel on part of aft Starboard bearings.
Complement	2 Officers, 3 Petty Officers, 12 Ratings.

Remarks on machinery
The turbine designs were being prepared by Metropolitan Vickers, but the EinC was prepared to accept equally suitable designs from other firms if they wished it. Metro Vick expected to produce the first set in six months and two or three sets per month thereafter. Auxiliaries were to be produced by the ordinary makers and fitted by the builders.

Boilers
The Lamont boiler was produced by Messrs J Thompson of Wolverhampton. The Foster Wheeler boiler could be produced by any firm under licence. The proportion of each boiler type to be used was a matter for later consideration. The EinC wanted to know if firms preferred to build their own boilers.

(Source: ADM 229 24. DNC file, June 1940-March 1941)

Appendix Two

The Anti-E Boat. 2 December 1940
(Paper for Board of Admiralty)

Length on waterline	135ft
Length overall	143ft 11in
Breadth extreme	23ft 4in
Displacement	135 tons
Draught (forward)	3ft 9in
Shaft Horse Power	8000
Speed in standard condition	36kts
Speed in deep condition (20 tons oil fuel):	34kts
Oil fuel capacity	20 tons
Oil fuel capacity (emergency):	30 tons additional
Endurance	awaiting result of trials
Complement of Officers and Men:	17
Armament	One 2pdr HA single on power mounting
	1150 rounds per gun
	0.5in machine guns on twin power worked mountings
	2400 rounds per gun
	Lewis shoulder shooting
	2500 rounds per gun
Armour	Bullet proof plating – wheelhouse & bridge.
Weights (tons):	
General equipment	7.5
Machinery including water & lubricating oil:	52
Armament	7
Protection	2
Hull	66.5
Standard Displacement	135

General Description of Steam Gunboats (abbreviated)

Genesis of the Design.
A counter was required to the German E-boats, particularly where conditions were unsuitable for motor torpedo boats. We are largely dependent on internal combustion engines from abroad, the Engineer in Chief has designed a steam machinery of low weight and high power which can be produced in this country.

Dimensions.
In working out the design it was found that the estimated displacement was too small. The best way to increase dimensions was to increase length, as this improves propulsive efficiency and seaworthiness.

Form and Seaworthiness.
Estimated turning circle at full power is about 500yds. The reputation these boats will win for seamanship will depend to a great extent on seamanship. Speed in rough weather will be limited but they should be superior to E-boats in this respect.

Construction.
The hull is of ungalvanised steel, rapid construction being more important than long life.

Armament.
The armament has not been definitely decided beyond the detail quoted. A magazine and space aft have been arranged for another 2pdr (Power or Rolls Royce). The structure and space amidships would permit the fitting of two torpedo tubes but fitting would reduce speed by about half a knot. A 20in searchlight (worked from a battery) is provided.

Machinery, Speed and Endurance.
A single boiler and two sets of geared turbines will drive the propeller shafts at 900 revolutions per minute giving a speed of 34-36kts according to loading. The first set is being built rapidly for extensive testing. Pending results endurance at various speeds cannot be given. Additional oil load of 30 tons means the vessel will have to be nursed in a seaway if serious strains are to be avoided.

Appendix Three

The Steam Gun Boats

	Job Number	Builder	Laid down	Launched	Completed
SGB1	J6066	Thornycroft	Not laid down – cancelled		
SGB2	J6087	Thornycroft	Not laid down – cancelled		
SGB3 *Grey Seal*	J1874	Yarrow	24.141	29.8.41	21.2.42
SGB4 *Grey Fox*	J1875	Yarrow	24.1.41	25.9.41	15.3.42
SGB5 *Grey Owl*	J4273	Hawthorn Leslie	17.4.41	27.8.41	1.4.42
SGB6 *Grey Shark*	J4275	Hawthorn Leslie	28.3.41	17. 11.41	30.4.42
SGB7	J1261	Denny	3.2.41	25.9.41	11.3.42
SGB8 *Grey Wolf*	J1262	Denny	3.2.41	3.11.41	17.4.42
SGB9 *Grey Goose*	J6059	White	23.1.41	14.2.42	4.7.42

Note: Other records say that SGB 5 laid down 28.3.41 and SGB 6 laid down 17.4.41.

(Source: Warships Supplement 76, World Ship Society, Spring 1984)
(Job Numbers source: CB 3064. Copy held at the Naval Historical Branch)

Wireless Telegraphy Arrangements.
Radio Direction Finding – Type 286 and Wireless Telegraphy – Type T/W 12D provided.

Protection.
3/8in protective plating for bridge and wheelhouse. Extent – to be discussed. Provided no extra weight involved arrangement can be modified.

Accommodation.
Generally similar to that fitted in motor torpedo boats. Provisions, including water, carried on basis of a single operation (3 days supply). For a longer sea passage temporary arrangements would have to be made and such old fashioned hardships as no fresh water for washing purposes accepted.

(Signed) S V GOODALL. 2nd December, 1940.

THE BRAZILIAN IMPERIAL NAVY IRONCLADS, 1865-1874

The Brazilian Imperial Navy of the 1860s faced two problems, to protect the coastline from its unstable and sometimes quarrelsome neighbours, and to keep the major rivers open for commerce. Not surprisingly, the War of the Triple Alliance forced its administrators to look for solutions similar to those developed by the Union Navy in the American Civil War. **George A Gratz** provides a detailed study of these armoured ships and their experiences.

The first ironclad projects

Concerned about news of the construction of armoured ships in Europe, and naval warfare in the US Civil War, the Brazilian Imperial Navy Minister, Rear Admiral Joaquim de Lamare, presented a report to Parliament in May 1862, describing the latest innovations in naval technology. That report opened the way for future acquisition of modern warships for Brazil's Navy.

In a series of more practical measures, de Lamare asked Lieutenant (Armament Engineer) Henrique Antonio Baptista (who was in Europe), to write a report on naval guns. He created a committee to study US riverine warfare, and sent the Navy's Director of Naval Construction, Lieutenant (Naval Constructor) Napoleão Level, to the United Kingdom and France to acquaint himself with the latest technical advances in armour and steam propulsion. In March 1863, when Level returned to Brazil, he brought back plans and models, and an estimate for a corvette and two gunboats to be built in France. In fact, he recommended that the gunboats should be built in Brazil, in order to train the dockyard engineers and workers, and this was duly approved by the Navy Minister.

These vessels were adequate for the envisaged war scenario: coastal and riverine. At the end of the 1850s, as a result of tension between Brazil and Paraguay about navigation rights on the Paraguay River and the expansion of Brazilian interests in the River Plate region, the navy ordered fourteen screw gunboats from abroad, suitable for river operation, and built two more at the Royal Naval Arsenal, Rio de Janeiro. After the Paraguayan War this policy was continued, so that similar requirements led to the construction in the 1870s of the powerful French-built 3700-ton monitors *Javary* and *Solimões*, and also influenced the design of the British-built battleship *Aquidaban* in the 1880s.

Details of these first projects are as follows:

Ironclad corvette

Dimensions :	60.96m (pp) x 10.67m x 4.04m
Depth in hold:	4.04m
Cassette length:	15.85m
Tonnage:	1450-tons (bom)
Propulsion:	200hp (nominal)
Speed:	10.5kts
Armament:	Eight guns
Cost:	£56,640

Gunboat

Dimensions :	54.86m (pp) x 9.15m x 2.44m
Depth in hold:	3.27m
Casemate length:	8.53m
Tonnage:	775-tons (bom)
Propulsion:	100hp (nominal)
Speed:	10.5kts
Armament:	Four guns
Cost:	£34,488

Both ships had iron hulls with an 114 mm thick iron belt along the entire length, forming a casemate of uniform thickness.

The First Ironclad

The corvette project materialised, with some modifications, as the first Brazilian ironclad, the *Brasil*; built in France, the contract for its construction was signed on 5 January 1864. This ship, as foreseen in the initial studies, had an iron hull, and the original contract specified that she should have the same rig as the Italian *Maria Pia*, and the armour of the same quality and thickness of the

The armoured corvette Brasil *after combat with Paraguayan batteries in Curupaity, 22 September 1866.* (Author's collection)

Spanish *Numancia*, both ironclads being built at the time in the shipyard.

The Paraguayan Challenge - An Ironclad Race Begins

Beginning in November 1862, John & Alfred Blyth Engineering of Limehouse presented several ironclad designs to the Paraguayan Government. They acted as consulting engineers, furnishing the basic specifications and also acted as intermediaries in negotiating and ordering these ironclads from various shipyards. In November 1864, Captain Cowper Coles was contracted to design the revolving turrets for two of the vessels, a job that was finished on 31 December of that year, when the drawings and specifications were furnished. Before that, in October 1864, the building of two ironclads had already been authorised by Lord John Russell, the British Foreign Secretary. The ships finally ordered were the *Minerva* and *Bellona* from William Laird & Sons, of Birkenhead, the *Triton* and *Meduza* from Dudgeon Brothers, of Limehouse, and the French *Nemesis*. These ironclads, as well as Krupp guns and Enfield-pattern rifles ordered by the Paraguayan Army, would, if delivered, drastically alter the balance of power in the South in favour of Paraguay.

As soon as the war began, the Paraguayan diplomats directed all their efforts to blocking the delivery of the *Brasil*, the only armoured ship near completion; but Baron Penedo, Brazil's ambassador in Europe, succeeded in getting clearance for the ship. She sailed from Toulon on 1 July 1865, and was given a salute by all of the

Ironclad Corvette *Brasil* - Particulars as built

Laid down in 1864, launched 23 December 1864 and completed 2 March 1865 by Forges et Chantiers de la Mediterranée at La Seyne, France, at a cost of £60,000.

Dimensions:	60.10m (pp); 61.70m (wl); 63.41m (oa) x 10.75m x 3.50 m (bow); 3.81m (aft)	
Armament:	Four 70pdr Whitworth muzzle-loading (ML) guns	
	Four 68pdr smooth-bore (SB) guns	
	One 12pdr SB gun	
Propulsion:	The entire system was built by Forges et Chantiers de la Mediterranée: single- expansion engine developing 250hp (nominal); two boilers and one four-bladed cast iron propeller	
Speed:	10.5kts (designed); on the Rio de Janeiro measured mile she averaged 11.7kts	
Armour:	Iron; hull belt 114mm (maximum), tapering to 90mm at bow and stern; casemate 102mm. Both hull and casemate had 230mm wood backing	
Weights (tons):	Hull and fittings:	520
	Guns and ammunition:	82
	Armour and wood backing:	418
	Two boilers (loaded with water) and machinery:	190
	Coal:	170
	Sail and masts (sail area 550 m2):	42
	Stores and water:	96
	Total:	1518

Armoured corvette Brasil*. General arrangement as originally rigged and built.* (Drawn by the author)

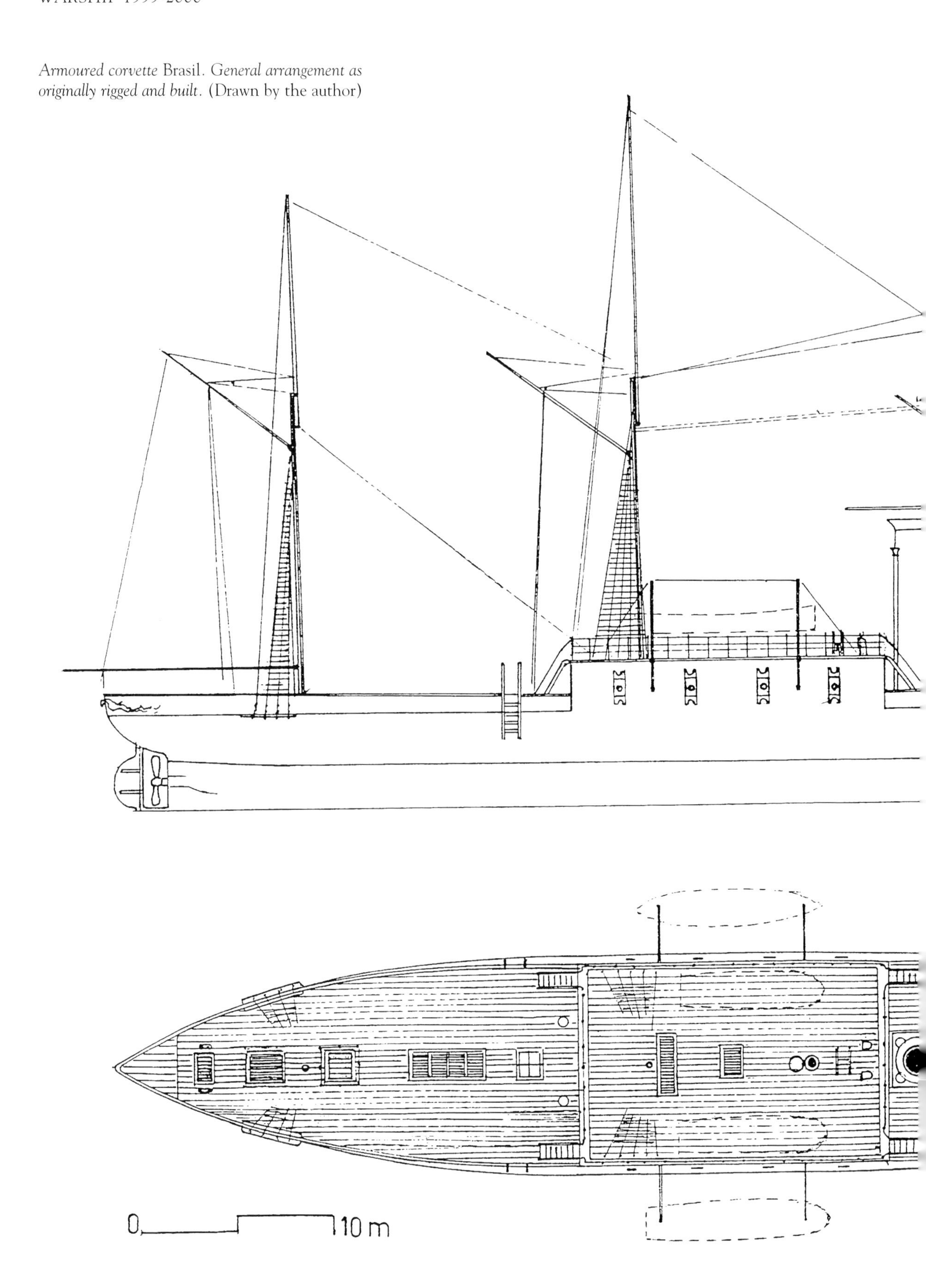

French ships in the harbour. A steamer escorted the ship as far as the Island of Madeira to bring back the shipyard workers who were engaged in the final trials. The ship arrived in Rio de Janeiro on 29 July and was commissioned in the Brazilian Navy two days later. The outbreak of war cut off Paraguayan contact with Europe, and the government was unable to maintain the payments for the ships, and as a result all the ironclads ordered were finally sold to Paraguay's enemy Brazil, and used against the Paraguayan Navy.

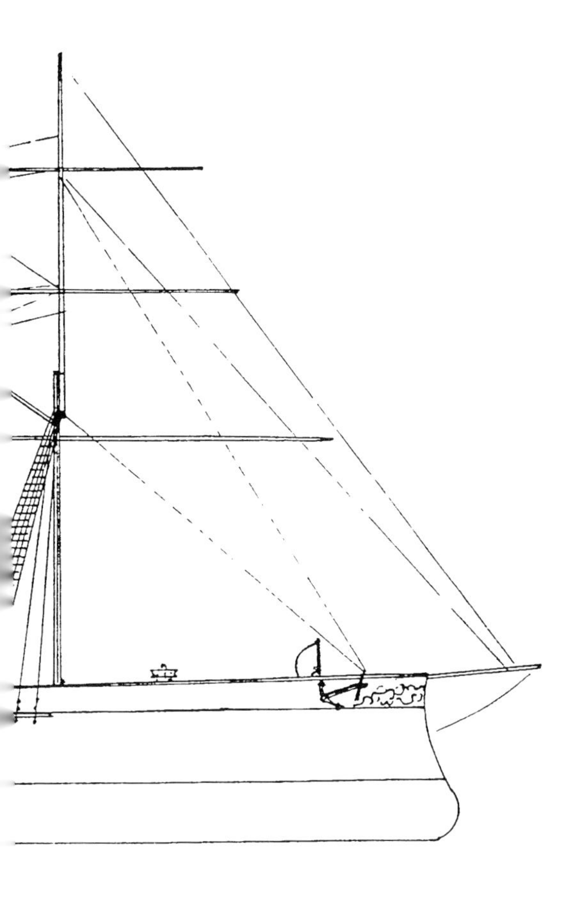

The Brazilian Reaction

Apart from the ships ordered in the United Kingdom (*Cabral* and *Colombo* built by A C Rennie of Greenwich), or in negotiation for purchase in Europe, the Brazilian Navy also hoped to acquire redundant warships from the US Navy after the Civil War. In October 1865 Captain Joaquim de Azambuja from the Brazilian navy, with William H Webb as technical adviser, inspected several monitors put for sale, such as the *Yazoo* of the infamous *Casco* class, and the *Canonicus* and *Saugus*. None were purchased however, because Azambuja and Webb doubted if the monitors could face the Atlantic Ocean waters, with their low freeboard and structural faults pointed out by Webb. Two of the best monitors for sale, the *Catawba* and *Oneota* of the *Canonicus* class, were sold to Peru and arrived by way of Cape Horn after a troublesome voyage that took all of fifteen months. By way of comparison, the Laird-built *Bahia* (ex-*Minerva*) crossed the Atlantic in thirty days.

The Three Ironclad Gunboats

At the same time, the Brazilian Navy had started work on three First Class Armoured Gunboats in the Royal Naval Arsenal. Their delivery took from six to eight months each, the first ship (the *Tamandaré*) being sent to the theatre of operations with workers on board finishing the assembly of the casemate armour plates. 'Here it may be remarked that every protracted war will develop new requirements, which must be met by the rapid construction of special types. The Crimean War produced the floating battery, the Civil War in America the monitor, and the Paraguayan War a new class of large, armoured, gunboat', noted Sir Thomas Brassey in *The British Navy* Vol 1 (1882).

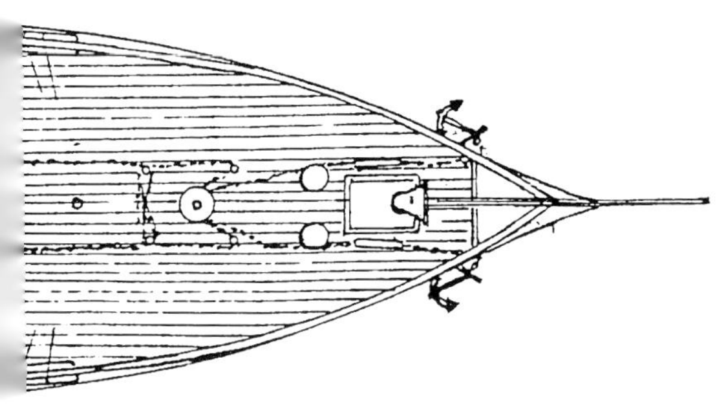

The First Class Armoured Gunboats *Tamandaré*, *Barrozo* and *Rio de Janeiro*, were built to the same general design, based on the 1863 project. There were, however, some differences. The *Rio de Janeiro* was longer than the *Tamandaré*, to provide space for bigger engines and boilers, and the *Barrozo* was a scaled-up version – longer, wider beamed and with a bigger casemate than the others. This third unit was sometimes described as an Armoured Corvette in official papers. They all proved good sea boats, and in river navigation the *Barrozo* performed very well, but the *Rio de Janeiro* did not perform as well, and the *Tamandaré* was decidedly poor, because of her old

TABLE 1: *TECHNICAL DATA OF THE FIRST CLASS ARMOURED GUNBOATS*

Name of the ship	*Tamandaré*	*Barroso*	*Rio de Janeiro*
Classification: *Canhoneira Couraçada*	Nr. 1	Nr. 2	Nr. 3
Laid down	31 May 1865	21 February 1865	26 June 1865
Launched	21 June 1865	4 November 1865	18 February 1865
Completed	16 September 1865	11 January 1865	1 March 1866
Removed from the list	1879	1881	1866 (sunk)
Cost	£40,506	£55,046	£47,409
Builder:	Arsenal de Marinha da Côrte (Royal Naval Arsenal) at Ilha das Cobras, Rio de Janeiro		
Dimensions (in meters)			
Length (oa)	51.36	61.44	56.69
Beam	9.19	10.97	9.19
Depth of hold	3.04	3.34	3.04
Draught (mean)	2.44	2.74	2.62
Draught (designed)	2.59	2.59	2.59
Midship submerged section (designed) in sq meters	18.00	21.50	18.00
Displacement (tons)			
Normal	754	980	871
Full load	845	1354	1001
Machinery	Two tubular boilers; Penn & Sons trunk engine, with two cylinders, single-expansion; one two-bladed screw propeller. Coal for six days.		
ihp/knots	273/8	420/9	320/9
Armament: (all the MLs were Whitworth guns)			
120pdr ML	none	1	none
70pdr ML	1	2	2
68pdr SB	3	2	2
12pdr SB	2	2	none
Armour: wrought iron			
Belt: 51 mm<102 mm>51 mm; Deck: 12.7 mm; Casemate: 102 mm with 609 mm wood backing, top 12.7 mm			
Crew (Officers and ratings)	120	149	148

Note: The engines of the *Tamandaré* were taken from the British-built gunboat *Tietê* (450-tons, length 45.72m pp)

engines. The *Barroso*, together with the French built *Silvado*, was considered the more manoeuvrable ship for riverine operations. They were originally schooner-rigged for sea passages, their freeboard being 1.7m, including 1.1m bulwarks removable in riverine operations, as well as the masts, to permit all-round fire.

Hulls

The original specification envisaged iron hulls, but the difficulty of obtaining all the materials in time, allied to the lack of experience in this type of construction, led to their being built of wood, with iron parts only to support the armoured deck and the top of the casemate plates. Their hulls were made of three 203mm thick layers of wood at the sides, decreasing progressively to thinner layers at the keel. They were sheathed with Muntz metal, and were fitted with a 1.4m (1.8m in the *Barroso*) bronze ram bow. Both the deck and the top of the casemate were curved and fitted with iron plates with a 102 mm plank above. The whole superstructure was supported by I-beams 203mm high, athwartships, which were fastened to L-brackets screwed on the wooden sides. As normal in wooden hulls, they had no bulkheads, which led to the *Rio de Janeiro* sinking rapidly after hitting a mine.

Bahia *photographed after 1885, when she was reboilered, and had the wooden decking changed, the bulwarks removed and a bridge added.* (Author's collection)

Meduza *(later the Brazilian* Herval*), as rigged for sea travel.* (Author's collection)

Nemesis *(later the Brazilian* Silvado*). General arrangement. This monitor was very manoeuvrable due to its twin screws and rudders.* (Drawn by the author)

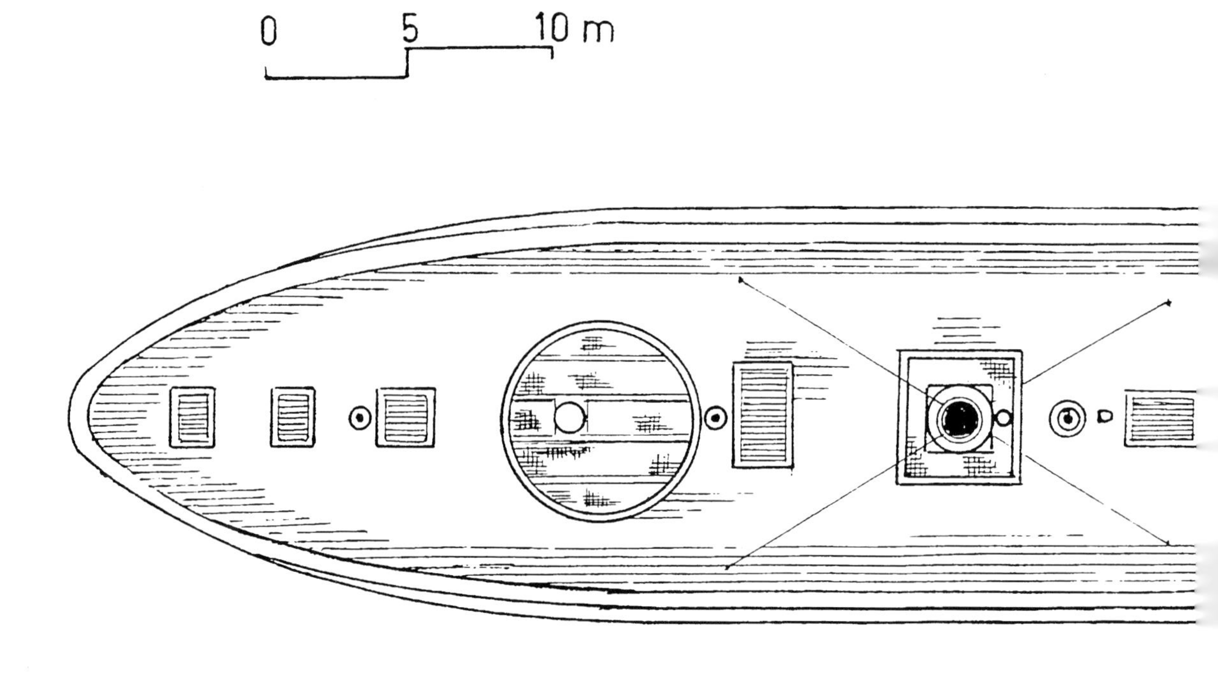

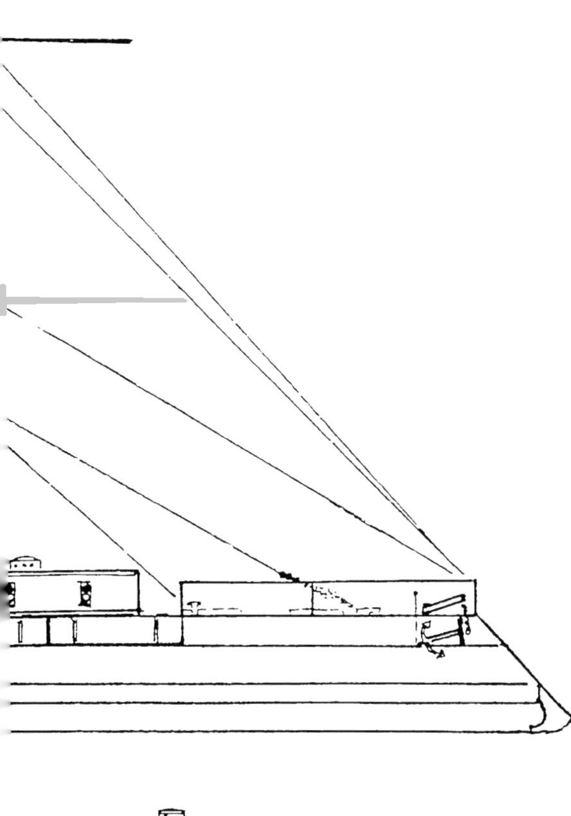

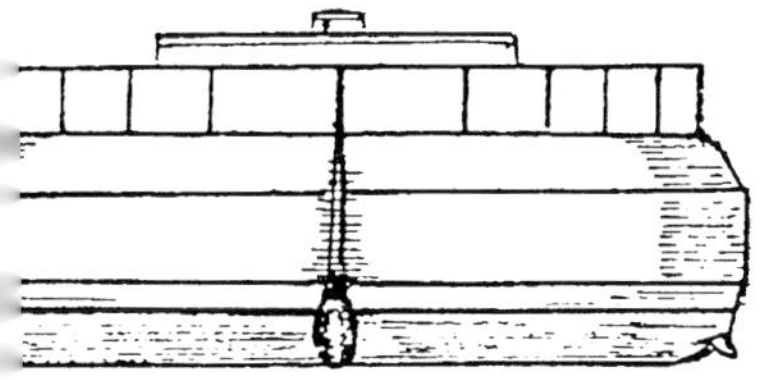

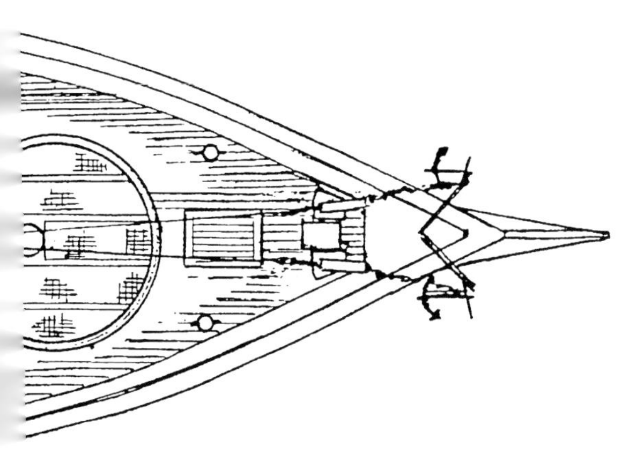

Protection

These ships' hulls had a complete 1.52m deep iron belt. It was 102mm thick in the engine, boiler and magazine areas, while in the remainder of the ship it was 51mm thick. The casemate also had 102mm of armour with 609mm hardwood backing. It was capped with a 102mm thick layer of peroba hardwood. The 12.7mm iron plates that covered the structure of the curved deck and of the casemate completed the above water protection. The rectangular casemate, 9m in length (9.8in the *Barrozo*), was pierced for two guns at the sides, front and rear, the height of the gunports above the waterline being 1.6m, as designed.

The trials for the *Tamandaré* and her near-sister's armour were held at the fortress of São João, Rio de Janeiro, in July 1865. A 70pdr Whitworth rifled gun and a 68pdr smooth bore were fired at a distance of 278m at a wooden target 3m high and 2.4m wide and 609mm thick, covered with 102mm iron plates. The 68pdr gun, firing solid round shot, caused indentations on the plates and displacement of some bolts. The Whitworth, using a propellant charge of 10lbs, made indentations, and a 450mm crack on the plates, without reaching the wood backing.

The hull armour extended below the waterline to protect against floating mines, which were recognised as a serious threat. The *Tamandaré* was the first ship of the Brazilian Navy to be protected by a net-defence against these mines. This protection, to be used when the ship was at anchor, was devised by James Hamilton Tomb, who had been working for the Brazilian Navy as a mining expert since 1866. The successful use of this device was extended to other ships in the combat zone, and Tomb was transferred to the steamer *Apa*, which was used as a 'torpedo spotter' for the fleet.

Guns

The number of non-standard guns that armed these and other ironclads of the Brazilian Navy were the result of alterations to the schedule for the delivery of the guns from Europe. The pressing need for guns meant that, as soon as one arrived, it would be installed in the first available ship. The only ironclads to carry their designed armament were the *Bahia*, *Lima Barros*, *Silvado* and *Herval*. The others shipped with a mixed battery of whatever guns were available. The guns of the casemate ships, including the *Brasil*, were mounted on iron carriages designed by Lieutenant Henrique Baptista. They were simple mountings, designed for easy and rapid construction, which was the main criterion at the time.

In order to decrease the possibility of shots coming through them, the gunports were as small as possible, allowing for a horizontal firing angle of only 12°. Crude pointing of the guns at the target was therefore done by aligning the anchored ship against the river current, by using the rudder, the engine and the anchor cables, since most of the firing was done upriver against enemy field fortifications. After some months of action, the consensus of opinion was that the best guns were the smooth-

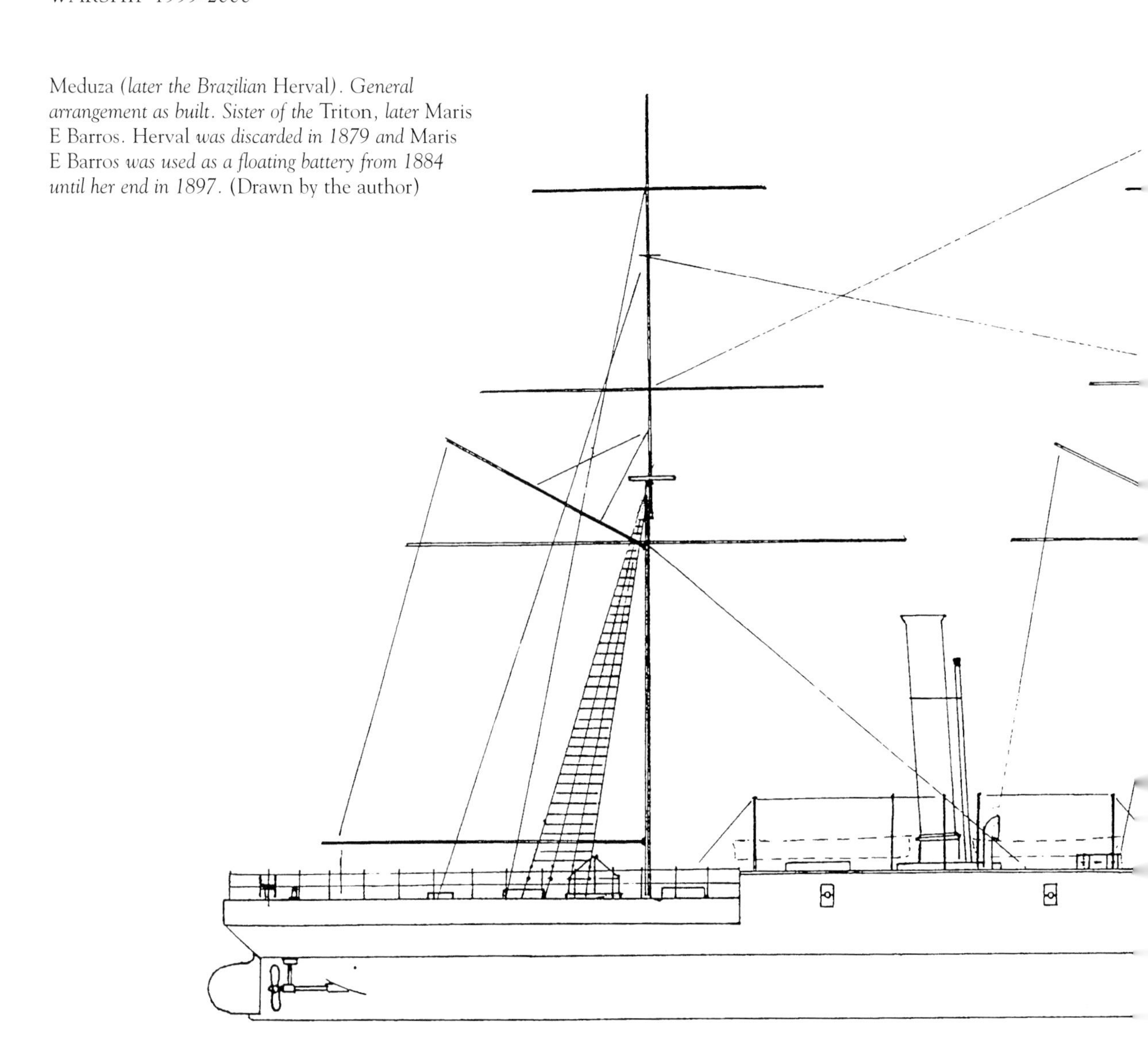

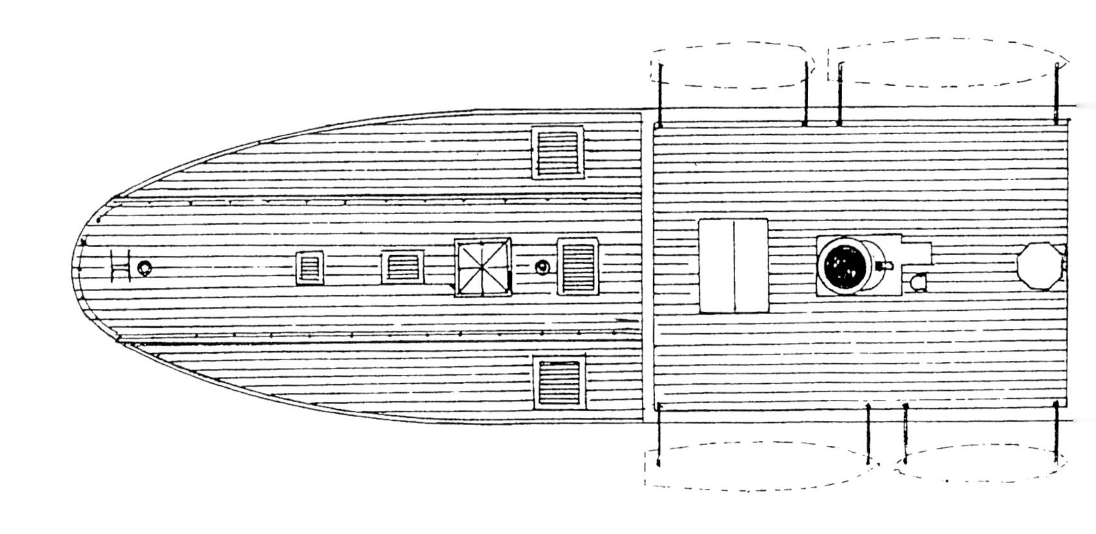

Meduza *(later the Brazilian* Herval*). General arrangement as built. Sister of the* Triton, *later* Maris E Barros. Herval *was discarded in 1879 and* Maris E Barros *was used as a floating battery from 1884 until her end in 1897.* (Drawn by the author)

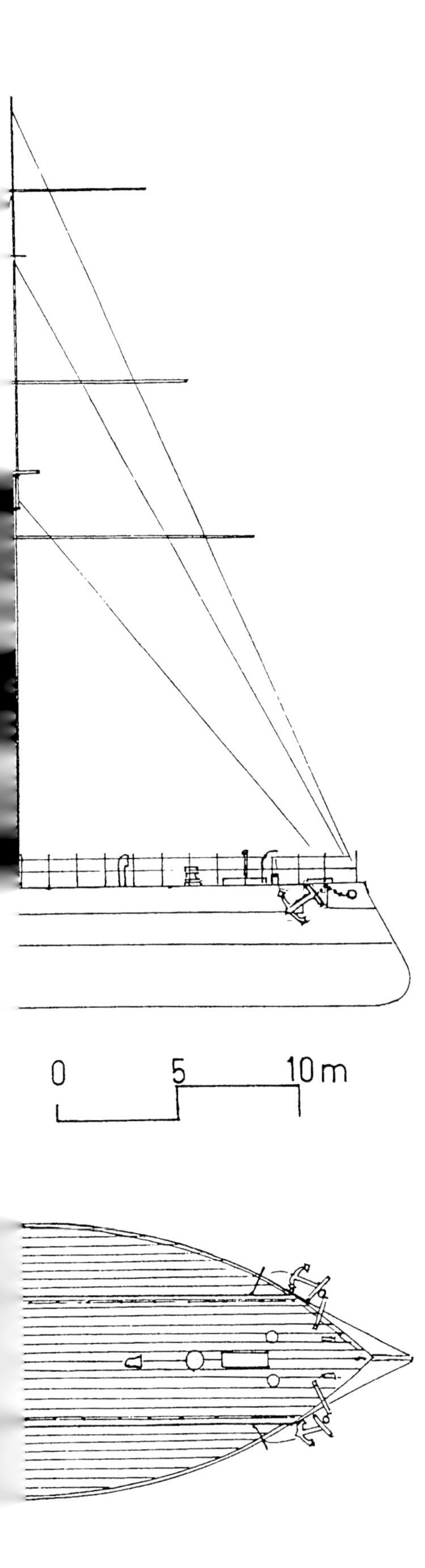

bores. The main reason for this was the lack of armoured targets, that would justify using of the powerful Whitworths, and the fact that the firing was at ranges that varied between 100m and 400m, only rarely reaching 1000m. The smoothbores were also easier to serve, faster in reloading, less prone to firing accidents; there was also a dearth of the special ammunition needed for the modern guns.

Careers

Tamandaré was commissioned in September 1865 and sent to the combat zone. She arrived at Corrientes on 16 March 1866 and joined the fleet. On 17 March, with the ironclad gunboats *Brasil*, *Barroso* and *Bahia*, thirteen wooden gunboats, five *avisos* and twelve transports, she sailed upriver to the confluence of the Paraná and Paraguay rivers to start the operations against the Paraguayans. On 26 March she shelled the Itapirú Fort and sank one of the three *chatas* destroyed between 24 and 28 March. On 27 March during an attack at Itapirú a 68pdr shot penetrated a gunport, despite the chain curtain protected it, wounding twenty men and killing fourteen including the commanding officer Lieutenant Mariz e Barros. On 1 September, together with the *Barroso*, *Rio de Janeiro*, *Brasil*, *Bahia*, and *Lima Barros*, she shelled Curuzu Fort. Between 24 and 29 December, the *Tamandaré*, *Barroso* and *Brasil*, eleven gunboats, two bomb vessels and three bomb *chatas* shelled Curuzu. Again on 8 January 1867, the *Tamandaré*, *Bahia* and *Colombo* shelled Curupaity. On 15 August, *Tamandaré*, *Barroso*, eight other ironclads, one *aviso* and two towed *chatas* crossed Curupaity under intense fire. The *Tamandaré* had an engine breakdown in front of the batteries and was towed clear by the *Silvado*. On 16 August, she shelled the Timbó Batteries. On 19 February 1868, the Third Division formed by the *Barroso*, *Bahia* and *Tamandaré*, with the newly arrived monitors *Rio Grande*, *Alagoas* and *Pará*, managed to pass by the main Paraguayan fortress of Humaitá. For the passage the monitors were lashed to the gunboats in case engines were disabled by the fortress guns. The *Barroso* was leading with the *Rio Grande*, followed by the *Bahia* with the *Alagoas* and the *Tamandaré* with the *Pará*. During the passage *Tamandaré* sufferd 120 hits and *Alagoas* 200 hits. Both ships, together with the *Pará*, which had also been severely handled, had to be beached after the battle to prevent them from sinking, and were under repair at the forward naval repair base at Cerrito until 11 March. On 25 November she shelled Assunción. On 23 March 1869 the *Tamandaré* and *Alagoas* shelled and destroyed the Timbó battery. After the war, she served with the Mato Grosso Flotilla, based on Ladario, being decommissioned on 18 April 1879 and scrapped afterwards.

Barroso was commissioned in January 1866, and was sent immediately to the combat zone. Between 26 and 28 March she shelled Itapirú, sustaining twenty hits. On 4 September she shelled Curupaity, suffering four more hits. On 15 August 1865, she crossed Curupaity towing the *chata Cuevas* until the cable parted. On 20 February

1868 the *Barroso*, *Bahia* and *Rio Grande*, the remaining battleworthy ships of the Third Division, sailed upriver to Assunción, shelling the city on 24 February and destroying the telegraph lines en route.

They met the Paraguayan steamer *Piraveve* and gave chase, but she managed to escape. On 23 March 1868, near Timbó, the *Barroso* and *Rio Grande* pursued and sank the steamer *Igurey*, while the *Bahia* gave chase to the *Tacuary*, managing to sink her. On 9 July 1868 at 11pm, the *Barroso* and *Rio Grande* were boarded by Paraguayan soldiers from twenty canoes, but managed to repel the boarders. On 17 May 1869 she was blockading the rivers Jujuy and Araguay. After the war she served with the Mato Grosso Flotilla, where she was decommissioned on 1882, but was not scrapped until 1937.

Rio de Janeiro was commissioned in April 1866, and sailed to the combat zone on 4 May. In July 1866, she arrived at Corrientes with the *Lima e Barros*. On 1 September 1866, while shelling Curuzu, took a hit from a 68pdr that penetrated through a gunport, injuring five men and killing four. On 2 September, after having the damage repaired, tried to navigate a passage on the River Apa discovered by Tomb, in order to join the *Lima Barros*, *Brasil*, *Bahia* e *Barroso* in the bombardment of Curupaity. The ship drifted broadside down stream and her stern passed over one of three 'torpedoes' discovered earlier. There was an explosion, and the ship broke in half and sank in a few minutes. The *Rio de Janeiro* remains where she was sunk, covered by some 15m of sand accumulated over a century and more.

A new Naval Programme

In October 1866, Brazilian naval minister Affonso Celso de Assis Figueiredo (later Viscount of Ouro Preto), prepared a questionnaire for the ship's commanders and officers involved in the war. In addition to questions relating to their ship's performance and armament, the question of casemate or turret was put forward. The questionnaire was an important study for future construction; the great majority of officers replied that the turret afforded much better protection for the crew. Upon this being discovered, casemated ships were no longer considered to be suitable for future riverine operations. It was also noted that the large rectangular holes on the *Silvado* turrets did not provide the necessary protection to the gun crews; this was also taken into consideration in the new designs.

All of the information collected was used to orientate the plans for the new naval programme, which was scheduled to start in 1867. The basic characteristics of the planned ironclads were as follows:

Due to the financial troubles caused by massive war expenditure, the Naval Program was never completed. Only one 1st Class Gunboat (the *Sete de Setembro*) and six 2nd Class Gunboats (*Pará* class) were built. The *Pará* class ships were laid down towards the end of 1866, to fulfil the pressing demands of the war. Four years after the end of the war, a large armoured frigate, the *Independência* (later HMS *Neptune*) and two monitors, *Javary* and *Solimões*, were ordered. The monitors could be classed as

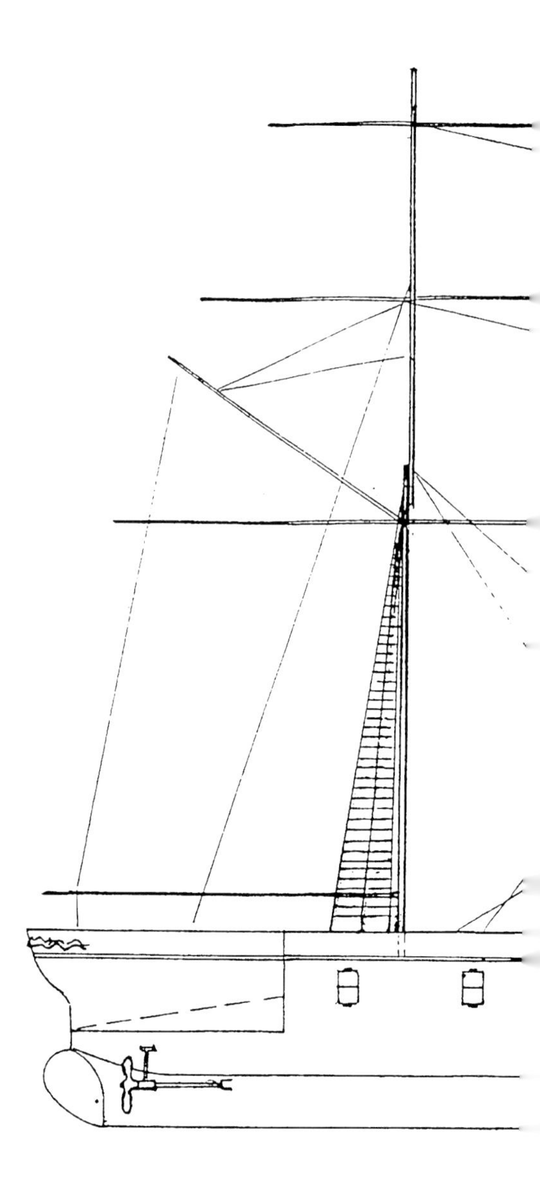

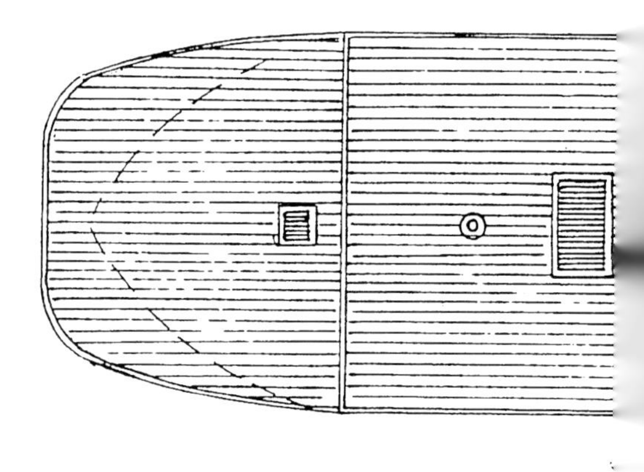

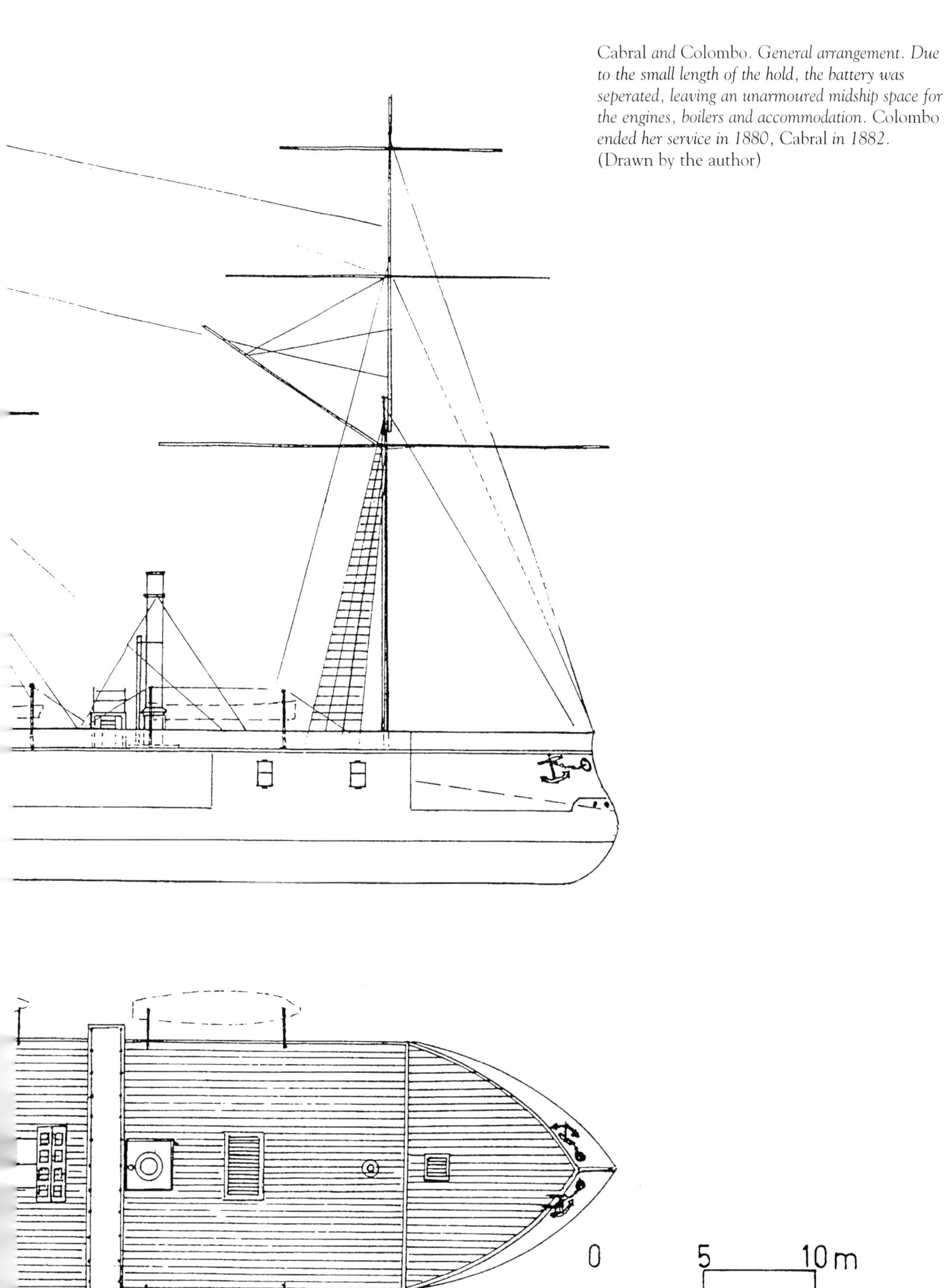

Cabral *and* Colombo. *General arrangement. Due to the small length of the hold, the battery was seperated, leaving an unarmoured midship space for the engines, boilers and accommodation.* Colombo *ended her service in 1880,* Cabral *in 1882.* (Drawn by the author)

The armoured gunboat Tamandaré *after combat against the Curupaity batteries, 22 September 1866. The illustration shows that indentations made by Paraguayan shots 35-70mm deep, and hit on the belt with a shot that penetrated 95mm.* (Author's collection)

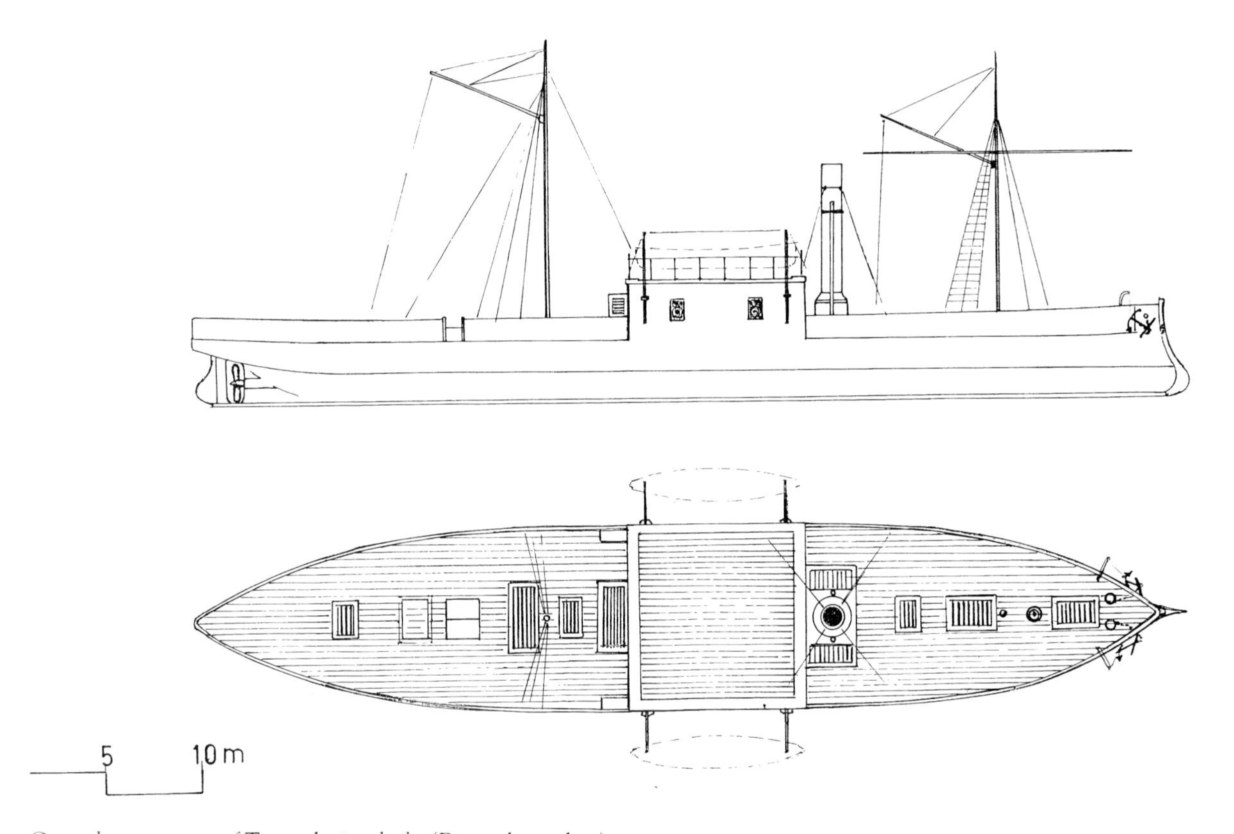

General arrangement of Tamandaré *as built.* (Drawn by author)

Table 2: *Naval Programme Ironclads*

Type of ship	Number	Speed	Draught	Armour	Guns	Coal
Frigate	1	15kts	7.90m	203mm	16*	4-5 days
Corvette	4	14kts	6.70m	152mm	10*	5 days
1st Class Gunboat	6	10kts	3.65m	152mm	6**	5-6 days
2nd Class Gunboat	16	6kts	1.52m	102-152mm	5***	1 days

Notes: * Frigates and Corvettes had guns of the same calibre.
** Designed to have 6-150pdr ML guns in a central casemate, or 4-300pdr ML guns in two revolving turrets.
*** Displacement 500 tons (full load). Two shaft engines. Dimensions: length 36.57m pp; draught 1.52m. Armament: 1-120pdr ML gun and 4-6pdr guns.

1st Class Gunboats, as they had the same gun layout, speed and draught as was originally proposed.

The Pará *class river monitors*

The need for light draught, small and mobile ships capable of withstanding heavy fire, without ineffective casemate gunports, led to the design of this class of highly specialised ironclads. These monitors were only suitable for riverine operations; with limited seaworthiness they had to be towed between Rio de Janeiro and the theatre of operations. The monitors did not have sails, only possessing two signal masts which could be lowered when needed.

Hull and armour

The strong wooden hulls, with a 0.3m freeboard, were made from three layers of wood: two horizontal and one vertical in the middle. This amounted to a thickness of 457mm, which was capped with a 102mm thick layer of peroba hardwood. A bronze ram was fitted, and the hull was sheeted with Muntz metal.

The iron belt around the hull was 0.91m high, with a maximum thickness amidships of 102mm, decreasing to 76mm, and finally to 51mm at the extremities. The curved 12.7mm armoured deck protected all of the ship, including the rudder mechanism. The top of the deck was 0.45m above the waterline, and the combat steering wheel was positioned ahead of the turret in a low, iron plated square cabin.

Turret

Official papers described the turret as 'a prismatic rectangular form with curved faces'. The unique design was developed by Lieutenants Level and Braconnot; the theory behind the shape was to add weight to the turret's structure, and to present the minimum front surface to enemy fire, reducing the possibility of a hit.

The original design was later modified, due to the difficulty encountered in bending the 152mm plates into position on the front face. The turret was redesigned to be assembled in a twelve-sided shape. The side armour was 102mm thick, and the rear was 76mm thick. Beneath the armour plating lay 457mm thick wooden backing, capped with a 102mm thick layer of peroba hardwood. The top protection of the turret had 12.7mm iron plates.

The iron carriage was designed by Lieutenant Baptista to have the vertical centre of inclination centred at the turret opening; this reduced the size of opening needed for the gun barrel. This idea was successful, as the gun opening was finally reduced to only 320mm diameter (for a 70pdr gun); this greatly reduced the possibility of splinter and enemy shot from hitting the gun crew.

The oblong turret was built on top of a horizontal circular platform, which was protected by 12.7mm iron plates. The bottom was reinforced by 203mm beams, to support the gun and carriage. The turret's rotation, guided by a central fixed pivot, was made by means of an iron rod collar over a turntable; movement was effected by a system of gears and Galle chains, actuated by four men, who needed 2.25 minutes to complete a full 360o rotation. The height of the turret was 1.67m.

Table 3: *70pdr Gun Ranges*

Gun angle	7 pound powder charge		10 pound powder charge	
	Range	Time of flight	Range	Time of flight
0o	425m	2 secs	450m	2 secs
1o	710m	3.5 secs	830m	3.5 secs
5o	2070m	9.5 secs	2290m	9.5 secs
6o	–	–	2630m	11 secs
10o	–	–	4000m	17 secs
15o	–	–	5540m	25 secs

Table 4: TECHNICAL DATA OF THE PARÁ CLASS MONITORS

Classification	Monitores Encouraçados (without numbering)	
Laid down	8 December 1866	
Floated out	*Pará*	21 May 1867
	Rio Grande	17 August 1867
	Alagoa	29 October 1867
	Piauí	8 January 1868
	Ceará	22 March 1868
	Santa Catharina	5 May 1868
Completed	*Pará*	15 June 1867
	Rio Grande	3 September 1867
	Alagoa	November 1867
	Piauí	January 1868
	Ceará	April 1868
	Santa Catharina	June 1868
Removed from list	*Pará*	1884
	Rio Grande	1907
	Alagoa	1900
	Piauí	1893
	Ceará	1884
	Santa Catharina	1882
Builder	Court Naval Arsenal, Rio de Janeiro	
Dimensions	Length 36.59m pp, 39.00 oa; Beam 8.54m; Depth in hold 1.66m; Draught 1.51m to 1.54m; Submerged section (as designed) 11.36sqm	
Displacement	500 tons full load	
Machinery	Two tubular boilers; two one cylinder engines; two shafts and two screw propellers. Normal coal provision: one day	
	ihp/kts	180/8
Armament: (Whitworth ML guns)		
70pdr	*Pará*	1
	Rio Grande	1
	Alagoa	1
	Piauí	–
	Ceará	–
	Santa Catharina	–
120pdr	*Pará*	–
	Rio Grande	–
	Alagoa	–
	Piauí	1
	Ceará	1
	Santa Catharina	1
Armour: wrought iron	Belt: <51m -76mm-102mm-76mm-51mm>; Turret: Front 152mm; Sides 102mm; Back 76mm	
Weight distribution (tons):		
	Turret and base without gun	50
	Gun and carriage	6 (70pdr)
	Fittings	4
	Engines, boilers, etc.	23
	One day coal provision	7
	24 ratings and one day supply	3
	Complete hull	245
	Total	338
Crew	8 officers plus 35 ratings	

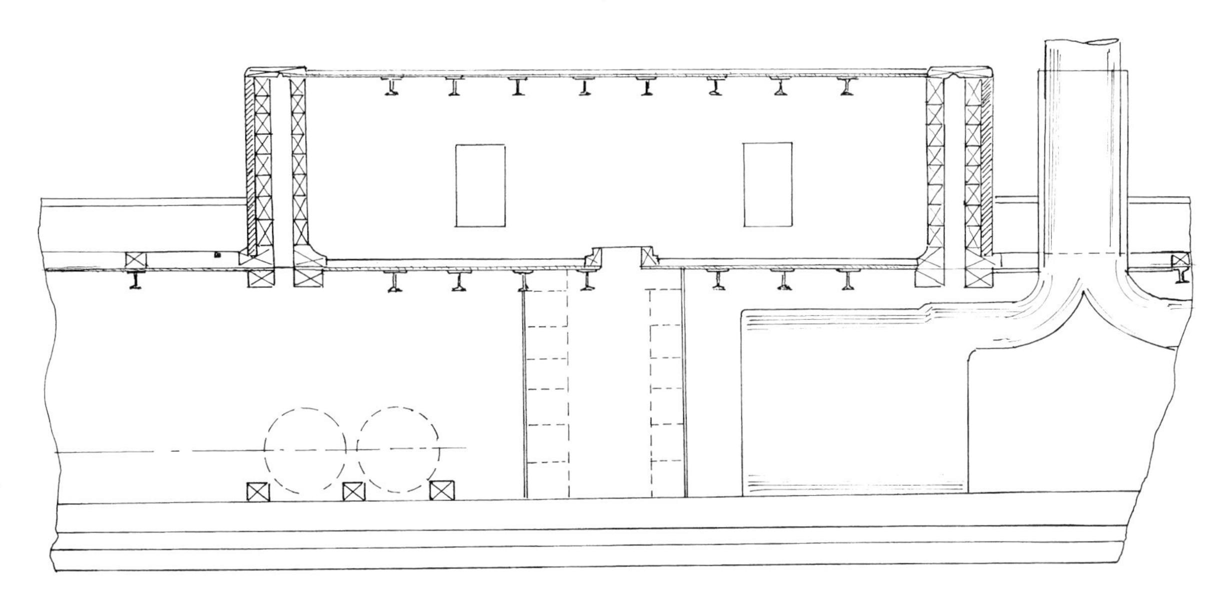

Internal view of the casemate, magazine, engine and boilers of Barroso. (Drawn by the author)

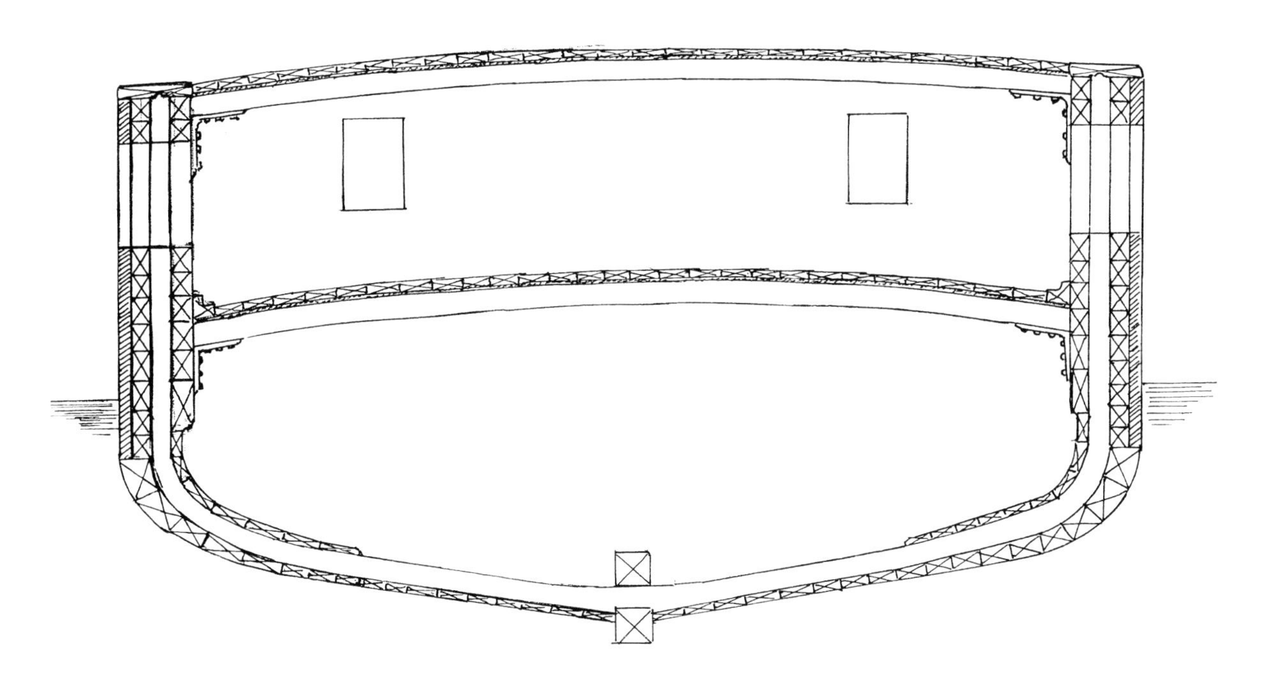

Cross-section of Barroso's *casemate, 1908. (Drawn by the author)*

Guns and gunnery

The gun barrel lay 0.85m above the waterline, and had a maximum elevation of angle of 15° for the 70pdr Whitworth ML gun; the 120pdr Whitworth which was used on the final three monitors had a lower maximum elevation due to the greater length of barrel. In the 1880s, *Alagoas* and *Piauí* both had two 11mm machine guns added.

The range of the 70pdr is shown in Table 3. The 120pdr had a similar range despite its lower elevation, due to the weight of the shell.

Propulsion plant

Each monitor had two high-pressure, direct-acting engines without condensers; each engine had one cylinder with a 381mm bore and 280mm stroke. The two boilers worked at a pressure of four atmospheres. The

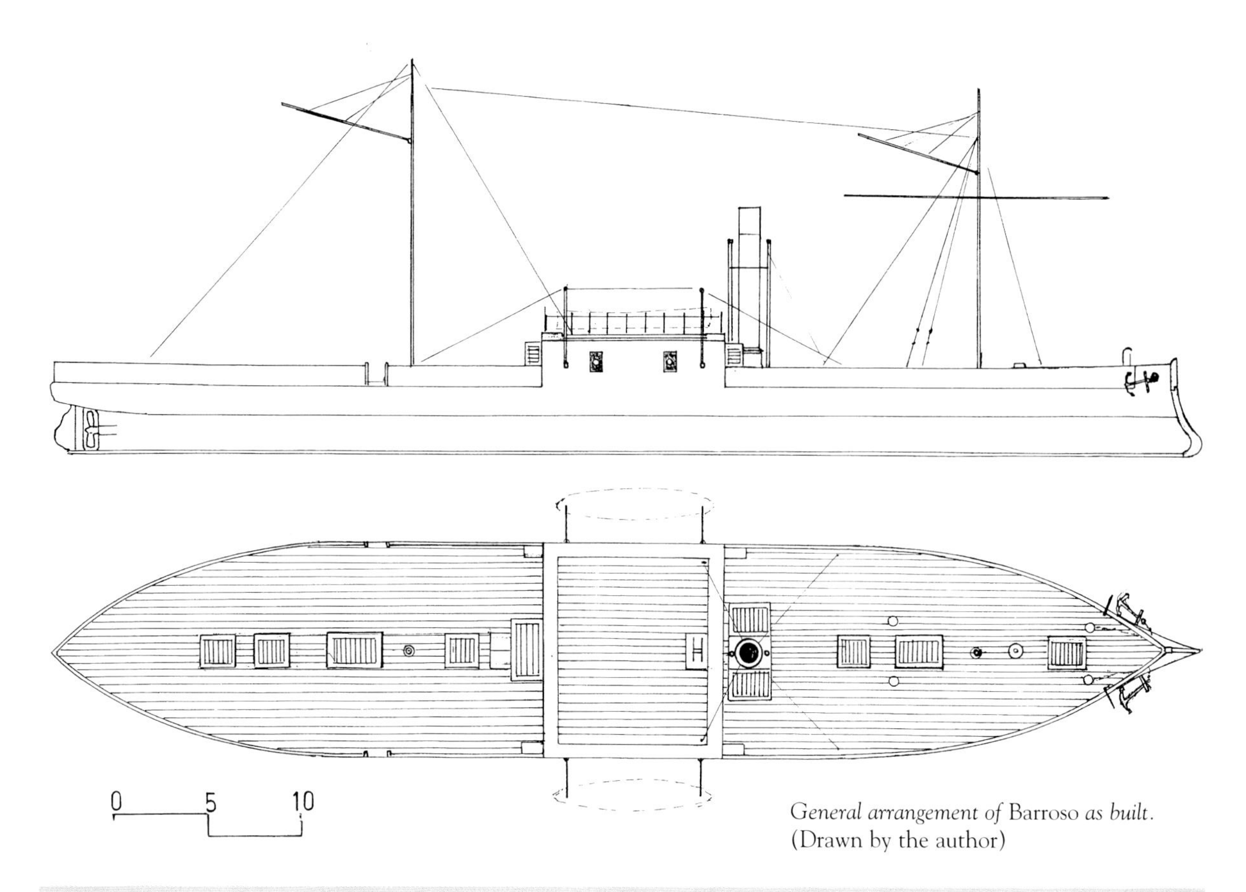

General arrangement of Barroso *as built.* (Drawn by the author)

Alagoas. *The only photograph still in existence of a* Pará *class monitor, probably taken in the 1890s in Rio de Janeiro.* (Author's collection)

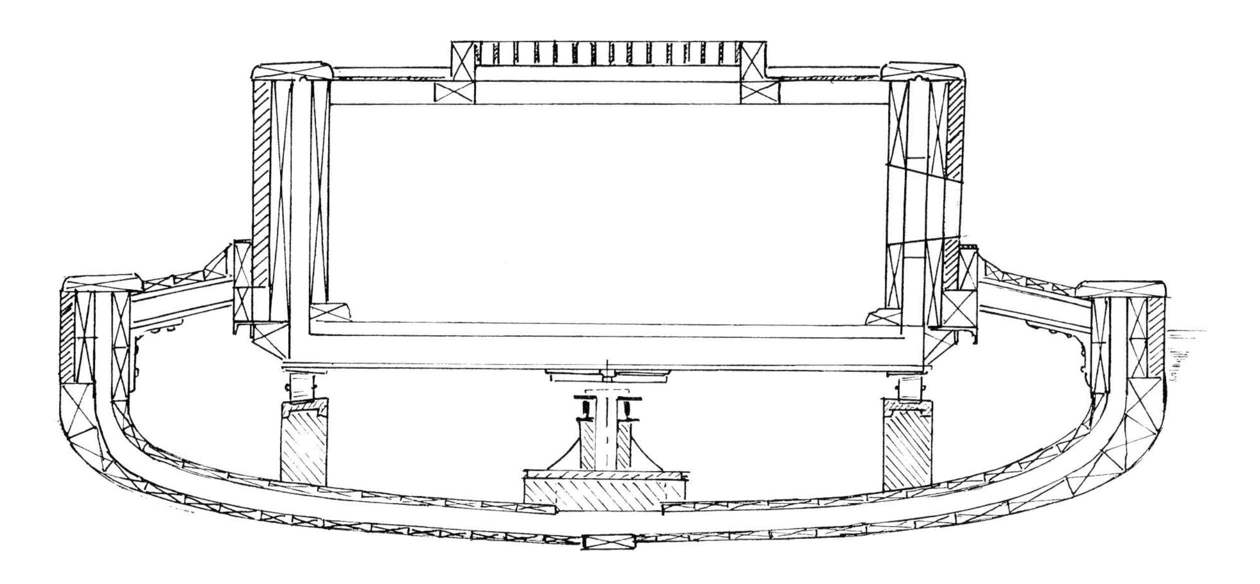

Cross-section of the Pará *class turret.* (Drawn by the author)

engines and boilers were designed by Lieutenant Braconnot and were built at the machine shop of the Royal Naval Arsenal. The only imported parts in the ship were the six 114mm Downton pumps. The engines developed 180ihp, giving a speed of 8kts maximum in calm waters. Their bronze screws had a diameter of 1.30m and a pitch of 1.67m.

Careers

Pará was sent on 20 June 1867 to the theatre of operations. On 13 February 1868, *Pará*, *Alagoas* and *Rio Grande* passed by Curupaity In order to join the fleet. On 27 February, it sailed with a squadron to seize the city of Laureles. On 15 October, with *Brasil*, *Silvado*, *Ceará* and *Rio Grande*, she shelled Angostura Fort. 17 May 1869 saw *Pará* sail as part of a blockading force on the rivers Jejuy and Araguaya. After the war, she was commissioned in the Mato Grosso Flotilla; in 1884 she was disarmed and discarded at Ladario.

Rio Grande arrived in Montevideo on 6 January 1868. After the war, she was commissioned with the Alto Uruguai Flotilla, based at Itaqui. In 1899, she was docked for rebuilding at Ladario; this work was never completed, and she was scrapped in February 1907.

Alagoas arrived in the theatre of operations in January 1868. On 21 July, she forced the Timbó battery and took station at Tagí. On 23 July she shelled the San Fernando batteries and Tibicuary at short range; she shelled Tibicuary again on 24 August. On 10 October 1868, accompanied by the *Lima Barros*, she shelled Angostura. After the war, she served in the Alto Uruguai Flotilla. In the 1890s, *Alagoas* returned to Rio de Janeiro and participated in the Fleet Revolt of 1893-94 as part of the revolutionary force. By this time, she was engineless, and was towed into position to fire upon the government forts. She was scrapped in 1900.

Piauí arrived in the theatre of operations in February 1868. On 21 July, together with the *Cabrai* and *Silvado*, she forced passage by the Humaitá defences to join the rest of the fleet; on the same day, she shelled Assumpción. On 31 August 1869, *Piauí* unsuccessfully tried to locate and give battle to the remainder of the Paraguayan fleet on the Manduvirá River. After the war, she served with the Mato Grosso Flotilla, and was scrapped in 1893.

Ceará arrived in the theatre of operations in May 1868. On 31 August, she was on the Tibicuary River, shelling enemy positions to cover the advance of the Allied Army. On 18 April 1869, she destroyed defences along the Manduvirá River. On 29 April, she was shelling enemy defences again, this time at Guaracy. *Ceará* served on the Mato Grosso Flotilla after the war, serving until she was scrapped in 1884.

Santa Catharina was sent to the front in mid 1868. In April 1869, she was in action pursuing the remnants of the Paraguayan Navy on the Manduvirá River. After the war, whilst serving on the Mato Grosso Flotilla, *Santa Catharina* was docked for repairs, but sank due to the poor condition of her hull, near the Ladário naval base.

Sete de Setembro: *the forgotten ironclad*

The Sete de Setembro was originally conceived as a First Class Gunboat, as laid down by the 1867 Naval Programme; however, she was finally classed as an armoured frigate. *Sete de Setembro* was the only seaworthy ironclad to emerge from this era of Brazilian warship construction – she was also the last ironclad to be built. The original design envisaged a scaled-up version of the *Barroso*, with the deck and top of the casemate flat

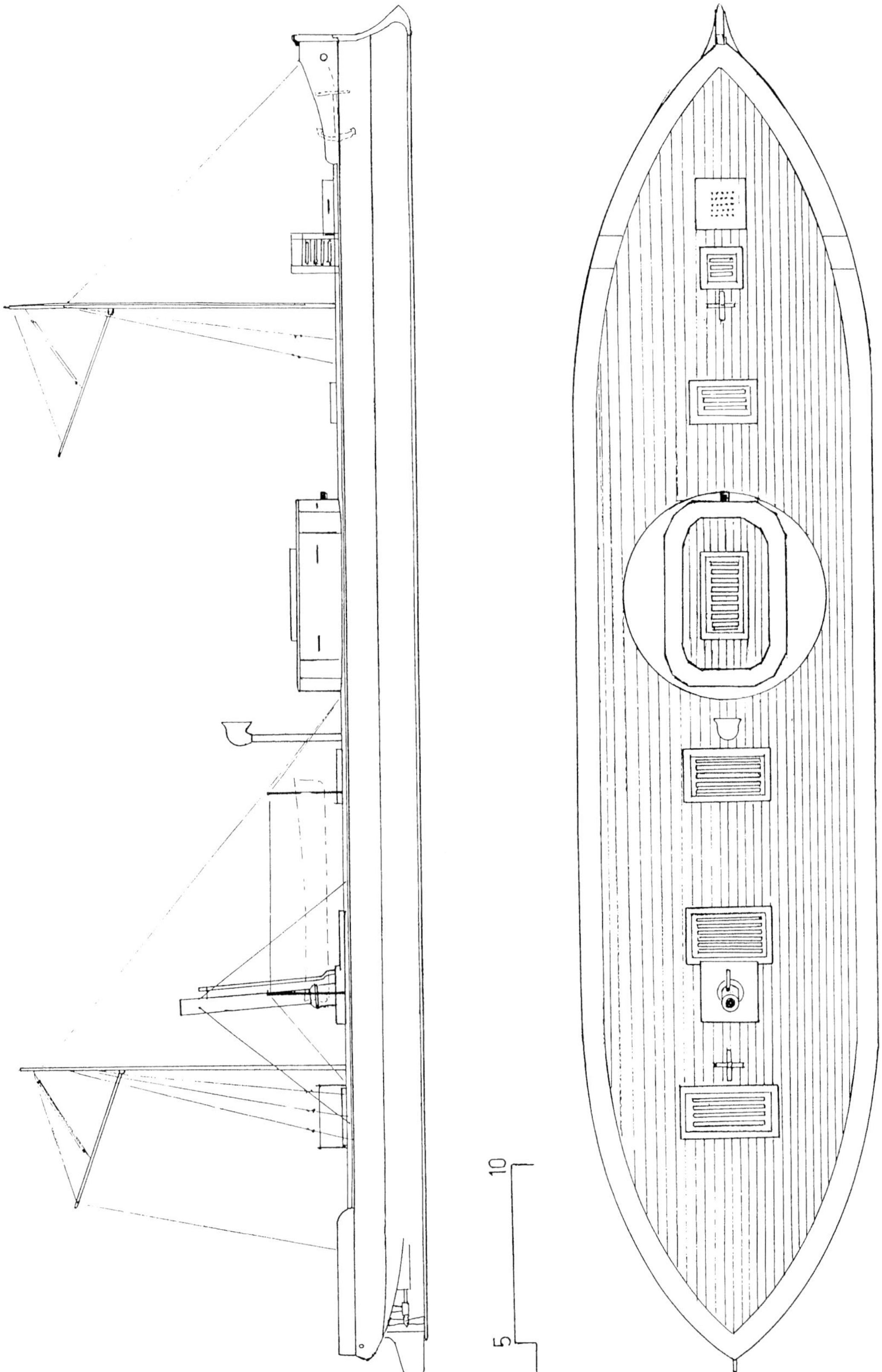

General arrangement of the Pará *class monitors.* (Drawn by the author)

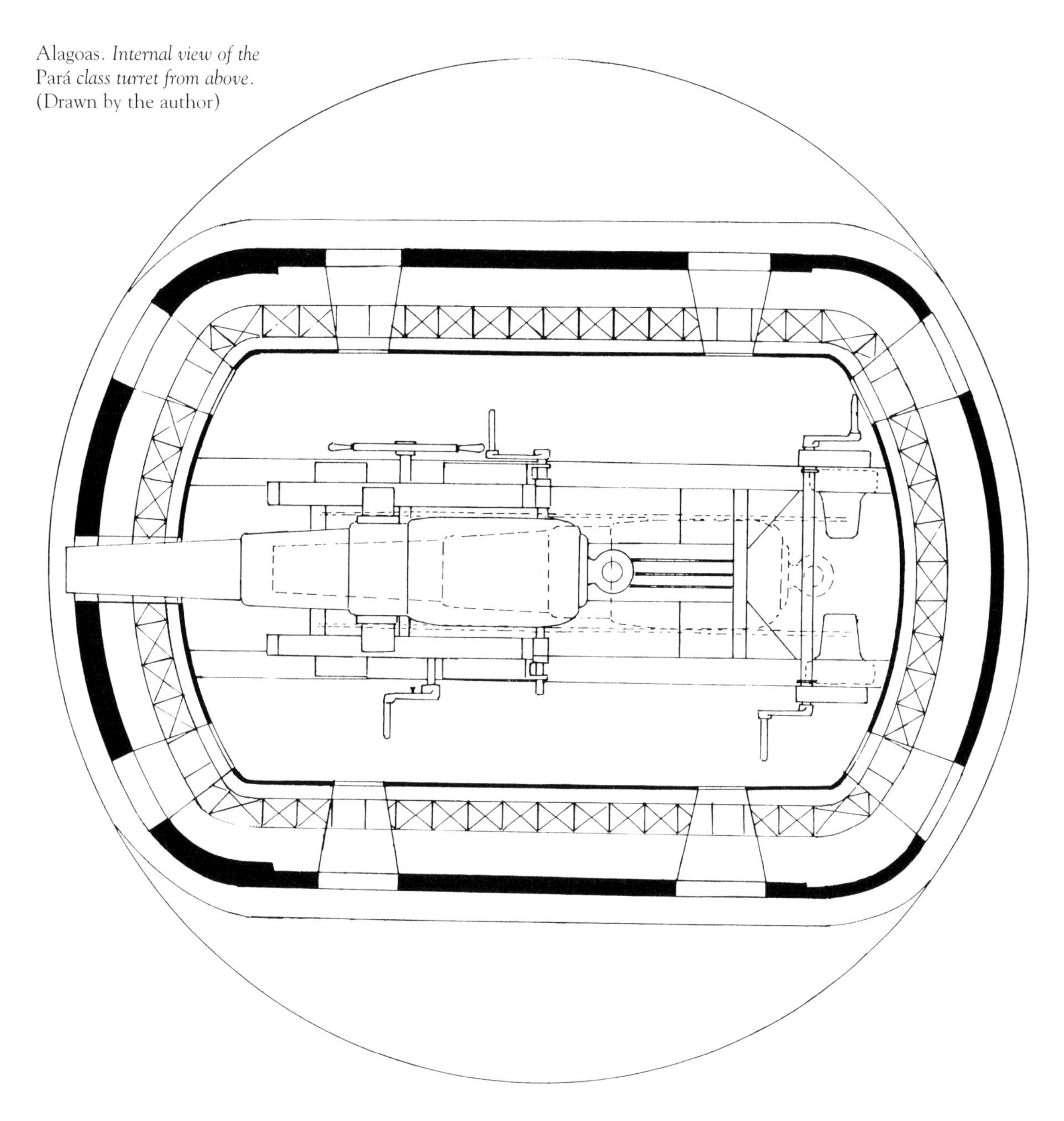

Alagoas. *Internal view of the* Pará *class turret from above.* (Drawn by the author)

instead of curved. These original plans were later modified with the addition of weather decks fore and aft (as on Dudgeon's *Herval*); these added to comfort and sea-worthiness, but also protected the capstans, where many casualties had been wounded during the war.

Hull and armour

In construction terms, *Sete de Setembro* followed the armoured gunboat layout. She had the usual wooden hull, sheathed with Muntz metal and fitted with a 2.40m long bronze ram. Without any watertight compartmentation or bulkheads, the ship had a 3.20m freeboard, which included 1.1m bulwarks (which were removable to allow for gunfire ahead and astern).

The 3.04m high iron belt armour had a maximum thickness of 114mm, the same as the casemate, and both had a backing of 593mm of wood. The casemate was pierced for two guns in the front, in the rear, and on the sides; these portholes were 2.30m above the waterline. The flat deck and the casemate top were protected by 12.7mm thick armour. After 1879, this armour was considered to be too weak, and the *Sete de Setembro* was reclassified as a mobile floating battery. Despite this, she served with the ironclad squadron of the Evolution Fleet.

Guns

As noted above, the 1867 Naval Programme presented two choices for the location of armament. The first was a

General arrangement of Sete de Setembro *as built.*
(Drawn by the author)

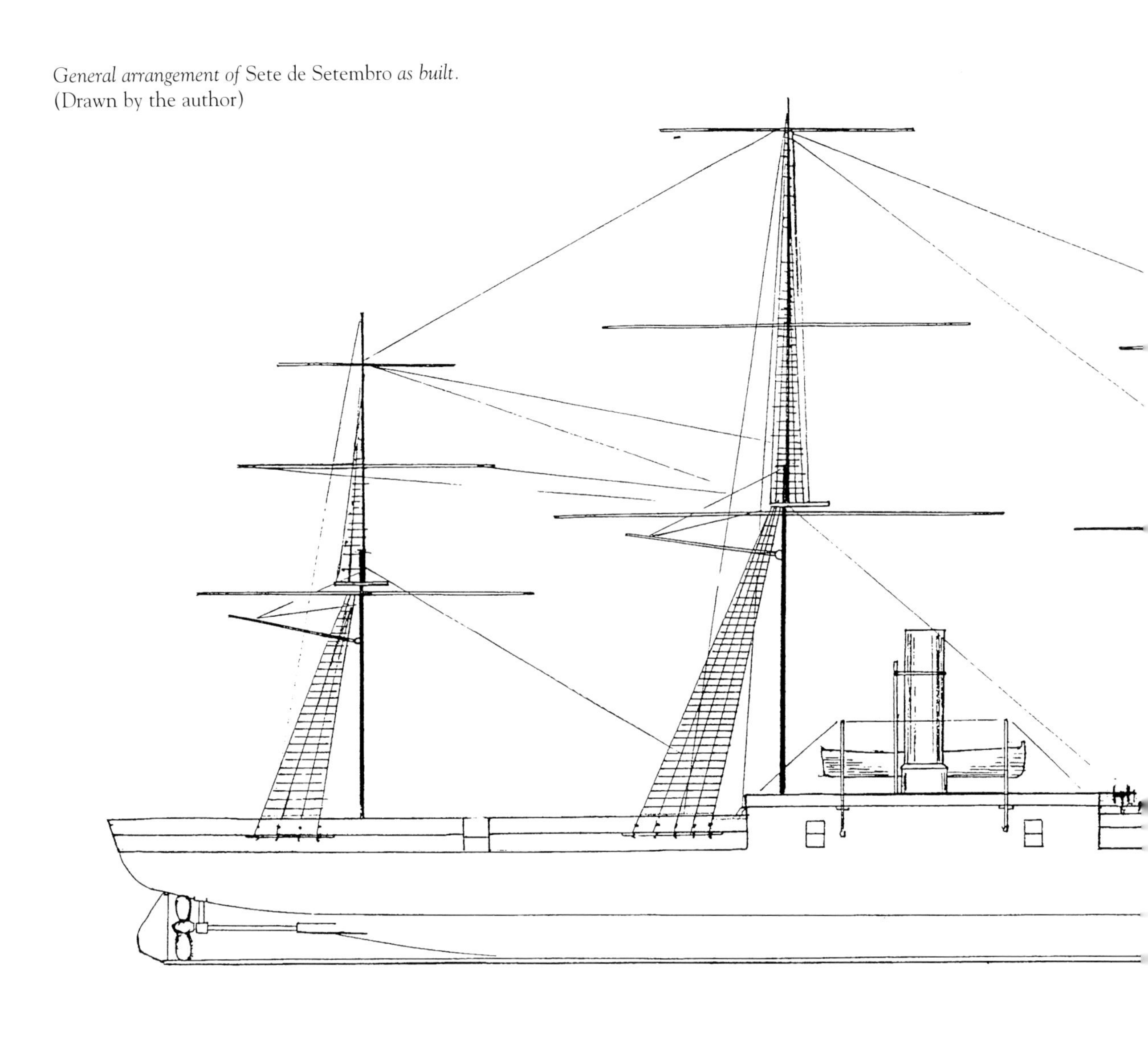

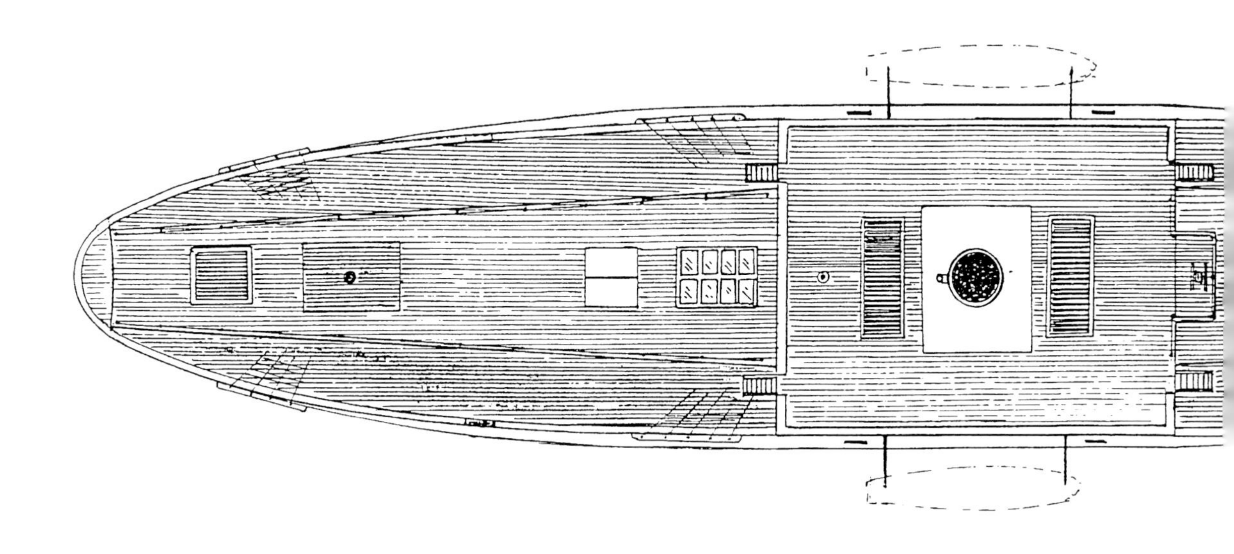

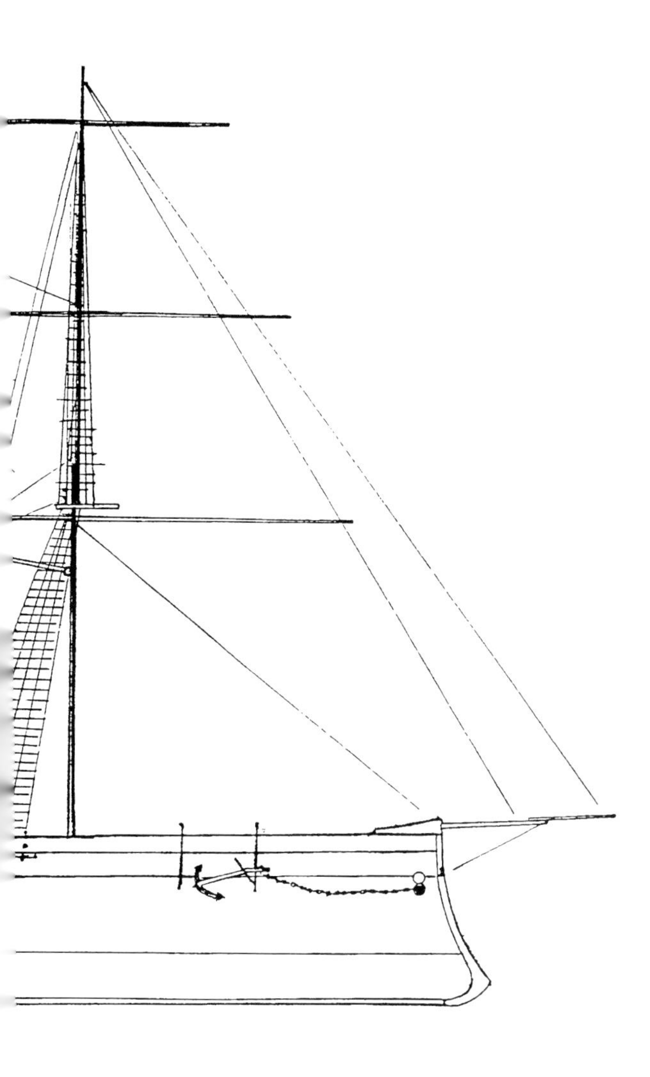

central casemate ship, with two gun ports in the front and in the rear, and three on each side; this layout was designed to carry six 150pdr Whitworth guns, the four nearest to the corners being intended to fire to the sides, and to either the front or rear. The second option was for a twin turreted ship with four 300pdr Whitworth guns. A final compromise was reached: a central casemated ship with four 300pdr (9in) Whitworth ML guns.

The chosen layout found opposition within the navy, as their preference was for Armstrong guns. This controversy went into an extended discussion between the two factions, spreading to include the views of the Rio de Janeiro newspapers, the general public, and the Emperor Dom Pedro II. The Navy Minister appointed a committee, which finally decided to continue using the Whitworth guns. The armament issue held up the ship's construction, which eventually saw completion in four years!

General remarks

The *Sete de Setembro* was completed after the war had ended, at a time when the Navy Dockyard was in decline. Due to the lengthy construction period, she was obsolete by the time of completion – the new, foreign ships had thicker armour, and hulls constructed fully from iron with watertight compartments. Before being launched in 1874, a Brazilian Navy mission was in Europe, negotiating the purchase of *Independência* (a 3600-ton ironclad frigate), and two monitors named *Javary* and *Solimões*. Official resources then concentrated on these vessels, neglecting the *Sete de Setembro*.

Career

Completed on 8 January 1874, *Sete de Setembro* went into reserve in August 1876; she was recommissioned in June 1877. Early in the 1880s, she was stationed at Montevideo, returning to Rio de Janeiro in 1884. In November 1885, she became part of the Evolution Fleet, together with the *Riachuelo*, *Javary* and *Solimões*. During the Fleet Revolt of 1893, *Sete de Setembro* was captured by the revolutionary forces, and despite being engineless, she was towed and stranded near to Armação Beach, to be used as a stationary defence post. The army took her back on 16 December 1893, sacking and sinking her.

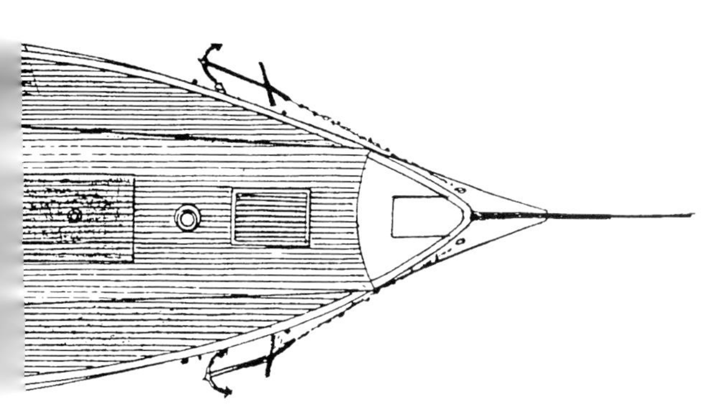

Sources

Relatorio do Ministerio de Marinha 1862 to 1903

Ordens Gerais: Ministerio da Marinha 1866 to 1874

Arquivo Nacional Ship's log entries of all ships except Rio de Janeiro

Boiteaux, Lucas L. 'Das naus de ontem aos submarinos de hoje, 1822-1946'. *Subsidios para a historia maritima do Brasil* Vols XVII, XVIII, XIX, XX, XXIII, XXIV.

Paris, Francois E. *L'art Naval a la Exposition Universel de Paris de 1867*. Paris, 1869.

Gardiner, R. *Conway's All the World's Fighting Ships 1860-1905*. CMP.

Table 5: *TECHNICAL DATA OF THE* SETE DE SETEMBRO

Laid down	8 January 1868
Floated out	16 May 1874
Completed	4 July 1874
Removed from list	16 December 1893 (sunk after catching fire)
Dimensions	Length 67.05m pp, 73.40m oa; Beam 14.20m; Depth in hold 4.75m; Draught 3.81m (mean); Submerged section (amidships) 40.89sqm
Displacement	2174 tons (normal load)
Machinery	Four rectangular boilers; two Penn & Sons direct action two cylinder trunk engines; two screw propellers of 3.70m diameter; coal 177/263 tons
ihp/kts	2000/12
Armament	four 300pdr (9in) Whitworth ML guns
Armour: wrought iron	belt: 114mm (max); casemate 114; deck and casemate top 12.7mm
Complement	185

Ferreira, Julio M. 'Vapores encouracados e monitores – uma industria estavel no Arsenal de Marinha da Corte 1850-1890'. Unpublished thesis.

Acosta, J P. *Carlos Antonio Lopez, Obrero Maximo*. Assuncion, 1948.

Acknowledgements

Thanks are due to Mr Reginaldo J da Silva Bacchi for the incentive and suggestions; to Mr Jean Michel Adnauer, who kindly allowed me to use his private library and archives on the war with Paraguay; and to Ligia B de Souza Neves for his general and generous help.

Riverine action in the War of the Triple Alliance. (Author's collection)

NAVAL BOOKS OF THE YEAR

Nigel West, The Secret War for the Falklands. *Little Brown & Co, London, 1997. 260pp, 17 illustrations.*
ISBN 0 316 88226 7. £17.50

I cannot ever recall being so infuriated by a book. Although this alleged account, sub-titled *The SAS, MI6 and the War Whitehall Nearly Lost*, might superficially appeal to *Warship* readers interested in the naval side of the Falklands War in 1982, they should beware. To adapt an old quote, candidates sitting an O-Level history examination should take care not to base their answers on this text.

Apart from a profusion of spelling errors, the book contains so many idiotic mistakes about the Royal Navy (RN) that the author's claimed expertise on the murky world of counter-intelligence must be called into question. He repeatedly claims that RN ships were fitted with an electronic warfare system called Agave, when a quick check would have told him that it is the target-indicating radar in the Super Etendard strike aircraft. 'Chaff' is not an American codename for 'Window'; it is the technically correct term for the payload of a variety of anti-missile decoy systems. A map of Argentine air bases includes the Chilean port of Punta Arenas! Was there secret collusion between Argentina and Chile?

Lest this be seen as nit-picking, a more serious criticism is West's silence on the technical background to the sinking of the cruiser *General Belgrano*. The real reason for sinking her and the associated security risk ought to be known to a self-proclaimed expert on the security aspects of the Falklands campaign. Nor does he even hint at the role played by three nuclear submarines in monitoring sorties from southern Argentine air bases, or the crucial work done by GCHQ at Cheltenham and the RN's electronic warfare specialists. Instead we are offered a rambling narrative taking in the Banco Ambrosiano and the Entebbe Raid, among other side-issues. It reads as if gabbled into a tape-recorder, or even worse, like a trawl through a tabloid newspaper's cuttings-library. Definitely not recommended.

Antony Preston

John Roberts, Battlecruisers. *Chatham Publishing, London 1997. 121pp, 100 drawings and photographs.*
ISBN 1 86176 006 X. £30.00.

Another volume in the 'Ship Shape' series, this covers the short and violent reign of the battlecruiser in the Royal Navy. Although the origins and achievements of these handsome but flawed ships have been chronicled many times, this volume brings together the design-history and operational lives of the ships and adds a magnificent collection of photographs and drawings.

John Roberts also subjects the arguments to close scrutiny, making it clear that Admiral Fisher was hardly consistent in his reasoning about the role envisaged for these advanced and very expensive combatants. In his concluding chapter he points out that Fisher did nothing more than create a hybrid type with 'excellent short-term prospects but dubious long-term value'. In other words, even if the inherent flaws of unstable cordite, defective shells and sub-standard protection of magazines against flash had been eliminated before the outbreak of war, they would still have been an aberration.

The book will be a joy to the technical historian, the modeller and the rank-and-file warship-lover. Photographs and drawings are clear, and the luxury of a double-sided sheet of 1:250 profile, deck plans, sections and lines of the tragic *Queen Mary* (as completed in 1913) is included in a pocket in the back cover (as with the *Early Destroyers* reviewed in last year's *Warship*). Expensive, but very attractive.

Antony Preston

Michael Wilson and Paul Kemp, Mediterranean Submarines. *Crécy Publishing, Wilmslow, 1997. 219pp, 55 illustrations.*
ISBN 0 947554 57 2. Price unknown.

Sub-titled *Submarine Warfare in World War One*, this detailed operational history is a very important contribution to submarine literature. For the first time we can study the achievements of all of the belligerents in the Mediterranean theatre in 1914-1918.

The Mediterranean is the forgotten theatre, with most submarine-historians fascinated by the slaughter of shipping around the British Isles. British writers seem by and large to bask in the reflected glory of the campaign in the Sea of Marmora in 1915-16, playing down the efforts of French submariners. Yet, as the authors show, the deadly war in the Adriatic accounted for heavy losses, not only in warships and merchantmen, but in submarines also. No fewer than 16 major warships (battleships and large cruisers) were sunk by torpedoes and submarine-laid mines, and a further five were damaged. The overlapping national Allied commands failed to co-ordinate anti-submarine measures, resulting in appalling losses to U-boat attack.

It is a measure of the objectivity of this study that the heroes who emerge are the Austro-Hungarian and French submariners who battled for control of the Adriatic. Both navies had a large percentage of obsolescent, inefficient submarines, the KuK Navy having the additional handicap of very small numbers. The Italian Navy showed very little initiative, the Russian submariners showed a lack of professional competence in all but a few instances, and the Royal Navy, for all its resources and ill-concealed contempt for its allies, achieved very little in the Adriatic. The French made repeated attacks on the main Austro-Hungarian base at Pola, showing great heroism in tackling the minefields and nets. Only very late in the war did the Italians develop a range of special assault craft, and even their greatest success, the sinking of the battleship *Viribus Unitis*, was only achieved after the Austro-Hungarian forces had surrendered.

One of the authors is an ex-submariner, and so the exploits are put in their proper context. The extent to which Austrian, French, German, Italian, Russian, Turkish and even Bulgarian records have been consulted is revealed in the photographs and the bibliography.

Antony Preston

Janusz Skulski, Anatomy of the Ship Series: The Battleship Fuso. *Conway Maritime Press, 1998. 256 pp, 900 illustrations. ISBN 0 85177665 5. £35.00.*

In 1912, the battlecruiser *Kongo*, the last major Japanese warship to be designed and built by a foreign constructor, was launched at the Vickers shipyard in Barrow. She was followed by three sister ships constructed in home yards and then by two battleship versions of similar design. The lead ship of this latter class, *Fuso*, is the subject of the authors third contribution to the now well established *Anatomy of the Ship* series.

At the time of her completion in 1915, *Fuso*, with a displacement of 30,000 tons, was the largest battleship in existence. Heavily armed, with twelve 14in guns in six twin turrets, and with a speed at the top end of the standard speed range for the dreadnoughts of the period, she demonstrated the Japanese inclination towards a qualitative advantage to counterbalance the numerical superiority of her potential naval rivals. In this period of rapid technical development, she and her sister, *Yamashiro*, were soon dislodged from their front rank position but they continued to occupy an important place in the Japanese battle-fleet up to the early years of the Second World War. Between 1930 and 1941, *Fuso* was heavily reconstructed in several stages, seeing service for only short periods in 1933-34, 1935-37 and 1938-40. During this time her machinery was replaced; the adoption of fewer, yet more powerful, boilers resulted in a 2kt increase in speed and in the removal of the original forward boilers and their funnel. The superstructure was substantially altered, resulting in a distinctive profile that included an impressive bridge structure of considerable complexity and height. In addition her main armament mountings were modified, the AA armament and armour protection augmented and torpedo protection bulges added to the hull. Her wartime service was comparatively uneventful until the Battle of Leyte Gulf in October 1944, when she was sunk in the Surigao Strait with the loss of her entire crew.

This *Anatomy* book follows the standard format for the series with an introductory text (23 pages), photographic section (40 pages) and the drawings (184 pages). Despite its considerable size – the largest in the series – it cannot be called comprehensive, however, this is an observation not a criticism. The historical documentation, particularly original drawings, available on the ships of the Imperial Japanese Navy is severely limited as much of this material was lost or destroyed at the end of the Second World War. In these circumstances it is hardly surprising that there are gaps in this publication and it is surprising that the author has managed to gather together as much detail as he has. The drawings concentrate primarily on the ship's external appearance and fittings from

1933 onward – that is after her first and most comprehensive reconstruction. There are general arrangement drawings of the *Fuso* as completed and in 1925, which cover her appearance prior to modification. Internal detail is limited to plans of the upper and main decks and longitudinal and transverse sections of the ship in 1935, plus two constructional sections, an internal section of one of her 14in mountings and some detail of the 14in gunhouse ; all are dated 1933. The 14in mounting section is of considerable interest, as it is shown after modernisation with the maximum elevation of the guns increased to 43o, for which the working chamber had to be lowered to give sufficient clearance in the gun well for the cradle. The shell room and handing room are on the upper platform, above the magazine – the reverse of the standard arrangement in British mountings of the First World War period. As Vickers originally designed these mountings it seems that the reconstruction included the reversal of the shell room/magazine positions and the shortening of the loading trunk in consequence. The only British vessel to have this type of modification carried out to her old mountings was the new battleship *Vanguard*, although whether the Japanese carried out these modifications for the same reason (improved magazine safety) is not clear. In all other respects the ship's appearance from 1933 to 1944 is covered in great detail. There are general arrangement views of her in 1933, 1935, 1938, 1941 and 1944, together with details of her superstructure and its modifications, the rig, armament, fire control gear, radar, fittings, aircraft and boats. There are also complete sets of lines and body plans covering all variations in *Fuso*'s hull form.

The photographic section includes over sixty views, some familiar, some not, of which about 20% are of the author's very detailed model of part of the ship (from forward of No.2 turret to abaft the bridge structure) in 1934-35. The latter reveals the author to be a superb model maker as well as draughtsman. The text covers the ship's history both in service and technically, and gives particularly detailed information about the ship's armament. There are some typographical errors (mostly obvious) and some of the drawings are not to the stated scale, but the publisher hopes to issue a list of corrections on its website in the near future. For the model maker looking to build a Japanese warship, this book is indispensable – no other drawing information would be required to build a detailed model of the *Fuso* (the text includes notes on colour schemes) and the details of armament, boats, fittings etc. would be equally applicable to many other Japanese warships. For the enthusiast there is a great deal of new information and considerable insight into the detail of one of the first generation of Japanese dreadnoughts.

John Roberts

Richard Brooks, Fred T Jane – An Eccentric Visionary. *Jane's Information Group, Coulsdon, 1997. 260pp, 240mm x 160mm, B&W illustrations.*
ISBN 0 1706 1751 8. Price unknown.

I must confess that I had a stereotype image of Fred T Jane in my mind, a naval enthusiast and wargamer, even a crank, who managed to make his hobby pay, and founded the most famous naval reference book in the world.

As this book shows, Jane was a much more complex character, with a much wider range of interests. He had something of the fantasist about him, as many defence journalists do, who did not contradict (false) rumours that he took part in a South American revolution, but was also a patriot who ran unsuccessfully for parliament. He was a practical joker, who got into trouble for 'kidnapping' the Labour MP Victor Grayson to prevent him from addressing a rally in Portsmouth.

Fred T Jane was a talented illustrator who earned a living supplying illustrations to the national press. This talent served him well when illustrating science fiction, although today his paintings of warships are much better known. Although Jane clearly believed in the British Empire and the need for a strong Royal Navy to protect it, when war broke out in 1914 he followed a prudent line. He derided the belief in an imminent Battle of Trafalgar in the North Sea, and although he was temporarily infected by the spy mania which swept country in the first weeks of the war, he deplored the crude bigotry of the press.

Moving to more familiar ground, it is amusing to read of his swordplay with the naval establishment. As it still does, the Navy tried to have it both ways, arguing that Jane's information compromised the nation's security, and almost in the same breath poured scorn on his 'amateur' opinions. His riposte was brisk and to the point: the information was available to any trained observer, and he devoted a large amount of time to studying subjects, on which a naval office might spend only ten minutes. How many naval commentators recognise that exchange or a close equivalent?

Sadly Fred Jane's career ended in decline. The outbreak of war was a disaster for *All the World's Fighting Ships*, as the Admiralty severely restricted and distorted the information released. No attempt was made to use his formidable knowledge in intelligence-assessment, reflecting the scorn which the Navy felt for civilians. His health deteriorated, and the author raises a reasonable doubt about his death. If he did commit suicide (as his descendants believe) his doctor must have falsified the death certificate. It was typical that such a complex man should die in questionable circumstances.

Antony Preston

H T Lenton, British and Empire Warships of the Second World War. *Greenhill Books, London, 1997.*
ISBN 1 85367 277 7. Price £100.00.

Over thirty years ago, Trevor Lenton and the late Jim Colledge produced their excellent work *Warships of World War II*, which up to now has been the only single-volume source giving comprehensive details of the vast fleet which comprised the Royal and Commonwealth Navies in 1939-45.

Trevor Lenton has now produced a monumental book containing over 700 pages of detailed information about the ships, and in many cases a basic outline of the *raison d'être* for the design. Particularly welcome is the flood of new information about the smaller types of warship, and in many cases details of their fates. The subject is colossal, and it would be an impossible task to produce work accurately listing *all* the facts that a reader might want to know, for not all relevant material reaches the Public Record Office. The new book has, however, not been produced under the constraints of the old Fifty Year Rule covering the release of government records, so there should have been a revision of the data listed in some sections. An example is the cruiser-section, in which particulars were taken straight out of the authors' pocket history published twenty-five years ago. The *Hawke*, for example, was not a unit of the *Neptune* class, whilst the later *Minotaur* design was a post-war project. There are also many small factual errors in the text. The *Lion* class battleships are quoted as being cancelled in 1941, whereas the ships were not finally abandoned until after the war (a version featured in the draft 1945 programme). Another case is the 'Loch' class frigates, considerable numbers of which were said to have been cancelled at the end of the war. In fact the cancellations took place in December 1943 as their machinery was required for the new LST Mk 3 tank landing ships.

This lack of attention spoils the book, but, treated with caution, it is a useful tool for the serious naval historian and the enthusiast alike. I have one other small quibble: it would have been nice to have a list of sources, always a help for the student undertaking original research. Nevertheless, I like this book, in spite of its drawbacks. It is well illustrated, logical in its approach and a major achievement by the author.

George L Moore

Gerhard Koop & Klaus-Peter Schmolke, Battleships of the Bismarck Class. *Greenhill Books, London, 1998. 159pp, 185 photographs, 15 line drawings.*
ISBN 1 85367 320 X. Price £25.00.

This book is primarily a picture book, and bearing in mind the short life of these two ships, the authors deserve considerable praise for the very large number of photographs which they have brought together. Understandably, the quality is variable; there are numerous good pictures backed by 'atmospheric' ones of snap shot style.

The text comprises 27 pages on *Bismarck*, a further 12 pages on *Tirpitz*, and 4 pages of conclusions. This text is superficial and sometimes seriously misleading; the *Deutschland* class ('pocket battleships') were not 'around this limit' of 10,000 tons but varied from 10,600 to 12,340 tons standard. The claim that the two *Bismarck* class were designed for 35,000 tons seems unlikely since they completed either side of 42,000. The suggestion that Ballard's expedition to the wreck shows that 'The hull does not appear badly damaged' is quite wrong; Garzke has written 'there are over 400 holes' to disprove such stories.

If you want the pictures, this book is for you.

Eur Ing David K Brown RCNC

Roger D Thomas & Brian Patterson, Dreadnoughts in Camera. *Sutton, Stroud, 1998. 192pp, 150 illustrations.*
ISBN 0 7509 1446 7. Price £19.99.

This book contains a magnificent collection of photographs of *Dreadnought* battleships and battlecruisers under construction. They are mainly drawn from the archives of John Brown, Beardmore, Vickers and Portsmouth Royal Dockyard. The section on propulsion has 16 photos of machinery being assembled or installed and the gunshop is well represented. The captions are clear and generally accurate but not very technical.

The text is generally sound and is most interesting on labour relations. It is, perhaps, a little biased to the Union side but the authors are right in pointing out that the work was often uncomfortable, sometimes dangerous and not well paid. Just think what a modern safety inspector would make of the staging shown in many pictures – and it was little changed until well after World War II. The description of the design and building process is sound – with the exception of one howler: having begun the section on models correctly by saying that Froude's model tests were to 'analyse and find' the hull form, the text continues 'The major function of the wax models ... was to obtain a complete presentation of the shell plating'. This was the function of the (wooden) half block model!

Anyone interested in warship building at the beginning of the century will find much of interest in this book and it is strongly recommended.

Eur Ing David K Brown RCNC

Leonard C Reynolds, Dog Boats at War. *Sutton Publishing, with the Imperial War Museum, Stroud, 1998. 299pp, 154 illustrations.*
ISBN 0 7509 1817 9. Price £25.00.

The 'Dog' boat – properly the Fairmile D type MGB/MTB – was based on a design by W J (Bill) Holt RCNC, adapted by Noel Maclin's Fairmile organisation for easy production. The only engines available were Packard marine engines giving 1250bhp and running on 100 octane petrol; 5000 gallons were carried below deck and more in cans on the upper deck for long-range work. The first boats had a speed of 32kts, but ever increasing armament reduced this to about 30kts. By the end of the war the usual armament included two semi-automatic 6pdrs on power mounts, a twin Oerlikon, four 0.5 inch and four 0.303 machine guns together with a couple of torpedo tubes.

The author served in *MGB 658* for three years, publishing a book on his experiences in 1955. Many years of research has enabled him produce this very detailed history of the 'Dogs'. They were involved in 273 actions, 136 in home waters, 104 in the Mediterranean and 33 in Norwegian waters. The treatment is a mixture of geographical and chronological; for example, the Mediterranean is covered in three chapters with visits elsewhere in between.

The illustrations include some clear maps, line drawings of the craft and weapons (by John Lambert) and many photographs. Most of the photos were taken by crew members at the time and are fascinating, even though the quality of wartime film was not always good. I particularly enjoyed a shot of two Norwegian MTBs camouflaged in a fjord – it took me some time to find them. The very hazardous work by these Norwegian boats is a high point of a fascinating book.

Eur Ing David K Brown RCNC

I L Buxton, Warship Building and Repair During the Second World War. *The Centre for Business History in Scotland, Glasgow, 1998. 20pp, 12 photos, 4 graphs.*
ISBN 0 9520160 2 8. Price £5.00.

This is another research monograph from the British Shipbuilding History Project. Rarely can so much fascinating material have been packed into 20 pages but it can still be read with enjoyment. As is well known, the shipbuilding industry shrank drastically during the slump when some 30 shipyards closed and the number of slipways declined from 459 in 1939 to 266 in 1939. The loss of skilled manpower was even more important, particularly the lack of young apprentices entering the industry. Despite this, British shipyards built during the war 1192 warships of 1.8 million tons (displacement), and 6000 smaller craft of 700,000 tons as well as 1576 merchant ships of 6.25 million gross tons. The Royal Navy had about 1.5 million tons of ships at the outbreak of the war and grew to 4.5 million at the end, despite the loss of 1.1 million tons, due to the building of 2.4 million tons in the UK and the great assistance from the USA.

The feats of US shipyards in rapid building are well known, but the author points out that they typically needed twice the man-hours of comparable ships in British yards and were more than twice as expensive. The average weekly pay in shipyards rose from £3.50 to £7 during the war (RN Petty officer £2.50 to £3.50). Despite this, there were frequent strikes, infuriating sailors risking their lives for half the pay. Poor management and obsolescent equipment was partly to blame.

There were fourteen firms on the Admiralty list for steam turbines, and despite an output roughly double the best pre-war year, most smaller ships had to have reciprocating engines. Between September 1939 and December 1945 the industry produced some 880 turbine sets totalling 12,658,500shp and 942 sets of reciprocating engines of 1,800,700ihp.

The illustrations are well selected and, as usual, Dr Buxton has done an excellent job in the captions, identifying all the ships in the background as well. Any serious student of naval history in World War II needs this book.

Eur Ing David K Brown RCNC

J Rohwer, Axis Submarine Successes of World War II. *Greenhill Books, London, 1998. 382pp, 10 maps.*
ISBN 1 85367 340 4. Price £30.00.

This book is a statistical record of every successful attack by Axis submarines during World War II. It is the result of 50 years study by the author and is an update of an early book in German (published 1968) and an American version in 1983. While there are still a few gaps here and there, Rohwer's book must be seen as the definitive word on the subject. The author acknowledges help from historians world-wide including the RN Historical Branch.

The main part of the book describes each incident, in simple abbreviated form, in 15 columns. The columns are Date/time, Nationality of submarine, Name or number, Name of CO, Position (Based on the U-boat grid, reproduced in the book), Submarine's estimate of target type and size, Weapon, Convoy designation, Date/time of hit, Nationality of target, Type of vessel, Name, Actual tonnage, Position of attack (Allied records), all supported by numerous fascinating footnotes.

The author makes an interesting point in his preface. It is usually believed that the over-estimates of hits and sinking made by Axis submarines were due to falsification either by the commander or by propaganda departments. It is pointed out that attacks on unescorted vessels are usually reported accurately, that attacks where visual observation was possible are fairly accurate, but things go wrong in a convoy battle. Here, an explosion at roughly the right time is claimed as a hit while it might be exploding due to a faulty magnetic pistol, at the end of its run, on hitting the bottom or, most often, the explosion of a torpedo from a different submarine which might be claimed by every boat in the area. The conclusion is that most incorrect claims were genuine errors rather than falsehoods.

All too often, even today, writers draw conclusions from inaccurate data published either during the war or soon after that cross checking was not possible. It is strongly recommended to serious students of the submarine war.

Eur Ing David K Brown RCNC

R J Winklareth, The Bismarck Chase: New Light on a Famous Engagement. *Chatham Publishing, London, 1998. 192pp, 90 illustrations.*
ISBN 1 86176 076 0. Price £20.00.

The book opens with a brief summary of the history of the *Dreadnought* battleship and the corresponding battlecruiser up to the design of the *Hood*. There follows a similar chapter outlining the inter-war limitation treaties leading to the design of the *King George V*. A third chapter discusses the rebirth of the German navy and the genesis of the *Bismarck*. Though he points out that the *Bismarck* displaced more than 6000 tons over the treaty limits which Germany had just signed, he fails to point out that this was deliberate cheating.

Bismarck's one and only voyage is followed in some detail. The author has used his background in military analysis to re-examine track charts and gun alignment, in the course of which he shows that many of the German photos have become reversed. Numerous charts help to clarify the action.

It is interesting that none of the shells which hit *Prince of Wales* detonated properly: *Hood* was very unlucky. The author says that *Hood* was sunk by a hit in the after 15in magazines; contrary to the board of Inquiry and to Juren's detailed re-examination. While generally accurate there are some important errors. He claims the *Victorious*' torpedo hit did no damage; in fact, it dislodged the temporary repairs made after *Prince of Wales*' hit in the forward fuel tanks and flooded a boiler room.

Bismarck's rapid rolling in the final action is blamed on 'little stability' – in fact, the problem was excessive stability. It is said that *Dorsetshire*'s third torpedo added to the underwater damage whereas it actually hit 01 deck as *Bismarck* went under. The claim that this book sheds a new light on *Bismarck* is not justified. The author does not seem to have read any of the recent papers by Garzke *et al* based on examination of the wreck.

Eur Ing David K Brown RCNC

Peter Brook, Warships for Export: Armstrong Warships 1867-1927'. *World Ship Society, Gravesend, UK, 1999. Paperback, 243 x 187mm. 244pp, 162 photographs, 98 drawings and plans. ISBN 0 905617 89 4. Price £19.00 (WSS members), £28.00 (non-members).*

This book describes the designs and service careers of the 159 warships built by the once-great Armstrong's armament firm at its Tyneside shipyards between 1867 and 1927 (the year of the company's financial collapse). The ships, ranging in size from small gunboats to battleships, were built to over 100 basic designs, for Britain, three Australian colonies, and seventeen other countries,. Between them, they played a prominent part in every significant naval war from 1891 to 1945. A further eleven cancelled units are also covered. The book omits non-combatant warships, such as yachts and ice-breakers.

Peter Brook's text is the fruit of extensive archival research, together with wide reading in secondary sources. Both are summarised, though unfortunately the original critical apparatus has been omitted. The text is beautifully illustrated with photos, some previously unpublished, and by Ian Sturton's line drawings.

The author devotes substantially more space to ships designed by Armstrong's themselves than to those built from Admiralty designs. As the latter are described in detail elsewhere, this is justifiable. In some cases, mainly battleships and armoured cruisers, considerable detail is provided on preliminary and alternative designs to those finally selected.

Dr Brook is candid about the limitations of Armstrong's design practice. The protected cruisers that made the firm's reputation impressed technologically inferior foreign customers with their heavy armament and fast trial speed, the latter obtained at lightly-loaded displacement with heavily-forced boilers. Endurance and sea-keeping qualities were often sacrificed, with consequent loss of service speed and reduction of the original battery. Further, Armstrongs failed as destroyer builders; the author's use of RN comments is telling. Ironically, three of Armstrong's very able principal naval architects succeeded one another as DNC.

The book contains a few errors, mostly misprints. However, the statistics of Vickers' warship construction are flawed (Tables 1/2 and 1/3); *Sao Paulo* fired on *Minas Geraes*, not vice versa (p.136); *Malaya* never made 25kts, and was not present on D-Day (p151); and *Zieten* never mounted 120mm guns (p160).

Overall, this is a fascinating, informative and well-produced book, reflecting great credit on its author, editor and publisher alike.

The book can be ordered from WSS, 11 Beechwood Road, Nailsea, North Somerset, BS48 2AF, UK. UK price £19.00 (Society members only), £28.00 (non-members), plus £3.00 postage (cheques made payable to World Ship Society).

Andrew Smith

D Miller, The Cold War: a Military History. *John Murray, London, 1998. 496pp, 16 illustrations, 3 maps. ISBN 0 7195 5618 X. Price £25.00.*

The author takes the Cold War as lasting from 1949 until 1991, pointing out that his military career spanned 36 years of this time: your reviewer claims 39 years! The first impression is one of surprise that one had forgotten so many incidents, and this book is an invaluable reminder.

Part I outlines the organisation of NATO and the Warsaw Pact, Part II with strategic weapons and the philosophy of deterrence. The next three parts cover sea, land and air warfare dealing both with strategy and technology. Part VI deals with the problems of going to war such as mobilisation. There are numerous appendices, mainly tabulated particulars of rival weapon systems.

There is an interesting section on intelligence concerning the performance of Soviet aircraft. The initial report would usually overestimate the significance and performance. The next Middle East war would usually show poorer performance due to less skilled maintenance and ground control particularly since the 'export' model did not always have the full range of equipment of the Soviet versions. Since the Cold War ended, Western pilots have found that performance was better than expected, but reliability and serviceability were worse. It would have been of interest if the overall intelligence assessments of the Soviet 'threat' at various times had been compared with the reality.

The author has no doubt that NATO won in the long term but 'the fact that there is a long term to look forward to is a tribute to men of good will, sound judgement and common sense on *both* sides'.

It is a very readable book and seems free of serious errors. There is a rather muddled account of two RN battleships lent to the Soviet Union of which one was said to have been scrapped at Sevastopol in 1957. In fact only one, *Royal Sovereign*, was lent and she was returned. On a personal note, he sets the invasion of Czechoslovakia on Sunday, 20 August 1968 – since it was my wedding day, I know that it was a Tuesday!

Eur Ing David K Brown RCNC

W A Haskell, Shadows on the Horizon: The Battle of Convoy HX233. *Chatham Publishing, London, 1998. 192pp, 75 illustrations. ISBN 1 86176 081 7. Price £20.00.*

This book takes the story of one convoy, HX 233, in which the author sailed in a US tanker, and sets it in the context of tactics and technology of the whole battle. The convoy assembled in New York and was met by its escort on 12 April 1943 by which time the Battle of the Atlantic had been won, though few on either side would have realised it. The escort was commanded by a USN officer in the coast guard (USCG) cutter, *Spencer*, the ship being under the command of a USCG officer. This was different from the RN system, in which the senior commanding officer also commanded the group. The author is very critical both of the group commander and the ship's discipline, apparently justified by the considerable number of casualties from blast and flash from the ship's own guns amongst spectators allowed on deck whilst she was in action with a U boat.

There were originally fifty-seven merchant ships, but some dropped out with engine trouble and fifty-two finally set out for the crossing. Eight U-boats made contact, but only four made effective attacks, sinking one merchant ship. The escort consisted of two US CG cutters, a destroyer and two corvettes and the RCN and three RN corvettes. One U-boat was sunk, *U175*, and the author makes good use of survivors' accounts to paint a vivid picture of life in a U-boat at the climax of the Battle of the Atlantic.

The photographs are clear and interesting, particularly wartime shots of the merchant ships. (The photo of *Skeena* is not 1944 as captioned, but pre-war). It is an interesting book and well worth reading.

Eur Ing David K Brown RCNC

A Niestle, German U-boat Losses of World War II. *Greenhill Books, London, 1998. 314pp, 9 maps. ISBN 1 85367 352 8. Price £25.00.*

The main part of this book consists of a tabular statement of U boat losses. The columns are: Number of U-boat, date of first commissioning, date of last departure, abbreviated name of port of departure, rank and name of CO and, lastly, a brief account of the loss.

The introduction explains the need for revision of the wartime lists of sinking, still often quoted (it is noted that the author exchanged information with Naval Historical Branch, UK). Chapter 1 explains the very cautious assessment procedure used during the war. Chapter 2 has a list of U-boat numbers grouped in numerical order giving their type number. The main part of the book, Chapter 3, gives the data, by type, and then in numerical order. This is the one drawback of the book; since another book that I have reviewed in this issue has much about the sinking of *U175*, I decided to look up that boat. First of all, one goes to Chapter 2 to find that she was a type IXC, and then to find IXC in Chapter 3; this is a time-consuming process.

Appendix 1 is a chronological list, Appendix 2 is a very interesting tabular statement showing number lost each month from some fifteen causes. The most obvious aspect is the almost total lack of success of shore-based aircraft in early years, followed by domination later. There follow appendices listing U-boats surrendered, charts showing the location of each sinking and lists of commanding officers. There are extensive notes mainly explaining the reasons for changes from earlier lists.

Eur Ing David K Brown RCNC

SHORT NOTICES

Donald L Canney , Lincoln's Navy. *Conway Maritime Press, 1998. 240pp, 295mm x 248mm, B&W illustrations.*
ISBN 0 85177 669 8. £40.00

Donald L Canney's book is the first major, in-depth study exploring all aspects of the Union Navy. In addition to this, the book includes an overview of the associated naval forces of the conflict.

Daniel Mersey

Richard Boswell, Weapons Free. *Crécy Publishing, Wilmslow, 1998. 256pp, 246mm x 187mm, B&W and colour illustrations.*
ISBN 0 947554 67 X. £19.95.

This is the story of a Gulf War helicopter pilot, recounting his experiences flying the Lynx of the Royal Navy's destroyer HMS *Manchester*.

Antony Preston

Bernard Ireland, Jane's Naval History of World War II. *HarperCollins Publishers, 1998. 256pp, B&W and colour illustrations.*
ISBN 0 00 472143 8. £29.99.

Bernard Ireland's book covers naval aspects of the entire conflict in six chapters, entitled: 'The War against Commerce', 'The War against the U-boat', 'The American Submarine War against Japan', 'Amphibious Warfare', 'Aviation at Sea' and 'Last Days of the Battleship'. A well-designed book, illustrated with a pleasing selection of colour images.

Daniel Mersey

Lincoln P Paine, Ships of the World. Conway Maritime Press, *1998. 712pp, 254mm x 200mm, 200 paintings, drawings and plans.*
ISBN 0 85177 739 2. £35.00

A comprehensive encyclopedia describing more than a thousand of the world's best known merchant and naval ships. Unusually for a book of this kind, *Ships of the World* also includes a chapter focusing on vessels of literature and legend.

Daniel Mersey

Norman Polmar and Samuel Loring Morison, PT Boats at War: World War Two to Vietnam. *MBI, USA, 1999. 160pp, B&W illustrations.*
ISBN 0 7603 0499 8. Price unknown.

A well illustrated book detailing PT Boats from their role in the Second World War to their involvement in Vietnam.

Antony Preston

NAVIES IN REVIEW 1997-1999

Antony Preston looks at current naval developments around the world.

The gap between the front-line navies and the 'also-rans' is wider than ever. 'Front-line' in this context takes account of capabilities rather than numbers, even if those capabilities are only exercised in concert with allies (the NATO navies) or in specific areas (non-aligned countries like Sweden).

Western European Navies

Belgium: The paid-off frigate Westhinder was sold for scrap in May 1997, reducing the class to three. Three of the Tripartite type minehunters were transferred to France in 1997 after short refits, but work started in 1998 on the long-delayed Kustmijnenveger (KMV) coastal minesweepers. Only one of the support ships, the Godetia, remains in commission and both are to be retired in 2004-2005.

Denmark: The Royal Danish Navy's (RDN) plans for long-term restructuring have been threatened by budget cuts. The RDN had hoped to build a 'Large Standard Vessel' displacing about 4600 tonnes for the surface fleet. These ships would enable the RDN to partake in peacekeeping operations well outside the NATO area, and would extend the modular weapons concept developed for the Stanflex-300 54-metre patrol craft and the *Thetis* class frigates.

In the first decade of the next century it had been hoped to order six ships to replace the ten *Willemoes* class fast attack craft (FACs), the three *Niels Juel* class corvettes and the four *Falster* class minelayers. Each ship would have six or eight container-positions and be able to operate two helicopters. Two will be configured as command and support vessels, and four as patrol vessels. Naval capabilities would include anti-surface warfare (ASuW), anti-submarine warfare (ASW) anti-air warfare (AAW), minelaying and mine clearance (using drones). Civil tasks would include hydrography, pollution-control and search-and-rescue (SAR). The recommendations also cover the previously announced plans for 'Minor Standard Craft'.

All five submarines will be discarded in 2001-2006, but until the recent budget cuts were proposed they were to be replaced by four fitted with an air-independent propulsion (AIP) system and capable of operating out-

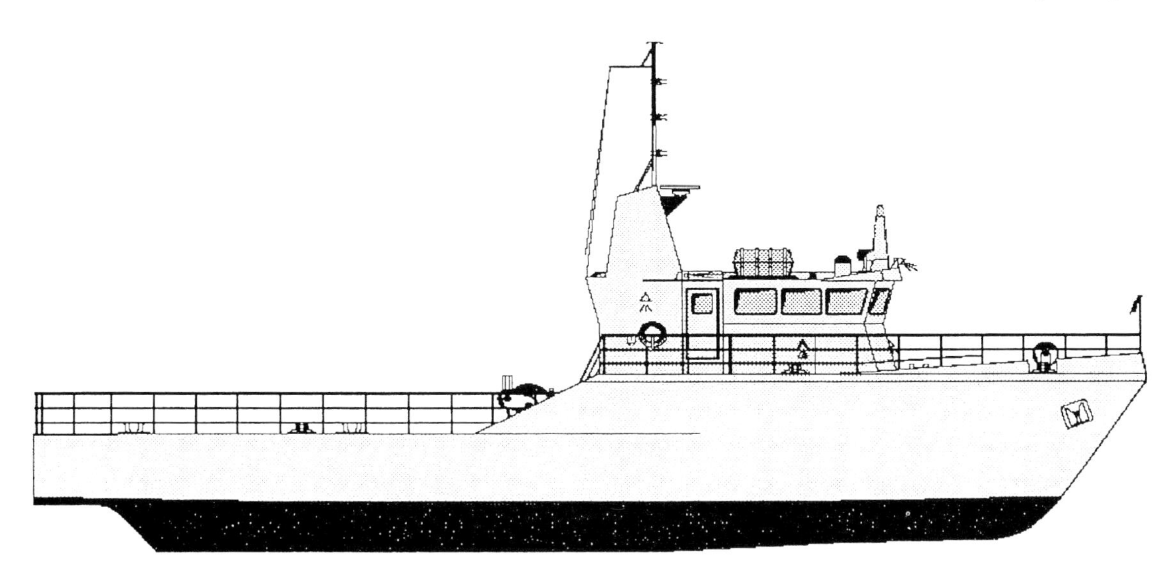

The Danish navy's SF100 *type drone mine sweeper.* (Author's collection)

Jaureguiberry, the French Navy's latest Lafayette *class frigate.* (Author's collection)

side coastal waters. The design may be the 'Viking' project to build a common-hull submarine with Norway and Sweden, which has been under discussion for some time, but as an interim measure four second-hand *Västergotland* class may be acquired from Sweden. The budget cuts proposed by the coalition government early in 1999 may result in some of the projects being cancelled but others may be deferred.

Estonia, Latvia and Lithuania: In 1997, the three Baltic Republics agreed to form a joint Baltic Squadron, but funds do not run to a programme of new construction. In the summer of 1997 Estonia's *Eesti Merevagi* received two ex-Type 394 inshore minesweepers from the German Navy, the *Kalev* (ex-*Minerva*) and *Olev* (ex-*Diana*). Latvia's *Latvijas Juras Speki* took delivery of an ex-*Volksmarine* Project 205 'Osa' type FAC in 1995, but she is laid up in reserve until funds are available for a refit. Two earlier 'Osa' FACs have been scrapped, leaving only the *Zibens* in commission.

Lithuania's Lietuvos Respublikas Karines Juru remains the most powerful of the three navies, but plans to refit and rearm the two Project 1124M *Grisha* type corvettes have not yet materialised.

France: The ship for which the Marine Nationale has sacrificed so much, the nuclear-powered aircraft carrier *Charles de Gaulle*, started her sea trials in 1999, but they were marred by a machinery breakdown. The first Rafale-M squadron will not join the ship until 2002, and there is some doubt that she will be able to operate the E-2C Hawkeye aircraft because the flight deck is too short. Hopes that the *Clemenceau* could be saved as a museum of French naval aviation have been dashed as the ship was 'cannibalised' wholesale to keep her sister *Foch* running. Then, in April 1998, the Defence Minister Alain Richard confirmed that the *Foch* will also be disposed of as soon as the *Charles de Gaulle* becomes fully operational. This leaves the French Navy with only one carrier until a second carrier can be funded, which seems very unlikely, although some interest has been expressed in building a ship modelled on the Royal Navy's CV(F) design (see below).

The second of the new generation of strategic submarines (SSBNs), *le Teméraire*, started her trials in April 1998 and started operational patrols in July 1999. This allows the *Foudroyant* to be taken out of service, leaving a force of four SSBNs. Only two of the diesel-electric *Agosta* class boats (SSKs) are still operational, and when *la Praya* is paid off in 1999, only the *Ouessant* will be left, serving as a trials boat.

The tribulations of the surface fleet continue, and with the British withdrawal from the 'Horizon' programme a variant of the Saudi *La Fayettes* will be built instead. Thus the burden of defending the *Charles de Gaulle* falls on the *Cassard* and *Jean Bart*, because the *Suffren* and *Duquesne* are approaching obsolescence. Only two of the *Tourville* class large anti-submarine ships will be upgraded to operate the SLASM sonar system, casting doubts on plans to fit the 'mini-SLASM' to five of the *Georges Leygues* class.

The third *La Fayette* class frigate became operational in July 1997, and her sister *Aconit* will follow in 1999. The fifth unit, *Guepratte*, was laid down in September 1997 and will be launched in 1999. The coastal escort *Detroyat* was retired in May 1997 and three more will follow in 1999, reducing the class to 13 units.

The purchase of three *Tripartite* minehunters from Belgium in 1997 brings the *Eridan* class up to 13 units, but in September 1997 all five of the older *Circé* class were sold to Turkey.

Rapid-reaction forces have been given priority, and the second *Foudre* class amphibious dock transport LPD *Siroco* was planned to come into service by April 1998. Two more, currently designated L-9013 and L-9014, will be in service in 2004 and 2006 respectively. Despite their age the *Orage* and *Ouragan* will not be retired until 2000.

Germany: Also beset by funding problems, the German Navy is trying to adapt to the changing needs of the next decade. The first of the new Type 212 submarines, *U-31*, was laid down in September 1998 and should be in service by 2003. When funds permit, another eight will be built, allowing all the ageing Type 206A SSKs to be retired. Two unmodernised Type 206 boats, *U-19* and *U-21*, are laid up for possible sale.

The air defence frigate *Sachsen*, first of the Type 124 ships, was laid down in February 1999. Two more, to be named *Hamburg* and *Hessen*, are to be started in 2001-2002, but the option on the fourth has not been taken up. The three *Lütjens* class destroyers (Type 103B) will be replaced as the *Sachsen* class come into service. Plans for up to 15 Type 130 corvettes have not been dropped, but the first will not be ordered until 2000.

The FAC force is being steadily reduced by sales to Chile and Greece and probably other countries. Only fourteen Type 148, ten Type 143 and ten Type 143A remain. The deferment of the corvette programme means that they will be modernised to serve for another ten years. The mine countermeasures (MCM) force has been strengthened by the delivery of the last two Type 332 *Frankenthal* class minehunters. Five are to undergo a major modernisation from 2000 onwards, as will the ten Type 343 *Hameln* class. This will enable the current minehunters and inshore minesweepers to be replaced.

Great Britain: Despite unfavourable comparisons with the French Navy made by some commentators in the recent years, in 1999 the Royal Navy (RN) looked in much better shape. The Ministry of Defence (MoD) drive for efficient procurement shows in the control over naval acquisition costs. In retrospect the decision to go for Short Takeoff and Vertical Landing (STOVL) technology has ensured the survival and prosperity of the Fleet Air Arm. The policy of buying off-the-shelf weapons has given the RN capabilities which other European navies envy, but where political interests supervene the story is not so encouraging.

The RN has opened the debate on future aircraft carriers early, arguing that the three *Invincible* class should be replaced by two much larger (40-50,000 tonnes) carriers. The Strategic Defence Review (SDR) published in July 1998 confirmed that future funding is earmarked for them. If everything goes to plan they will operate the supersonic Joint Strike Fighter (JSF) currently under development in the United States. The flexibility of the *Invincibles*, despite the strictly limited scope of the original design, proves what good ships they are, but their most serious weakness remains the small air group. In the 1998 Gulf emergency HMS *Invincible* embarked an air group of sixteen F/A.2 Sea Harriers, RAF GR.7 Harriers and Sea King helicopters, not counting six Sea Kings sent ashore at Fujairah. Starting with HMS *Illustrious* in September 1998, all three will be modified, sacrificing the GWS.30 Sea Dart missile system to make room for an extended forward flight deck. The magazine will be modified to accommodate ordnance for the GR.7s. HMS *Illustrious* returned to service in April 1999 and HMS *Ark Royal* arrived at Rosyth a month later to start her two-year modernisation.

With the commissioning of the third *Vanguard* class SSBN, HMS *Vigilant*, and work on the *Vengeance* well advanced, the Trident programme is virtually complete. Despite claims that it would run over budget, the whole programme is comfortably within the limits predicted, according to the National Audit Office. Under the SDR the total of warheads will be reduced to 48 per SSBN (three warheads per missile instead of six). The SDR confirmed that the nuclear attack submarine (SSN) force will be cut by two to ten, but two more *Astutes* will be built. The third unit of the *Astute* class, *Artful*, will not be ready until 2010, and the fifth boat cannot be ready before 2014-2015, by which time the two earliest *Trafalgar* class will be replaced. The *Swiftsure* class SSN HMS *Splendid* completed her capability upgrade programme (CUP) at Rosyth in May 1998, and sailed for the United States to carry out test-firings of the Tomahawk Block III land-attack cruise missile. The SDR predicts that all SSNs will receive Tomahawk, rather than the seven previously earmarked, and HMS *Splendid* fired the first against Serbian targets this year. On 6 April 1998 Canada's Ministry of National Defence announced that it would lease the four *Upholder* class SSKs at a cost of Can$750 million, including all support-costs. At the end of the lease the Canadians will have an option to buy the boats outright.

The RN was the major player in Project 'Horizon', with a continuing commitment to build twelve ships, although sceptics predicted that the order might well be cut to eight because of the spiralling cost. With the older Type 42 destroyers now close to the end of their effective lives (HMS *Birmingham* has already been laid up), their replacement is urgent. A service-life extension programme (SLEP) is not a serious option as their combat system, weapons and radars will not be adequate to handle future threats. In April 1999, the MoD finally lost patience with its partners, and announced that a national programme will take the place of 'Horizon', although the new Type 45 destroyers will be armed with the Principal Anti Air warfare Missile System (PAAMS), and the order was announced at the same time as the cancellation of the collaborative programme.

Two 'Duke' class frigates joined the fleet in 1997, HMS *Grafton* and HMS *Sutherland*; the fourteenth, *Kent*, was launched at GEC Marine's Yarrow shipyard on 27 May 1998, and started trials in May 1999. The *St Albans* was launched in November 1998 and the *Portland* on 15 May 1999; they will join the fleet in 2000-2001, completing the class. These ships remain remarkably cost-effective, costing considerably less than comparable foreign frigates, and all now have fully functioning DNA(1) command systems. On 28 July 1998 it was announced that the Defence Evaluation & Research Agency (DERA) would order a 90-metre, 1100-tonne trimaran demonstrator, RV *Triton*, from Vosper Thornycroft, to evaluate the trimaran hull as a basis for future frigates. First steel was cut at Woolston on 11 January 1999; launching is planned for April 2000 and the ship will be delivered to DERA five months after that.

The cancellation of a major refit for HMS *Beaver* in spring 1998 was the precursor of the bad news that three of these Type 22 Batch 2 ships will be offered for sale as part of the reductions called for in the Strategic Defence Review. Brazil has been cited as the likely candidate.

The MCM force is being scaled down, reflecting a reduced priority. Plans for a major modernisation of the Hunt class were dropped in 1996, but a 'minimum update' is planned to start around 2000, with an upgraded sonar system. In the meantime three have been transferred to patrol duties, with their minehunting sonars and control systems inoperative, and deck equipment removed. The seventh *Sandown* class minehunter, HMS *Pembroke*, was launched on 15 December 1997, and came into service in November 1998, the *Grimsby* was launched on 10 August 1998, followed by the *Bangor* on 16 April 1999. The last five ships will be commissioned in 1999-2001.

The new amphibious assault helicopter carrier (LPH) HMS *Ocean* suffered a slight delay into service, and had to be repaired at Yarrow's yard on the Clyde and at Portsmouth before commissioning in June 1998. The machinery plant for the assault dock transports (LPDs) *Albion* and *Bulwark* was formally accepted in March 1998, and their keels were laid on 22 May. After major cost-overruns on the SLEP of the logistic landing ship RFA *Sir Bedivere* it has been decided not to waste any more money on her sisters *Sir Geraint* and *Sir Percivale*, and two new LSLs will be built instead. BAeSEMA (now BAe Defence Systems) won the

The Royal Navy's new frigate, HMS Kent. (Yarrow Shipbuilders)

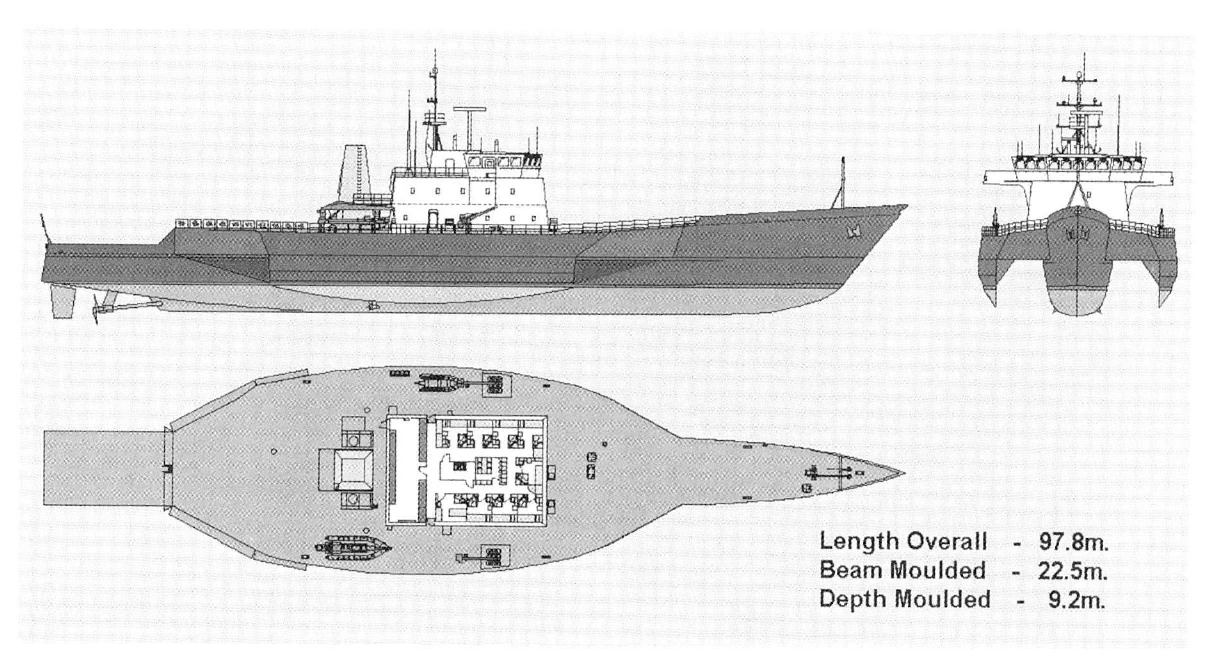

RV Triton, *The DERA Trimaran Demonstrator research vessel.* (DERA)

design contract for the new Mk 10 utility landing craft (LCUs), eight of which will operate with the LPDs. The second Ro-Ro ship chartered for the Rapid Reaction Force, RFA *Sea Chieftain*, was officially named in Gothenburg in May 1998.

Greece: The Hellenic Navy is being modernised to face the perceived threat from Turkey. With the completion of the modernisation of the four *Glavkos* class Type 209/1100 SSKs, funds are now available to bring the slightly larger *Poseidon* class Type 209/1200 boats to the same standard. In October 1998 an order was announced for three IKL Type 214 SSKs, one to be built in the contractor's shipyard and the others locally.

The four *Kidd* (DDG-993) class destroyers have been offered by the US Navy as replacements for the four ex-*Charles F Adams* class, but these very large and complex ships require a large number of specialists, and they will prove a liability. With the commissioning of HS *Kontouriotis* (F-462) on 13 December 1997 the Navy now has six ex-Royal Netherlands Navy *Kortenaer* class frigates. The third MEKO-200 type frigate, HS *Psara*, was completed in April 1998 and her sister *Salamis* was completed in January 1999.

After nine years under construction the tank landing ship *Ikaria* was commissioned in July 1997, followed by the *Lesbos* in January 1999, but there is no indication of when the last, the *Rodos*, will appear. The Eleusis shipyard will build three 62.5-metre missile-armed FACs to a Vosper-Thornycroft design, with options for two more.

Italy: The new STOVL aircraft carrier (*Giuseppe Mazzini* or *Conte di Cavour* are possible names) may be ordered in 1999. The *Nuovo Maggiore*

The Vosper Thornycroft fast attack craft ordered for the Hellenic Navy in September 1999. (Author's collection)

Unitá (NUM) design is emerging as an enlarged LPD, with a secondary amphibious warfare capability.

The SSK *Enrico Toti*, last of her class, was laid up in 1997 ready for disposal. The four *Nazario Sauro* class are planned to be replaced by the new Type 212A boats built at Muggiano, rather than the traditional Fincantieri yard at Monfalcone, outside Trieste but at least two may be offered for export as part of a sales drive to win the South African submarine contract.

The Italian Navy is still the partner of the French after the collapse of the 'Horizon' programme, but has already tried to substitute a more modest design as a replacement for the *Maestrale* class. Having originally bid for six 'Horizons' to win a major work-share, the requirement will be met by two modified *La Fayettes*.

Four new 65-metre offshore patrol vessels (OPVs) are planned, replacing plans for four more *Cassiopea* class. The first three *Esploratore* class 36-metre patrol vessels were commissioned in 1997, and the fourth, the *Vedetta*, was commissioned in June 1998.

The Netherlands: The first two air defence frigates, the *de Zeven Provincien* and the *Tromp*, have been laid down at Schelde Shipbuilding in Vlissingen, and will be completed in 2001 and 2002 respectively. The *de Ruyter* was laid down in 1998, and the *Evertsen* will follow in 2000, but they will not have the full command facilities of the first two. To provide funds for the last two, the proposed mid-life modernisation of the *Jacob van Heemskerck* and *Witte de With* has been cancelled. Only four of the *Kortenaer* class frigates remain, and of these only HNlMS *Jan van Brakel* and *Pieter Florisz* are likely to remain in commission.

The new 11,000-tonne amphibious dock transport (LPD) *Rotterdam* was delivered in December 1997, and deliveries of her new LCUs started in 1998. Funds are being sought for a second LPD.

Norway: Although discussions continue on the submarine project, the frigate programme took a step towards fruition in May 1999, when EN Bazán's design was nominated as the most suitable, subject to final negotiations on local industrial participation. If these are not satisfactory Blohm+Voss will be asked to make a fresh presentation. Work may start in 2000, with delivery of the sixth frigate in 2012.

The prototype surface-effect FAC *Skjold* was delivered in July 1998, and is running an extended series of first-of-class trials lasting at least two years. Only eight of the *Storm* class remain in service, but one is laid up. The 14 *Hauk* class will be fitted with the same SENIT 8 combat system as the *Skjold* class when they start their upgrade (the last will be completed in 2003).

Portugal: The *Marinha Portuguesa* announced in 1998 that it is seeking bids for three of four submarines to replace its three *Albacora* class boats dating from the late 1960s. The obvious solution is to participate in the Spanish programme, which implies the Franco-Spanish 'Scorpène' design. The frigate *Comandante Roberto Ivens* was taken out of commission in 1997 as a result of damage sustained during a collision with a Canadian oiler two years earlier. The other three completed modernisation at the end of 1997 to allow them to serve for another ten years.

Spain: Although suffering from budget constraints, the *Armada de España* continues its modernisation programme. After years of delay a decision is close on replacements for the four *Delfin* class submarines, built to the French *Daphné* design a quarter of a century ago. The 1500-tonne 'Scorpène', designed by DCN and Empresa Nacional Bazán, seems to be a certain choice, especially as it is currently building for export in France.

The first *Alvaro de Bazán* class Aegis frigate was laid down at Ferrol in November 1997, and she is likely to be completed in 2002. The remaining three will be built in 1999-2006, giving the Spanish Navy the most powerful air defence ships in Europe. They will replace the five *Baleares* class from 2003 onwards.

The minehunter *Segura* was launched at Cartagena in August 1997 and was delivered in May 1998. When the fourth is launched at the turn of the century it is hoped to start work on the second batch of four, fitted for minesweeping. The new amphibious dock transport *Galicia* was delivered at Ferrol in April 1998, and her sister *Castilla* was launched in June 1999.

Sweden: The 'Viking' project, to design a future submarine not only for the Royal Swedish Navy but also for the other Scandinavian navies, is moving ahead slowly. As so often happens, the other partners' operational requirements are so different that collaboration may ultimately be confined to systems and weaponry, rather than a common hull, and major cuts in defence spending are also planned. The third and last unit of the A 19 *Gotland* class, HSwMS *Halland*, was delivered by Kockums at the end of 1997. The building facility at Malmö is closing, and all future submarines will be built by Karlskronavarvet, also a member of the Celsius Group. The sale of four *Sjöormen* class (A 11B type) to Singapore reduces the submarine force to ten boats; the remaining pair have already been taken out of service, and the four *Västergotland* class may offered for sale.

The new 'stealth' corvette *Visby* was launched in mid-1999. Six of the *Norrköping* class FACs ('Spica II' type) were taken out of service in 1997, reducing the FAC force to only ten units. The minehunter *Sturkö* was delivered at the end of 1997, bringing to an end the first batch of four, but no orders have been placed for the planned second batch of four.

The United States Navy, Canada and Latin America

United States: The commissioning of the USS *Harry S Truman* (CVN-75) in July 1998 goes some way to relieving the strain on the aircraft carrier force, but the forty-year old *Independence* (CV-62) was finally decommissioned shortly before, so new construction is barely keeping pace. Work started on the *Ronald Reagan* (CVN-76) in February 1998,

A scale model of the Netherlands' LCF frigate de Zeven Proviecien. (Hollandse Signaalappparaten BV)

but she will not be ready until the end of 2002. Design work on CVN-77 is well advanced, and she may incorporate different flight deck features, notably a reconfigured island (one, two or even three have been suggested), while much more advanced ideas are planned for CVNX and her successors.

The USS *Seawolf* (SSN-21) has proved very quiet in service, and her sister *Connecticut* (SSN-22) came into service in December 1998. The third and last of the class will be named *Jimmy Carter* (SSN-23). Work has already begun on the *Virginia* (SSN-774), the first of the New Attack Submarines (NSSNs), a 'cheap' 7700-tonne design costing only $3.372 billion. Only 54 of the *Los Angeles* (SSN-688) class remain in service, and a further 23 are being retired prematurely to avoid the cost of recoring their reactors. For similar reasons the *Sturgeon* (SSN-637) class is down to ten units.

Unofficial reports say that the first five *Ticonderoga* (CG-47) class Aegis cruisers will be laid up or offered to another navy, the reason being the relative inefficiency of their twin Mk 26 missile-launchers as compared with the Mk 41 vertical launch system (VLS). With all twenty-eight Flight I Blocks I and II *Arleigh Burke* (DDG-51) class Aegis destroyers now in service, construction has switched to the Flight IIA design, with a flight deck and double helicopter hangar. Twenty-four of these ships are planned to come into service from 2000 onwards, and the 33rd unit of the class, the *Howard* (DDG-83), was laid down in December 1998. The 26th, the USS *Higgins* (DDG-76), was formally commissioned in April 1999.

To follow this programme the US Navy hopes to build a new generation of advanced ships, known generically as the 'Surface Combatant, 21st Century' (SC-21). The first priority is to be given to land attack, and so the design-study is referred to as DD-21. In all thirty-two 'Battlespace Dominance Ships' are planned (DDG-103 etc.), displacing some 10,000 tonnes and armed with a variety of air defence and land attack missiles. Although the 'Arsenal Ship' was cancelled, many of the concepts such as low manning and signature-management developed for it are being fed back into the DD-21 design-studies. The later 'Sea Dominance Combatant' variant would have anti-submarine, anti-surface and mine warfare capabilities, while the 'Full Multimission Capability

USS Bonhomme Richard *(LHD-6) on pre-delivery sea trials.* (Ingalls Shipbuilding)

Combatant' or 'Power Projection Ship' would combine every conceivable capability in one hull.

It seems likely that more *Oliver Hazard Perry* (FFG-7) class frigates will be offered to other navies. Only forty-five remain in service, eight of them in reserve. Even the *Spruance* (DD-963) class are beginning to come out of service, as well as the *Kidd* (DDG-993) air defence variants.

The completion of the coastal minehunter USS *Shrike* (MHC-62) in December 1998 completed the *Osprey* (MHC-51) class. The US Navy's enthusiasm for conventional mine countermeasures seems to have waned, although great attention is being paid to beach clearance, the so-called 'surf zone', using a variety of high-technology systems.

The modernisation of the amphibious forces continues. The large assault ship *Bonhomme Richard* (LHD-6) was commissioned in July 1998, and her sister *Iwo Jima* (LHD-7) was launched in December 1997. A planned upgrade of defensive systems for the earlier *Tarawa* (LHA-1) class has been cancelled, and unofficial reports say these 40,000-tonne ships may be retired within the next few years. They have seen arduous service since they were built in the 1970s, and their steam plant is expensive to run.

Work has started on the *San Antonio* (LPD-17) class of amphibious dock transports, with a second contract for the *New Orleans* (LPD-18) awarded to Avondale Industries at an estimated cost of $4 billion. The Avondale Alliance will share work with partners Bath Iron Works, Raytheon Systems and Intergraph. The *San Antonio* is still in the engineering and design phase, but construction will start in 1999, with delivery planned for 2002.

Canada: In March 1998 it was announced that the four *Upholder* class 2400-tonne diesel-electric submarines would be acquired from the UK Royal Navy at a cost of Can$750 million. This includes an eight-year lease with an option to buy, as well as training and support. Even that modest price will be set off against continuing use of Canadian training facilities by British forces. The costs will be met by paying off two destroyers earlier than planned and the cancellation of a refit for one of the *Ojibwa* class submarines. Names will be *Chicoutimi*, *Cornerbrook*, *Victoria* and *Windsor*.

All the *Kingston* class maritime coast defence vessels (MCDVs) have been delivered, with HMCS *Summerside* the last, early in 1999.

Brazil: The fourth *Tupí* class submarine, BNS *Tapajó* (S-33), was launched in mid-1998, and the *Tikuná*

(S-34) will be laid down the following December. She will be slightly longer to accommodate more powerful machinery and other improvements. The official plan is to straight to an indigenous nuclear-powered design when the diesel-electric programme is complete, so the SNAC-1 diesel-electric design will not be built.

The new frigate *Barroso* is believed to be close to launching as her stabilisers have been delivered, and delivery could take place next year. After severe setbacks the modernisation of the *Niteroí* class frigates is in hand, and *Liberal* was completed in June 1998. The programme is to run until 2001, but it is not clear if all six will be modernised.

The eleventh and twelfth *Graúna* class 46-metre patrol craft have not yet been ordered. Plans to modernise the river flotilla include five helicopter-capable patrol vessels, three smaller patrol vessels and twenty launches. Three more *River* class minesweepers have been bought from the Royal Navy, for conversion to navigation tenders.

Chile: The order for two *Scorpène* type submarines in December 1997 put an end to months of speculation, and on 29 July 1998 first steel was cut at DCN Cherbourg. Trials of the first boat are tentatively set for 2004. They will replace the British-built *O'Brien* and *Hyatt*, and by the time they are both in service the *Armada de Chile* may have ordered more.

The availability of British destroyers and frigates in the wake of the 1998 Strategic Defence Review may prove a blessing, by solving the problem of replacements for the elderly destroyers *Prat* and *Latorre*. Four more Type 148 FACs have been acquired from the German Navy in 1998, bringing the total up to six.

Venezuela: The long-delayed modernisation of the frigates *Mariscal Sucre* and *Almirante Brion* began at Ingalls Shipbuilding in Pascagoula, Mississippi in December 1997, and will take about two years to complete. The remaining four might be brought to the same standard later.

The Russian Navy

The long struggle to re-create a credible force continues, but the parlous state of the economy makes this more difficult than ever. The legacy of the Soviet Union, a hugely bloated military establishment, is not easily dismantled, not least because of the risk of dumping large numbers of impoverished military personnel on the civilian economy.

Efforts to get the 60,000-tonne carrier *Admiral Flota Sovetskogo Soyuza Kuznetsov* fully operational seem to have failed; a major refit started in 1996 was still unfinished in December 1997. The largest number of fixed-wing pilots to operate aircraft from her deck is fourteen, according to *Combat Fleets*. The smaller hybrid carrier-cruiser *Admiral Goshkov* (the honorific Admiral Flota Sovetskogo Soyuza or Admiral of the Fleet of the Soviet Union has apparently been dropped) is the subject of protracted negotiations with

Russian Project 667BDRM Delfin *class submarine* ('Delta 4). (Author's collection)

Kuwait's Failaka *(P 3715) with dummy Sea Skua missile canisters visible aft*. (CMN)

India. It is hard to reconcile the reality with the gloomy predictions uttered when these ships first appeared; 'the Bear has Wings' etc.

Work on the submarine fleet proceeds slowly. The first Project 955 SSN, the *Yuri Dolgoruky*, was laid down in 1996 but was reported to be only 1 per cent complete three months later. Work on the *Severodvinsk*, the first Project 885 SSN, is even slower: laid down in 1993 but not due for delivery until 2002 at the earliest. Only four Project 941 'Typhoon' type SSBNs remain, and the burden of maintaining the strategic deterrent falls mainly on the Project 677 'Delta' series (twelve 'Delta IIIs' and seven 'Delta IVs'). All the Project 671 'Victor I' and 'Victor II' series have been decommissioned but eighteen Project 671RTM and RTMK 'Victor IIIs' remain.

The conventional submarine force has shrunk to twenty-one Project 877 *Kilo* type and two Project 636 'Improved Kilos', and ten obsolescent Project 641B *Tango* class and three Project 641K *Foxtrots*. The first Project 677 boat, codenamed *Lada*, has apparently been laid down as the *St Petersburg*. She is almost certainly intended as a 'pump-primer' for export sales, the domestic variant of the Rubin Bureau's 'Amur' series, and would be sold off the stocks if a buyer materialises.

Only two of the four Project 1144 nuclear-powered missile cruisers are in commission, the *Petr Veliky* and the *Admiral Nakhimov*. A 'Squadron Surface Ship', a 10,000-tonne missile-armed cruiser, is reported to be on order from the Yantar Zavod yard in Kaliningrad, but in the present economic climate it is doubtful if such a ship is affordable, and in any case the shipyard is in receivership.

The economic crisis seems to have no effect on the shipbuilders' determination to offer designs for export. The Project 1166.1 'Gepard' programme resulted in three frigates being ordered by the Zeledenosk Zavod in Tatarstan, of which the *Yastreb* has been built, but her trials were suspended for lack of money. The same yard laid down the Project 1244.1 light frigate *Novik* in October 1997, despite being in receivership and unable to deliver two frigates to the Navy.

Middle East and Indian Ocean

Bangladesh: A 2000-ton frigate was ordered from Daewoo Heavy Industries in South Korea in October 1997. The cost is being met from a Saudi Arabian grant of US$100 million.

Egypt: The Egyptian Navy has made no decision on new submarines, and it is possible that the plans might be deferred indefinitely.

In addition to the three *El Arish* class missile-armed frigates, the US Navy transferred two more *Oliver Hazard Perry* class in 1998, the USS *Fahrion* (FFG-22) and *Lewis B Puller* (FFG-23). The delivery of the last of ten SH-2G Super Seasprite helicopters in October 1998 for these ships and the two ex-*Knox* class frigates will enhance anti-submarine capabilities.

India: The search for a carrier to replace the *Vikrant* has been a long one, and finally even the *Viraat* will have to be paid off earlier than hoped. Faced with such a humiliating loss of prestige and striking power, the Indian Navy's only affordable option seems to be the purchase of the Russian Navy's *Admiral Gorshkov*.

The submarine force was enhanced by the arrival of the ninth Project 877 *Kilo* type *Sindhurakshak* in 1997, but the number of Project 641E *Foxtrots* will fall to four by 1999. In addition, two Project 636 boats were ordered from the Admiralty Yard in St Petersburg in February 1998, for delivery in 2001-2002. Although plans exist to build two more IKL Type 1500 boats at Mazagon Dock in Bombay, at the time of writing funds have not been voted.

The commissioning of the destroyer INS *Delhi* at the end of 1997 marked the completion of the first major warship built in India, but the cost has been heavy. Similarly the protracted process of enlarging the British *Leander* design to produce the *Godavari* and *Brahmaputra* designs has consumed resources better devoted to keeping the fleet efficient. Significantly, the latest development is the ordering of three (later increased to six) Project 1135.6 modified *Krivak III* frigates from Russia; a slap in the face to Indian shipbuilding interests but a better deal for an under-funded Navy.

Israel: The submarine *Dolphin* was completed by HDW in Kiel in September 1997, and the *Dakar* and *Leviathan* are fitting out. Sales to Chile and scrappings have reduced the FAC strength to only seven units, of which the *Sa'ar 4s* are nearly twenty years old. The two *Aliyah* (*Sa'ar 4.5*) class are believed to be up for sale, along with the remaining four *Dabur* type patrol craft.

Kuwait: The first five P-37BRL type *Um Almaradim* class missile-armed patrol craft have been completed by CMN in Cherbourg in conditions of secrecy. The *Al Fahaheel* (P-3716) is expected to carry out the first firing of the BAe Sea Skua missile system by December 1999, but retrofitting of the first batch of operational missiles will apparently be done at Ras al Qalayah, whereas the last three boats will be delivered with missiles installed.

The plans to build up to five 1200-tonne corvettes have not yet reached the point of awarding a contract.

Pakistan: The first *Agosta-90B* type submarine was rolled out at DCN Cherbourg on 8 August 1998, and sea trials will start later in the year. In April sections were sent by sea to Karachi Naval Shipyard for the second boat. These boats will be armed with F-17 Mod 2 wire-guided wake-homing torpedoes and SM-39 Exocet anti-ship missiles, the first export order for both weapons. When the first boat is fully worked up it is likely that one of the thirty-year old *Hangor* class will be paid off.

The ex-Royal Navy frigate *Tariq* (now rated as a destroyer) is the second of the class to be modernised, starting in 1998. The minehunter *Mahmoud* was delivered in December 1997, the first fibreglass-reinforced plastic (FRP) vessel built at Karachi Naval Shipyard. The

Jalalat, delivered in August 1997, is reported to be a missile-armed FAC, and was also built at Karachi Naval Shipyard, proof of the growing diversity of the yard.

Qatar: With the arrival of the second pair of *Barzan* class FACs, QENS *Al Udeid* and QENS *Al Debeel* in May 1998, the next step is to order two 46-metre patrol craft. A letter of intent has been given to Vosper Thornycroft (UK) Ltd, but at the time of writing no contract has been signed.

Saudi Arabia: Work started on the first of three *Arriyad* class *La Fayette* type air defence frigates at DCN Lorient in 1997. Under the 'Mouette' programme the four *Al Madinah* class frigates are being overhauled at DCN Toulon. The first, *Al Madinah*, returned to Saudi Arabia in mid-1997, and the last, the *Taif*, is to be finished in March 1999.

Turkey: The submarine force continues to be modernised, and in 1998 it was announced that four more IKL Type 1400 boats are to be built at Gölcük Naval Shipyard. The *18 Mart* (S-355) was launched in 1998; her name commemorates the Turkish defeat of the British and French fleets' attempt to force the Dardanelles in 1915. The seven old ex-US Navy boats are restricted to harbour training, and will eventually be scrapped.

As new surface ships come into service, the old ex-US Navy destroyers are also being decommissioned. After a long delays, the ex-*Oliver Hazard Perry* class frigates *Gaziantep*, *Giresun* and *Gemlik* were commissioned early in 1998, and *Gelibolu* and *Gokceada* in February 1999. The third *Barbaros* class, TCG *Sahilreis*, started her sea trials in Hamburg in April 1998.

The third *Yildiz* class 57-metre FAC, TCG *Kiliç* (P-330) was delivered in 1998. The ex-French Navy minehunters are named *Edinçük*, *Edremit*, *Enez*, *Erdek* and *Ermenit*, and they have been refitted by DCN

The Republic of Korea Navy's first KDX-1 type destroyer, Kwang-Gaetto, *on trials. (BAe Defence Systems)*

Lorient before delivery. Three new minehunters have been ordered from Germany.

United Arab Emirates: No progress has been made on the 'LEWA 1' project, to build six 65-metre FACs, and 'LEWA 2', the construction of 90-metre corvettes, is as far away as ever. In March the 'LEWA 3' programme for small fast patrol craft was said to be about to be awarded to CMN of Cherbourg.

The Asia-Pacific Region

Australia: With three of the *Collins* class submarines now in service the Royal Australian Navy is wrestling with software problems in the combat system, and the *Collins*, *Farncomb* and *Waller* will not be fully operational before 2000. The construction schedule for the remaining three is running at least five months late.

Although only two of the *Anzac* class frigates are in service the Navy is already asking for tenders for a Warfighting Improvement Programme (WIP) for all eight. This will involve the retrofitting of Harpoon anti-ship missiles, replacing the VL Sea Sparrow air defence missiles with the Evolved Sea Sparrow Missile System (ESSM) and adding a second silo aft, adding a second tracker and various other improvements. An upgrade is also planned for the six *Adelaide* class, and a contract has been awarded to ADI.

The second *Huon* class minehunter, the *Hawkesbury*, was launched on 24 April 1998 and started sea trials in March 1999, the same month in which HMAS *Huon* was handed over to the Navy in March. The third, *Norman*, was launched at Newcastle, NSW on 4 May 1999, and the keel of the last unit, the *Yarra*, was laid the following month.

In a surprise reaction to events in East Timor, the Navy leased a fast catamaran transport from the builders INCAT Australia, to enter service on 1 June 1999. The 86-metre ship can carry 500 troops and their vehicles and equipment at over 40kts, and has a maximum range of 1000 miles. She will bridge the gap until the converted LSTs *Kanimbla* and *Manoora* become operational in mid-to-late 2000.

Brunei: After a delay of six months to select weapons and sensors the order for three corvettes was finally placed with GEC Marine's Yarrow shipyard in January 1998. They will come into service in 2001-2003, and will have Thomson-Marconi sonars.

China: Intentions and capabilities of the People's Liberation Army-Navy (PLAN) remain obscure, and much of what is known is based on outside observers' opinions and information released by Western intelligence agencies. According to US Navy sources up to four Project 094 SSBNs are planned, to be armed with JL-2 missiles capable of reaching a distance of 8000 km. A new SSN, Project 093, is also said to be under construction at Huludao, and likely to be launched early next century. Work on the diesel-electric Project 039 *Song* type continues, and Western sources suggest that European equipment has been supplied for this class. The second Project 636 improved *Kilo* type was reported to be completed by the Admiralty Yard in St Petersburg in June 1998, the first having been delivered by heavy-lift ship at the end of 1997.

New construction of surface warships continues at a slow pace. Combat Fleets gives a tentative completion date of 1999 for the first of the two Project 956A *Sovremennyy* class destroyers bought from Russia, although late payments have held up delivery of the Kh-35 anti-ship missiles. No other additions of major warships has been reported, and the rumoured purchase of the hulk of the carrier *Varyag* from a Macao gambling syndicate turned out to be untrue

Indonesia: The financial and political instability in Asia hit Indonesia very hard, and although the deal with Germany to buy five Type 206A submarines had seemed watertight (names had been allocated), it has since been cancelled. The only other important programme, the PB 57 Variant V patrol craft, seems unaffected, and the first two were scheduled for delivery in 1998.

Japan: Despite financial cutbacks the Maritime Defence Force continues to procure ships at a rate which all navies can envy. The *Oyashio* (SS-590) class of submarines is to run to ten units, of which the *Oyashio* herself came into service in March 1998, *Michishio* (SS-591) was commissioned in March 1999, SS-592 is fitting-out, and SS-593 was launched in June 1998. The tenth boat is to be in service by 2007.

With the completion of the *Chokai* (DDG-176) in March 1998 the *Aegis* destroyer programme is complete. Two 4600-tonne *Aegis* destroyers are projected, presumably successors to the latest *Murasame* (DD-101) class, of which the *Yudachi* (DD-103) and *Kirisame* (DD-104) were commissioned in March 1999, and six are under construction or funded.

Mine warfare plays an important role, and since the Gulf War, capabilities are being upgraded. The second *Uraga* (MST-463) class mine countermeasures support ship, the *Bungo*, started sea trials in December 1997. The first of a new class of coastal minehunters, the *Sugashima* (MSC-681), was launched in August 1997 and was commissioned in March 1999, at the same time as the *Notojima* (MSC-682). Two more are under construction and four more have been approved.

The controversial flat-deck tank landing ship *Osumi* (LST-4001) was completed in March 1998, a second ship having been approved in December the previous year, and two more projected. She is described as controversial because she is construed by political opponents of the government as having an offensive capability. In fact the ships are 14,000-tonne amphibious dock transports (LPDs), capable of operating two air-cushion landing craft (LCACs), helicopters and even STOVL aircraft if they become available. However, the Maritime Self Defence Force is becoming involved in peacekeeping operations, a role for which large amphibious ships are ideal.

Malaysia: Another South East Asian country hit by the regional financial

The Royal Malaysian Navy's new frigate, Lekiu, *accepted in August 1999.* (Author's collection)

crisis, Malaysia did not take delivery of its frigates *Lekiu* and *Jebat* from GEC Marine's Yarrow shipyard until April 1999. The second pair of ex-Iraqi corvettes bought from Fincantieri are expected to be commissioned in 1999, but names have not been announced. Other programmes, particularly replacements for the FACs, will be deferred until finances improve.

New Zealand: The second *Anzac* type frigate, HMNZS *Te Mana*, started sea trials in March 1999.

Philippines: In August 1998, the government announced that the financial crisis has forced the cancellation of the offshore patrol vessel (OPV) programme, but in the light of several serious confrontations wit the Chinese PLA Navy the government has agreed to reinstate part of the naval budget.

Singapore: The patrol craft *Independence* (87), the last of the *Fearless* class, was launched in April 1998 by Singapore Technologies Marine (formerly SSE), at Jurong. Her sisters *Unity* (83), *Sovereignty* (84), Justice (85), and *Resilience* (86) were commissioned in a single ceremony on 7 February 1998. The tank landing ship *Endurance* was launched by Singapore Technologies in March 1998, the first of four replacements for superannuated ex-US Navy LSTs. The *Persistence* was launched in April 1999. The ex-Swedish submarines *Centurion* and *Conqueror* were commissioned a month later.

WARSHIP NOTES

This section comprises a number of short articles and notes, generally highlighting little known aspects of warship history.

NAVAL SURFACE WARFARE CENTER, CARDEROCK DIVISION, BETHESDA, MARYLAND, USA

David McLean visits a major Naval Research establishment in the United States.

The largest naval testing tank in the world is known as the David Taylor Model Basin, twelve miles northwest of Washington, DC. The tank is so long that the surface of the water is not exactly level, but follows the curvature of the earth's surface. It was built in the 1940s and is covered by an arched reinforced concrete roof with a span of 110ft. The actual building is 3200ft long and contains a Shallow Water Basin, a Deep Water Basin, and a High Speed Basin, the longest of which is nearly 3000ft long, 50ft wide and with water to a depth of about 15ft. The towing carriages run along rails which follow the earth's curvature and are built on bedrock. The largest tank contains 16 million gallons and all the tanks are kept in darkness to prevent the growth of algae. For practical reasons fresh water is used, so test results have to be calibrated to represent sea water testing. The towing carriages are powered by electric motors and tow models up to 20kts in the Deep Water Basin and up to 70kts in the High Speed Basin. The water surface is kept dust-free by a neat system of skimming. The scale of the tanks is awesome, the darkened tunnel seems to disappear over the horizon.

Elsewhere in the Research Centre, known as the Carderock Division, NSWC, are the Manueuvering and Seakeeping Basin, used to test the performance of vessels in realistic waves, and the Rotating Arm Facility in a 260ft diameter circular basin used to tow models in circular paths and test propulsion systems in turns. Attached to the rotating arm during my visit was the sleek model of a still-secret submarine just visible as a shimmering dark shape below the surface. In the Maneuvering and Seakeeping Basin, a diagonal bridge on rails enables models to be towed into or with waves, generated by pneumatic wavemakers, at any angle from 0° to 90°. These basins are used to test hulls of surface ships, submarines, platforms, mooring facilities, and other structures. Going through tests during my visit were futuristic assault craft designed to hit the beach at 25-35kts rather than around 8-10kts as at present. Also on site were floating platforms designed to be coupled together to make an aircraft runway.

To complement the basins are various water tunnels – the marine equivalent of wind tunnels – with cross-sections varying from 12 to 36ins and operated at speeds from 12 to 50kts. Once models were positioned in the tunnel they could be observed through reinforced windows. Dyes and threads, and sheets of laser light are all used to research flow characteristics.

The Carderock Division boasts the largest basin facilities in the world and is now offering commercial and private testing for cargo ships, oil platforms and even racing yacht hulls. Their fees are high but any refinements in a tanker's hull design can save a fortune over the working life of the vessel. For a world-class racing yacht, cost is rarely the most important issue. Nevertheless, most of the work is on the next generation of formidable warships, submarines and various weapons systems. At Carderock they test every part of a ship which deforms the air or water flow – rudders, masts, antennae, fins, bows, sterns – and even the missile launchers, and the external fire mains.

As in all fields of research computer simulation is playing an increasing part. Although much can be learned from it, it is only useful up to a point. Tests with real models in real water show up many things not remotely mentioned in the printouts.

In one room we were shown several 20ft long hull models made of wood with detachable bow sections used for testing different designs of bow bulbs. At the other end of the vessels is the propeller and this is where some of the most intense and secret research is going on at Carderock. Not only is it a vital part of any ship (without which it can't move) but the effect of cavitation (bubbles created and destroyed by the rotation of the blades) is loss of thrust, heavy vibration within the ship, and noise which can be detected and followed from 200 miles away. There was talk of propellers with flexible blades to reduce cavitation. It is likely that some important refinements in propeller technology, coming in over the next decades, will have been developed and tested at Carderock.

With today's emphasis on stealth and detection and the constant interplay of these two disciplines, it comes as no surprise that Carderock is testing the radar reflections of frogmen,

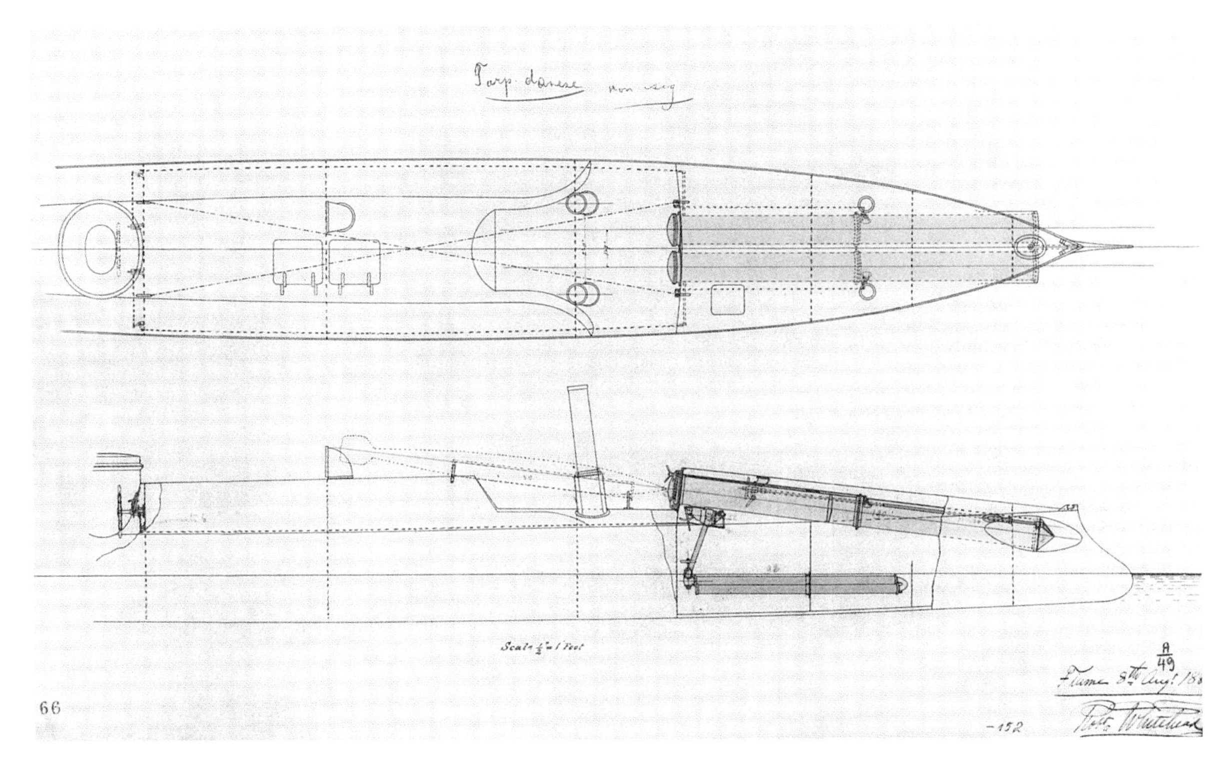

unmanned intelligence gathering devices, and the materials from which they are made.

Today the Carderock Division's technical research areas include ship systems, hydromechanics, materials, structures, survivability (in explosions of various kinds), signatures, ship propulsion systems, etc. Besides Carderock there are facilities in Alaska, California, Idaho, Florida, and Washington DC, employing a total of 16,000 people.

As part of Carderock's submarine development programme, a quarter-size radio-controlled model is built and tested in a deep lake in the Rockies. During the noise test, it lies on the lake floor while each piece of equipment is turned on independently and tested. Everything is considered – down to the commander's desk fan. When sensitive seabed microphones line an enemy coast, close to where a submarine might be operating, all this testing is vital. Every warship has unique signatures (heat, radar, sound, magnetic, vision, influence on the earth's magnetic field, etc.) and each can be measured, recorded and stored. Advanced navies now have databases of 'signatures' helping individual captain's ships to quickly recognise any vessel detected. While a captain is reading the printout of another vessel's identity, he had better remember that someone else may be reading his signature. This is just what the scientists at Carderock are working on at the moment.

WHITEHEAD TORPEDO-TUBES

Antony Preston comments on two unusual drawings from the original Whitehead torpedo factory at Fiume.

These two drawings, reproduced from the archives of Italian torpedo-manufacturer Whitehead SpA, show details of torpedo-tube installations for two Danish warships of the 1880s. Both are the equivalent of Admiralty 'as fitted' drawings, and the written details are in English.

The first is identified simply as '*Torp Danese*' (this title probably being added much later), but the date, 8 August 1881, suggests that it is the Royal Danish Navy 1st class torpedo boat *Svaerdfisken* (Swordfish), built by Thornycroft and armed with twin 15in (38cm) bow tubes. The second carries the legend '*Valkyrien* stern-tube' and is dated 22 August 1887. The ship which fits this is the 2972-ton protected cruiser of that name, launched at the Royal Dockyard in Copenhagen in 1888. She is listed in *Conway's All the World's Fighting Ships 1860-1905* as having five 15in tubes. The only other realistic candidate is a Norwegian destroyer launched in 1896, but she has a very different configuration. Further information will be welcomed.

VICTORIAN TORPEDO DISCOVERY AT SOUTHEND

Antony Preston describes a chance find by a trawler along the British coast.

In June 1999, the trawler *Hornet* fished up what appears to be the remains of a 14in Whitehead torpedo, two miles off of Southend. A somewhat garbled account in *The Times* of 15 June described it has having a 'sharp nose', a body of iron (?), and a copper head, indicating an early model Whitehead. The owner

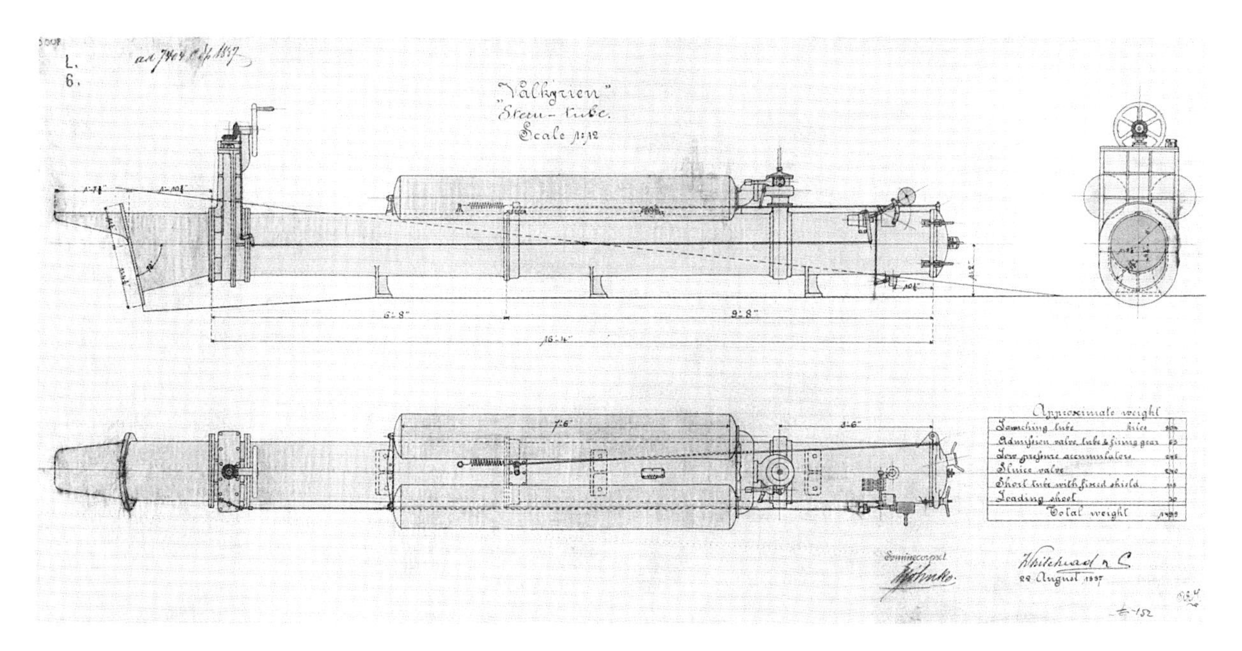

Whitehead torpedo-tube plans. (Antony Preston)

of the trawler is quoted as saying that his research shows that the torpedo was one of two fired from a paddle-steamer in Sheerness, and that it could be the first Whitehead ever fired in England. Such precise provenance should sound some warning bells – several hundred torpedoes were launched by torpedo boats, cruisers and even battleships, and inevitably some went astray.

The sequel to this story descends into farce. When the trawler owner called the Royal Navy to report his find, bomb disposal experts advised him to throw it overboard in case it exploded! The likelihood of a torpedo being fired with a live warhead is very remote; by the Victorian Navy's standards, they were very expensive weapons, and were intended to be re-used as often as possible; inevitably, this led to eruptions of argument when one was not recovered. We await the next act in the unfolding drama.

AUSTRALIAN SUBMARINE WRECK FOUND AFTER 80 YEARS

Antony Preston reports on the recent discovery of the wreck of HM Australian Submarine AE-2, the first submarine to get through the Dardanelles.

The October-December 1997 issue of *The Navy*, the journal of the Navy League of Australia, reported the discovery of the wreck of the Royal Australian Navy's submarine *AE-2* in the Sea of Marmora. The wreck was identified by sonar, lying in 80 metres of water, upright and partially covered in fishing nets.

The find is understandably important to Australian and Turkish historians because *AE-2* was the first submarine to reach the Sea of Marmora in 1915, to attack Turkish shipping carrying reinforcements and supplies to the troops fighting at Gallipoli. The *B-11* had penetrated the minefields to sink the old coast defence ship *Messudieh*, but the *E-15* and the French *Saphir* both ran aground and were lost. *AE-2*'s success and the feats of the British and French submarines which followed heartened the Allies at a bad time for the Allied forces struggling to maintain their bridgeheads. Although *AE-2* under Lt Cdr H G Stoker RAN caused havoc in the Sea of Marmora, her career was ended after four days, on 30 April 1915, when she was sunk by gunfire from the Turkish torpedo boat *Sultan Hissar*. Over the years both Australian and Turkish authorities tried to locate the wreck, but without success.

The work has been done under the energetic leadership of Selçuk Kolay, Director of the Rahmi M Koç industrial museum in Istanbul. He went to the length of consulting the CO's surviving relatives, and began a search to the north of the reported position of the sinking. Based on memories of Stoker's aunt, who remembered him shouting "North" in his sleep many years later, Selçuk Kolay decided that *AE-2* had been heading north to try to escape. Although the official theory is that Stoker was trying to stop the Turks from acquiring details of the latest Royal Navy submarine design, a more prosaic explanation may be that the submarine's navigation was only approximate.

The museum is keen to raise the wreck and display it as an attraction for the many Australian visitors to Gallipoli, and hopes to attract Australian finance for a joint venture. Mr Kolay's estimate of US $1 million seems very low, and corrosion

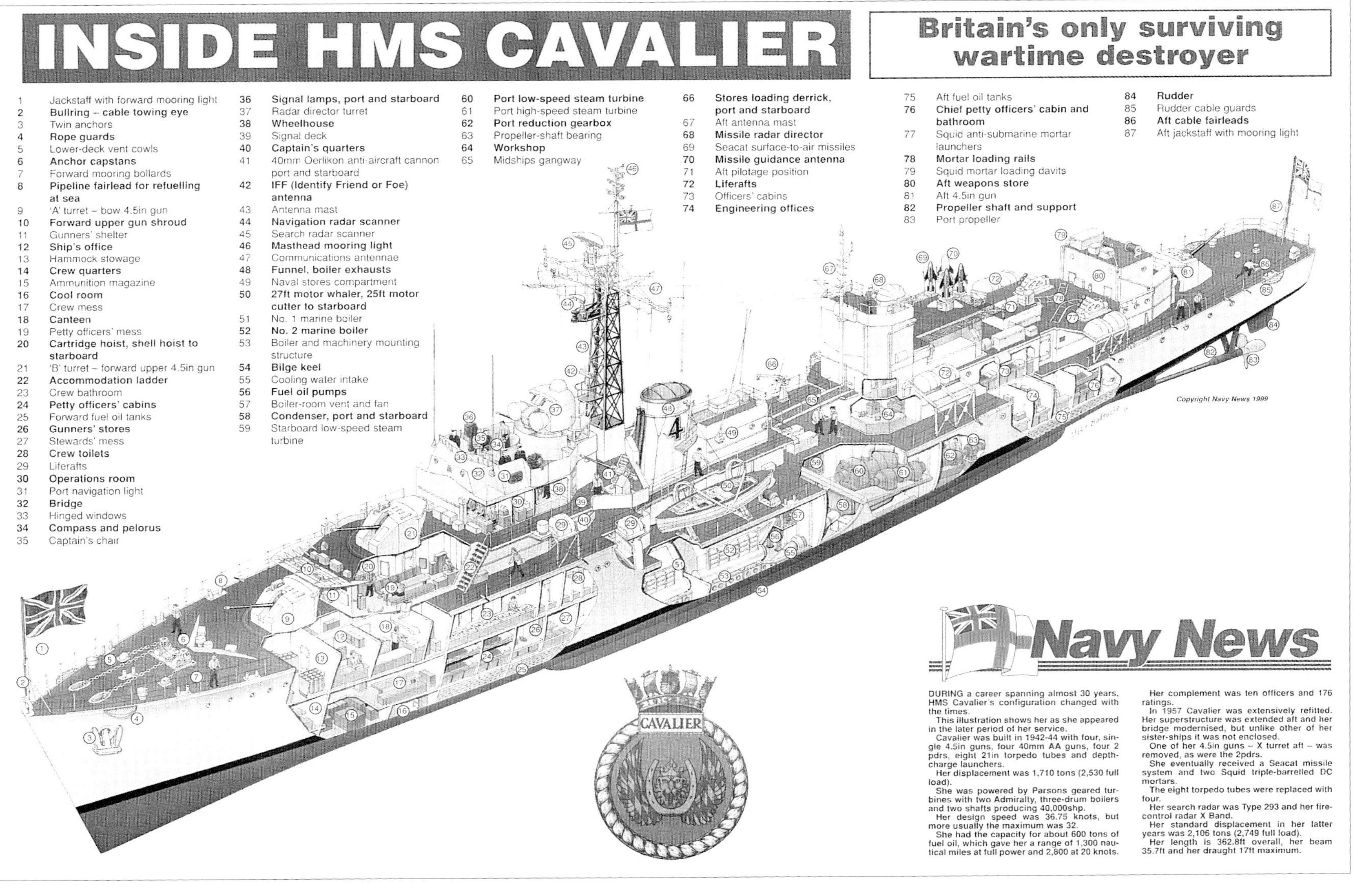

INSIDE HMS CAVALIER

Britain's only surviving wartime destroyer

1 Jackstaff with forward mooring light
2 **Bullring – cable towing eye**
3 Twin anchors
4 **Rope guards**
5 Lower-deck vent cowls
6 **Anchor capstans**
7 Forward mooring bollards
8 **Pipeline fairlead for refuelling at sea**
9 'A' turret – bow 4.5in gun
10 **Forward upper gun shroud**
11 Gunners' shelter
12 **Ship's office**
13 Hammock stowage
14 **Crew quarters**
15 Ammunition magazine
16 **Cool room**
17 Crew mess
18 **Canteen**
19 Petty officers' mess
20 **Cartridge hoist, shell hoist to starboard**
21 'B' turret – forward upper 4.5in gun
22 **Accommodation ladder**
23 Crew bathroom
24 **Petty officers' cabins**
25 Forward fuel oil tanks
26 **Gunners' stores**
27 Stewards' mess
28 **Crew toilets**
29 Liferafts
30 **Operations room**
31 Port navigation light
32 **Bridge**
33 Hinged windows
34 **Compass and pelorus**
35 Captain's chair
36 **Signal lamps, port and starboard**
37 Radar director turret
38 **Wheelhouse**
39 Signal deck
40 **Captain's quarters**
41 40mm Oerlikon anti-aircraft cannon port and starboard
42 **IFF (Identify Friend or Foe) antenna**
43 Antenna mast
44 **Navigation radar scanner**
45 Search radar scanner
46 **Masthead mooring light**
47 Communications antennae
48 **Funnel, boiler exhausts**
49 Naval stores compartment
50 **27ft motor whaler, 25ft motor cutter to starboard**
51 No. 1 marine boiler
52 **No. 2 marine boiler**
53 Boiler and machinery mounting structure
54 **Bilge keel**
55 Cooling water intake
56 **Fuel oil pumps**
57 Boiler-room vent and fan
58 **Condenser, port and starboard**
59 Starboard low-speed steam turbine
60 **Port low-speed steam turbine**
61 Port high-speed steam turbine
62 **Port reduction gearbox**
63 Propeller-shaft bearing
64 **Workshop**
65 Midships gangway
66 **Stores loading derrick, port and starboard**
67 Aft antenna mast
68 **Missile radar director**
69 Seacat surface-to-air missiles
70 **Missile guidance antenna**
71 Aft pilotage position
72 **Liferafts**
73 Officers' cabins
74 **Engineering offices**
75 Aft fuel oil tanks
76 **Chief petty officers' cabin and bathroom**
77 Squid anti-submarine mortar launchers
78 **Mortar loading rails**
79 Squid mortar loading davits
80 **Aft weapons store**
81 Aft 4.5in gun
82 **Propeller shaft and support**
83 Port propeller
84 **Rudder**
85 Rudder cable guards
86 **Aft cable fairleads**
87 Aft jackstaff with mooring light

Navy News

DURING a career spanning almost 30 years, HMS Cavalier's configuration changed with the times.

This illustration shows her as she appeared in the later period of her service.

Cavalier was built in 1942-44 with four, single 4.5in guns, four 40mm AA guns, four 2 pdrs, eight 21in torpedo tubes and depth-charge launchers.

Her displacement was 1,710 tons (2,530 full load).

She was powered by Parsons geared turbines with two Admiralty, three-drum boilers and two shafts producing 40,000shp.

Her design speed was 36.75 knots, but more usually the maximum was 32.

She had the capacity for about 600 tons of fuel oil, which gave her a range of 1,300 nautical miles at full power and 2,800 at 20 knots.

Her complement was ten officers and 176 ratings.

In 1957 Cavalier was extensively refitted. Her superstructure was extended aft and her bridge modernised, but unlike other of her sister-ships it was not enclosed.

One of her 4.5in guns – X turret aft – was removed, as were the 2pdrs.

She eventually received a Seacat missile system and two Squid triple-barrelled DC mortars.

The eight torpedo tubes were replaced with four.

Her search radar was Type 293 and her fire-control radar X Band.

Her standard displacement in her latter years was 2,106 tons (2,749 full load).

Her length is 362.8ft overall, her beam 35.7ft and her draught 17ft maximum.

Cutaway of HMS Cavalier. (Navy News / M Badrooke)

may turn out to be a much bigger problem than predicted, as it has with *Holland No.1* at HMS *Dolphin* and other preserved submarines.

CAVALIER'S EPIC STORY

Daniel Mersey reports on the destroyer's homecoming and display at Chatham Historic Dockyard.

HMS *Cavalier* is Britain's only surviving wartime destroyer, which served in the Royal Navy for almost thirty years. Commissioned at the end of 1944, she saw only a few months active service in European waters, but was awarded with her sole Battle Honour, Arctic 1945, for her escort services with convoy RA 64 – generally acknowledged as having survived the worst weather experienced on the Murmansk run. After this, HMS *Cavalier* sailed for the Far East, and became involved in the political upheavals following the surrender of Japan. Later, she participated in the nuclear bomb tests at Christmas Island in 1958; the final years of her tour of duty were spent in home waters. In July 1972 her extended service came to an end, and campaigns to prevent her being scrapped were launched; a Trust was organised and the long battle to save HMS *Cavalier* began.

On 16 May 1999, HMS *Cavalier* arrived back at Chatham Historic Dockyard, towed from Hebburn by the tug *Sun London*. She was welcomed home by the paddle steamer *Kingswear Castle*, *MTB 102*, and a flotilla of other historic vessels including the Dunkirk little ships. HMS *Cavalier* has now been transferred to dry dock, on display as a worthy memorial to the 30,000 who gave their lives in destroyers in the Second World War. This was made possible by the HMS *Cavalier* (Chatham) Trust, a consortium of campaign groups whose aim was to berth the ship beside a planned memorial museum in Chatham; a National Heritage Lottery grant of £830,000 helped the consortium to achieve their goal.

THE ANGLO-GERMAN ARMS RACE

Antony Preston notes an interesting tale of espionage pre-dating the First World War.

Recently declassified British Secret Service (MI5) files reveal details of the only British subject to be prosecuted for spying for Germany before the First World War. He was Warrant Officer George Parrott, gunner in the battleship HMS *Agamemnon*.

According to the MI5 files Parrott was recruited in 1910, and soon handed over a four-volume report on RN gunnery in 1908-09, followed by a report on the 1909 Annual Manoeuvres. They allege that he smuggled the German agent Karl Hentschel on board the *Agamemnon*, and that the two men quarrelled in 1911. He was sentenced to four years in prison.

The case is no more than a footnote to the Anglo-German naval arms race, but it reflects German interest in keeping abreast of the developments in RN long-range gunnery (see *Warship 1996*).

ARMSTRONG GUNS IN ACTION

Antony Preston details an article relating to Armstrong breechloading guns.

In the May 1999 issue of *The Mariner's Mirror* (pp.205-212) Colin Jones analyses the notorious Armstrong breechloading guns' performance during two bombardments in Japan dated to 1863-64. The guns had been brought into service with the Royal Navy after a concerted campaign of lobbying by both Press and Parliament, yet seven years later all of the larger calibres were withdrawn, although the 40pdr remained in service for two decades longer.

Colin Jones points out that the list of gun-accidents listed by Parkes and other authorities refer to two actions, whereas most authorities have assumed that the figures referred only to the 1863 bombardment of Kagoshima. More relevant, he shows that many of the accidents were related to faults in the carriages, and possibly errors in loading drill. In many ships, the Armstrongs were in a mixed battery, alongside muzzle-loaders, so some crews were likely to be confused in the heat of battle. Several reports praised the Armstrong gun's phenomenal range and accuracy (3500yds) and the accuracy of the time-fuzes, and some officers suggested improvements to drill to get the best out of the new guns. The main weakness appeared to be the vent-piece, which often cracked or blew out; the lack of spare vent-pieces meant that these guns were then useless. Some of the accidents were caused by the failure of the men serving the gun to tighten the breech-screw properly.

The Navy adopted five types of Armstrong:

Calibre/ length	*Type*	*Gun Weight*	*Projectile Weight*
7.2in/13.8	110pdr	81cwt 2lbs	109lbs
4.96in/21.4	40pdr	31cwt 4lbs	40lbs 1oz
3.94in/21.3	20pdr	16cwt	21lbs 8oz
3.2in/19.2	12pdr	8cwt	11lbs 3oz
3.2in/16.4	9pdr	6cwt	8.5lbs

Editorial Note: Navies using (or debating the use of) Armstrong guns can be read about in George Gratz's and Peter Brooks' articles in this volume of *Warship*.

THE *MELIK* SOCIETY

Daniel Mersey details a society dedicated to the gunboats and history of the Re-conquest of the Sudan.

The purpose of the *Melik* Society is to advance public awareness of British and Sudanese history, especially the development of river gunboats and their achievements in the military campaigns between 1883 and 1899. Foremost among the Society's objectives is the preservation, restoration and exhibition of the gunboat *Melik* and the steamer *Bordein*.

THE MELIK SOCIETY

Registered Charity 1049646

Kitchener, Sirdar (Commander-in-Chief) of the Egyptian Army, set out to re-conquer the Sudan in 1898, eleven years after the death of General Gordon at Khartoum. Against a host of Mahdist warriors, he had to face the logistical nightmare of supplying 25,000 men and 10,000 beasts in one of the world's most inhospitable climates. He knew that control of the River Nile was vital, and succeeded in this with a flotilla which rose to ten vessels.

Melik was a twin-screw armoured gunboat, which was transported by river and train to aid in Kitchener's reconquest of the Sudan. She mounted a powerful searchlight, to guard against Mahdist night attacks, and played a decisive part in the Battle of Omdurman before carrying troops to Khartoum for General Gordon's memorial service (*Melik*'s commander was Major "Monkey" Gordon – a nephew of the General). *Bordein* was one of General Gordon's steamers.

The Society aims to research and publish information about engineering aspects of the campaigns and conservation of artifacts. It also wishes to promote goodwill and co-operation between British and Sudanese organisations involved in similar projects.

The *Melik* Society was formed in 1994 by a group of individuals with a common interest in the history of the Sudan and her relationship with Great Britain. If you are interested in the Society's objectives, contact them at: The *Melik* Society, 202 Lambeth Road, London SE1 7JW, UK.

NAVAL RESEARCH USING THE INTERNET

Stuart Slade offers useful information for those Warship readers who have access to the Internet.

According to a recent report in the *New York Times*, the number of Internet users is doubling every 100 days. In less than a decade the Internet and its backbone, the World Wide Web, have evolved from an obscure research tool into a major source of information and a means of dissemination and exchange.

This change has revolutionised the study of naval affairs. Once equipped with a modern personal computer (PC), a modem, an Internet service-provider and a search engine, the researcher can access a previously unimaginable range of technical information services. Searches quickly reveal a wide range of high-quality sites that provide data on naval topics around the world. The Net is growing so fast that any attempt to list all of the appropriate sites would be futile. Instead, some indication can be given of the major classes sites on the Net, with some caveats.

THE 'OFFICIAL SITES' OF THE WORLD'S NAVIES

There are a number of such sites, those run by the US Navy (http://www.navy.mil/), the Royal Navy (http://www.royal-navy.mod.uk/index.htm), Japanese Maritime Self Defence Force (http://cssew01.cs.nada.ac.jp/~yas/JDA/MSDF/defense.html), Republic of Singapore Navy (http://www.mindef.gov.sg/) and a number of others. They feature many pictures of smart, well-disciplined sailors going happily about their duties in sleek, well-maintained warships. The Royal Australian Navy site (http://www.navy.gov.au/) gains immense credibility and admiration by including photographs of what happens when operations do not go entirely to plan. Many such sites have a news section with details of current operations and more illustrations of smart, well-disciplined sailors rendering humanitarian aid to photogenically-grateful victims of natural disasters. But, amid the public relations hype, these sites really do contain a good deal of useful information. The Singapore MinDef website contains fact-sheets on warships and weapons in naval service. As one might expect, the US Navy site contains copious data on ships and aircraft, as well as links to other sites run by individual ships, bases and units. The site for the USS *Enterprise* (CV-65) Battle Group (http://bgmain.apptechsyse.com/aldevwev) is typical. Some of them even allow users to e-mail questions directly to officers of the ships.

UNOFFICIAL SITES

In addition to the official websites there are a large number of sites dedicated to specific navies, but run without official approval. The content of these sites and the reliability is variable, and tends to be of a less formalised nature. The sites dealing with the Chinese People's Army-Navy (http://wwwcsif.cs.ucdavis.edu/~wen/plan.html), German Navy (http:///wwww.un-karlsruhe.de/~unit/enavy.html) and Royal Malaysian Navy (http://maf.mod.gov.my/homepage/mainrmn/htm) are typical. Unofficial websites often have the virtue of providing links to other sites, so that the researcher can find additional material easily. Unfortunately they are more transient than the official sites. When they publish photographs, these are from private collections and are more revealing than official views. On these sites naval enthusiasts are putting up a stunning variety of photographs which, a few years ago, would have driven Western intelligence services mad with envy, and possibly also have sent the photographers to the Gulag.

COMPANY SITES

Run by individual companies to further their commercial interests, these sites are a valuable source of data, an invaluable but often neglected source. By placing data on their productions on the Internet, companies make this information easily accessible to anybody with the energy to search for it. Authors now have no excuse for ignoring this resource. The sites run by DCN International (http://www.dcnintl.com/), Northrop Grumman Oceanic Systems (http://www.essd/oceanic/overview.html), GEC plc (http://gec.comb/b.htm) and Newport News (http://.nns.com/) are typical.

ENTHUSIAST SITES

The meat of the Internet can be found at these sites. Like the unofficial naval sites (and with extensive linking between the two), they are run and used by those who love ships and the sea. Typically, they contain photographs, information on specific areas of interest and 'Bulletin Boards' where news, information and opinions can be exchanged. The acknowledged leader in this category is *Battleships, Carriers and All Other Warships* (http://warships.4biz.net/index2.htm) run by Guy Derdall. This site has the benefit of a well-informed manager who supervises the content closely, eliminating material that is absurd or in bad taste. A site of similar quality is *Battleship Comparison*, a site which attempts to compare the various building-styles of Second World War battleships. Its prime virtue is the careful analytical approach of the author and the presentation of his methodology, allowing his results to be evaluated. Even the most knowledgeable of enthusiasts can learn from this Internet site. Of even higher quality is *Guns & Armor* (http://www.skypoint.com/members/jbp/okun_biz.htm), which contains an exhaustive treatise on the armouring of Second World War capital ships. This study finally and totally dispels the myth of the *Bismarck*'s 'invincibility', for example. The Pacific War is the subject of *Japanese Naval Power* (http://www2.gol.com/users/billise/jnp/), containing much strange and obscure data. Finally, the more general site *Navis* (http://navismagazine.com/f-right.html) is an Internet version of a conventional naval magazine.

FAKES, FRAUDS AND LIARS

After a short time an Internet researcher becomes uneasily aware of the major drawback of the Internet as a research tool. There is no control whatsoever over the information presented, and no guarantee that any data found on the Net is even remotely accurate. Sites may purport to belong to any of the previous four categories, contributors may not know what they are talking about, they may be spreading false data deliberately in pursuit of an agenda of their own, or may simply be pathological liars. Such fraudulent offerings can be easily recognised; one rapidly-deleted contributor claimed to have commanded a US Navy *Montana* class battleship completed in secret after the end of the Second World War. Other examples of disinformation are more subtle and may take a lot of trouble to flush out. Experience can be invaluable; when several contributions from the same source are available the validity or otherwise of the information becomes easier to judge. The primary rule must be that any information taken from the Net must be carefully checked and the source-site verified before it can be used with confidence.

This caveat notwithstanding, the Internet has revolutionised the way we gather information. By providing a medium by which data and opinions can be shared, all the users benefit and new insights are possible, even in apparently exhausted subject areas. Perhaps its most valuable attribute is the Net's international nature, which highlights differing perceptions. This factor alone has cast new light on many long-standing debates.

Editorial Note: The Conway website (www.conwaymaritime.com) now has a section where you will find a full list of available titles. The site features on-line ordering, bargain books, extracts and a bookclub. The bookclub not only entitles members to substantial discounts, but also provides an e-mail notification service to keep members up to date on new titles and special offers.

OBITUARY

Stephen McLaughlin writes in remembrance of the late RD Layman.

It is with great sadness that *Warship* reports the death of RD Layman on 22 June 1999 after a brief illness; he was 71 years old. Layman had become fascinated in naval history as a boy, despite growing up in land-locked Utah, and while working for a variety of newspapers, he managed to amass an enormous amount of material on early naval aviation in all its forms – man-lifting kites, balloons, airships and heavier-than-air craft. His career as a writer of naval history began in the 1970s, and his first book, *To Ascend from a Floating Base*, appeared in 1979. Four other books followed: *The Cuxhaven Raid* (1985), *Before the Aircraft Carrier* (1989), *The Hybrid Warship* (with Stephen McLaughlin, 1991) and finally *Naval Aviation in the First World War* (1996). Layman was also a regular contributor to *Warship*, and was proud of the fact that he had an article or photo feature in every issue from 1989 to 1997/1998. His death is a great loss to the field of naval history.

WARSHIP GALLERY

In this section, we publish photographs of warships which are unusual, remarkable as images, mysterious or otherwise of special interest to readers. The section is not intended for standard ship portraits, but for out-of-the-ordinary pictures which illuminate aspects of warships not evident in the usual views. This year's annual includes a special feature on the German Kreigsmarine towards the end of the Second World War. The editor would be happy to hear from readers with any unusual pictures which might appear in future issues.

HMS Lancaster. *A Type 23 'Duke' class ASW frigate*. (Royal Navy)

Royal Navy Type 23 frigate. The fore mast, with GSA8, UAF/UAT and 911 clearly shown. (BAe Defence Systems)

The high-tech end of modern naval warfare – the DNA(1) command systems in a Type 23 frigate. (BAe Defence Systems)

Two Kuwaiti missile boats, the Fallaka *(P3715) and* Maskan *(P3717) on trials off Cherbourg. (CMN)*

US Navy personnel boarding U-858 shortly after her surrender on 14 May 1945. One of the destroyer escorts to which the U-boat surrendered can be seen in the background.

The Prinz Eugen *after her surrender to the Allies at Copenhagen. The troops in the foreground are German-equipped Danish troops, keeping guard over the heavy cruiser in Copenhagen Harbour.*

U-996 *photographed in a London dock after her capture, showing masts and navigation equipment on the conning tower.* (Antony Preston)

A second view of U-996 showing the snorkel mast and the AA gun on its 'bandstand' at the after end of the conning tower. (Antony Preston)

The German light cruiser Köln *in Wilhelmshaven. The ship is resting on the floor of the harbour, having sustained damage from allied bombs.* (Antony Preston)

Three Type XXI U-boats under construction at the Blohm & Voss shipyard in Hamburg. Directly behind can be seen two more partly finished, while on the left of the picture another three wait on the slipway. (Antony Preston)

The end of the war. The Royal Navy are photographed taking over the German naval port and dockyard at Kiel. The assembled U-boat crews give their names and numbers to German personnel under the supervision of British naval officers. (Antony Preston)

INDEX

Page references in *italics* refer to illustrations.